Praise for previous editions of The Alyson Almanac

The Alyson Almanac is a lot of fun. This so-called "treasury of information for the gay and lesbian community" contains just about everything a Gay person could ever want to know about Gay life ... Readers are bound to annoy their companions by asking them: "Did you know this?" —*THE WASHINGTON BLADE*

The Alyson Almanac is the first lesbian and gay almanac of its kind. It turns out to be a really good idea. Alyson Publications should be commended for this first attempt and I hope it will become an annual or at least regular publication. The almanac is chock full of valuable information and will make an excellent gift. —*EDGE* (Los Angeles)

In the tradition of excellence we have come to expect from Alyson Publications, these folks have given us a second Alyson Almanac, expanded, updated, and revised from last year's model.
  —*ALABAMA FORUM*

The Alyson Almanac is a remarkable book. In its second edition much has been rewritten, redesigned, and updated. It might as well be considered an entirely new book.
  —*THE (ELECTRONIC) GAY COMMUNITY MAGAZINE*

An extremely wide spectrum of information for and about lesbians and gays has been brought together in this useful and entertaining almanac. This is a great summary of all kinds of information relating to gays and lesbians. All libraries will want it.
  —*AMERICAN REFERENCE BOOKS ANNUAL*

A warehouse of information. —*SOUTHERN EXPOSURE*

A delightful collection of facts, lists, and trivia.
  —*THE WEEKLY NEWS* (Miami)

A unique addition to any library's popular reference shelf. —*BOOKLIST*

THE
ALYSON
ALMANAC
1994–95 EDITION

___

THE FACT BOOK
OF THE LESBIAN AND
GAY COMMUNITY

BOSTON • ALYSON PUBLICATIONS, INC.

Copyright © 1989, 1990, 1993 by Alyson Publications, Inc.
All rights reserved.
Typeset and printed in the United States of America.

Published as a trade paperback original by
Alyson Publications, Inc.
40 Plympton St.
Boston, Massachusetts 02118
Distributed in the U.K. by GMP Publishers.

Third edition, November 1993

This book is printed on acid-free, recycled paper.

Portraits of Elizabeth Cady Stanton and Bayard Taylor
are reproduced from *The Dictionary of American Portraits*,
Dover Publications, Inc., 1967.

ISBN 1-55583-242-3

Library of Congress Cataloging-in-Publication Data

The Alyson almanac : the fact book of the lesbian and gay community. -
- 1994–95 ed.
    p.   cm.
    "3rd ed."—T.p. verso.
    Includes bibliographical references and index.
    ISBN 1-55583-242-3
    1. Homosexuality—History—Miscellanea. 2. Lesbians—History-
-Miscellanea. 3. Gay men—History—Miscellanea. I. Alyson
Publications.
HQ76.25.A48 1993
305.9'0664—dc20   93-37642
                                     CIP

CONTENTS

ACKNOWLEDGMENTS

Although I act as overall editor, much of the research and writing for *The Alyson Almanac* is done by the staff of Alyson Publications. Past and present staff contributors include: Tony Grima, Karen Barber, Joe Chapple, Wayne Curtis, Doug Dittman, Lori Freedman, Dan O'Connell, Dianna ONeill, Darryl Pilcher, and Tina Portillo.

Many others provided advice, information, photographs, and help. In addition to those credited in specific chapters, we'd like to thank the following individuals and organizations for contributions that appear in this edition: Hubert Kennedy; David J. Coynik, M.D.; Eric Garber; Barbara Grier; Terry Helbing; Richard Labonté; Merril Mushroom, Jim Morrow; ONE, Inc.; Peri Jude Radicic and the National Gay and Lesbian Task Force; Leigh Rutledge; and Vito Russo.

In preparing his book, we often referred to back issues of two publications: *The Advocate* and the *Washington Blade*. We benefited from their reporting, and recommend them to readers.

—Sasha Alyson

INTRODUCTION

The Alyson Almanac represents a new step for the gay and lesbian community. It's a reference book that's fun to read. You'll find these pages packed with facts about our past, as well as where we stand now. For this third edition, the *Almanac* has been completely revised. New listings and information have been added to nearly every chapter. Every address and phone number has been checked. One entirely new chapter describes laws and attitudes in the major nations of the world. Another new chapter summarizes the major studies of lesbians and gay men. (You may be surprised to find that the Kinsey report doesn't say just what you've been hearing it said.)

The *Almanac* can be read in several different ways. Sometimes you'll refer to it for specific facts or advice. Is Election Day approaching? You can look up the voting records of the politicians who currently represent you. Looking for something to do tonight? Experts on gay films, books, plays, and music have suggestions about the best and worst that those fields have to offer. Is it time you finally joined the National Gay and Lesbian Task Force? Their address and phone number are here — along with those of other national organizations and publications.

You'll also enjoy just browsing through the *Almanac*. At a time when AIDS, gay-bashing, and anti-gay initiatives have many of us discouraged, it's important to keep a perspective on the overall progress that we're making. The chronology in the first chapter provides that perspective. It also calls attention to the deep roots of the modern gay movement.

And if you have trouble finding something, please check the index. Many books these days skimp on the index. We've gone to great pains to provide an extensive index that makes it easy to find whatever you're looking for.

The Alyson Almanac is meant to provide a continuing record of the lesbian and gay community. Every two years, we'll revise and update it. Your suggestions, corrections, and additions are welcome; please enclose documentation (clippings or source references) when relevant and send to: *The Alyson Almanac*, Alyson Publications, 40 Plympton St., Boston, Mass. 02118. If you're the first person to send material that we incorporate into the next edition, we'll send you a free copy as soon as it's published.

HIGHLIGHTS OF HISTORY

There's more to gay and lesbian history than you'll find in the history books. Here are a few highlights from our past.

c. 1900 B.C.: The cities of Sodom and Gomorrah, according to Chapter 19 in the Book of Genesis, are destroyed with fire and brimstone. Centuries later, this was interpreted by Philo of Alexandria, and then by religious writers, as an angry God's punishment for the homosexuality of the inhabitants.

That interpretation, although common, hinges on an unlikely translation of the ambiguous Hebrew word meaning "to know." The term is used 943 times in the Old Testament; only 15 of those times is it a euphemism for sexual activity. Father John McNeill, who has written extensively about the Church and gay liberation, notes that "in the New Testament, the only reference to Sodom (Luke 10:10) identifies the sin as inhospitality." The story of Sodom and Gomorrah probably had nothing to do with homosexuality.

c. 730 B.C.: "Krimon warms the heart of Simias." This personal revelation is one of several lines of homosexual graffiti, dating back perhaps to the time of Homer, that constitute one of the earliest known uses of the Greek alphabet.

594 B.C.: Solon is elected ruler of Athens, and is empowered to write a new code of law. He declared the death penalty for any unauthorized adult male who mingled in a schoolyard with boys below the age of puberty. Yet he had no problem with relationships involving older youths; his own poetry includes such homoerotic lines as "Boys in the flower of their youth are loved."

580s B.C.: Sappho's famed girls' school flourishes on the isle of Lesbos. Her exquisite love poems to students are the earliest known lesbian writings.

c. 393–387 B.C.: Plato writes *The Symposium, Phaedrus,* and other works celebrating homosexual love.

c. 371 B.C.: The Sacred Band of Thebes forms in Greece. This military unit, consisting of 150 male couples, was based on the belief that men fighting alongside their lovers would die rather than shame

Sappho is believed to have loved both men and women, but she is remembered today for her lesbian love poetry.

one another. The Sacred Band was annihilated thirty-three years later by Phillip of Macedon and his son, Alexander the Great, at the Battle of Chaeronea.

c. A.D. 60: Saint Paul writes several Biblical passages (especially Romans 1:26–27 and I Corr. 6:9) that have been used to support homophobia. However, as scholar John Boswell points out, the translations that lead to this interpretation probably do not reflect Paul's real intent.

314: The Council of Ancyra establishes sodomy as a crime.

342: The emperors Constantius and Constans, having inherited much of the empire of their father, Constantine, call for "exquisite punishment" for homosexuality. By 390, that decree was broadened into a call for gay people to be burned alive.

533: Byzantine emperor Justinian I, combining Roman law and Christian morality, decrees that homosexuality and blasphemy are equally to blame for famines, earthquakes, and pestilences; he orders castration for offenders.

c. 650: The Cummean Penitential, a manual used by priests, provides them with guidelines for homosexual sin. The nature of the offense, and the age of the offender, were taken into account. "Simple kissing" by two males under the age of twenty called for six special fasts; kissing "with emission or embrace" called for ten special fasts. Mutual masturbation by men over twenty made the offenders liable to twenty days' penance; for anal intercourse, the period jumped to seven years.

1073: All known copies of Sappho's lesbian love poems are burned by ecclesiastical authorities in Constantinople and Rome. As a consequence, today we have only one-twentieth of Sappho's total output, and even that exists only because of an 1897 archeological discovery.

1210–1215: The Council of Paris declares sodomy to be a capital offense. This marked the start of a militant anti-sodomy campaign by the Catholic Church.

1252: St. Thomas Aquinas begins his theological teaching. Aquinas declared that God created the sex organs exclusively for reproduction; homosexual acts were thus "unnatural" and heretical. He was not the first to take such a stand, but because of his enormous influence within the Church — continuing even today — Aquinas's statements greatly encouraged intolerance.

c. 1260: The legal school of Orleans orders that women found guilty of lesbian acts have their clitoris removed for the first offense; that they be further mutilated for a second offense; and burned at the stake for a third.

1292: Europe's first known execution for sodomy takes place in Ghent.

1310: On October 12, King Philip the Fair of France orders the arrest of all French members of the Order of Templars. They were charged with heresy, sodomy, and being in league with the Moslems; many were tortured and executed. Philip benefited enormously from property confiscated as part of the arrests, and modern-day scholars still

England declared sodomy to be a capital offense in 1533. One victim of that law was Bishop John Atherton, executed for buggery in 1640.

disagree about the accuracy of the allegations.

1323: In one of the earliest recorded trials for sodomy, Arnold of Verniolle is found guilty and sentenced to life imprisonment with a diet of bread and water. Despite stiff church prohibitions against sodomy, the trial record shows that Arnold had little trouble finding sex partners.

1450–1453: Pope Nicholas empowers the Spanish Inquisition to investigate and punish homosexuality.

1513: Balboa, on his explorations of present-day Panama, reports that "the most abominal and unnatural lechery is practiced by the King's brother and many other younger men in women's apparel." He threw forty of the offenders to his dogs.

Balboa's observation of homosexuality was echoed by others of his time. In 1519, an anonymous conquistador reported the Mayan people of Mexico to be "great sodomites"; a later European wrote that everyone in the New World seemed to practice sodomy.

In reality, it appears that homosexuality was accepted by the Mayan civilization (centered chiefly in the Yucatan Peninsula), which often portrayed anal intercourse between men in its art. Both male homosexuality and lesbianism were practiced, but less accepted, by the more authoritarian cultures of the Aztecs and Incas. On occasion, these two civilizations are known to have punished such acts by death.

1533: The "buggery" law is passed in England, decreeing a penalty of death for "the detestable and abominable Vice of Buggery committed with mankind or beast." This marked the first time that the crime was covered under civil law in England; previously, it had been considered a church matter.

1583: The Third Provincial Council of Lima, in Peru, in promulgating Christianity to the native Indians there, tells them that "sodomy, whether with another man, or with a boy, or a beast ... carries the death penalty, ... and the reason God has allowed that you, the Indians, should be so afflicted and vexed by other nations is because of this vice that your ancestors had, and many of you still have."

1585: In one of the earliest recorded cases of masochism, Sister Mary Magdalene de Pazzi begs other nuns to tie her up and hurl hot wax at her. She also made a novice at the convent thrash her.

1610: The Virginia Colony passes the New World's first sodomy law, decreeing the penalty of death for offenders.

1624: Richard Cornish of the Virginia Colony is tried and, despite flimsy evidence, hanged for sodomy. He is the first person in America known to be convicted of this offense.

1631: Mervyn Touchet, the earl of Castlehaven, is put on trial for sodomy. He was found guilty and was beheaded. Touchet's was one of the best publicized of many sixteenth- and seventeenth-century sodomy trials, and set the legal precedent for such trials for the next two centuries.

1641–1642: The Massachusetts Bay Colony incorporates the language of Leviticus 20:13 into its laws: "If a man lyeth with mankinde, as he lyeth with a woman, both of them have committed abomination, they both shall be surely put to death." Other New England colonies soon followed suit.

1649: Mary Hammon and Goodwife Norman are charged with "lude behavior uppon a bed" in Plymouth, Massachusetts. The charges against Hammon were dropped, but Norman was convicted and had to make a public confession. She is the first woman in America known to be convicted of lesbian activity.

1655: The colony of New Haven expands its definition of sodomy — a capital offense — to include sexual relations between women.

1682: *Venus in the Cloister* is published in France. The book caused a scandal — it was about lesbian nuns. But it seems to have been written merely to titillate male readers rather than to portray real life.

1730–1731: Authorities announce the discovery of an extensive homosexual network in Amsterdam. Three hundred prosecutions resulted and seventy people — including boys as young as fourteen — were executed. Although a few executions for sodomy had taken place before 1730, persecution seems to have increased thereafter.

1740: China's first sodomy laws are enacted by the Manchu Qing regime, which outlaws male homosexuality. The new laws were probably a reaction to the increased visibility of homoeroticism in literature, and even in everyday life. Female homosexuality, which did not threaten the tradition of passing down the family name through the male, does not appear to have been punished.

1790s: Moreau de St. Mery, a Philadelphia bookseller, remarks on the "almost unbelievable" phenomenon of women who were "not at all strangers to being willing to seek unnatural pleasures with persons of their own sex."

1805: The first homoerotic book in the German language is published. It was *Ein Jahr in Arkadien (A Year in Arcadia),* by Herzog August von Sachsen Gotha.

1810: The Napoleonic Code is instituted in France. As part of this wide-sweeping reform, Napoleon eliminated all laws forbidding homosexuality. This influential penal code served as a model for other Catholic countries to also abolish sodomy laws in the first years of the nineteenth century.
• The mother of a schoolgirl accuses Marianne Woods and Jane Pirie, mistresses at a boarding school for girls, of "improper and criminal conduct" with each other. The British courts debated whether a sexual relationship between women was even possible. Lillian Hellman used this plot 120 years later as the basis for her play *The Children's Hour.*

1828: The English Parliament closes a loophole in its definition of the capital crime of buggery. It would no longer be necessary to demonstrate "the actual Emission of Seed" to convict someone of buggery or rape; "carnal Knowledge shall be

Napoleon eliminated all laws forbidding homosexuality in France, and his Napoleonic Code influenced other countries to do the same. His aide Jean Jacques Régis de Cambacérès, a homosexual man, played a key role in this reform.

deemed complete upon Proof of Penetration only."

1834–1836: Heinrich Hössli, a Swiss milliner, publishes his two-volume set *Eros: On the Love of Men,* in German. It collected all the examples he could find of homosexual love in ages past — Greek, Roman, and Persian love poems and manuscripts — and was one of the first books in modern times to give a positive view of homosexuality and to urge the repeal of anti-homosexual laws. Hössli was well ahead of his time, and his work went largely unnoticed. But thirty-one years later, it provided encouragement to Karl Ulrichs, who by then had already begun his own pioneering work.

Elizabeth Cady Stanton organized the first Women's Rights Convention in 1848.

1836: The last execution for homosexuality takes place in Britain, although the death penalty for homosexuals would remain on the books until 1861.

1848: The first Women's Rights Convention passes a "Declaration of Sentiments and Resolutions," based on the Declaration of Independence. This convention is generally seen as the precursor of the modern feminist movement, and provided support and communication for many lesbian and bisexual women.

1860: Walt Whitman brings out the second edition of Leaves of Grass, which is more homoerotic than the first. The book provoked much public debate about Whitman's possible homosexuality, and inspired other gay poets in the years to come.

1861: England eliminates the death penalty for male homosexual acts; offenders are now subject to impri-

sonment for ten years to life. This change, however, reflected a rethinking of capital punishment more than a change of attitude about homosexuality. Since 1826, the British Parliament had reduced the number of capital crimes from some two hundred to only four.

1863: Karl Ulrichs writes two short pamphlets in German — *Vindex* and *Inclusa* — that attempts an unbiased and scientific explanation of homosexuality.

1867: On August 29, while speaking to a conference of jurists in Munich, Karl Ulrichs becomes the first known person in modern times to publicly declare himself a homosexual and to speak out in favor of gay rights.

1869: Karl Maria Kertbeny publishes an anonymous pamphlet urging

When Karl Ulrichs publicly came out in 1867, the word *homosexual* had not yet been coined. He instead called himself a *Uranian*. (In English, that translated into *Urning*.)

Courtesy Tamiment Institute Library

repeal of sodomy laws. In this pamphlet, Kertbeny first introduced the term *Homosexualität (homosexual)*.

1870: The first American novel to touch on gay themes, *Joseph and His Friend,* is published. Written by the prominent poet Bayard Taylor, it is dedicated "to those who believe in the truth and tenderness of man's love for man, as of man's love for woman." But the homosexual elements were so subtle that a nongay reader could easily have missed them.

1872: The newly formed German empire adopts a penal code that includes the infamous Paragraph 175, outlawing male homosexuality. The new law became a catalyst for the nascent German homophile movement.

Karl Maria Kertbeny was a contemporary of Karl Ulrichs, but they disagreed about the nature of homosexuality. Ulrichs believed that homosexual men had a woman's soul; Kertbeny rejected the notion that homosexual men were effeminate.

1885: Britain broadens its laws so that any form of homosexual expression, if a jury deems it "filthy and offensive," becomes criminal. Previously, proof of sexual penetration had been required.

1886: The first edition of the perennial best-seller *Psychopathia Sexualis* is published in Germany. The author, Richard von Krafft-Ebing, was primarily responsible for the medical view that homosexuality is a symptom of degeneracy.

1889: The Cleveland Street Affair shakes Victorian England. A male brothel was discovered at 19 Cleveland Street in London's West End. The scandal became the talk of society, and while few prosecutions resulted, many important figures — including Prince Albert Victor, second in line to the throne — were rumored to be implicated.

1891: John Addington Symonds's book *A Problem in Modern Ethics* is published, providing a systematic review of scholarly literature on homosexuality.

1894: One of the earliest known gay organizations is formed by George Cecil Ives, a friend of Edward Carpenter. The Order of Chaeronea took its name from the Greek battle of 338 B.C. at which the Sacred Band of Thebes, a military unit made up of male couples, was annihilated by the Madeconians. The organization had religious and spiritual overtones, and is known to us today because of the extensive diaries that Ives kept.

1895: Oscar Wilde is convicted of committing "indecent acts" with young lower-class men. His trial caused a public sensation, and the

By the time this issue appeared in 1906, *Der Eigene* was openly gay.

playwright was condemned to two years' hard labor. The ensuing anti-gay hysteria proved a serious setback for the emerging gay movement in England.

1896: The first known gay periodical, *Der Eigene,* is founded in Germany by Adolf Brand. Many related ideas came together in the new magazine: anarchism, theosophy, nudism, and especially the idealization of the male nude. Within two years, *Der Eigene* was openly gay; it continued until 1931.

• For the first time, two actresses on an American stage are seen to kiss one another. Immediately afterward, writes historian Kaier Curtin, ushers rushed down the aisles to offer ice water to any patron on the verge of fainting. *A Florida En-*

chantment, however, had nothing to do with lesbians; the play's plot focused around a young woman who magically changed into a young man.

1897: Havelock Ellis publishes *Sexual Inversion* in England. It was the first book to present a comprehensive and sympathetic perspective on homosexuality. He argued that much of the unhappiness associated with homosexuality was a result of intolerance. Ellis withdrew the book soon after publication, and not until a revised U.S. edition was published in 1901 did it gain wide circulation.

• The Scientific Humanitarian Committee (Wissenschaftlich-humanitäre Komitee) is formed in Berlin by Dr. Magnus Hirschfeld and others. The committee's main purpose was to decriminalize homosexuality by working for the removal of the anti-gay Paragraph 175. The effort failed, but the committee did a great deal of important work until the Nazis forced it to disband in 1933.

1899: Magnus Hirschfeld publishes the first issue of the *Jahrbuch der sexuelle Zwischenstufen (Journal of Sexual Intermediates).*

1903: The Gemeinschaft der Eigenen (Community of Self-Owners) is founded by Adolf Brand (1874–1945) in Berlin. Its goal was to work for a rebirth of the "love of friends" in union with the first known gay journal, *Der Eigene,* which Brand also published. *(See listing for 1896.)*

1906: Maximilian Harden, publisher of Berlin's *Die Zukunft,* publishes an editorial warning of the danger presented by the homosexual conspiracy. Homosexuals, he wrote, form "a comradeship ... which brings together men of all creeds, states, and classes. These men are to be found everywhere, in the army and navy, in newspaper offices, behind teachers' desks, even in courtrooms." Harden specifically charged that Prince Philip Eulenburg and Count Kano Moltka had created a homosexual clique around Kaiser Wilhelm II. His editorial lent support to a public reaction against the growing gay movement. The controversy stretched out until 1909, when Moltka won a libel suit against Harden.

1907: A crowd of 2,000 shows up for a debate about Germany's sodomy law, the notorious Paragraph 175, sponsored by the Scientific Humanitarian Committee

1908: Edward Carpenter's *The Intermediate Sex* is published in England. In it, Carpenter idealizes the concepts of friendship, "comrade attachment," and homosexuality.

1909: Two black men are accused of oral sex with one another in Kentucky. They were not convicted because the judge couldn't find any law on the books under which to find them guilty. He urged that lawmakers remedy this problem, and soon many states had outlawed oral sex.

1911: A law is passed in the Netherlands prohibiting sexual contact between members of the same sex under the age of twenty-one. The law sparked a Dutch nobleman named Jacob Schorer to form the group NWHK (Nederlandsch Wetenschappelijk Humanitair Komitee), modeled after Hirschfeld's Scientific Humanitarian Committee in Germany. The NWHK provided support to homosexuals until 1940, when Schorer destroyed its records to prevent them from falling into the hands of the Nazis.

1912: The Scientific Humanitarian Committee, which has been gaining influence since it was founded in 1897, polls candidates for the forthcoming Reichstag election to learn their views on gay issues. Amazingly, ninety-one out of ninety-six who responded said that they favored gay rights.

1913: Alfred Redl, head of Austrian Intelligence, is exposed as a double agent working for the Russians. He committed suicide the next morning. When they searched his room, Austrian authorities found photographs of nude men, a perfumed love letter from another man, and other indications that Redl had been homosexual. The widely publicized case gave prominence to the idea that homosexuals are security risks, and thirty-seven years later, Joseph McCarthy used the Redl case to raise similar fears.

1917: The new revolutionary government of the Soviet Union abolishes the sodomy laws of the tsarist regime.

• On July 28, some 12,000 black Americans silently march down the streets of New York to protest the widespread lynchings of the era. This marked the beginning of the Harlem Renaissance, two decades of remarkable literary, artistic, and intellectual activity centering around Harlem's black community. Many leading personalities of the period were gay or bisexual, including Langston Hughes, Alberta Hunter, and Alain Locke.

1919: Magnus Hirschfeld founds the Institute for Sexology in Berlin. In a huge palace in Berlin, which Hirschfeld purchased, the Institute combined the world's first sex counseling center, a museum, and an ongoing series of educational events. The institute devoted its work to the fields of civil rights for women and gay people, legalization of contraception and abortion, sex education, and confidential treatment of sexually transmitted diseases. Hirschfeld co-starred with Konrad Veidt in *Anders als die Andern (Different from the Others),* one of the earliest films to offer viewers a gay-positive perspective; it was first shown on May 24.

1920: Natalie Barney's *Pensees d'une amazone* is published. It was a collection of thoughts on homosexuality that included references to Whitman, Ulrichs, Symonds, and Wilde.

1921: Marcel Proust's *Sodome et Gomorrhe* is published in France. Despite the book's stereotyped ideas, it contributed greatly to the demystification of homosexuality in France and elsewhere. The book was noteworthy for its depiction of homosexuality as a social world, rather than as just a few isolated individuals.
• The First Congress for Sexual Reform opens on September 16 at Berlin's Institute for Sexology.
• The Theater des Eros, the first theater devoted exclusively to gay plays, is founded in Berlin.

1922: Despite protests from many, the Soviet Union re-introduces the concept of "crimes against nature" and begins the process (finished by Stalin in 1933) of recriminalizing homosexual acts.
• *The God of Vengeance,* a play by Sholom Asch featuring a lesbian relationship, is produced in Provincetown. It was the first play on an American stage to depict gay or lesbian characters, and created an outcry the next year when it reached Broadway.
• A petition to abolish Paragraph 175, Germany's sodomy law, is presented to the Reichstag, but without success. The petition was largely the work of Magnus Hirschfeld and his Scientific Humanitarian Committee, and was signed by such prominent intellectuals as Albert Einstein, Herman Hesse, Thomas Mann, and Leo Tolstoy.

1924: On Dec. 10, Henry Gerber and others incorporate the Society for Human Rights as a nonprofit corporation in the state of Illinois. Gerber had lived in Germany and was influenced by the gay movement there; his is believed to have been the first homosexual organization in the United States. It lasted only a few months but during that time Gerber brought out two issues of the country's first gay liberation magazine, *Friendship and Freedom.* The group dissolved after the wife of one member found literature that she turned over to police. Gerber and other officers were arrested. Although the charges were dismissed, Gerber lost his job and was psychologically devastated by the lack of support from gay friends. He moved to New York and joined the

In the late 1920s and early 1930s, the German magazine *Die Freundin (Girlfriend)* openly discussed lesbian issues. This drawing appeared in 1932.

army, and the Society for Human Rights disbanded.

• In his book *The Doctor Looks at Love and Life,* Dr. Joseph Collins includes a lengthy chapter about homosexuality. Collins concluded that "the majority of homosexuals ... are not degenerates" and that anti-homosexual prejudice reflected a lack of enlightenment. A *New York Times* review of the book, on Oct. 24, marked the first use of the word *homosexual* in that newspaper.

• André Gide, in *If It Die,* makes his homosexuality public. He was the first prominent individual in modern times to do so.

1928: Radclyffe Hall's *The Well of Loneliness* is published. Calling for "the merciful toleration of inverts," it became the best-known book in English with a lesbian theme. Merely by breaking the silence surrounding the subject, it gave hope to many lesbians.

1930: Several gay magazines flourish in Berlin. According to scholars David Galloway and Christian Sabisch, one magazine, *Die Insel (The Island),* boasted a circulation of 150,000 — more than any gay magazine currently publishing in the U.S.

• Denmark repeals its sodomy laws. It was the first European nation to respond to the early homophile movement. Poland, Switzerland, and Sweden all followed suit within fifteen years.

1933: On January 30, the new Hitler regime bans the gay press in Germany. Five gay papers had their offices raided. Four months later, Nazis raided Magnus Hirschfeld's Institute for Sexology in Berlin and burned an estimated twelve thousand books, periodicals, and other documents from the Institute library. Many irreplaceable items were lost, including unpublished manuscripts by Karl Ulrichs and Richard von Krafft-Ebing. This bonfire marked the death of the early gay rights movement in Germany.

• Mammina, a Swiss woman, founds the Swiss Friendship Bond, the earliest gay organization in that country and one of the first anywhere. She also (in 1932) began publishing a monthly magazine of stories, art, and photography — George Platt Lynes was among the photographers represented in it. In 1937 the group and magazine were renamed Manschenrecht (Human Rights). In 1942 Mammina turned over leadership of the organization to Roberto Rolf, and the next year it became all-male and the name was changed to Der Kreis (The Circle). Under that name, the organization continued until 1967. The magazine became trilingual — German, French, and English — and gained a reputation for high production and writing standards.

1934: On June 28, the anti-gay holocaust in Germany begins. In the early morning hours of what became known as "The Night of the Long Knives," German S.S. troops rounded up some 200 people, including Nazi officials who had fallen into disfavor, and executed many of them. Hitler announced that the purge victims were "homosexual pigs who have besmirched the honor of the party." High-ranking Hitler deputy Ernst Röhm was the most prominent official arrested; he was briefly imprisoned and was asked to commit suicide; when he declined, he was murdered. Throughout the year, the danger intensified as the Nazis rounded up gay people from German-occupied countries and sent them to concentration camps.
• Meanwhile, the Soviet Union back-pedaled on its early sexual reforms. A new law decreed a minimum five-year sentence for homosexual acts, which were seen as a sign of "the degeneracy of the fascist bourgeoisie."

1935: The Nazis expand their anti-gay laws; kissing and embraces between men, and even gay fantasies, are criminalized.

1936: Mona's, the first lesbian bar in San Francisco and among the first in the U.S., opens at 140 Columbus Street. For over a decade it was an important gathering spot for women, although eventually (with a marquee that read "Where Girls Will Be Boys") it focused more on the tourist trade.

1937: The Nazi regime introduces the inverted pink triangle as a way of identifying gay people in the concentration camps.
• The first issue of *Bachelor* hits the stands. It promised to mirror "the varied interests of the discerning cosmopolite in society as well as in business or profession, in politics as well as in sport or the theater, in adventure as well as in the arts and sciences." Hunks of the day such as Buster Crabbe and Tyrone Power appeared in swimsuits or gym shorts. If that wasn't enough to define the magazine's intent, there was a cartoon showing two naked women emerging from the water, with one saying to the other, "Don't look now, but I think we've come up in the wrong magazine!" *Bachelor* folded the following year, after publishing only nine issues.

1941: The United States enters World War II. The war brought together millions of young men and women in sex-segregated environments; many discovered their gay feelings. Gay historians consider the dramatic growth of a gay consciousness in the following decade to be a direct consequence. Much hidden gay history of World War II would still be hidden except for the work of gay historian Allan Bérubé. His book *Coming Out under Fire* gives us a much better understanding of this pivotal period.

1942: The U.S. military issues its first official prohibition against allowing homosexuals to serve. The psychiatrists who suggested the policy advised commanding officers to watch for limp wrists, as one way of distinguishing who was gay. Enforcement of the policy was haphazard and inconsistent. The U.S. Surgeon General declared that homosexual relationships should be tolerated as long as they were kept private, and WAC officers were told to tolerate lesbian relationships as much as possible. "Any officer bringing an unjust or unprovable charge against a woman in this regard will be severely reprimanded," said one edict.

1945: World War II ends, but gay people who survived the German concentration camps are not freed, but are forced to serve out their sentences in post-war prisons. Homosexuality remained illegal in Germany until the late 1960s.

• Bob Mizer founds the Athletic Model Guild in Los Angeles, which will become a leading source of erotic male photography — published, however, under the guise of "physique" and "physical culture" magazines.

1946: A homosexual organization known as the Shakespeare Club forms in Amsterdam. In 1948 the name was changed to the C.O.C. (for Cultuur en Ontspannings Centrum, or Cultural and Recreational Center) and within two decades, it had grown into the largest such group in the world.

1947: Under the pseudonym of Lisa Ben (an anagram of "lesbian"), Edythe Eyde begins publishing *Vice-Versa,* the first U.S. lesbian magazine. She typed each issue manually, making about seven carbons with each retyping, during her lunch break at RKO studios. Copies were circulated clandestinely from one reader to another. *Vice-Versa* was remarkably open for its time: the subtitle read "America's gayest magazine," and an editorial in the first issue stated that the magazine was dedicated "to those of us who will never quite be able to adapt ourselves to the iron-bound rules of Convention." Four decades later, history repeated itself in Russia as Olga Lipovskaya published an underground *samizdat* newsletter about feminist and lesbian issues, using the same carbon-paper method. She, too, got about seven copies from each typing.

1948: The Kinsey report is published on Jan. 5. Sex researcher Alfred Kinsey found that 4% of the adult men he interviewed were exclusively homosexual, 13% were more than incidentally homosexual for at least three years after the age of sixteen, and 37% had a homosexual experience in their adult lives. The fact that homosexual activity was so commonplace surprised gay and straight readers alike, and offered hope to millions of closeted gays.

Kinsey also found that over 90% of males engaged in masturbation, a practice that was still in considerable disrepute. As Kinsey noted, "The United States Naval Academy at Annapolis rules that a candidate 'shall be rejected by the examining surgeon for ... evidence of ... masturbation.'"

The report became an instant best-seller, and went back to press six times within two months of publication.

• Gore Vidal's novel *The City and the Pillar* is published. Although hardly the first American gay novel, it received more widespread attention than its precedessors, and marked the beginning of a post-war surge in gay writings.

• In August, Communist Party activist Harry Hay proposes the formation of a group called Bachelors for Wallace, ostensibly to promote the presidential campaign of progressive candidate Henry Wallace but also "devoted to the protection and improvement of Society's Androgynous Minority." But it would be two years before he found any support for such an idea.

1950: On July 9, Harry Hay writes a prospectus calling for the "Androgynous Minority" to unite. Four months later, on November 11, the idea took hold. Five men met at Hay's home in Los Angeles and gave birth to what soon became known as the Mattachine Society. (The name Mattachine came from medieval French history, when it referred to jesters who always wore masks in public.) Some of Mattachine's earliest organizers — Hay, Chuck Rowland, and Bob Hull — had been members of the Communist Party. They combined the politics and strategies of that group with the elaborate initiation rites and secrecy of the Masons. Although it was not the first gay organization in the U.S., Mattachine was the first to grow and give rise to other organizations. It represents the start of today's organized gay movement.

• The McCarthy witch-hunts begin. A subcommittee of the U.S. House Committee on Un-American Activities reported in December that

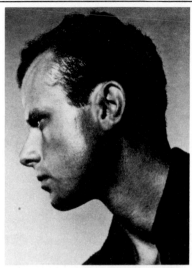

LeRoy Robbins

Harry Hay wanted to start a gay organization in the summer of 1948, but didn't find enough support to go ahead until November 1950.

"those who engage in overt acts of perversion lack the emotional stability of normal persons ... Even one sex pervert in a Government agency tends to have a corrosive influence." A purge of lesbians and gay men from the government and military soon followed.

1951: The California Supreme Court unanimously rejects an effort to close the city's most famous gay bar. The state Alcoholic Beverage Control Department had tried to close the Black Cat in 1949, charging that it was a "disorderly house" and a "meeting place for persons of known homosexual tendencies." Owner Sol Stouman called on employees and patrons to join in defending the bar, and they succeeded when the court ruled that mere "patronage of a public restaurant and bar by homosexuals" was not sufficient reason to close it. It was the first time the gay community had legally won the right to gather openly and publicly.

• The group Arcadie is created in France. It sought to be a ministry to homosexuals suffering from oppression.

• In Los Angeles, Dorr Legg, Merton Bird, and others form Knights of the Clock, an interracial gay social group.

1952: Marking an important shift from discussion groups to activism, the Mattachine Society rallies behind Dale Jennings, a Los Angeles man accused of solicitation. Jennings acknowledged in court that he was gay, but denied having solicited for sex; the charges against him were dismissed. The Jennings case became a local cause célèbre. It provided Mattachine's first media coverage, and a consequent surge in both membership and morale.

• On Oct. 15, the founders of ONE, Inc., an early gay organization, hold their first meeting at the apartment of Dorr Legg. Legg is generally considered the moving force behind the new group. The other six founders were Martin Black; Dale Jennings; Guy Rousseau; Merton Bird; Don Slater; and Tony Reyes. Rousseau, a black man, suggested the name, which came from a quote by Thomas Carlyle: "A mystic bond of brotherhood makes all men one."

1953: In January, ONE begins publishing the country's first openly gay magazine to achieve wide circulation. It promptly ran into problems with the U.S. Post Office, which claimed that articles about homosexuality were inherently obscene, and specifically objected to an arti-

cle on gay marriages. The attempted censorship continued until January 1958, when the U.S. Supreme Court ruled in ONE's favor.

• Sex researcher Alfred Kinsey, who five years earlier had released his report on male sexuality, follows up with a study of women. He announced that about 2% of the women in his study were exclusively lesbian during their adult lives, and 13% had engaged in homosexual activity at least once.

• In one of his first acts upon taking office, President Dwight Eisenhower issues an executive order prohibiting the employment of gay people in federal jobs. State and local governments, and government contractors, followed suit; by the mid-1950s, estimates historian John D'Emilio, over 20% of the workforce faced loyalty-security investigations.

• The Mattachine Society is split by political differences. At a conference in May, newer members of the organization demanded (and got) the resignation of the founders, and of any other members who were affiliated with the Communist Party, threatening to turn their names over to the FBI otherwise. The depoliticized group virtually disappeared in Los Angeles, but gained new members elsewhere, especially in San Francisco.

1955: The Daughters of Bilitis, the first lesbian membership organization in the United States, is formed in San Francisco. Originally a social club, it grew into a national organization with educational and political as well as social goals. Among the eight lesbians who founded it were Del Martin and Phyllis Lyon.

• In January, the first issue of *The*

Ruth Mountaingrove

Del Martin (left) and Phyllis Lyon co-founded the Daughters of Bilitis in 1955 and are still active today.

Mattachine Review is published. It included articles by sex researcher Evelyn Hooker and *Quatrefoil* author James Barr.

• For the first time, a national magazine provides sympathetic coverage of a gay organization. *People Today* ran an article about ONE, Inc., titled "Third Sex Comes Out of Hiding."

• The American Law Institute publishes its Model Penal Code, recommending the decriminalization of private sexual acts between consenting adults. It was adopted six years later by Illinois, which became the first state to decriminalize homosexual acts.

• Three men are arrested in Boise, Idaho, for homosexual activity. This marked the start of a major witch-hunt. In a city of only 40,000, over a thousand men were questioned; ultimately, nine were sentenced to prison terms of up to fifteen years each. Years later, former *Time* and *Newsweek* editor John Gerassi investigated the story. In his book The Boys of Boise, he reported his findings: that the investigations were politically motivated by a mayor, prosecuting attorney, and police who wanted to capitalize on homophobia to build their own political base.

1956: In San Francisco, the Daughters of Bilitis begins publishing *The Ladder,* a lesbian magazine. Phyllis Lyon was the first editor.

• The Church of ONE Brotherhood is founded in Los Angeles by Chuck Rowland. It lasted only a year, but was the first documented gay church.

• Police raid the Alamo Club, a lesbian bar, on Sept. 21. Forty-one patrons were arrested on charges of visiting a disorderly house. Four women pleaded not guilty and demanded jury trials; all four were acquitted. This marked the beginning of a movement by lesbians to challenge such arrests. The Daughters of Bilitis worked with the American Civil Liberties Union to support such challenges, which became increasingly successful.

• The Florida legislature initiates a massive witch-hunt for homosexuals in education and public life. For nine years the Johns Committee (named after chairman Charley Johns) interrogated thousands of individuals, often pressuring them to name suspected gays. Over a hundred teachers lost their jobs as a result. The full extent of the committee's activities didn't come to light until 1993.

1957: The British government publishes the Wolfenden Report, recommending that homosexual acts between consenting adults be legalized. The British Medical Associa-

The Ladder, begun in 1956, quickly established itself as the leading lesbian publication in the U.S.

tion endorsed the report and even the Catholic Church, while emphasizing that it believed homosexuality to be a sin, recommended decriminalization. A nationwide debate ensued. Three years later, a proposal to adopt these recommendations was defeated by a two-to-one margin in the House of Commons.

• The Crittenden Report, sponsored by the U.S. Department of Defense, concludes that security concerns about homosexuals in the military are exaggerated. It wasn't what the Pentagon wanted to hear, and the report was ignored.

• In the U.S., the American Civil Liberties Union expresses disinterest in pursuing gay rights cases. The government was correct, the ACLU said, in classifying gays as security risks.

• Sex researcher Evelyn Hooker issues the first of several reports disputing the belief that homosexual men and women are likely to have psychological problems. Previous studies were flawed, said Hooker, because they focused on people who sought help. For her own studies, Hooker found subjects through gay groups such as Mattachine.

1958: The late 1950s were a difficult time for gay people. A sense of the era comes from longtime activist Jim Kepner's recollection that after *ONE* magazine ran the headline "I'm Glad I'm Homosexual" in 1958, "unnerved subscribers cancelled in droves."

• The first East Coast chapter of the Daughters of Bilitis forms in New York. Barbara Gittings was elected its first president, serving until 1961.

Letters

UNDER NO CIRCUMSTANCES DO THE EDITORS FORWARD LETTERS FROM READERS TO OTHER PERSONS NOR DO THEY ANSWER CORRE-SPONDENCE MAKING SUCH REQUESTS.

Dear ONE:

I did not like the story "A Place to Go" (December, 1958). It reads too much like too many of my own experiences. In the letters you print I note that every now and again some reader refers to ONE Confidential. What is it? I'd like to know more about it. (ONE Confidential is a monthly newsletter sent to the "Friends of ONE," or voting and non-voting Members of the Corporation—those who support the Corporation's work financially and in other ways. EDITOR.)

Have been interested in your comments about Police Chief Cleon Skousen. I heard that one of his "boys" had a very torrid date with a fellow in a bath house. Then donned his clothes and left. His partner did not know he was a policeman until he got dressed. The sad part is that this policeman would not hesitate to arrest his bed partner under different conditions, calling it "his duty."

Mr. W.
SALT LAKE CITY, UTAH

Dear Sir:

I have not forgotten ONE but I have been in jail. I had been arrested for attempting a "pick-up." When arrested I was threatened with bodily harm by the police, not allowed to contact a lawyer or to notify my parents. The judge was "lenient" however. As there had been no sexual contact I was sentenced to **only** 364 days. I had to agree to surrender my driver's license, agree not to even own a car, have psychiatrist's treatment for a "cure," and be on five year's probation. Even after I agreed to all that the judge backed down and wouldn't release me.

An interesting sidelight was that while in jail I was in solitary confinement. One of the prisoners who brought me food was a "voo-doo murderer" who cut off a thirteen-year-old boy's head to make a love potion. Being homosexual I was, naturally, more dangerous. So, to protect the other prisoners I was kept in solitary for damn near four months.

You can bet that from now on I'll be one of your staunchest supporters. The "dark age" witch hunters scream loudly, but you have shown great courage in standing up for our rights. As soon as I can get back on my feet you can count on me.

Mr. H.
TRENTON, NEW JERSEY

Dear Sir:

I think that you are doing a terrific job of educating the public as to homosexuality. The colored people in the face of prejudice have gotten together to form a union (just as the United States itself once did) to fight this prejudice and they are defeating their enemies by getting laws passed. Why cannot all of the homosexuals do the same thing, form a union, collect funds and fight for legalization of this way of life—**so long as they do not use violence and both parties are willing participants?** All that it would take would be a few, good strong leaders to approach the Senators and Congressmen in Washington to sponsor such a bill. There is no reason to consider sex a crime, except our narrow-minded upbringing and training.

The only reason that I can see for homosexuality being scorned by the people is that the homosexual will not get up and fight for his ideas and beliefs. Until the colored people fought for their rights they got nowhere. The world is ready for a change but it will take funds and strong leadership to put it across. The great psychiatrists all agree that the sex laws are inadequate, having been written in olden times by superstitious, ill-informed people.

Another thing that I think should be done is to stop the harrassment of homosexuals by the police. If a policeman knows of a homosexual, or one who has been arrested for a homosexual act, what is to stop him from blackmailing him for life? You should also fight to have all previous arrest records for homosexual acts removed from the records and destroyed so that a man will not have to be exposed to public ridicule when he goes to apply for a job. I believe the questionnaires for jobs which ask, "Have you ever been arrested?" are against a man's civil rights, and leave him wide open for blackmail. It would be at least better to change the question to, "Were you ever **convicted** of a crime?"

Nothing is gained without fighting for it. You will run into prejudice, but follow the example of various unions, such as the labor unions. With a union you can get the voting power and by showing the homosexuals who have done great things, and by using the writings of modern psychiatrists I don't see how you can lose.

Mr. A.
UPPER DARBY,
PENNSYLVANIA

This page of letters from *ONE* magazine (May 1959) gives a sense of the concerns and perspectives of that era.

1961: Illinois becomes the first state to repeal its sodomy laws, effective January 1962.

• Franklin Kameny founds a chapter of the Mattachine Society in Washington, D.C.

• The first television special on homosexuality, titled "The Rejected," is aired by station KQED in San Francisco. Margaret Mead was among the guests.

• Jose Sarria pulls 5600 votes when he runs for the office of San Francisco city supervisor. He is believed to be the first openly gay person to run for public office in the United States. Sarria was a legendary entertainer at the Black Cat, a bohemian bar with an international reputation as a gay meeting place. His primary difficulty in running for office, he recalled years later, was that he had no appropriate men's clothing to wear on the campaign trail.

1962: A well-publicized study by Dr. Irving Bieber claims to analyze homosexuality scientifically, and concludes that it is caused in large part by seductive mothers and hostile fathers. This theory had been heard before, but only with Bieber's study did it gain widespread currency.

1963: New York activist Randy Wicker organizes what is believed to have been the first gay rights picket. It was a protest of unfair treatment of gays by the military, at a Draft Induction Center.

1964: The Society for Individual Rights (SIR) is founded by disgruntled members of an earlier gay organization, the League for Civil Education. By the end of year, SIR had brought out the first issue of its

Reproduced from Before Stonewall

**HOMOSEXUALS (ARE)
DIFFERENT...**

but...

we believe they have the right to be. We believe that the civil rights and human dignity of homosexuals are as precious as those of any other citizen . . . we believe that the homosexual has the right to live, work and participate in a free society.

Mattachine defends the rights of homosexuals and tries to create a climate of understanding and acceptance.

**WRITE OR CALL:
MATTACHINE SOCIETY INC.
OF NEW YORK**

A Mattachine Society ad from the early sixties reflects the sentiments of the day.

magazine *Vector,* and it soon became the leading gay advocacy group on the West Coast.

1965: The year opens with San Francisco's first drag ball. As early activist Del Martin told the *Bay Area Reporter* twenty-five years later, "We consider that ball to be our Stonewall, because 500 lesbians and gay men crossed a picket line of cops to go in, and that was while the entrance was floodlighted and photos were being taken of everybody who went in and out." Subsequent publicity lead to the appointment of a police liaison to the gay community.

• The State Department is picketed by the Daughters of Bilitis, the Mattachine Society, and other gay organizations, protesting its security policies. There were also public demonstrations at the Civil Service Commission, the Pentagon, and the White House, and at Independence Hall in Philadelphia, calling for homosexual rights.

• In Amsterdam, the fast-growing C.O.C. becomes the world's largest gay organization; membership was pegged at 4000 in 1965, far surpassing any group in the U.S. From its three-story stone headquarters, the C.O.C. sponsored lectures, plays, dances, and several periodicals.

• On August 26, Secretary of State Dean Rusk issues a statement that the department did not knowingly employ homosexuals, and would discharge any such employees if they were identified. It was to be twelve years before the department publicly made any modification to this policy.

1966: Police raid a gay party in a wealthy suburb of Johannesburg, South Africa, spurring a parliamentary committee that investigates the extent of homosexuality. Two years later, the committee recommended that homosexual acts be outlawed. "All levels of society practice homosexuality on a scale which was hitherto unthinkable," reported the committee.

• Forty delegates from various local and regional groups meet in Kansas City to form the North American Conference of Homophile Organizations (NACHO). At that first meeting, NACHO adopted the slogan "Gay Is Good." It also made plans for a nationwide day of protest on May 21 to draw attention to the military's discriminatory policies. On that date, a motorcade of thirteen cars, with pro-gay placards, made its way through Los Angeles. Smaller protests took place in other cities. NACHO was dissolved in 1970.

• Police raid the Yukon Club, a popular Los Angeles gay bar, handcuffing forty patrons and hauling them off to jail. Such raids were too common to be noteworthy — except that one of the patrons was forty-year-old Dick Michaels. Michaels was so outraged that he joined PRIDE, an early gay rights organization, and the next year he founded the *Los Angeles Advocate*. From an initial investment of $200 and a press run of 500 copies, the paper grew to a 3500 circulation within a year and soon became the country's most prominent gay publication.

• In San Francisco, radical street people form Vanguard, a new kind of gay liberation group that brought together anarchists, communists, hippies, and hustlers.

• Dick Leitsch, president of the Mattachine Society of New York, decides to challenge a New York law stating that any meeting of three or more homosexuals in a bar would be considered grounds for suspending the bar's license. Although Leitsch was ready to go to court over the issue, he never got a chance; as soon as the test case began, the New York Liquor Authority changed the policy, realizing that it would never hold up in court. Gay bars, at least in New York state, were legal.

• The Society for Individual Rights (SIR) holds its historic first Candidates' Night in San Francisco, in which politicians running for office came to court the gay vote.

• In July, *The Mattachine Review,*

publishes its last issue. Founded in 1955, the magazine filled a valuable function for many years, but by the mid-1960s, newer publications better reflected the direction of an increasingly militant community.

1967: Several hundred activists gather in Los Angeles to protest police raids on gay bars. It was believed to be the largest gay demonstration up to that time.
• Britain legalizes homosexual activity between consenting adults, except for those in the military and police forces.
• Robert A. Martin, a student at Columbia College in New York City, obtains a school charter for a Student Homophile League. It was the first gay campus group.
• The American Civil Liberties Union, previously unsympathetic to gay cases, calls for an end to sodomy laws in a statement dated Aug. 31. In security cases, said the ACLU, the burden of proof should be on the government to prove that a gay employee was a security risk. It also called for an end to police harassment and to nondiscrimination in immigration policy and government employment.
• In its first episode, on September 5, the television show *N.Y.P.D.* features a story about a blackmail ring that preys on gay people. A black policeman, seeing the correlation with his own situation, supports the gay characters. According to gay activist and media historian Vito Russo, this was the first network portrayal of gay characters.
• A CBS Special Report on "The Homosexual" also appears. Mike Wallace, as commentator, reported that "the average homosexual, if

there be such, is promiscuous. He is not interested in, nor capable of, a lasting relationship, like that of a heterosexual marriage. His sex life, his love life, consists of a series of chance encounters at the clubs and bars he inhabits, and even on the streets."
• One of the first economic boycotts on behalf of gay rights is announced in San Francisco. The Glide Methodist Church and the Glide Foundation announced that they would not buy goods and services from companies that discriminated against homosexuals, and encouraged others to do the same.
• Der Kreis, the gay Swiss group founded thirty-five years earlier, folds, and is replaced by the Swiss Organization of Homosexuals (also known as Club 68), with younger leaders. Many gay organizations, in the U.S. as well as Europe, were experiencing a shift toward a more radical leadership.
1968: The gay movement did not begin at Stonewall. The 1968 convention of the North American Conference of Homophile Organizations (NACHO) was attended by representatives of *twenty-six* gay groups.
• A dozen members of the Daughters of Bilitis, Mattachine Society, and Society for Individual Rights picket the Federal Building in San Francisco on July 3, calling for an end to employment discrimination by the government.
• The Metropolitan Community Church meets for the first time on Oct. 6 in Los Angeles. Founded by the Reverend Troy Perry as a nondenominational church for the gay community, it rapidly grew from its

ALTERNATE LIFESTYLES OF FAMOUS PEOPLE
...OUT OF THE CLOSET...

FROM THE COLLECTION OF
PAUL HENNEFELD

STONEWALL STA.
20 YEARS 1969-1989
LESBIAN & GAY PRIDE
JUNE 25, 1989
NEW YORK, NY 10199

In 1969, no one would have guessed that twenty years later, the U.S. Postal Service would issue a special postmark honoring the Stonewall riots and Lesbian and Gay Pride.

original congregation of twelve members to some five hundred members just two years later.

1969

Spring: Leo E. Laurence and Gale Wittington come out in an article titled "Don't Hide It," published by the underground newspaper *The Berkeley Barb.* The next day, Wittington was fired from his job at States Steamship Company. The Committee for Homosexual Freedom was formed in response; it organized a picket line at States and demonstrations elsewhere, and became an early voice of the nascent gay movement.

June 28–29: The Stonewall riots forever change the shape of the gay movement.

Early in the morning of June 28, a routine police raid on the Stonewall Inn at 53 Christopher Street, in New York City, turned into history's first gay riot when the patrons put

up unexpected resistance. A group of uniformed policemen arrived at the bar about 3:00 a.m. They ordered customers to leave, then began arresting employees, as well as several drag queens.

Although such arrests had occurred routinely in the past, this time the crowd reacted. Patrons chanted "Pigs!" at the police, then threw pennies, followed by beer bottles, bricks, and even a parking meter. The police barricaded themselves inside the bar, which itself came under attack from the crowd. Someone attempted to set it on fire. According to one observer, the riot was escalating and the trapped police were about to begin firing on the crowd when reinforcements arrived, and the group dispersed. Estimates of the crowd's size ranged from 200 to 400.

The following day, the Stonewall Inn re-opened but the management, which had been charged with selling liquor without a license, gave away drinks. A crowd gathered, soon spilling over to nearby Sheridan Square Park. The riots resumed that night, and continued for the next several evenings.

July 1: The Gay Liberation Front, a militant leftist organization, forms at Alternate U in New York City. The GLF repesented a dramatic change from the homophile movement of the 1950s and 1960s, with its emphasis on social respectability. The new organization was noteworthy for its lack of structure. There was no official leadership; meetings consisted of open discussions that continued until a consensus was reached, an approach that some members found too open to manipulation. Many GLF activists were allied with other leftist groups, some of which still had homophobic positions or members. Consequently, late in 1969, dissatisfied GLFers split off to form the Gay Activists Alliance, which sought to combine elements of structure and democracy.

Sept. 1: Soon after East Germany repeals its sodomy laws, West Germany finally drops Paragraph 175 of its penal code, the law used by Hitler to send gays to concentration camps. It was the first time since German unification in 1871 that homosexual activity was legal. Germany, the homeland of the earliest gay rights movement, was among the last major nations to abolish these laws; after 1969, the U.S. and Soviet Union were the only major countries in the West to retain sodomy laws.

Sept. 3: The American Sociological Association condemns "the firing, taking economic sanctions, and other oppressive actions against any persons for reasons of sexual preference." It was the first professional organization to take such a stand.

October: A government report that favors decriminalization of homosexuality is pushed under the carpet. In September 1967, President Johnson had appointed Dr. Evelyn Hooker to head a Task Force on Homosexuality for the National Institute of Mental Health. In October, the Task Force submitted its report. It concluded that three or four million American adults were predominantly homosexual, and recommended the repeal of sodomy laws and better public education about homosexuality. The report was largely ignored by the newly elected President Nixon, and by the press. But two years later Frank Kameny and other activists used it as they began their campaign to get homosexuality removed from the American Psychiatric Association's list of psychiatric disorders.

1970

Jan. 28: A Daughters of Bilitis chapter forms in Melbourne, Australia, marking the start of the organized lesbian movement in that country.

June 27–28: Gay activists in four cities commemorate the first anniversary of the Stonewall riots. A New York march was estimated to draw (depending who you believed) 2,000 to 20,000 participants, while rallies in Chicago and San Francisco each attracted several hundred. In Los Angeles, 1200 people, many in costume, took part in a festive parade down Hollywood Avenue. The 10,000 to 20,000 spectators got to see a band of paper-winged "fairies"; a float with a huge jar of Vaseline; a tanned and muscular model with a live python; and the winner of the *Advocate*'s Groovy Guy contest. It was these anniversary events that established the Stonewall riots as the beginning of the modern gay movement.

July 10–13: The national convention of the Daughters of Bilitis votes to replace its formal national structure with a loose federation of autonomous local chapters.

August: Huey Newton, leader of the Black Panther Party, acknowledges his own discomfort with homosexuality but calls for political solidarity with the gay liberation movement.

Aug. 25–28: The split between early homophiles and the new gay liberationists is highlighted by clashes at the North American Conference of Homophile Organizations (NACHO) convention in San Francisco. Among other issues, delegates divided over whether to support the militant Black Panther Party, and whether heterosexuals should be welcome to participate in the gay movement. NACHO dissolved soon after the convention.

September: A gay organization at the University of Minnesota finds only one major employer in the state that is willing to admit it would discriminate against a gay person in their hiring practices. Twelve companies were polled about their policies, and eight did not respond. Three (General Mills, Pillsbury, and Dayton's department store) said they would not discriminate. Only Honeywell said it would, explaining that "our practice is the result of actual adverse prior experience."

Sept. 30: The federally sponsored Commission on Obscenity and Pornography urges the repeal of most anti-pornography laws. The Commission found that adult sex offenders had less exposure to erotica, as adolescents, than did the population at large, and that most adults, at some point in their lives, had voluntarily seen sexually explicit material. It also urged a massive increase in sex education programs for parents, teachers, doctors, and children. Three of the commission's eighteen members dissented; one dissenter was Charles Keating, better known for the loot he hauled off two decades later as a key figure in the Savings and Loan scandals.

Oct. 13: The first British Gay Liberation Front is founded at a meeting at the London School of Economics.

November: The country's first legislative hearing on gay rights is held at the New York Bar Association in New York. It was called by assemblymen Franz Lichter, Tony Olivieri, and Steve Solarz.

• Rita Mae Brown and other lesbians are purged from the National Organization for Women.

1971

March 23: Franklin Kameny draws 1841 votes (1.6% of the total) in a campaign to become the District of Columbia's nonvoting delegate to the U.S. House of Representatives. Kameny was president of the Mattachine Society of Washington.

April 7: Jack Baker is elected president of the student association at the

University of Minnesota. He was the first openly gay person elected to such a position anywhere in the United States.

Sept. 6: Only a year after purging certain lesbian members, the National Organization for Women at its annual convention acknowledges the "oppression of lesbians as a legitimate concern of feminism."

October: The Gay Community Services Center opens in Los Angeles. It provided counseling, rap groups, and other services, and soon became — and today remains — the largest gay social service agency in the country.

Nov. 26: A group of Italians living in the Netherlands issue their *Manifesto for a Moral Revolution,* which is considered to mark the founding the the gay and lesbian movement in Italy.

Jack Baker — MSA President

Jack Baker was fully out of the closet when he ran for student association presidency at the University of Minnesota in 1971, as this campaign poster shows. Baker ensured that gay issues stayed visible in other ways, too. In 1970 he and his lover Jim McConnell unsuccessfully applied for a marriage license, and they filed joint tax returns in 1972 and 1973.

1972

January: Naiad Press forms. From small beginnings, it would become the world's largest lesbian publishing house.

April 30: The United Church of Christ becomes the first major denomination to approve the ordination of an openly gay person. For about an hour, William Johnson fielded questions from delegates at the UCC's San Francisco area Ecclesiastical Council, which then voted 62 to 34 in favor of ordination. He was ordained on June 25.

May: The Washington, D.C., school board becomes the first in the country to prohibit anti-gay discrimination in the hiring of teachers. The

action came at the urging of the local Gay Activists Alliance.

June 8: Camille Mitchell becomes the first open lesbian to win custody of her children in a disputed divorce proceeding. But her victory was only partial: the judge required that "Mrs. Mitchell be precluded from having [her lesbian lover] and her family move into her home. The rationale for this is that Mrs. Mitchell and the children need to develop a firmer base of understanding, particularly regarding the homosexual issue, prior to the children's becoming more intensely exposed to it."

July 12: San Francisco gay activist Jim Foster addresses the Democratic

National Convention. Foster and Madeline Davis were the first openly gay delegates at the national convention of a major party. George McGovern, the party's nominee for president, endorsed gay civil rights.

Aug. 22: John Wojtowicz, 27, makes national news in a different way. Wojtowicz and a companion entered a Chase Manhattan bank heavily armed and scooped up $29,000. In the lengthy confrontation that followed, Wojtowicz's companion Sal Naturale was killed and Wojtowicz was arrested. He explained that he was gay and needed the money to pay for a sex-change operation for his lover. He got a twenty-year jail sentence for the crime, and $7500 for film rights. The film (which the producers originally planned to call *The Boys in the Bank*) became a major hit as *Dog Day Afternoon*.

Nov. 1: *That Certain Summer* airs on ABC network television. This made-for-TV film, about a fourteen-year-old boy who learns that his divorced father is gay, was the first television drama to focus on gay issues from a nonhomophobic perspective. The show generally received extensive advance publicity and generally good reviews; the *New York Times* wrote that it "can lay claim to some of the most impressive and sensitive acting ever contributed to television."

1973

February: Gail Bates and Valerie Randolph are married in San Francisco by the Reverend Ray Broshears, a gay minister whose penchant for publicity has made him a controversial figure in the community. The two women were army WACs, and Broshears called a press conference to announce that he had married them and two other lesbian WAC couples. The media played the story up, and the two women were discharged from the military.

March 4: Betty Friedan, founder of the National Organization for Women, charges in a *New York Times* article that lesbians had plotted to seduce and blackmail her, and were trying to take over NOW. Three years earlier, Friedan had succeeded in inciting anti-lesbian sentiments within NOW. This time, attitudes had changed. Many prominent feminists and feminist organizations rallied in support of lesbian rights. Robin Morgan spoke for many when she urged the public to dismiss "Ms. Friedan's pathetic demands that we all now go backward."

Oct. 3: Dr. Howard J. Brown, who had been New York City's health commissioner under Mayor John Lindsay, comes out via a page-one interview in the *New York Times*.

Oct. 15: The formation of the National Gay Task Force is announced by Dr. Howard J. Brown, who had come out just two weeks earlier. The new organization's founders had asked Brown to make the announcement because of his stature. Dr. Bruce Voeller was the first executive director of the group.

1974

The United States elects its first openly gay elected officials.

The first of them was Kathy

Kozachenko. Running as a member of the Human Rights Party, she was elected in the spring by a nine-vote margin to the Ann Arbor (Michigan) City Council. But the city council had fewer openly gay members after her election than the year before: Two outgoing council members, Nancy Wechsler and Gerald De-Grieck — had come out the previous fall, after winning election on April 3, 1972.

On Nov. 5, Elaine Noble was elected to the Massachusetts state legislature, becoming the first openly gay person to win election to a state office. However, she was not the first to *hold* a state office.

On Dec. 9, encouraged by Noble's victory but before she took office, Minnesota state senator Allan Spear publicly declared his homosexuality. He had been elected in 1972 on a progressive platform, and was already known within the gay community, and privately to the press, as being gay. In fact, he had been the main speaker at the Minneapolis Gay Pride rally the preceding June. Voters in Spear's district, which included the University of Minnesota, were undisturbed by his revelation, and the governor called that week to offer his full support. Spear kept winning re-election and twenty years later, he was named president of the senate.

April 9: The membership of the American Psychiatric Association votes to remove homosexuality from its official diagnostic manual of mental disorders. The vote, approved by 58% of the membership, ratified a recommendation the APA Board of Trustees had made the previous Dec. 15.

May 14: The "Equality Act of 1974," HR 14752, is introduced in Congress by representatives Bella Abzug and Edward Koch, both Democrats from New York. It would have amended the 1964 Civil Rights Act to prohibit discrimination based on "sex, marital status and sexual orientation." The bill had twenty-four cosponsors, but did not pass.

Oct. 8: An episode of *Marcus Welby, M.D.,* titled "The Outrage," portrays a junior high school teacher who sexually assaults a student. Hearing in advance of the storyline, the National Gay Task Force coordinated a nationwide protest. Dozens of prominent officials, representing organizations such as the United Federation of Teachers and the American Psychiatric Association, joined the protest. ABC aired the show anyway, but several advertisers withdrew their support; five local affiliates refused to air it; and others allowed time for rebuttals by gay advocates. It was the first time the lesbian and gay community had exercised such power in responding to prejudicial coverage.

Nov. 8: NBC airs a *Policewoman* episode titled "Flowers of Evil," featuring three stereotyped lesbians as murderers. The show was offensive enough in itself; NBC further outraged lesbian and gay activists when it agreed to edit out the offensive references, then reneged on that promise and moved the airing up a week in an effort to short-circuit the protests that had been planned.

Dec. 18: The first International Gay Rights Congress opens in Edinburgh, Scotland. Over 400 delegates attended.

1975

January: Charles "Valentino" Harris, with his disco single "I Was Born This Way," becomes the first performer to come out on a record. "I'm gay... 'Tain't a fault, 'tis a fact," he sang.

Jan. 24: The American Psychological Association, lagging a year behind the psychiatrists, changes its policy on homosexuality, concluding that "homosexuality *per se* implies no impairment in judgment, stability, reliability or general social or vocational capabilities." It further urged "all mental health professionals to take the lead in removing the stigma of mental illness that has long been associated with homosexual orientations." The action came after extensive work by the Association of Gay Psychologists.

July 3: The U.S. Civil Service Commission repeals its blanket ban on employing gay people. Some agencies, however, including the CIA and the FBI, are allowed to continue to discriminate.

Sept. 8: Sgt. Leonard Matlovich, discharged from the air force after he came out, appears on the cover of *Time* magazine. The cover story in that issue, combined with the image of this conservative, flag-waving gay man, was one step in changing the public perception of homosexuality. On Sept. 9, 1980, a federal court ordered the air force to reinstate him; Matlovich instead accepted a $160,000 settlement from the military. It was the first major blow against the Pentagon's anti-gay policy.

Doug Hinckle/The Washington Blade

1975: Leonard Matlovich's battle with the air force, which landed him on the cover of *Time* magazine, shattered many popular stereotypes.

Dec. 11: Football player David Kopay comes out. He was the first major-league athlete to do so.

• Ernest O. Reaugh is appointed by New York state senator Manfred Ohrenstein to act as liaison to the gay community. Reaugh is believed to have been the first gay liaison appointed by any public official in the U.S. Today, hundreds of mayors, governors, and legislators have such positions.

• The National Organization for Women defines passage of federal rights legislation to protect lesbians as a top priority, and commits one percent of its dues-generated income to working for lesbian rights.

1976

Feb. 10: *Doonesbury* character Andy Lippincott comes out. In a comic strip sequence that continued for four days, Andy put off the romantic advances of Joanie Caucus by explaining that "I'm gay." At least five of the 450 papers that carried *Doonesbury* refused to run the strip; the Miami *Herald* explained that "We are more sensitive about the comic section than we are about other parts of the paper ... We just decided we weren't ready for homosexuality in a comic strip."

May: *Christopher Street,* which aspires to be the gay *New Yorker,* publishes its first issue.
• The country's first openly gay law enforcement officer is hired in San Francisco, as Sheriff Richard Hongisto hires Rudi Cox to be a deputy. In the same year, San Francisco's police department became the first in the country to urge gay officers to come out.
• The first Michigan Womyn's Music Festival is held. It will become a major annual event for the lesbian community.

1977

Orange juice was the watchword of 1977, as singer (and Florida citrus industry spokeswoman) Anita Bryant waged a highly emotional campaign to repeal a gay rights ordinance in Dade County, Florida. On Jan. 28, the Dade County Commission — the governing body for the city of Miami — passed an ordinance banning anti-gay discrimination in jobs, housing, and public accommodations. Within six weeks, opponents had formed the Save Our Children committee and collected enough signatures to force a ballot referendum on the subject. The campaign took on massive proportions, mobilizing both gay and anti-gay forces nationwide. Because of Bryant's ties to the citrus industry, orange juice became taboo in many households and bars. On June 7, the ordinance was repealed by a two-to-one margin.

Jan. 10: Ellen Marie Barnett is ordained in New York City as an Episcopal priest. She was the first open lesbian to be ordained by a major Christian denomination.

Feb. 7: The U.S. State Department announces that it will no longer automatically bar lesbians and gay men from employment, but will make such decisions on a case-by-case basis. An official explained homosexuality would be considered relevant if it violated local customs; could be used to coerce or blackmail an individual; or was believed to reflect an emotional disorder.

Feb. 8: Midge Costanza, acting as community liaison in the new Jimmy Carter administration, receives the first official lesbian and gay delegation to the White House.

July: At its annual convention, the National Education Association calls for the removal "by statute and practice" of discrimination based on sexual orientation.

July 12: Denis Lemon, editor of the London *Gay News,* is convicted of blasphemy. The newspaper had printed a poem by Professor James Kirkup depicting a Roman centurion who had sexual fantasies about Christ. Lemon was the first person convicted of blasphemy in fifty-five years.

Nov. 8: Harvey Milk is elected to the San Francisco Board of Supervisors, becoming the first openly gay city official in a major city. Milk was endorsed by the mainstream San Francisco *Chronicle,* but many local gay activists opposed him.

November: A sweeping gay rights resolution passes overwhelmingly at the National Women's Conference of International Women's Year, held in Houston. At a similar conference two years earlier in Mexico City, lesbian concerns had been ignored. Thanks to the advance work of several women, including Bella Abzug and Jean O'Leary, that didn't happen again. Even early feminist and National Organization for Women founder Betty Friedan, who had once attacked "the lavender menace" of lesbianism, now joined in supporting the resolution.
• Two lesbians win favorable rulings in child custody cases. In Michigan, Jacqueline Stamper won joint custody rights for her two children after her estranged husband charged that she was "morally unfit" because she was a lesbian. The other case, in Denver, was more complicated: Donna Levy won custody of the daughter of her deceased former lover, successfully fighting off claims by the girl's aunt and uncle. Neither case set a wide legal precedent, but both provided important momentum for lesbian mothers in custody disputes.
• Although no one has yet identified it, the AIDS virus is already relatively widespread.

1978

It is a year of losses for the lesbian and gay community. Emboldened by their success in Dade County the previous year, conservatives in St. Paul, Minn., Wichita, Kan., and Eugene, Ore., got voters to repeal local gay civil rights laws. A Seattle law, however, was upheld at the polls.

August: Gay Bob, the world's first gay doll, gets the fifteen minutes of celebritydom to which Andy Warhol said everyone is entitled. Produced by Out of the Closet, Inc., Bob was advertised as "anatomically correct," and was sold complete with a plaid shirt, jeans, boots, and an earring. *Time* magazine published a caricature depicting Gay Bob with false eyelashes, lipstick, and a limp wrist — none of which the real-life doll possessed. Called to task, they apologized privately for "reinforcing stereotypes."

Nov. 7: In the gay community's one major victory of 1978, Proposition 6 — better known as the Briggs initiative — is soundly rejected by California voters. Had it passed, the measure would have banned gay people, or anyone "advocating a homosexual lifestyle," from teaching in the public schools. Opponents believed that an important factor in the initiative's defeat was support from an unlikely source: former California governor and future president Ronald Reagan. After the Dade County defeat of eighteen months earlier, it was a much-needed victory for gay people.

Nov. 27: San Francisco mayor George Moscone and openly gay

ILLUSTRATIONS FOR TIME BY SANDY HUFFAKER

The Gay Bob doll walked out of the closet in 1978, but he didn't look quite like this. *Time* magazine apologized (but only in private) for the stereotyping.

city supervisor Harvey Milk are assassinated by homophobic ex-cop Dan White. Milk became the first modern-day gay martyr.

• The Civil Service Reform Act bars discrimination against gay people in the federal government's civilian positions.

1979

Apr. 13: The first International Gay Association conference opens held in Bergen, The Netherlands. It was attended by sixty-five delegates representing seventeen countries. The group, which remains active (although less known in the U.S. than elsewhere) later changed its name to the International Gay and Lesbian Association.

May 21: Dan White is found guilty on the reduced charge of voluntary manslaughter, rather than of first-degree murder, for killing San Fran-

cisco mayor George Moscone and openly gay supervisor Harvey Milk. White's defense was built around the controversial Twinkie defense: He claimed that a diet of too much junk food had impaired his reasoning. Gay people were outraged and that evening, a march on San Francisco's City Hall turned into rioting. On the eve of what would have been Harvey Milk's birthday, police and marchers clashed in what becomes known as the White Night riots. As for Dan White, he was released from prison after serving only five years, and committed suicide on Oct. 21, 1985.

Sept. 17: Stephen Lachs becomes the country's first openly gay judge when California governor Jerry Brown appoints him to the State Superior Court. The next three openly gay judges appointed in the U.S. were also Brown's appointees.

Oct. 14: An estimated 50,000 to 100,000 lesbians, gay men, and supporters show up for the first National March on Washington for Gay and Lesbian Rights. It was, up to that time, the largest such march ever held. Just before the march, hundreds of men and women met in Washington for the first National Lesbian/Gay Third World Conference.

• The San Francisco Gay Men's Chorus forms early in the year. It was the country's first gay chorus.

1980

Gay people are evident in the 1980 presidential campaign as never before. Activist Mel Boozer's name was put in nomination for the vice-presidency at the Democratic National Convention on Aug. 14. He told the convention, "I know what it means to be called a nigger, and to be called a faggot. The difference is none." That convention also included some seventy-six openly gay delegates, and the Democrats had their first gay rights platform plank. Meanwhile, the Socialist Party's candidate for president was David McReynolds, a longtime political activist who had been publicly out since 1969.

Feb. 15: The first national conference for black gay men opens in Atlanta, Georgia.

Apr. 26: CBS broadcasts *Gay Power, Gay Politics,* a supposed documentary about San Francisco's gay community. The program focused on gay men to the exclusion of lesbians; it focused on sex (especially S/M, transvestism, and public sex) to the exclusion of other issues; and used deceitful editing to support the producer's preconceived findings. Millions of lesbian and gay viewers were dismayed. San Francisco journalist Randy Alfred went one step further: he documented the program's bias, and filed a formal complaint with the respected National News Council, which publicly rebuked CBS for its distortions.

May 30: Aaron Fricke, a Rhode Island high school student, takes a gay date to his high school prom. The school administration tried to stop him, but a court order forced the school to back down. The nationwide publicity that ensued provided moral support and a positive role model for hundreds of thousands of gay teenagers. He was not the first, however. In June of 1979,

Aaron Fricke made national news when he took a male date to his high school prom in 1980.

seventeen-year-old Randy Rohl of Sioux Falls, South Dakota, took a date to his high school prom, though the event received far less media attention.

Aug. 9: The second quadrennial Gay Games ceremonies open in San Francisco.

Nov. 4: Longtime community organizer Karen Clark is elected to the Minnesota House of Respresentatives by a two-to-one margin. Clark was open about her lesbianism during the campaign, and became one of the nation's most prominent and active openly gay elected officials.

Nov. 19: Two gay men are killed and six more wounded in Greenwich Village as a 38-year-old man, armed with a submachine gun, goes on a rampage in front of the Ramrod bar.

• The government of Holland, in a remarkably strong official statement, informs the governments of

Ireland and New Zealand that it considers their sodomy laws to be unacceptable.

• Norway institutes a comprehensive gay civil rights law, making it a crime to threaten or scorn anyone because of their sexual orientation.

1981

It is a bad year for closeted conservatives. Mississippi congressman Jon Hinson was arrested on Feb. 4 for having sex with a man in a House office building restroom; he resigned his seat shortly afterward. Congressman Bob Bauman of Maryland, a Moral Majority supporter, found himself out of a job following his October 1980 arrest for soliciting sex from a sixteen-year-old boy. And the head of Taxpayers Against Smut pleaded no contest after being arrested for sexual misconduct with an eight-year-old girl and a teenage boy.

Jan. 20: Ronald Reagan takes office, and the Reagan era begins.

Apr. 7: Norway becomes the first country in the world to specifically outlaw discrimination based on sexual preference.

June 5: The Centers for Disease Control announces that five previously healthy gay men in Los Angeles have been diagnosed with pneumocystis carinii pneumonia (PCP), a rare disease that was previously unknown in people with healthy immune systems. This was the first official warning of what would become the AIDS epidemic. At first, the disease was known as GRID — Gay-Related Immunity Disorder.

July 3: "Rare Cancer Seen In 41 Homosexuals," reports the *New York Times,* reporting on an outbreak of Kaposi's sarcoma. This story first brought the yet-unnamed AIDS epidemic to the attention of the general public.

Aug. 26: Mary Morgan is appointed to the San Francisco Municipal Court by California governor Jerry Brown; she is the first openly lesbian judge in the U.S. The appointment came after the lesbian and gay community in San Francisco actively organized to get an openly gay judge appointed, and urged Morgan, an attorney active on women's and gay issues, to apply for the position.

Nov. 8: Forty delegates attend India's first conference on gay rights, held in Hyderabad.

November: NBC evening news prominently covers allegations that homosexuals present a "nightmare" to national security officials. Later evidence indicated that this report was prepared with the help and encouragement of FBI officials, in an effort to persuade Congress that the Bureau should be exempt from budget cuts. The story ultimately developed into the made-up scandals of July 1982.

• In Strasbourg, after lobbying by the International Gay Association, the Council of Europe votes overwhelmingly to encourage member countries to pass gay civil rights legislation. Among their recommendations: abolish laws against homosexual acts; ban job discrimination against gay people; eliminate discriminatory child-custody laws; and destroy police files on gays.

1982

Mainstream films feature lesbian and gay themes on a level never before reached. *Personal Best* (released Feb. 5) starred Mariel Hemingway and Patrice Donnelly as competing athletes who have a lesbian affair. Critics, however, charged that the film depicted lesbianism as merely a phase. *Making Love* (released Feb. 12) starred Harry Hamlin, Michael Ontkean, and Kate Jackson, in a drama about a married man who realized he was gay. The comedy Victor/Victoria, with Julie Andrews and Robert Preston, got the highest praise from gay critics, while *Deathtrap,* featuring two gay murderers, rounded out the year.

Feb. 25: Following a lengthy effort by Rep. David Clarenbach, Wisconsin becomes the first state to get a wide-reaching gay rights law. Governor Lee S. Dreyfus, a Republican, as he signed the bill into law, expressed his belief in the "fundamental Republican principle" of restricted governmental involvement in the lives of citizens.

March 2: Lambda Indonesia, the first open gay organization in that country, is formed in Djakarta.

March 31: Dan Bradley becomes the highest-ranking government official up to that time to publicly come out. Bradley had been head of the Legal Services Corporation, a federally funded agency providing legal services for the indigent. He came out in an interview with the *New York Times.*

April 22: A federal judge in San Francisco rules that the Immigration and Naturalization Service may not bar entry to foreign visitors simply because they are gay. The INS had tried to prohibit Carl Hill, a British journalist, from entering on the grounds that his homosexuality constituted a "psychopathic personality." The injunction was made permanent in July, and was upheld by the 9th Circuit Court of Appeals in 1983.

July 13: Charges of homosexual misconduct in Congress dominate the news. CBS interviewed former House page Leroy Williams, who claimed to have engaged in sex with members of Congress. ABC found a self-proclaimed hustler who, without revealing his name, alleged that foreign agents had approached him for the names of closeted gay people in the government, ostensibly so they could be blackmailed. On July 13, the U.S. House of Representatives voted to investigate the issue.

By late August, it became clear that the stories were fabricated. Leroy Williams flunked a lie detector test, then admitted that he had lied; ABC's hustler turned out to be an FBI informant; and the Justice Department admitted that there was no evidence that any congressmen had exploited pages. Many observers speculated that the FBI had created a scandal, in hopes of generating increased funding for investigative work. But as has so often happened with invented gay scandals, the press paid less attention to the truth than it had to the false allegations.

Aug. 3: Police mistakenly show up at the Atlanta home of Michael Hardwick with a warrant to arrest him for a ticket that he had actually already paid; they walk into his

Making Love, in which a married man comes out, was seen as a ground-breaking film of 1982, though not a record-breaking one.

bedroom and find him engaging in gay sex. Hardwick's arrest eventually led to the landmark 1986 Supreme Court decision upholding the right of states to enforce sodomy laws.

Aug. 28–Sept. 5: The first international Gay Games are held in Kezar Stadium in San Francisco, with 1300 gay and lesbian athletes from some two dozen countries competing. The Games had originally been called the Gay Olympics, but a lawsuit filed by the U.S. Olympic Com-

mittee against the organizer, Dr. Tom Waddell, forced the change of name.

• The U.S. military refines its anti-gay policy, declaring that it is homosexuality itself, not homosexual sex, that is forbidden. Personnel who engage in homosexual sex, said the Pentagon, would be excused if it was deemed to be merely a lapse, while any soldiers who declared they were lesbian or gay would be discharged, even if they were celibate.

1983

Apr. 30: More than 17,000 people fill Madison Square Garden for the Ringling Brothers, Barnum & Bailey Circus. The event, which benefited the Gay Men's Health Crisis, was by far the largest AIDS fundraiser held up to that time.

July 14: Congressman Gerry Studds becomes the first politician elected to national office to openly and unapologetically state that he is gay. Studds had been charged by the House with making improper advances to a male page ten years earlier. Rather than blaming it on alcohol, as politicians in similar situations had done in the past, he decided not to contest the charge. Instead, he talked openly about the difficulties of combining a closeted gay identity with a public life, and expressed relief at finally being out. Six days later, Studds was officially censured (rather than receiving a reprimand, the less severe step originally proposed) by the House.

Aug. 26: On the eve of a major civil rights march, Coretta Scott King and other black leaders announce their support for gay civil rights. Several days earlier, Walter Fauntroy, the black congressional delegate from the District of Columbia, had tried to prevent any gay presence at the march, saying it would be divisive. Following a long conference phone call that included King, Fauntroy, lesbian activist Virginia Apuzzo, and black gay leader Gil Gerald, march organizers agreed to reverse that position. It was the first time that black civil rights activists had come together so visibly to endorse gay rights.

Nov. 13: A drunk driver crosses the highway and strikes a car driven by Sharon Kowalski. Kowalski lay in a coma for several months, becoming quadriplegic and suffering severe brain damage. Her parents refused to give their daughter's lover, Karen Thompson, full access to Kowalski or input into her care. Thompson fought for those rights, and also used the case to emphasize to other lesbians and gay men the importance of putting onto paper the rights that they want to grant to a partner. Not until 1991, after numerous court hearings that sometimes supported her and sometimes went against her, did Thompson finally win legal guardianship of Kowalski. Kowalski had already indicated that this was what she wanted.

• Openly gay mayors take office in both Santa Cruz and Laguna Beach, California.

1984

As evidence mounts that AIDS is caused by a virus and is sexually transmitted, health authorities emphasize the importance of "safe sex." Many gay men, however — especially outside the urban areas already hard hit by AIDS — were slow to take the advice, and the epidemic continued to spread.

April 23: Margaret Heckler, U.S. Secretary of Health and Human Services, announces at a media conference that the virus that causes AIDS has been identified. Heckler credited Dr. Robert Gallo with the discovery, which she termed "the triumph of science over a dread disease." She predicted a test for the virus within six months, and a cure

Lisa Means

Sharon Kowalski (right) was disabled in a 1983 auto accident. Her partner, Karen Thompson, struggled for eight years before finally winning legal guardianship of Kowalski. During that time, Thompson tirelessly encouraged lesbian and gay couples to establish living wills, partnership agreements, and other legal protections for themselves.

within two years. It soon became clear that the media conference was a triumph of PR over substance. The virus had already been discovered by French researchers, and U.S. politicians and scientists were merely trying to horn in on the credit. A blood test for HIV antibodies became available in 1985, but predictions for an early cure were entirely unfounded.

October: The General Accounting Office reports that the U.S. military's anti-gay policies cost $23 million in the previous year alone. Most of that amount represented wasted training costs for lesbians and gay men who were discharged from the service merely because of their sexual orientation.

Nov. 6: The voters of West Hollywood, California, vote to incorporate as a new city. The first five-member city council included two gay men and one lesbian. Top vote-getter Valerie Terrigno became the nation's first openly lesbian mayor. West Hollywood was the first U.S. city to have an openly gay majority on its governing body, and was promptly dubbed the "gay city" by the media. Twenty-three days after the election, the council passed a broad-reaching gay rights law.

Dec. 5: Berkeley, California, becomes the first U.S. city to pass a "domestic partners" law for city employees. Gay, lesbian, and unmarried heterosexual couples could file an affidavit with the city to receive comparable benefits to married couples in areas such as health and dental care, bereavement leave, and leave to care for a sick partner.

• Robert Ebersole, the town clerk of Lunenberg, Massachusetts, comes out, and later is easily re-elected. He was the country's first openly gay Republican elected offical. Barney Frank, the Massachusetts congressman who came out three years later, cited Ebersole's experience as a factor in his own coming out.

• The National Organization for Women sponsors its first conference devoted to lesbian rights.

1985

Mar. 26: The U.S. Supreme Court strikes down an Oklahoma law banning the favorable mention of homosexuality in schools as an unconstitutional interference with free speech.

May 12: A small memorial stone is laid at Neuengamme, the site of a Nazi concentration camp, to commemorate the gay victims of the Holocaust. Hundreds of memorials already existed throughout Germany for other targets of Nazi persecution, but this marker, paid for by a gay organization in Hamburg, was the first in Germany to recognize homosexuals.

June 11: The Los Angeles Republican Party officially charters the Log Cabin Republican Club which, although not defined as a gay club, consisted predominantly of lesbians and gay men. It was the first time a gay Republican group had received any formal party recognition.

July: Disneyland announces that it will allow same-sex partners to dance together. Officials — who acknowledged the change without formally announcing it — explained that it was made to accommodate teenage girls who came without dates and wanted to dance together, but the amusement park had also lost a much-publicized lawsuit by two gay men who had been evicted for dancing together.

Oct. 2: Rock Hudson dies from AIDS-related complications. He was diagnosed in mid-1984, but denied rumors of his illness until July 1985, when he went to Paris for an experimental treatment. Hudson's illness and death made AIDS strike home for Americans in a way that thousands of previous deaths had not.

1986

June 1: The Danish parliament takes a first step in recognizing same-sex couples, as it grants lesbian and gay partners the same break on inheritance taxes that married couples have received.

June 30: The U.S. Supreme Court upholds the right of states to enforce sodomy laws. In a 5–4 decision, the Court ruled in the case of *Hardwick* v. *Bowers* that Georgia's sodomy law was constitutional. Justice Byron White, writing for the five-member majority, stated that the right to privacy has "little or no textual support" in the U.S. Constitution. In dissent, Justice Harry Blackmun argued that "the right of an individual to conduct intimate relationships in the intimacy of his or her home seems to be the heart of the Constitution's protection of privacy."

Gay legal activists expressed anger and dismay at the ruling, which suggested that anti-gay discrimination could be justified because it had been going on for centuries. Four years later, retired justice Lewis Powell commented that his support of the majority position had probably been a mistake. But it was too little, too late.

Oct. 30: Pope John Paul II issues a fourteen-page letter calling gay people "intrinsically disordered" and maintaining that homosexuality can never be reconciled with Church doctrine. He ordered Church officials to withdraw all support from gay organizations such as Dignity. Many complied, and Dignity chapters nationwide had to search for new places to meet.

Dec. 4: A settlement is announced between Pacific Bell and the National Gay Rights Advocates, in which the utility agrees to compensate individuals for anti-gay discrimination. This closed a lawsuit initiated eleven years earlier, when several gay job applicants learned they were turned down because of the company's anti-gay policy. The settlement cost Pacific Bell about $3 million, and was larger than any previous gay rights litigation victory.

1987

Jan. 14: KRON in San Francisco becomes the first television station to run condom ads. The major networks continued to refuse such advertising, explaining that such ads would be "intrusive to the moral and religious beliefs of many of our viewers," in the words of a CBS spokesman.

The announcement in 1985 that Rock Hudson had AIDS made the disease seem real, for the first time, to millions of Americans. Contributions to AIDS organizations skyrocketed.

March: The AIDS Coalition to Unleash Power (ACT-UP) forms in New York. ACT-UP advocated an aggressively confrontational style, and similar groups soon formed in other cities.

May: The Danish parliament votes to ban anti-gay discrimination.

May 30: U.S. congressman Barney Frank comes out in an interview with the *Boston Globe.* He explained that he did not feel his gayness was really relevant, but that to continue to skirt the issue would suggest that he felt it was something to hide. He was the first person elected to national office to come out strictly of his own choice. He easily won reelection the following year, with 70 percent of the vote.

June 15: The *New York Times* finally decides the word *gay* is acceptable to use, as an adjective. Previous policy, under editor Abe Rosenthal,

Doug Hinckle/The Washington Blade

The 1987 March on Washington was the largest gay and lesbian gathering anywhere, up to that time. The crowd was variously estimated at 200,000 to 600,000 people.

had forbidden the term except as part of an organization's name. Rosenthal was replaced in 1986 by Max Frankel, who improved overall coverage of lesbian and gay issues. "We're inching into the twentieth century," commented one *Times* employee. The equally staid *Wall Street Journal* had accepted the term *gay* back in 1984.

Summer: President Ronald Reagan announces appointees to the Presidential Commission on the Human Immunodeficiency Virus Epidemic. Many on the commission were right-wing ideologues with little or no AIDS-related experience or special knowledge. One appointee, how-

ever, was Dr. Frank Lilly, an openly gay biomedical expert. Lilly was believed to be the first openly gay person ever appointed by a United States president to a public position.

Sept. 9: A San Francisco jury awards over $2 million in palimony to James Short after he broke up with his lover of nineteen years. Reports at the time indicated that it was the first time a jury had settled a gay palimony case.

Oct. 10–13: Hundreds of thousands of gay people and supporters descend on Washington, D.C. (see photo). The focus of the weekend was the Oct. 11 March on Washing-

Doug Hinckle/The Washington Blade

The same weekend as the national March on Washington, the Names Project unveiled for the first time a giant quilt containing nearly two thousand panels, each commemorating a person who had died of AIDS.

ton, protesting anti-gay discrimination and calling for a stronger government response to AIDS. Other events of the weekend included:

• Some 2000 same-sex couples took part in a mass wedding on Oct. 10. The ceremony was held on the steps of the Internal Revenue Service building, to dramatize the fact that gay people are denied the tax benefits that heterosexual couples receive.

• The Names Project unfolded the memorial quilt for the first time on Oct. 10. Some two thousand panels made up the quilt at that first showing, each panel memorializing an individual who had died of AIDS.

• Two days after the march, on Oct.

13, the largest civil disobedience action since the Vietnam War took place. In a long and carefully planned action, 600 protesters allowed themselves to be arrested on the steps of the Supreme Court building, protesting the Court's upholding of sodomy laws.

• Threatened with a gay boycott, Delta Airlines apologizes for past homophobia and announces that it will not discriminate against passengers with AIDS. The airline came under fire in 1986 after its attorneys argued that the life of a gay passenger killed in a Delta crash was worth less money than that of a heterosexual passenger, because the gay passenger might have had AIDS.

1988

Feb. 12–14: The National Black Gay and Lesbian Conference in Los Angeles draws over four hundred participants, making it the largest such gathering ever. Organizers succeeded in including mainstream black organizations, such as the Urban League and the National Association for the Advancement of Colored People, in conference activities.

Feb. 24: The *Los Angeles Times* runs a prominent story about Lambda Delta Lambda, a lesbian sorority at UCLA. Soon the new sorority was getting attention on national network news, as well as on *Saturday Night Live*. The goals of Lambda Delta Lambda, as stated in its constitution, were to "promote awareness of women's, minorities' and gay issues on campus and in the community." A month later, the nation's first gay fraternity received official recognition at the same school.

Feb. 26–28: Nearly two hundred gay and lesbian activists meet at a first-of-its-kind "War Conference" to plan goals and strategies for the movement. The most lasting effect of the conference was the proposal to begin "outing" public officials who took anti-gay positions.

Feb. 29: Svend Robinson comes out, the first member of the Canadian Parliament to do so.

March: The federal government issues its first employee AIDS policy, banning discrimination against people with AIDS.

June: The president's commission on AIDS surprises observers with

In 1988, ROTC featured Jim Holobaugh as an all-American cadet in their recruiting ads. Two years later, they threw him out for being gay, and demanded that he repay a $35,000 scholarship.

the tone of its final report. A year earlier, most AIDS activists had expected the commission to merely serve as a mouthpiece of administration policy. Instead, it urged the government to ban discrimination against people who are HIV-positive, to protect the confidentiality of HIV status information, and to begin AIDS education as early as kindergarten. But on August 2, when President Reagan announced his new strategies for fighting AIDS, he ignored most of the commission's recommendations.

Summer: The U.S. Public Health Service brochure "Understanding AIDS" is mailed to every household in the country. It was the first time the government had done such a massive mailing on a health issue. Most AIDS activists felt the brochure, while long overdue, was useful in reducing AIDS hysteria.

Dec. 1: World AIDS Day is observed for the first time, under the sponsorship of the World Health Organization.

• Sweden passes legislation protecting the rights of lesbian and gay couples with regard to tax breaks, inheritance, and certain social services; it is the first country to do so.

1989

After some fifteen years of being played down, the subject of gay marriage and partnership rights once again becomes a focus of attention. In May, the Denmark legalized same-sex marriages. That was soon followed by a New York State ruling that a gay couple could be considered a family for purposes of rent control. In September, the California Bar Association urged that lesbian and gay marriages be legally recognized. And by year's end, Seattle, San Francisco, and several other cities had adopted "partners" regulations that extended certain protections and rights to unmarried couples — including those of the same sex.

January: Two studies undertaken by the U.S. Department of Defense find no reason to bar gay people from military service. The reports contradicted long-standing military policy, and the Pentagon tried to keep them secret. In October, word leaked to U.S. representatives Gerry Studds and Patricia Schroeder, who made the reports public. One researcher, psychologist Michael A. McDaniel, concluded that "the preponderance of evidence presented indicates that homosexuals show pre-service suitability-related adjust-ment that is as good or better than the average heterosexual."

April 19: Forty-seven sailors are killed as a gun turret explodes on the U.S.S. *Iowa*. Navy officials leaked speculation that the explosion was connected to a relationship between Clayton Hartwig, who was killed in the blast, and survivor Kendall Truitt. The explosion was variously rumored to have been the work of Truitt (to collect on an insurance policy Hartwig held with him as beneficiary); or of Hartwig (who was despondent over being rejected by Truit or, possibly, another sailor); or by both (as a double-suicide). Despite the murkiness and inconsistency of these rumors, the media widely reported them.

Eventually, on slim evidence, the Naval Investigative Service (NIS) concluded that Hartwig had caused the explosion; Truitt was cleared. But the NIS report was widely criticized. A House Armed Services subcommittee found that the NIS had literally thrown overboard "potentially significant evidence" during cleanup procedures, and one witness recanted crucial testimony, saying the NIS had pressured him to say what he did. A year later, the General Accounting Office concluded that the explosion could well have been an accident. Finally, in October of 1991, navy admiral Frank B. Kelso admitted that there was no factual basis for having suggested that the explosion was deliberately set by a gay sailor.

If the NIS did twist evidence to reach a predetermined conclusion, the motivation was clear. Their report buttressed the navy's long-standing argument that gay people are a security hazard, and it distracted attention from charges that lax safety practices or obsolete equipment were actually to blame.

May 26: Denmark, by a vote in parliament of 71–47, becomes the first country to legalize lesbian and gay marriages. The law took effect the following Oct. 1. Adoption rights were specifically excluded from the new legislation. Shortly thereafter, Swedish prime minister Ingvar Carlsson said the Danish move was "a strong argument for a similar move in Sweden."

June 13: Washington's Corcoran Gallery cancels a planned exhibit by photographer Robert Mapplethorpe. A few of the photographs to be shown depicted homoerotic or S/M activity, and conservatives such as Sen. Jesse Helms used it as an opportunity for grandstanding. The Mapplethorpe controversy was not over, however.

June 25: The U.S. Postal Service celebrates the twentieth anniversary of the Stonewall riots with the first gay postmark. It reads "Stonewall Sta., 20 Years 1969–1989, Lesbian & Gay Pride," and displays a drawing by gay pop artist Keith Haring.

July 6: The New York State Court of Appeals, in a 4–2 ruling, declares that a gay couple who have lived together for ten years can be considered a family for purposes of rent-control protection. It marked the first time a state's highest court had ruled that a gay couple could qualify as a family. While the ruling was narrowly written so as to apply only to New York City's rent-control regulations, the ACLU attorney who argued the case called it "the most important single step forward in American law toward legal recognition of lesbian and gay relationships."

On the same day, a newly passed ordinance offering limited protections to same-sex couples in San Francisco was suspended after opponents gathered enough signatures on a petition to force the issue to a November referendum. It lost that vote by a margin of just one percent.

Oct. 1: Eleven gay couples gather in Copenhagen for the world's first legally sanctioned same-sex marriages. The celebrities of the day were Axel Axgil, who founded the first Danish gay organization in 1948, and his life partner Eigil Axgil.

Oct. 6: The AIDS memorial quilt is unfolded in Washington, D.C., for the second time. In two years, it had grown from 2,000 panels to over 10,000.

November: Keith St. John becomes the first openly gay black person elected to public office. St. John, an attorney in Albany, New York, was elected to the Common Council of that city by a 4-to-1 margin over his closest opponent. Other election news was less encouraging: gay-related ballot measures in five cities (San Francisco; Concord, Calif.; Irvine, Calif.; Tacoma, Wash.; and Athens, Ohio) were all narrowly defeated.

December: Television commentator Andy Rooney comments on the air that "There was some recognition in 1989 of the fact that many of the ills which kill us are self-in-duced: too much alcohol, too much food, drugs, homosexual unions, cigarettes. They're all known to lead quite often to premature death." The gay community was outraged, but not until a month later — when *Advocate* writer Chris Bull interviewed Rooney and quoted him as saying that "blacks have watered down their genes," did the fuss receive wide attention. Rooney denied having made the comment about blacks. CBS suspended him briefly.

Doug Hinckle/The WashingtonBlade

For ten years, Sgt. Miriam ben-Shalom fought to be re-enlisted in the army. Despite some successes along the way, she ultimately lost an appeal to the U.S. Supreme Court.

1990

January: Only a month after his controversial ordination, openly gay Episcopalian priest Robert Williams comments publicly that "monogamy is as unnatural as celibacy," then further remarks that Mother Teresa would be better off "if she got laid." Williams resigned his priesthood in 1991.

February: A long battle between Sgt. Miriam ben-Shalom and the U.S. Army finally ends. For a decade, ben-Shalom had been challenging the army's right to discharge her for being lesbian. She won at a lower court level, and became the first openly gay person ever re-enlisted by the U.S. military. But that ruling was overturned on appeal. In February 1990, the U.S. Supreme Court refused to hear a challenge to that appeal, leaving ben-Shalom with no further legal recourse.

March: Anti-gay policies in college ROTC programs become the focus of controversy. After several ROTC cadets, including James Holobaugh, were forced to leave the program because they were gay, the military

demanded they repay scholarships of $25,000 to $35,000 each. U.S. representative Gerry Studds organized a congressional protest of what he called "an appalling meanspiritedness," and the army backed down in the cases that received the most attention — but continued to press for repayment in other cases.

April 23: As a number of gay rights activists look on, President George Bush signs a bill that covers anti-gay violence. The law authorized a detailed study of crimes motivated by racial, ethnic, or sexual prejudice. It was the first time a president had signed a bill that suggested parallels between homophobia and racism or sexism, and the first time that representatives of the gay community had been invited to a White House signing.

July 19: The House Ethics Committee votes to reprimand Rep. Barney Frank for his involvement with male prostitute Steven Gobie in the years before Frank publicly came out.

Aug. 4–11: Some 7,200 athletes gather in Vancouver, Canada, for the Gay Games III and Cultural Festival, making it the largest athletic event held anywhere in the world that year. An estimated 15,000 more lesbians, gay men, and supporters came to watch, and to participate in cultural activities. For the first time in the history of the Gay Games, a world record was set as swimmer Mike Mealiffe broke the former records in his age group for both the 50- and 100-meter butterfly.

Aug. 21: Although it was hand-selected by President George Bush, the National Commission on AIDS issues a scalding indictment of his administration for falling "far short of the mark" in the war on AIDS. It particularly criticized the slow pace of research, and the lack of any coherent research strategy.

September: A leaked navy memo describes the typical lesbian sailor as "hardworking, career-oriented ... and among the command's top professionals," then urges commanders to discharge them anyway because they were bad for heterosexual morale.

Sept. 7: Kimberly Bergalis embarks on a highly visible campaign to require that health-care workers reveal their HIV status. Bergalis charged that she had been infected with HIV when her dentist, David Johnson Acer, removed her wisdom teeth in 1987. Bergalis became a highly visible proponent of testing medical personel for HIV. "I blame Dr. Acer and every single one of you bastards" for letting her contract HIV, she wrote in a public letter. "If laws are not formed to provide protection, then my suffering and death were in vain." The popular media encouraged a hysterical response to the subject, even though health experts argued that testing dentists for HIV was a foolish and wasteful approach to the epidemic. "Of all the risks you face in your life, the chance of catching AIDS from your doctor is farcically small," wrote *New Republic* columnist Michael Kinsley.

Oct. 5: Dennis Barrie, director of the Contemporary Arts Center in Cincinnati, is acquitted on obscenity charges, following an exhibit of photographs by Robert Mapplethorpe. Five of the photos, which depicted homoerotic sex or children with their genitals exposed, became the focus of a nationwide debate about art and obscenity. The prosecution's case was weakened when one of their "expert witnesses" admitted that her artistic credentials consisted of having written songs for *Captain Kangaroo*.

Oct. 27: Congress drops a federal policy that bans lesbian and gay foreigners from entering the U.S. The 1952 McCarran-Walter Act included "sexual deviation" as basis for barring immigration; it was abolished as part of an immigration overhaul championed by openly gay congressman Barney Frank. At the same time, however, Congress refused to change a policy of denying entry visas to foreign visitors

Lisa Means

The army knew that Perry Watkins was gay, but nonetheless let him serve for fifteen years, including a stint in Vietnam. Then, *shocked* to discover a gay man in their midst, the brass discharged him. Watkins fought the ruling in court and won.

with HIV or AIDS. Instead, it gave to President George Bush the authority to change the policy; he did not do so.

1991

January: Perry Watkins ends a lengthy legal battle with the army. In return for a substantial out-of-court settlement, he agreed not to seek reinstatement. Army officials had known that Watkins was gay when he enlisted, but in 1981, after he had served for sixteen years, he was discharged for homosexuality. Courts had upheld Watkins in his battle for reinstatement.

Jan. 22: In a "Day of Desperation," protesters throughout New York City try to refocus media attention from the Gulf War to AIDS. Major demonstrations slowed activity on Wall Street and in Grand Central Station. Activists chanting "Fight AIDS, not Arabs" interrupted the CBS evening news; it was believed to be the first time since the Vietnam War that protesters had interrupted a national news broadcast.

Feb. 27: "Poppers," scientifically known as alkyl nitrites, are banned throughout the United States. In the 1970s and 1980s, many gay men used the inhalant to make sexual experiences seem more intense. Some researchers theorized that poppers were linked to AIDS, because the disease was more common in gay men who had used poppers. No clear evidence of a causal link ever turned up, however; in all likelihood, people who used poppers also had more sex partners, and had a higher incidence of AIDS for that reason.

March 16: New York mayor David Dinkins joins members of the Irish Lesbian and Gay Organization for the St. Patrick's Day march down Fifth Avenue. The Ancient Order of Hibernians, which organized the annual parade, had tried everything possible to keep the gay group out, before finally agreeing to a compromise that allowed ILGO to march, but without a banner. It was one of the year's most bitterly fought gay disputes.

June: A study published in *Pediatrics* magazine reports that nearly half of the gay and lesbian teenagers interviewed say they attempted suicide more than once.

June 13: Jeffrey Collins wins a $5.3 million settlement from Shell Oil, after it fired him for being gay. Collins had previously offered to settle out of court for $50,000, but Shell turned him down. It was the largest award ever made to a victim of anti-gay employment bias.

July 23–Aug. 2: The first gay conference in Russian history is held in Leningrad and Moscow.

August 27: A cover story in *The Advocate* reveals that Pete Williams, the assistant secretary of defense and a highly visible Pentagon spokesman, is gay. Although only one of many outings to take place during this period, this one became the focal point of a heated debate on the subject. Many mainstream media reported only that "a prominent Defense Department official" had been outed. Some gay activists denounced the action, calling it an invasion of privacy or a self-defeating action. *The Advocate* and its defenders replied that the Pentagon had outed 12,000 lesbians and gay men in the preceding decade, and that outing one more person was a small price to pay in the effort to stop the military ban.

Sept. 29: California governor Pete Wilson vetoes an anti-discrimination bill, despite promises during his candidacy that he would sign such legislation. The rage felt by California activists sparked protests up and down the state, and ignited a new wave of gay activism.

Nov. 5: Sherry Harris is elected to the Seattle City Council, becoming the nation's first openly lesbian black elected official.

Nov. 7: Basketball star Earvin "Magic" Johnson announces that he is infected with HIV. The news set off a flurry of AIDS coverage not seen since Rock Hudson's 1985 announcement that he had the disease although Hudson, unlike Johnson, had been noticeably ill when he made his announcement.

December: Patricia Ireland takes office as president of the National Organization for Women (NOW). Soon afterward, Ireland spoke openly about the fact that although she was married, she had also had a female "companion" for four years. Although Ireland was reticent about defining what she meant by "companion," most observers assumed that it meant NOW had a bisexual or lesbian president for the first time in its history. Lesbians had served as vice president on several occasions, starting as far back as 1977.

1992

January: Arthur Ochs Sulzberger, Jr., youthful new publisher of the *New York Times,* announces that "diversity" will be a priority at the paper. In the months that followed, Sulzberger made it clear that his idea of diversity included lesbians and gay men. This marked the culmination of a six-year odyssey, begun when Max Frankel became executive editor in 1986 and further influenced by Jeffrey Schmalz, a respected editor who was open about being gay and about having AIDS. By 1992, a newspaper that had once had embarrassingly weak coverage of lesbian, gay, and AIDS-related issues became a leader — on the news pages, on the editorial pages, even in the business pages. This, in turn, influenced other media, with far-reaching results.

Feb. 21: Levi Strauss & Co. extends full medical benefits to domestic partners of employees. With 23,000 employees, it was the largest U.S. company ever to have done so.

March: For the second year in a row, local media coverage in Boston and New York is dominated by controversy over the St. Patrick's Day marches. Ultimately, a Boston judge ordered the South Boston Allied War Veterans Council to allow lesbian and gay marchers, but the 25 marchers were pelted with beer cans and smoke bombs. A New York judge, however, ruled that parade organizers there had the right to exclude gay participants.

May: Deb Price begins a weekly column on gay and lesbian issues for the *Detroit News*. It was the first such column for a major U.S. daily, and was picked up in other papers, including *USA Today*.

May 8–12: The Asian Lesbian Network sponsors a conference in Tokyo, drawing almost 200 delegates from thirteen countries to discuss the status of lesbians in Asia. Lesbian invisibility was commonly cited as one of the biggest problems facing the participants.

May 19: Residents of Springfield, Ore., vote to prohibit the use of city funds to encourage homosexuality, and to ban the city council from passing gay civil rights legislation. On the same day, a similar measure was solidly defeated in the Oregon city of Corvallis.

June 19: The General Accounting Office reports that the Pentagon has spent $498 million (after adjusting for inflation) over the preceding decade to replace military personnel who were discharged for being gay or lesbian. It did not attempt to estimate the additional amount spent to identify and discharge such personnel.

June 25: The Vatican issues a four-page letter to U.S. bishops, titled "Some Considerations Concerning the Catholic Response to Legislative Proposals on the Non-Discrimination of Homosexual Persons." In a nutshell, it opposed such legislation. Bishops were urged to actively oppose gay civil rights laws. Bishops in Honolulu, Seattle, and elsewhere took the unusual step of publicly dissenting.

June 28: The first pan-European gay and lesbian pride march takes place in London. An estimated 100,000 people participated.

July: Epidemiologist Susan Haynes of the National Cancer Institute reports that because lesbians more often have several identifiable risk factors, they may be three times more likely than other women to develop breast cancer. Haynes notes that her conclusions are preliminary, but they spark a great deal of discussion among lesbian health activists. Some disagree; Susan Liroff of the Women's Cancer Resource Center warns of a "blame the victim kind of thing, ... like punishment for lack of babies or having higher body weight."

September: As school reopens, a Children of the Rainbow curriculum proposed for first-grade students becomes the target of heated attacks. City school chancellor Joseph Fernandez had required that schools "should include references to lesbians and gays in all curricular areas and should avoid exclusionary practices by presuming a person's sexual orientation, [or] reinforcing stereotypes." Some districts readily accepted the proposed curriculum. Others, led by District 24 in Queens, vehemently rejected it. Two children's books — *Daddy's Roommate* and *Heather Has Two Mommies* — were singled out from the 600-title bibliography for special attack. Eventually an uneasy compromise was reached, allowing some dissident school boards to postpone the point at which they will introduce gay subjects. However, the controversy seems likely to erupt again.

Sept. 26: In the midst of a heated campaign over an anti-gay referendum, a lesbian and a gay man are killed by a firebomb in Salem, Ore. Four youths described as skinheads were arrested in the attack.

October: The Canadian government opens military service to gay men and lesbians. There was little turmoil or protest over the decision, which had been mandated by a court ruling. Because Canada is both geographically and culturally close to the United States, the success of the new policy fueled attacks on the the Pentagon's anti-gay policies. The following month, Australia lifted its ban, as well.

Nov. 3: Bill Clinton, who has courted the gay vote more openly than any previous presidential candidate, defeats George Bush.

Colorado approves the now-notorious Amendment 2, which prohibited city and county governments from passing gay civil rights protection. Within a month, a nationwide boycott of Colorado was under full swing, endorsed by numerous celebrities and the *New York Times*. On Jan. 15, a judge temporarily blocked the amendment from taking effect, pending the outcome of a lawsuit. The following July 19, the state supreme court ruled 6–1 that the law seemed to violate the equal protection clause of the U.S. Constitution, and declared that it could not be implemented unless the state showed a "compelling interest" in doing so. It was left to a Denver district court to decide, in October 1993, whether such a "compelling interest" existed, and observers predicted that Amendment 2 would meet its final defeat at that time.

Other election news was mixed. Residents of Tampa, Fla., repealed a gay rights ordinance, but anti-gay initiatives were defeated in Oregon and in Portland, Maine.

1993

Jan. 1: For the first time, homosexuality is not identified as a "behavioral and psychological problem" in the World Health Organization's listing of diseases.

Jan. 5: The Federal Bureau of Investigation releases its first report on hate crimes. The agency was required by a 1990 law to prepare an annual report on bias-motivated crimes, but less than a fifth of the country's law-enforcement agencies participated. Based on available re-

FOR BETTER OR FOR WORSE

Gay teenager Lawrence Poirier made his debut in Lynn Johnston's daily comic strip *For Better or for Worse,* in 1993.

ports, the FBI tallied 4558 hate crimes nationwide in 1991; 422 of these were motivated by anti-gay bias. Clearly the report was only a first step in determining the actual extent of such crimes.

Jan. 28: A federal judge orders the navy to reinstate petty officer Keith Meinhold, who was discharged for being openly gay. Meinhold was re-admitted, but the following day, President Clinton asked the courts to delay further action on such cases pending a decision from the White House about gays in the military.

March-April: Lawrence Poirier, a character in Lynn Johnston's daily comic strip *For Better or for Worse,* comes out. Over a course of several weeks, seventeen-year-old Lawrence told his parents he was gay, and was thrown out of his home. It wasn't the first mainstream comic strip to deal with homosexuality (*Doonesbury, Life in Hell,* and *Outland* had all raised the subject), but it brought the reality of gay teens to millions of readers. Of the 1400 newspapers that carried the strip, five refused to run it during that period and two canceled it entirely.

April 15: The Guttmacher Institute

releases the results of a controversial study, claiming that only 1.1% of American men are exclusively homosexual. Statisticians and activists quickly pointed out flaws in the study, but for the most part, the media ran the 1% headline, and ignored the caveats.

April 16: President Bill Clinton holds an hour-long meeting with the heads of several gay and lesbian organizations — the first such meeting held by a U.S. president.

April 25: The National March on Washington for Lesbian, Gay and Bi Equal Rights and Liberation takes place in Washington, D.C., as the highlight of a weekend packed with meetings, memorials, celebrations, and parties. It was the largest gay gathering in history, though there was bitter disagreement over exactly how large. March organizers predicted that a million people would turn out, then claimed to have been right; the U.S. Park Police put the number at 300,000. The Washington Blade, a gay newspaper that used aerial photos and other techniques to get the best possible view, estimated a turnout of 750,000.

Cece Cox

The new Clinton administration got mixed reviews during the 1993 March on Washington. Based on the president's delay in appointing a so-called AIDS czar, and his failure to promptly lift the ban on gays in the military, these protestors gave him a thumbs-down.

May 5: The Hawaii Supreme Court rules (3–1) that the state's prohibition of same-sex marriages constitutes sex discrimination and is probably unconstitutional. A trial judge must now rule (probably in late 1994 or 1995) on whether there is a "compelling state interest" in the prohibition. Every state in the union currently recognizes marriages performed in the other states, so if Hawaii recognizes gay unions, the repercussions would be felt nationwide — and a bitter backlash is sure to follow.

May 18: Citizens of Cornelius, Ore., vote to ban civil rights protection for lesbians and gay men. The measure passed by a wide margin of 950–589, and activists fear it would provide encouragement for anti-gay initiatives in dozens of other cities and states.

May 24: After heated debate, Roberta Achtenberg is confirmed (58–31) by the U.S. Senate to become the assistant secretary for fair housing and equal opportunity at the Department of Housing and Urban Development. It marked the first time an openly gay person had been confirmed by the Senate for a high-ranking government position. Sen. Jesse Helms led the attack against her, opposing Achtenberg "because she's a damn lesbian. I'm not going to put a lesbian in a position like that. If you want to call me a bigot, fine."

June 11: The U.S. Supreme Court unanimously rules that hate crime laws are constitutional. Such laws provide a stiffer penalty for crimes if they are motivated by hatred of a specified group. In the Court's decision, which came in the case of

Wisconsin v. *Todd Mitchell*, Chief Justice William Rehnquist noted that such crimes "inflict greater individual and societal harm" and that society has a legitimate interest in punishing them more strictly. A year earlier, the court had struck down a related but distinctly different hate-crimes law, that had attempted to outlaw expressions of hatred such as cross-burning.

June 26: The second annual celebration of Europride Day is celebrated. Berlin was the center of the 1993 event, which was marked by a split between a political faction that wanted to protest increased racism and homophobia in the post-unification Germany, and a faction that was more interested in celebrating. Each of the two marches was estimated to draw about 15,000 participants.

July 16: A study published in *Science* magazine presents evidence that male homosexuality is often associated with a specific genetic marker. Dean Hamer of the National Institutes of Health studied forty pairs of gay brothers; he found that thirty-three had identical strands of DNA on a part of the X chromosome inherited from their mother. Activists disagreed as to whether this constituted good news (since in contradicts the argument of the religious right that being gay is a choice) or bad news (since some parents might abort fetuses that showed this marker).

July 19: Ending months of speculation, President Clinton announced his "don't ask, don't tell" plan for allowing lesbians and gay men to serve in the military provided they do not engage in gay sex on or off base, and generally remain secretive about being gay. Nobody was very happy with the compromise, and activists blasted the president for reneging on his campaign promise to lift the ban entirely.

July 26: Marcelo Tenorio becomes the first person to be granted asylum by the United States for reasons of anti-gay persecution. Tenorio claimed that he faced violence and human rights abuses in Brazil because of his homosexuality, and that the Brazilian government did little to prevent these attacks. An immigration judge in San Francisco granted the asylum request, but the U.S. Immigration and Naturalization Service vowed to appeal.

LIFE BEFORE STONEWALL

The Stonewall Riots of 1969 are often seen as marking the start of the modern gay movement, and the decade that followed saw a dramatic rise in the number of gay books being published. But gay literature existed long before that. Some of the leading examples of it are briefly described here.

JOSEPH AND HIS FRIEND, by Bayard Taylor, 1870. Taylor was an eminent poet and leading writer of his time. In the 1850s, he wrote several poems with subtle gay themes, including "To a Persian Boy." His novel *Joseph and His Friend* tells the story of Joseph Asten, a young blue-eyed Pennsylvania farmer who feels different from those around him, and who worries that love must be "hidden as if it were a reproach; friendship watched, lest it express its warmth too frankly." But never does he engage in homosexual activity, and the occasional hints of Joseph's gay feelings are counterbalanced by a marriage and other heterosexual musings on Joseph's part. A heterosexual reader could easily have missed the gay content completely.

Like most other gay-themed novels published for the next hundred years, *Joseph and His Friend* has an unsatisfying ending, as Joseph marries the sister of the man with whom he has fallen in love. Nevertheless, it was a breakthrough in American literature.

Poet and author Bayard Taylor wrote the first American novel known to portray gay characters.

NORMA TRIST, OR PURE CARBON: A STORY OF THE INVERSION OF THE SEXES, by Dr. John Wesley Carhart, 1895. This early novel featured a heroine, Norma Trist, who was physically and emotionally attracted to other women. The story, based on an actual event, is not a cheerful one — in a fit of anger, Norma murders a former female lover who is about to be married. The lesbian theme, however, is treated in a relatively positive light. Norma's lesbianism is presented as normal for her, and on the witness stand, she says that "My love for and relations with Marie afforded the highest and profoundest satisfaction of which the entire human being is capable in the realm of human love." Gay historian Jonathan Katz called this "probably the most explicit, unequivocating defense of genital-orgasmic relations between women published in English in the nineteenth century."

IMRE: A MEMORANDUM, by Xavier Mayne, 1906. For its time, *Imre* presented a remarkably positive portrayal of homosexuality. Presented as a true memoir, it describes the narrator's love affair with a handsome, virile Hungarian lieutenant named Imre. Mayne (a pseudonym for Edward I. Stevenson) identified with the philosophy of Edward Carpenter, the British socialist who saw homosexuality as the supreme form of friendship, and his novel ends with the two protagonists living happily together. The positive role models did little good for the average gay person, however; the book was published in English, in Italy, in a limited edition of 125 copies.

BERTRAM COPE'S YEAR, by Henry Blake Fuller, 1919. Set in the 1870s and told through the eyes of narrator Basil Randolph, *Bertram Cope's Year* portrays three characters who seem to be homosexual. Basil himself is a middle-aged bachelor with clearly repressed homosexual feelings. He becomes attracted to Bertram Cope, a likeable young professor at the local college, and makes thinly veiled passes at Bertram. Bertram is also being pursued by Arthur Lemoyne, a more overtly gay character with "dark, limpid eyes," and fingers that "displayed certain graceful, slightly af-

fected movements." Arthur is run out of town after trying to seduce another male student, and as the book draws to a close, Bertram also leaves town to join him. *Bertram Cope's Year* was turned down by the major publishers, and never achieved wide distribution.

DER PUPPENJUNGE, by John Henry Mackay, 1926. Mackay, a Scottish-born anarchist who lived in Berlin most of his life, was primarily attracted to teenaged boys. During the early 1900s, he devoted much of his energy to expounding the merits of man/boy love. In *Der Puppenjunge,* he depicted a young closeted gay man who finds himself irresistibly enamored with a street hustler he encounters in Berlin. The novel combines a poignant love story with a colorful portrayal of the gay subculture that thrived in Berlin during the 1920s. Mackay's depiction of the life of a Berlin hustler is especially illuminating. In 1985, Hubert Kennedy translated the novel into English, and it was published for the first time in the United States under the title *The Hustler.*

THE WELL OF LONELINESS, by Radclyffe Hall, 1928. The best-known novel before World War II to depict either a lesbian or gay male protagonist was certainly this one, brought out by a reputable London publisher. The protagonist, Stephen Gordon, is a woman who was born to parents who fervently wanted a boy; everything from her name to her upbringing reflects that desire. By the age of eight she has already developed a passion for an adult woman. Further infatuations follow, eventually culminating in a love af-

In 1933, Forman Brown (left) wrote the ground-breaking gay novel *Better Angel*, which was published under the pseudonym Richard Meeker. Fifty-four years later (right), Brown saw a new edition of the work and, for the first time, publicly identified himself as the author.

fair that might last except for the pressures of straight society. Hall was clearly familiar with the work of Karl Ulrichs, who believed that both lesbians and gay men represented the soul of one sex trapped in the body of another. Her book, although depressing, told lesbians of the time that they were not alone. For today's reader, however, Hall's characterization of a lesbian seems stale.

BETTER ANGEL, by Richard Meeker (pseudonym of Forman Brown), 1933. The first American novel to combine a positive gay character and a happy ending was probably *Better Angel,* in which a young man struggles successfully to find love and contentment in the years between the wars. The story behind *Better Angel* has an ending as happy as the novel itself. It was republished in 1987, with an introduction by Hubert Kennedy stating that the author had probably used a pseudonym and that "over a half century after the novel's original publication, we are unlikely to discover what became of Richard Meeker." But soon thereafter, an elderly man in Los Angeles came forth and identified himself as the author of the novel, which had been published pseudonymously. He and his lover and another gay friend — all of whom had provided the basis for characters in the book — had lived and traveled together for over sixty years. At the age of eighty-seven, Forman Brown finally received public credit for a pioneering work of gay fiction.

WE TOO ARE DRIFTING, by Gale

Gale Wilhelm stopped writing in 1945 and disappeared from public view. Forty years later, lesbian publisher Barbara Grier tracked her down and re-issued her two early lesbian novels. Today they are well known as treasured landmarks of lesbian literature. These photos of Wilhelm are from 1935 and 1985.

Wilhelm, first English publication in 1935. Although better written than *The Well of Loneliness,* Gale Wilhelm's work never received the public attention shown to Hall's earlier novel. *We Too Are Drifting* tells the story of Jan Morale, a young artist with decidedly masculine traits. Morale becomes sexually involved with an older married woman, while falling in love with another: the young and innocent Victoria. She is reluctant, however, to initiate Victoria into a world that for her has caused so much pain, and the pressure for Victoria to conform to her family's expectations proves too much for the relationship.

Wilhelm also wrote *Torchlight to Valhalla,* which has a happier ending. But she stopped writing in 1945. Forty years later, lesbian publisher Barbara Grier tracked her down: Wilhelm was then seventy-seven, living in Berkeley with a lover, and hospitalized with a broken hip. Through Naiad Press, Grier re-issued both books.

DIANA: A STRANGE AUTOBIOGRAPHY, by Diana Frederics, 1939. Published under a pseudonym, *Diana* purported to be a true autobiography and may actually have been so, but its often melodramatic tone suggests that the author took occasional liberties with the facts. The title character grows up surrounded by brothers and a father whom she loves. At the age of sixteen she falls in love with another schoolgirl, and is thoroughly frightened as she comes to realize the different nature of her sexuality. An older brother tries to help by introducing her to works of Havelock Ellis and Sigmund Freud, which portrayed homosexuality in a tolerant light, but Diana is still troubled. The road to self-acceptance is not easy, but by the end of the novel Diana has met a woman with whom she can live in happiness, and the author has presented a strong case for the validity of lesbian love. This upbeat ending, unusual for its time, and the widespread distribution of *Diana,* made the book a godsend for thousands of women.

THE CITY AND THE PILLAR, by Gore Vidal, 1948. The first gay American novel to get wide public circulation was unexceptional as far as its content. While in high school, Jim Willard and Bob Ford go on a camping trip together, where an evening swim and wrestling match by a campfire lead to sex. The incident becomes etched into Jim's mind as a perfect moment, which he seeks throughout his life to recreate. Years later he re-encounters and tries to seduce Bob, who is now married; when Bob refuses his advances, Jim rapes him. In the 1940s, however, this ending wasn't sufficiently gloomy for the book's New York publisher, who had Vidal write a new ending in which Jim strangles Bob to death. Only in the 1965 edition was the original ending restored.

QUATREFOIL, by James Barr, 1950. The decade following World War II saw a dramatic increase in both the quality, and quantity, of gay novels. Among the best was James Barr's story of Phillip Froelich, a brash young naval officer who is just realizing his homosexuality, and the

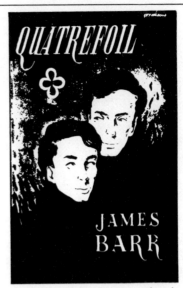

more experienced man who becomes his mentor and lover. An unwritten code dictated that gay novels written in this period should nearly always end with a death, and *Quatrefoil* is no exception, but Barr went as far as he could within the constraints of his time. The death is an accident rather than a suicide or murder, and the overall tone of the book is positive and uplifting. Many men who grew up in the 1950s remember *Quatrefoil* as one of the two books (Fritz Peters's *Finistere* is the other) that provided their most positive early role models.

WOMEN'S BARRACKS, by Tereska Torres, 1950. You won't find *Women's Barracks* on anybody's list of the best in lesbian reading. Yet it had a significance far beyond the storyline, which depicted two lesbian military officers in a relatively nonjudgmental light. In 1950, Fawcett Crest was among the first publishing companies to introduce a new type of book: the paperback original. Until World War II, a cloth jacket was the standard format for a book. With World War II came the practice of reprinting hardcover best-sellers in paperback. But not until the 1950s did publishers try eliminating the hardcover stage. The resulting low-priced books were marketed differently, and publishers experimented with manuscripts that would once have seemed too sensational. *Women's Barracks* was the first in a wave of lesbian pulp novels, cresting in the late 1950s, that gave women a chance to feel less alone. Although not often reviewed or recognized in the mainstream press, some of these books were phenomenally successful. Marion Zimmer Bradley broke into writing via the lesbian pulps, and Ann Bannon's *Odd Girl Out* was Fawcett's second-best-selling title in 1957.

THE CHARIOTEER, by Mary Renault, 1953. While recovering from war injuries in a British military hospital, a young soldier has time to wrestle with his gay feelings. In the hospital, he meets two people who symbolize his conflicting feelings: a young conscientious objector, and an old acquaintance from school who is already in the thick of gay life. Renault established her reputation with this hauntingly beautiful book (which was not published in the U.S. until six years later), but her future novels were set in classical Greece.

PATIENCE AND SARAH, by Isabel Miller (pseudonym of Alma Routsong), 1967. On a trip to New York, Alma Routsong serendipitously discovered a reference to painter Mary Ann Willson (c. 1820) and her "farmerette" companion, Miss Brundidge. She immediately tried to find out more about the women (one reference work described them as having a "romantic attachment") and soon used their relationship as the basis for a work of fiction. The finished novel was turned down by five or six publishers, Routsong later told historian Jonathan Katz, and in 1967 (under the title *A Place for Us*) she published it herself. Within five years McGraw-Hill had purchased rights to the book, and today it is considered a still-fascinating classic of lesbian literature.

STUDIES INVOLVING HOMOSEXUALITY

ULRICHS'S FIRST ESTIMATES

Karl Heinrich Ulrichs, the German lawyer who pioneered the early homosexual movment, published two short pamphlets — *Vindex* and *Inclusa* — in 1864, in which he attempted an unbiased scientific assessment of homosexuality. His estimate:

- One German in 500 was homosexual.

Critics said this was much too high.

Analysis:

Despite his scientific intentions, Ulrichs was still only making a stab in the dark, in an environment where it would have been impossible to get most homosexual men to acknowledge their orientation.

THE HIRSCHFELD REPORT

The first scientific attempt to measure the incidence of homosexuality was conducted in 1903 and 1904 by Dr. Magnus Hirschfeld, a German sex researcher. He distributed questionnaires to about 3000 college students and 5700 metal workers, and asked each one whether his libido had always been directed only to females, only to males, or to both.

About 49% responded, and Hirschfeld concluded that:

- 94.3% were exclusively heterosexual.
- 2.3% were exclusively homosexual.
- 3.4% were bisexual.

A German court ruled that Hirschfeld's study could have led impressionable young men toward "perverse tendencies," and fined him 200 marks for having sent out the questionnaires.

In a later study, Hirschfeld asked a number of men he knew to be homosexual to report how many men they knew at their workplace, in their fraternity, or in other groups where they spent time, and then to estimate how many were homosexual. By adding up the numbers, he concluded that out of 23,771 men, 525 were homosexual — 2.2%.

Analysis:

Hirschfeld's first effort was impressive for its day, but the two groups he surveyed were unrepresentative of the overall population. Even more troubling, 51% of those surveyed failed to respond. Without a better understanding of why they didn't respond, it's risky to draw many conclusions from his numbers.

His second study was an imaginative effort to overcome the dangers of self-concealment, but it introduced new limitations. Many homosexuals would not have been known to co-workers and associates, and probably a few heterosexuals were misidentified because of hearsay or wishful thinking.

THE KINSEY REPORTS

Alfred C. Kinsey never said that 10% of the population was homosexual. He would undoubtedly have been annoyed at such an oversimplification of his findings.

Kinsey's landmark 1948 study, *Sexual Behavior in the Human Male,* and his subsequent *Sexual Behavior in the Human Female* (1953), revealed a far more complex world. Kinsey considered sexual orientation to be a continuous spectrum, and for statistical purposes he rated it on a scale of 0 to 6, in which 0 represented someone who was exclusively heterosexual, and 6 was exclusively homosexual. For the total white male population, Kinsey concluded from his 5300 in-depth interviews that:

- 37% had at least some overt homosexual experience to the point of orgasm sometime between adolescence and old age.
- 30% rated 1 to 6 on his scale — they had at least incidental homosexual experience or reactions for at least three years between the ages of 16 and 55.
- 25% rated 2 to 6 — they had more than incidental homosexual experience or reactions for at least three years between the ages of 16 and 55.
- 18% rated 3 to 6 — they were at least as much homosexual as heterosexual for at least three years between the ages of 16 and 55.
- 13% rated 4 to 6 — they were more homosexual than hetero-

sexual for at least three years between the ages of 16 and 55.
- 10% rated 5 to 6 — they were more or less exclusively homosexual for at least three years between the ages of 16 and 55.
- 8% rated 6 — they were exclusively homosexual for at least three years between the ages of 16 and 55.
- 4% were exclusively homosexual all their lives.

Many observers also feigned surprise at Kinsey's statistics about masturbation:

- 44.9% of 13-year-old boys reported having masturbated.
- 91.8% of 18-year-olds reported having done so.
- 93.8% of 24-year-olds reported having done so.

In light of these numbers, it was hard for adults to maintain the myth that masturbation caused mental illness, hairy palms, nearsightedness, or pimples.

Five years later, in his report on female sexuality, Kinsey analyzed his data differently, so it's not possible here to give the same breakdowns as were given above for males. For the white female population, Kinsey concluded from his 5940 in-depth interviews that:

- 13% had at least some overt homosexual experience to the point of orgasm sometime between adolescence and old age.
- Between 3% and 8% of the unmarried females, and under 1% of the married females, rated 4 to 6 on Kinsey's scale — that is, they were primarily or exclusively homosexual — between the ages of 20 and 35.
- Of the 142 females with the

most extensive homosexual experience, exactly half (71) said they had no regrets.

- In comparing women in their fifth year of heterosexual marriage to women in long-term lesbian relationships, Kinsey found the latter group more likely to reach orgasm: 68% of lesbians, versus 40% of heterosexuals, experienced orgasm at least nine times out of ten.
- 12% of 12-year-old girls reported having masturbated.
- 20% of 15-year-olds reported having done so.
- 33% of 20-year-olds reported having done so.
- 57% of females (compared to 28% of males) learned to masturbate through self-discovery.
- 11% of females (compared to 40% of males) learned to masturbate through observation of and experience with others.

Analysis:

Kinsey's research methodology was far superior to that of any similar study, before or since. He went to great pains to ensure that respondents were honest. He often got the support of a minister or other influential member of a community, and used that support to create trust from the people he interviewed. He also promised confidentiality; names of interviewees were carefully encoded. His researchers were trained not to respond positively or negatively to what they were told. He developed careful procedures to detect exaggeration and cover-ups on the part of interviewees. Kinsey's first report includes 119 pages about his interviewing techniques, statistical concerns, and the steps he took to assure the validity of his data.

Kinsey's results have been criticized on the grounds of self-selection; that is, that he interviewed only those individuals who volunteered to participate. In fact, Kinsey was well aware of this potential for bias. As he himself noted, individuals who are "more prudish, restrained, apathetic, and sexually less active" are less likely to volunteer for a sex survey. Whenever possible, Kinsey tried to get 100% of the population within a certain group (a rooming house, a college fraternity or sorority, etc.) to participate. He used statistics from these "hundred percent groups" as an aid in evaluating the accuracy of his other samples.

Although he interviewed people in every state, most of Kinsey's subjects came from the Midwest and the Northeast. There is no evidence, however, that this created a significant bias in his results. Although he interviewed people of all races, Kinsey decided that he did not have enough nonwhites to make useful comparisons, and some of his results (including those above) were for the white population.

ASK *PLAYBOY* (1971)

The September 1971 issue of *Playboy* reported the results of a survey of male college students:

- 1% indicated a "same sex only" preference.
- another 1% preferred "same sex mostly."
- yet another 1% said they enjoyed sex with "either sex."

Analysis:

The magazine apparently did

make a reasonable effort to select a representative sample of colleges and universities for the poll. However, distribution of the actual survey was left up to *Playboy* representatives, a procedure that seems unlikely to have produced a random sampling of respondents. The survey presumably did help sell magazines — which is undoubtedly all it was intended to do.

GAY ATHLETES (1976)

Shortly after pro-football player David Kopay came out, speculation abounded about how many professional athletes were gay. Richard W. Smith and Bryan Garner, researchers at California State University, decided to find out. They conducted anonymous interviews with 82 team members within the National College Athletic Association. Of those men:

- 40% said they had engaged in sex to the point of orgasm with another man on at least two occasions in the preceding two years.

Trying to get a lower number, the researchers eliminated mutual masturbation from their list of gay sex acts. But even so:

- 33% still qualified as gay or bisexual, having engaged in either oral or anal sex with another man on two occasions in the preceding two years.

Analysis:

A sample size this small has a large margin of error. It's noteworthy, however, how closely these figures correspond to those of the Kinsey report.

THE MENDOLA REPORT (1980)

Mary Mendola, herself a lesbian, became interested in the experiences of lesbian and gay couples. She wrote a questionnaire for couples, and distributed 1500 copies through personal contacts, who in turn were asked to pass the questionnaire on to their friends, and so on. From the 27% that came back, she published *The Mendola Report: A New Look at Gay Couples*, in 1980. Among the results:

Monogamy:
- 83% of lesbians and 37% of gay men had sex exclusively with their partners.
- 14% of lesbians and 49% of gay men had sex mostly with their partners, but occasionally had outside affairs.
- 1% of lesbians and 8% of gay men had sex both in their relationsips and outside of their relationships on a regular basis.
- 2% of lesbians and 6% of gay men lived together but did not have sex, and were free to have sex outside the relationship.

Financial arrangements:
- 59% jointly owned household furnishings.
- 26% jointly owned cars or motorcycles.
- 24% jointly owned their residence.
- 8% jointly owned businesses.
- 4% had joint savings accounts and other investments.

Family relationships
- 40% said their parents accepted their relationship, and included partners in family functions.
- 53% said their siblings accepted their relationship.

- 36% said their parents were not aware of their relationship.
- 29% said their siblings were not aware of their relationship.
- 21% said their parents treat their relationship as simply that of two friends living together, with no special commitment.
- 16% said their siblings treat their relationship as simply two friends living together.

Analysis:

As Mendola acknowledged, a questionnaire distributed in this way will not represent the entire population. "The type of person [who responds to questionnaires] is better educated and of a higher socioeconomic background than the general population," she noted, and in fact, 54% of her respondents had professional backgrounds.

Statistics for monogamy, especially, have probably changed because of the AIDS epidemic.

NATIONAL ACADEMY OF SCIENCES (1988)

The National Opinion Research Council, under the auspices of the National Academy of Sciences, conducted a study based on data collected in 1970 and in 1988 through an anonymous, self-administered questionnaire for men. The results were reported in *Science* magazine, Jan. 20, 1989. Based on 1719 responses, they reported that:

- 1.6% to 2% had had sex to orgasm with another man within the past year.
- 20.3 had such sex at some point in their life.
- 6.7% had such sex after the age of 19.

- One in 16 had such experiences "fairly often" or "occasionally" at some point in his life.

The researchers noted that "given the history of discrimination and oppression — not to mention the fact that in many states sodomy statues would classify the reported behaviors as criminal," it is reasonable to expect that homosexual behavior would be underreported.

Researchers also noted that 20% of respondents skipped some or all of the questions about homosexual behavior.

Analysis:

A self-administered questionnaire is less accurate than a confidential, face-to-face interview with an experienced interviewer. However, given these limitations, the researchers here seem to have used solid methodology. They attempted to use statistical extrapolations to account for respondents who did not return the questionnaire or who responded only partially.

As the researchers noted, some respondents were probably reluctant to report homosexual activity. If we assume that most of the respondents who skipped these questions would have answered yes, and add that 20% to the 20% who acknowledged having engaged in homosexual sex at some point, we get 40% — again, remarkably close to Kinsey's 37%.

OVERLOOKED OPINIONS (Ongoing)

A Chicago-based research firm named Overlooked Opinions regularly announces the results of its surveys of the lesbian and gay population. Among its findings:

- 93.6% of lesbians and gay men voted in the 1992 presidential elections.
- 0% voted for George Bush in that election.
- 65.3% of lesbians go camping.
- 13.1% of gay men are Republicans.
- The average household income is $51,624 for gay men and $42,755 for lesbians.
- The average household size is 1.7 persons for gay men and 1.9 persons for lesbians.

Analysis:

The technique of sending a questionnaire to people, and asking them to mail it back, results in a process known as self-selection. If some recipients mail it back and others don't, then the people who mail it back are, inherently, not representative of the overall population that was surveyed.

Perhaps surprisingly, the use of decimal points — not 65% of lesbians, but 65.3% of lesbians, go camping — is a clue to its inaccuracy. However thoroughly it may be conducted, a poll of this sort will have a margin of error of several percentage points. Careful, systematic researchers will acknowledge this. They will not add a meaningless decimal digit to their numbers, and in most cases they will indicate their margin of error.

BATTELLE STUDY (1993)

A study suggesting that only 1% of American men are gay generated more coverage than any similar study since Kinsey's, as well as heated controversy.

In April 1993, the Battelle Human Affairs Research Centers in Seattle released the findings of a federally funded study on male sexual behavior. The study had been designed to study AIDS transmission, but the statistic that dominated the news was the small percentage of men who said they were exclusively homosexual. Researchers interviewed 3321 men between the ages of 20 and 39.

- 2.3% had had sex with men in the past ten years.
- 1.1% had had sex only with men in the past ten years.

Analysis:

The study was designed to look at heterosexual behavior, not to count the gay population. Although researchers initially made a point of grabbing headlines with their 1% estimate, they backed off as soon as questions about their methodology began to surface. "If we had wanted to count gays, we would have done a totally different study," explained one. And, in fact, several factors cast doubt on their results.

Respondents were asked for their social security number and the name of their employer. They were promised confidentiality, but not knowing the interviewers, they had no reason to feel confident about that. This would have greatly influenced the results.

Researchers took care to request interviews from a representative cross section of the population — a step not taken in most other studies. However, 27% of these randomly selected men refused to participate, and 3% did not answer all the questions. Researchers seem to have naively overlooked the importance of this self-selection bias. Since sodomy is still illegal in half the states, and workers can be fired for being gay in most states, many gay men were certainly hidden in this 30%. Koray Tanfer, a senior researcher involved in the study, made the remarkable statement (quoted in the *Washington Blade*) that "it's [gay men's] fault [if] their numbers aren't coming out more accurately.... [If the numbers are wrong, then] they should be more open so we can do our job."

U.S. CENSUS

The 1990 United States census, for the first time, included a question that more or less identified gay couples. It counted:

- 88,200 gay male couples, with average household income of $56,863, average age, 34.4 years.
- 69,200 lesbian couples, with average household income of $44,793, average age, 34.0 years.

Analysis:

The Census Bureau made no effort to notify people of these questions, and some individuals probably either answered wrong because they misunderstood the question, or didn't want to identify themselves as homosexual. In addition, the census question only counted gay people who were actually living together with someone in a relationship.

WE'RE NOT ALL ALIKE: FACTS ABOUT COUPLES

In the mid-1970s, with support from two major foundations, Philip Blumstein and Pepper Schwartz undertook a major study of how people relate as couples. Several thousand couples were interviewed and, unlike so many other researchers, Blumstein and Schwartz included not only married heterosexuals in their study, but also unmarried heterosexuals, gay male couples, and lesbian couples. They broke down their results according to these four categories, often finding significant differences between them. Some of these findings, revealed in 1983 in their book *American Couples,* are summarized here.

In general, the partner with the greatest income has more power within the relationship. In only one category was this not the general rule. For lesbians, the division of money and the division of power in a relationship were usually unconnected. The connection between power and income was stronger for gay male couples than for heterosexual couples.

Gay men enjoy their jobs more if they can be out at work. For lesbians, being out at work does not seem to make a difference in job satisfaction. This, the researchers speculate, may be because single women are not as-sumed to be lesbian as readily as single men are assumed to be gay.

During the first two years of a relationship, gay men have sex together more often than any other category of couple. After ten years, they have sex together much less often than do married couples. This reflects a common pattern by which gay male relationships turn into more of a friendship than a sexual relationship after a period of years, often with both partners having sex outside of the relationship. [Since this study was completed long before the full impact of the AIDS epidemic was felt, these figures might be different today.]

Lesbians generally have sex less frequently than do other types of couples. This study, however, only covered genital sexuality, and thus did not include what some participants would have considered to be fully satisfying but nongenital sexual experiences. After being together ten years or more, the percentage of couples who said that they had sex together no more than once a month was:

    Lesbians: 47%
    Gay men: 33%
    Married couples: 15%

The importance of kissing varies among types of couples. The percentage who said that they always kissed when they had sex ranged as follows:

Lesbians: 95%
Heterosexuals: 80%
Gay men: 71%

People who were disappointed with the amount of money they had, as a couple, were also less satisfied with the relationship — except for lesbians. The authors note that many lesbians are all too aware of the tendency in heterosexual relationships for differences in income to translate into differences in power. Lesbians, they speculate, "bend over backward to avoid letting money have that kind of control over their lives."

In general, men are more likely to approve of sex without love than are women. But lesbians are more likely to approve of it than are married men. Those who said they approved of sex without love broke down as follows, by category:

Gay men: 79%
Male co-habitors: 72%
Female co-habitors: 67%
Lesbians: 57%
Married men: 52%
Married women: 37%

Gay men are much less sexually possessive than are any of the other categories studied. When asked if they would be bothered were their partners to have sex with someone else, the percentage who said "Yes" in each category were:

Wives: 84%
Husbands: 79%
Lesbians: 74%
Female co-habitors: 72%
Male co-habitors: 68%
Gay men: 35%

...But when it came to "meaningful outside affairs," the differences were less dramatic. At least three-quarters of people in every category said that would bother them. The actual percentages were:

Wives: 93%
Female co-habitors: 89%
Husbands: 87%
Lesbians: 86%
Male co-habitors: 80%
Gay men: 76%

Gay men were far less monogamous than other couples. When asked if they had engaged in sex with someone other than their partner since that relationship started, the percentage who said "Yes" for each category was:

Gay men: 82%
Male co-habitors: 33%
Female co-habitors: 30%
Lesbians: 28%
Husbands: 26%
Wives: 21%

GAY SYMBOLS THROUGH THE AGES

Today the rainbow flag and the pink triangle are widely recognized symbols within the lesbian and gay community. But over the centuries, many other symbols have also represented homosexuality in one way or another.

BUTTERFLY. In the years soon after Stonewall, several gay liberation groups decided that the butterfly, resplendent and beautiful after emerging from its dark cocoon, perfectly symbolized the new movement. It is encountered less frequently today.

CALAMUS. Walt Whitman took the erect leaves of the calamus plant as a symbol of homoerotic love; the "Calamus" section of his book *Leaves of Grass* celebrates "manly attachments" and "the need of comrades." Whitman referred to the phallic symbolism of the plant and wrote that at a pond surrounded by the calamus plant, "I last saw him that tenderly loves me — and returns again."

CUT SLEEVE. Two thousand years ago, a Chinese emperor was resting next to his youthful lover. The young man fell asleep on the emperor's wide-cut sleeve, so rather than disturb his companion, the emperor cut off the sleeve. From this ancient legend arose the Chinese euphemism of the *cut sleeve* as a metaphor for homosexuality.

FREEDOM RINGS. The newest symbol of same-sex love has swept through the community like the storm before a rainbow. The six aluminum rings, brightly colored in red, orange, yellow, green, blue, and violet, were designed by David Spada, a New York artist, as a fundraiser for the 1991 Freedom Day Committee in San Francisco. Within year, over 100,000 sets had been sold. Some people wear them on a finger (stacked in rainbow sequence); more commonly they're displayed on a chain.

GREEN. According to historian Wayne Dynes, the color green was associated with homosexuality in ancient Rome, and again in late nineteenth-century England. Poet and writer Judy Grahn recalls that at her high school in the 1950s, anyone who wore the color green on Thursday was promptly labeled "queer."

In 1894, a satirical novel by Robert Hichens, titled *The Green Carnation*, included malicious attacks on Oscar Wilde's homosexuality, furthering the gay connotations of both the color green, and of the carnation. Detroit's first gay community center, formed in 1972, was called The Green Carnation.

HARE. In his book *Christianity, Social Tolerance, and Homosexuality,* John Boswell documents an early association of the hare with male homosexuality. It apparently began in the first century with the Epistle of Barnabus, which cited various prohibitions supposedly set forth by Moses. Eating a hare, the author said, would make one a pederast because the hare grows a new anal opening each year.

In the same vein of logic, this text forbade eating hyenas "because this animal changes its gender annually." It further condemned the weasels, "who we hear commit uncleanness with their mouths ... For this animal conceives through its mouth."

All three animals, Boswell shows, continued to be associated with homosexuality even into the Middle Ages.

HYENA. *See Hare.*

HARLEQUIN DIAMONDS. The Mattachine Society, formed in 1950, took its name from the medieval jesters who always wore masks in public. According to the International Gay and Lesbian Archives, the San Francisco chapter of Mattachine took this theme one step further in 1955, adopting a design consisting of four diamonds, which together form a larger diamond, from twelfth-century troubadors. This emblem appeared on their newsletter and on enameled pins.

LABRYS. The double-bladed ax known as a *labrys* appears in art dating as far back as ancient Crete, often as a symbol of female strength. The ancient Greeks portrayed members of the all-female Amazons carrying a labrys. In modern times, it has come to be a symbol of lesbianism, found most commonly in jewelry.

Barbara G. Walker, in her *Woman's Encyclopedia of Myths and Secrets,* traces the labrys back to mythological times when it was used as

a scepter by the ancient Amazon goddess Demeter (also known as Gaea or Artemis). Walker speculates that it may originally have been a battle-axe used by female Scythian warriors, who adopted it as a symbol when the goddess's shrine at Delphi was taken over by a male priesthood.

LADSLOVE. In the nineteenth and early twentieth centuries, some English poets used the plant ladslove as a symbol of homosexuality. Part of the appeal certainly derived from the plant's name. In addition, some said it had an odor like that of a man's semen.

LAMBDA. The Greek letter lambda was chosen by the Gay Activists Alliance in 1970 to become a symbol of the gay movement. Years later, one activist from that era recalled that the letter was chosen because in modern physics, the lambda signifies change. Others believe it was chosen because of its connotations, in ancient Greece, of justice and reconciliation of opposites.

The lambda's original militant connotations have softened, and it often appears on jewelry, as a sign that will go unrecognized by the uninitiated. The word has also been useful for organizations, such as Lambda Legal Defense and Education Fund, as a way of expressing the concept "lesbian and gay male" without quite so many syllables.

LAVENDER. Today, lavender is the color most often identified with gayness. The association goes back to ancient times, and has been strengthened by the fact that lavender or purple is the combination of blue and red (pink) — traditional male and female colors. The gemstone amethyst, because of its purple color, has acquired the same connotations.

MERGED SYMBOLS. The universal symbols for woman (a circle with a cross at the bottom) and man (a circle with an arrow at the top right) have been merged in various configurations to symbolize lesbians, gay men, or the full lesbian and gay community. The result is widely recognized, though not widely used — perhaps because it looks a bit too busy to satisfy a true gay sensibility.

MYRTLE. In 1894, poet and criminologist George Cecil Ives formed the Order of Chaeronea, one of the earliest known gay organizations. He designed rings for members that incorporated the number 338 (the original "army of lovers" — the Sacred Band of Thebes — was defeated in 338 B.C. at the Battle of Chaeronea), the letters Z, L, and D (for zeal, learning, and discipline), and wreaths of myrtle and calamus.

PHOENIX. The phoenix, a mythical bird of scarlet, blue, purple, and gold, was fabled to live five centuries, then to burn itself on a funeral pyre and rise from the ashes, each time grander than before. In a 1989 "Love letter to the movement," comedian Robin Tyler proposed the phoenix as a symbol of the lesbian and gay movement. "Like the phoenix, against all odds, we have risen again and again," she wrote. But so far, the proposal has not taken flight.

PEACH, HALF-EATEN. Chinese legend tells of an ancient emperor who was eating a peach as he enjoyed a walk with his male lover. In a spontaneous gesture of sharing, the emperor offered his companion the half-eaten peach, which then became a symbol of homosexual love. The story is recalled in Bret Hinsch's book *Passions of the Cut Sleeve.*

PINK TRIANGLE. The Nazis required known homosexuals to wear an inverted pink triangle (one pointing downward) on their clothing, so that they could be quickly picked out for special abuse. In the 1970s, gay activists began using this symbol as a way of identifying themselves while also calling attention to this long-forgotten chapter of gay history.

German historian Ilsa Kokula has found some evidence that

known lesbians were made to wear a black triangle in the concentration camps. Other scholars have been skeptical that the Germans even recognized the possibility of lesbian sexuality and believe that the black triangle was used for saboteurs and a wide range of other people who were considered misfits.

Q. The initial letter of the word *Queer* was introduced on t-shirts of Queer Nation members, then reappeared with the short-lived gay New York periodical, *QW.* It seems likely to take on an identity all its own in the years ahead.

RAINBOW FLAG. In 1978, Gilbert Baker of San Francisco designed the rainbow flag as a symbol of gay and lesbian community pride. The giant rainbow flag, dubbed "New Glory," made its first appearance in San Francisco's 1978 Gay and Lesbian Freedom Day Parade. It had eight stripes, adding pink and indigo to the six colors that remain.

Slowly the flag took hold, offering a colorful and optimistic alternative to the more common pink triangle symbol. Today it is recognized by the International Congress of Flag Makers, and is flown in lesbian and gay pride marches worldwide. It consists of six horizontal stripes, each an equal length. Starting at the top, the colors are red (for light); orange (for healing); yellow (for the sun); green (for serenity); blue (for art); and purple (for the spirit).

RED TIE. In the first few decades of this century, some men wore a red tie as a way of indicating that they were gay.

RHINOCEROS. Two Boston activists got tired of letting the mass media decide just how gay people were to be depicted to the public. In 1974, Bernie Toal and Tom Morganti initiated a media campaign using a lavender rhinoceros as a symbol of gay people. They prepared three placards for placement on the local subways, then hit a snag: the Massachusetts Transit Authority claimed the ads did not qualify for the public service rate of $2 per placement, and instead demanded the commercial rate of $7 each. The ensuing controversy provided valuable free publicity, but didn't change the rate. Ads were placed for three months, beginning in December of 1974; the organizers then decided to put their time and limited funds into other activities.

Why a rhinoceros? Toal explained that "The rhino is a much maligned and misunderstood animal and, in actuality, is a gentle creature — but don't cross him or her!" And, as someone else pointed out, it's always horny.

RING ON LITTLE FINGER. Wearing a ring on the little finger, especially the little finger of the left hand, has come to be a discreet way of indicating gayness. There is evidence that this tradition goes back many centuries, but its origins have been lost to antiquity. In her book

Another Mother Tongue, Judy Grahn notes that the occult sciences associated both the color purple and the little finger with spiritual knowledge and transformation. This connection may have given rise to the little-finger ring tradition.

VIOLETS. One of the earliest major plays to include a lesbian theme was Edouard Bourdet's *La Prisonnière,* which was translated and produced on Broadway as *The Captive* in 1926. In the play, a bouquet of violets symbolizes lesbian love, and theater historian Kaier Curtin writes that "As a result of the success of *The Captive,* French florists experienced a devastating drop in the violet market. The same thing happened in those sections of America familiar with the drama's lesbian love notoriety."

Curtin speculates that Bourdet, who was familiar with Sappho's lesbian love poems, selected this particular flower for his play because Sappho describes herself and her lover, in one poem, as wearing tiaras made of violets when they were happy together. Perhaps he also knew of the tradition in sixteenth-century England, reported by Judy Grahn, of violets being worn by men and women who did not plan to marry.

VULVA HANDS. Hearsay has it that this symbol originated in the 1980s at the peace camps in Europe when women inverted the old Italian curse-gesture meaning "pussy" (with the hands held over the crotch), reclaiming it as a symbol of women's power, especially women's sexual power. A "hearing-ism," it appears to have no connection to American Sign Language, although the sign for "vagina" is similar: the hands are held over the lower belly, pointing downward, with the tips of the thumbs and forefingers touching (the other fingers may be curled into the palms or extended). The hands have become a popular icon among lesbians, especially in the form of jewelry.

WEASEL. *See Hare.*

YANG AND YIN. A bulletin from the International Gay and Lesbian Archives notes that "our earliest known movement symbol was the ancient yang and yin adopted by The Circle in Switzerland," beginning in 1933. This symbol, consisting of a circle divided into two comma-like shapes, originated with the ancient Taoist philosophy and *I-Ching,* where it represents the balance of opposites: male and female, light and dark. According to the IGLA, a yang-and-yin flag flew over the headquarters of the International Committee for Sexual Equality in the 1950s, predating the modern rainbow flag by three decades.

A DICTIONARY OF SLANG AND HISTORICAL TERMS

These words and phrases have been used in the gay and lesbian community of past or present. Most of the listings are slang, but some, as indicated, are considered standard usage, or represent efforts to coin scientific or technical terms relevant to gay people.

AC-DC. Bisexual.

ACCORDION. A penis that becomes dramatically longer when erect.

ADAM'S PAJAMAS. A state of full nudity. ("There I was in Adam's pajamas.")

AMAZON. A strong woman; especially a lesbian. The ancient Greeks believed that a race of all-female warriors had flourished in about the twelfth century B.C.; according to Plutarch, they invaded Athens. A sixteenth-century Spanish explorer applied the name to a group of female warriors, and a river, that he found in South America. According to Kennedy Smith, who researched the term for the *Washington Blade*, Natalie Barney was the first person to equate the ancient Amazons with lesbians. Romaine Brooks, when she painted Barney's portrait, called the work *l'Amazone*.

AMY-JOHN. A lesbian. Derived from *amazon*.

ANDROGYNE. A effeminate-acting gay man. The term (coined from the Greek words for *man* and *woman*) was used in a scientific context around the turn of the century; it did not have the pejorative connotations of much slang of the time. The lesbian analogue was *gynander*.

ANDROPHILIA. The attraction of a man for another adult male. Magnus Hirschfeld, who produced a term for every variation of same-sex attraction, introduced this one early in the twentieth century. It is rarely used today, probably because such relationships are considered the norm for gay males. But in Hirschfeld's day, homosexual behavior in many cultures was closely linked to an age difference between the partners.

ANDROTROPE. A gay male. Kurt Hiller suggested this term in 1946 (and *gynaecotrope* for lesbians), because of what he considered the negative connotations of "homosexual." It never caught on.

ANGEL FOOD. A gay man in the Air Force.

ANGEL WITH A DIRTY FACE. [*Obsolete*] A man who wants to engage in gay sex, but is afraid to. From the 1930s film *Angels with Dirty Faces*.

AUNT FANCY. A male homosexual. The term is little used in the post-Stonewall era.

AUNTIE. An older gay man. This term is generally pejorative, and includes a sense of being dainty and gossipy.

B&D. Bondage and discipline. B&D enthusiasts find erotic satisfaction in sex that involves one person being tied up by the other and being disciplined. Related to, but by no means synonymous with, *S&M*.

BABY-BUTCH. A young, masculine-acting lesbian.

BALL-BEARING OIL. Semen, especially when used to lubricate a partner's penis.

BALLS. Testicles.

BAMBI-SEXUALITY. Physical interaction centered more about touching, kissing, and caressing than around genital sexuality. Not to be confused with *bestiality,* a very different concept.

BASKET. Male genitals, especially as emphasized by tight-fitting clothes.

BASKETBALL. *See Golf, Softball, and Basketball.*

BD. Abbreviation for *bull-dyke.*

BEADS. Several camp phrases incorporate the word *beads,* which seems to derive from the image of homosexual men wearing a string of pearls. To *drop one's beads* is to lose composure and become flustered. To *read the beads* is to give a tongue-lashing.

BEAN QUEEN. A non-Latino man who is attracted to Latino men.

BEAT OFF. To masturbate.

BEAT THE TOM-TOM. To masturbate.

BENT. [*British slang*] Homosexual.

BERDACHE. A member of an American Indian tribe who lived with, dressed as, or identified with the opposite sex. Berdaches often occupied a revered and unusual position within their tribes. The term comes from the Persian *bardag* (slave boy), via the French term *bardache.* It was first applied to Native Americans by French explorers in North America.

BILITIS. From *Chansons de Bilitis,* a collection of lesbian love poems published in 1894 by Pierre Louÿs and supposedly based on those by Sappho. The word is best known as part of the name of the Daughters of Bilitis (DOB), a pioneering lesbian organization founded in 1955 by Del Martin and Phyllis Lyon.

BIRD'S NEST. Pubic hair.

BISEXUAL. Attracted to people of both sexes. The word was originally a medical and scientific term, indicating organisms that include the anatomy or functions of both sexes. In his ground-breaking 1948 study of male sexuality, Alfred Kinsey bemoaned the fact that this usage was giving way to the new meaning, but he was helpless to stop the trend.

BITHYNIAN. Gay travel organizer Hanns Ebensten, in a 1993 *Christopher Street* column, recalled the love affair between Antinous, born in the kingdom of Bithynia (in what is now northern Turkey) and Emperor Hadrian. After Antinous drowned in A.D. 130, a grief-stricken Hadrian called for statues to be raised around the Roman empire to his beloved Bithynian. "I propose that homosexual men everywhere call themselves Bithynians," wrote Ebensten. Any takers?

BJ. Abbreviation for *blow job,* or fellatio.

BLIND MEAT. An uncircumcised penis.

BLINDS. The foreskin on an uncircumcised penis.

BLUFF. [*British slang*] A lesbian who on different occasions took both butch and femme identities. This synthesis of the terms *butch* and *fluff* also reminds us that in the 1950s, the lesbian community generally expected members to be either butch or femme, not both.

BONER. An erect penis.

BOSTON MARRIAGE. [*Obsolete*] A living-together relationship involving two women. This term was mainly used in nineteenth-century New England, and could refer both to actual lesbian relationships, and to situations where two women chose to live independently from men, often while they pursued their own careers.

BOTTOM. The receptive partner in anal intercourse (for gay men) or in vaginal intercourse with a dildo (for lesbians).

BROWN FAMILY, THE. [*Obsolete*] Bruce Rodgers, in his book *The Queen's Vernacular,* traces this term to the 1940s, when it referred to the homosexual subculture.

BRUSH YOUR TEETH. To perform fellatio on a man.

BUGGERY. Anal sex, usually between two men. The term is derived from *Bulgaria,* where an eleventh-century religious philosophy permitted sex but forbade its members to have children; an increase in homosexuality and in heterosexual anal intercourse were the natural consequences. As this philosophy spread into Germany, Italy, and France, its proponents were known as *Bulgars* or *Boulgars;* in France, this became corrupted into *bougre,* and ultimately the English word *bugger.*

BULL DYKE. A lesbian who dresses and behaves in a masculine style.

BUM BOY. [*British slang*] A male who prefers the receptive role in anal intercourse.

BUMPER TO BUMPER. Vagina-to-vagina. Generally used in reference to two lesbians engaging in sex, or dancing, etc. Occasionally used in referring to gay men or heterosexual couples.

BUNS. Buttocks.

BUTCH. Strong, tough, and aggressive; displaying traits considered masculine. The word is used to describe both physical build and personality, and may refer to either sex.

CALAMITE. A homosexual man. Algernon Swinburne combined the name of the *calamus* plant, with its gay symbolism, and the word *catamite,* to come up with this put-down of John Addington Symonds. The term is still occasionally used to describe gay poets and writers of past and present.

CAMP. An ironic, often gay-identified, approach to life, dress, and speech, that seems to defy exact definition. The term gained popularity with Susan Sontag's essay "Notes Toward a Definition of Camp" in the *Parisian Review* in 1964, but she was no help with defining it: "To talk about Camp is therefore to betray it," she wrote. Camp humor is not invariably marked by any one trait, but often includes elements of self-deprecation, exaggeration to the point of absurdity, and parodying of sex roles. Bruce Rodgers traces the term to Shakespearean England, when male actors who dressed as women were said to be *camping.* Most likely, the term derives from the French verb *camper,* "to play a role."

CANTONESE GROIN. [*Obsolete*] A dildo. The term appears in a medieval novel, describing a plant used in China for this purpose.

CATAMITE. A boy kept for sexual purposes, from "Catamitus," the cupbearer for the Roman god Jupiter. The term came into use in the seventeenth century. *See also Calamite; Ganymede.*

CATCHER. [*Prison slang*] The receptive partner in anal intercourse.

CHARLOTTE ANN. [*Obsolete*] A gay man. The term belongs securely in the pre-Stonewall era.

CHEEKS. Buttocks.

CHEESE. The accumulated smegma beneath the foreskin on an unwashed, uncircumcised penis.

CHERRY. A virgin, or someone new to gay or lesbian sex.

CHICKEN. A young gay male, usually in his teens or very early twenties.

CHICKEN HAWK. An older gay man who pursues boys or very young men.

CHUBBY CHASER. A man attracted to obese men.

CIAO. [pronounced *chow*] Goodbye. In Italian, the term can mean "hello" or "good-bye." As American slang, it has come to mean "goodbye for now; see you again soon."

CIRCLE-JERK. Simultaneous group masturbation. Once associated almost entirely with adolescent males, the term now — in an era of safe-sex consciousness — is used more widely.

CLONE. A gay man of a certain somewhat standardized appearance. The term arose in the early 1970s (often interchangeably with *Castro clone,* referring to the main street in the heart of San Francisco's gay community). The classic clone look consists of short-cropped hair and a trim moustache, a flannel shirt, and Levi's 501 jeans — all on a relatively well-sculpted body.

CLOSET. The place where gay men or lesbians hide, figuratively speaking, if they do not want their homosexuality to be known. "In the closet" means "not open about being gay." A *closet case* or *closet queen* is someone who is in the closet.

COCK. Penis. The modern slang usage seems to have derived from the tap, or cock, on beer barrels of yore.

COCK RING. A ring, usually made of leather or metal, secured around the base of the penis and testicles (or just of the penis) to increase an erection.

COLOR IN THE COLORING BOOK. To masturbate while looking at an erotic magazine.

COME or **CUM.** To reach orgasm. As a noun, this is also the most common slang term for semen. Some writers use the spellings *cum* for the noun and *come* (which thus lends itself to the past tense *came*) for the verb.

COME OUT. To acknowledge one's homosexuality, either to oneself or to others.

CORNHOLE. To be the insertive partner in anal intercourse.

COUCH AUDITION. A job interview that includes sex with the prospective employer.

COUNTERJUMPER. [*Obsolete*] Homosexual. The term was used occasionally in the 1940s and 1950s.

CREAM. Semen or vaginal fluid.

CROSS-DRESSING. To dress in a way usually identified with the opposite sex. *See also Drag; Transvestite.*

CRUISE. To actively look for a sex partner, generally in an area where others are engaging in the same pursuit.

CRUSH HOUR. The period late at night, just before a bar closes.

CUM. *See Come.*

CUNT. Vagina. The word is derived from *cunnus,* the Latin word for the female genitals. According to etymologist Eric Partridge, the Old English term *cwithe,* for *womb,* also influenced the term's pronunciation, giving it the final *t.*

CUPCAKES. Buttocks, especially when small and well rounded.

CURE THE BLIND. To perform fellatio on an uncircumcised penis.

CURTAIN(S). The foreskin on an uncircumcised penis.

CUT. Circumcised.

CUT SLEEVES. A Chinese phrase for male homosexuality. The term, *tuan hsiu* in Chinese, comes from a story about Emperor Ai-ti (6 B.C. to A.D. 2) of the Han dynasty. When a favored young man, Tung Hsien, fell asleep on the sleeve of the emperor's robe, the emperor cut off the sleeve rather than disturb his rest. According to Wayne Dynes, who relates this story in *Homolexis,* many Chinese rulers from the third century onward kept minions (*luan-tung*), and Buddhist monks and nuns often interpreted their vows of chastity as barring heterosexual affairs, but not homosexual ones.

DADDLE. To engage in lesbian sex, in a face-to-face position.

DAISY CHAIN. Three or more men engaged in simultaneous anal intercourse.

DAISY DUCK. A man who prefers the receptive role in anal intercourse.

DANGLER or **DANGLE QUEEN.** A male exhibitionist.

DASH. Open to experimenting with homosexuality, though not self-defined as gay.

DESPERATION NUMBER. A sex partner found just before closing time at the bar.

DICK. Penis. The term probably derives from *dirk,* an early English term for a short dagger.

DIESEL DYKE. A lesbian who dresses and behaves in a masculine style.

DILDO. A device shaped more or less like a penis and used as a sex toy.

DINGE QUEEN. A nonblack gay man who is attracted to black men. Often considered racist.

DIONING. [*Obsolete*] The heterosexual man to whom a homosexual is attracted. This term was coined in the 1860s by Karl Heinrich Ulrichs, who believed that homosexual males were generally attracted only to straight men. *See also Urning.*

DISHONORABLE DISCHARGE. To masturbate at home after unsuccessfully going out in search of a sex partner.

DOCKING. Inserting the head of one's penis into another's foreskin.

DONG. Penis.

DOUBLE RIBS. [*Obsolete Chinese slang*] A euphemism for male homosexuality, used in ancient China. The term appears in a story from 636 B.C., when the hosts of visiting Ch'in prince Ch'ung-Erh spied on him as he bathed to see if he really had "double ribs."

DRAG. Dressed in a way usually identified with the opposite sex. Drag differs from *transvestism* in that *drag* usually refers to a specific act of cross-dressing, while *transvestism* refers to a general (and often sexual) enjoyment of the act. In the movie *Some Like It Hot,* Jack Lemmon dresses in drag, but the character he played was not intended to be a transvestite. The term seems to have acquired its current meaning in the 1880s, when men who played female roles on the British stage wore *draggy* skirts and petticoats. *See also Transvestite.*

DRAG BUTCH. A butch lesbian who often passes as a man.

DRAG QUEEN. A man who dresses like a woman.

DROP A HAIRPIN. To give a clue that one is homosexual, by using slang or other clue words.

DUTCH BOY. A man who identifies with lesbians or is primarily attracted to lesbians. The term was coined in about 1990 by lesbian sex honcho Susie Bright.

DUTCH GIRL. A lesbian. Derived from the double meaning of dyke/dike.

DYKE. A lesbian. The term probably derives from the nineteenth-century slang word *dike,* which referred to male clothing, and when it was first used to refer to women, it carried a derogatory connotation of masculine appearance or behavior. The masculine connotation is often still present, but many lesbians have adopted *dyke* as their term of preference.

ENGLISH STYLE SEX. Sex between men in which one places his erect penis between the legs of his partner, under the testicles. The little-used term originated with the presumption that the practice is common in English boys' schools.

EONISM. [*Obsolete*] Transvestism. In eighteenth-century France, the Chevalier d'Éon gained notoriety for his love of dressing in drag. By some reports, he acquired the habit as a

spy for the French government; when it became clear that he enjoyed dressing in drag, King Louis XV forbade him to dress any other way. A century later, sexologist Havelock Ellis resurrected the legend of the chevalier to coin the term *eonism.* It never gained wide acceptance.

EPHEBOPHILIA. The attraction of a man for a post-pubescent youth. The term is rare, but is occasionally used to create a category distinct from *pedophilia,* and *androphilia.* Stephen Donaldson, in the *Encyclopedia of Homosexuality,* suggests that Magnus Hirschfeld probably introduced the term in a 1906 book.

EROTEM. A sex toy. Ted McIlvenna of the Institute for the Advanced Study of Human Sexuality seems to have coined this term.

FACE-FUCKING. Engaging in oral-genital sex.

FAG HAG. A heterosexual woman who socializes extensively with gay men. Sometimes pejorative.

FAGGOT, also FAG. A male homosexual. Like *dyke,* this term was originally used as an epithet, but has been adopted by many of the people to whom it refers. There is no general agreement about its origins. In the early years of the gay liberation movement, some activists proposed that it derived from *fagot,* the sticks used as kindling during the Inquisition when heretics, homosexuals, and others were burned at the stake, but there is no historical evidence to support this theory. Others have suggested it comes from *fag,* the younger boy required in British boys' schools to do menial tasks for an older student, but this seems unlikely; that usage was probably an unrelated contraction of *fatigue.*

FAIRY, also **FAERIE.** A male homosexual, especially one who acts or dresses in an effeminate manner. This was a common derogatory term for homosexuals during much of the twentieth century. Like *dyke* and *faggot,* it has been reclaimed by gay people, and a sizeable number of gay men now identify themselves as *radical faeries,* thus asserting pride in their refusal to accept traditional male roles.

FAN QUEEN. Someone who is entirely passive during sex and merely lies back, hands behind the head, as if fanning himself or herself.

FEIGELE or **FAYGELE,** A gay man, from the Yiddish for "little bird."

FEMME. A lesbian or gay man who acts and dresses effeminately.

FINGER or **FINGER-FUCK.** Using a finger to manipulate the clitoris, vagina, or anus of a partner.

FINOCCHIO. [*Italian slang*] Homosexual. The term sometimes carries a connotation of effeminacy, comparable to the American *fairy. Finocchio* is Italian for "fennel," and the origins of its slang meaning are unknown.

FISTFUCK or **FIST.** To insert part or all of one's hand into the anus or vagina of a sex partner.

FLIP. To make love to a butch woman. Also used passively: to flip for someone.

FLUFF. A femme lesbian.

FRENCH. To engage in fellatio. In its more common usage as an adjective, the term refers to a preference for oral-genital sex. *See also Greek.*

FRENCH EMBASSY. Any location, especially a gym or Y, where gay sex is readily available.

FRICATRICE. [*Obsolete*] A lesbian. In the sixteenth to nineteenth centuries, when such matters were rarely discussed, there was little standardization of terminology, and this term enjoyed a occasional popularity. It was derived from the Latin word for "rubbing together," but was never as widely used as the Greek equivalent, *tribade.*

FRIG. Sex between two women, often involving one rubbing the genitals of the other with her fingers; probably derived from *friction.*

FRUIT. A gay person. The etymology of *fruit* is similar to that of the word *gay.* In the early twentieth century, it referred to a sexually available woman. By the 1940s, with the stereotype of gay men as soft, it had acquired its present meaning.

FROG QUEEN. A French-Canadian gay man; also a gay man attracted to Frenchmen.

FUCK. To engage in sexual intercourse. The term is most often used for anal or vaginal intercourse. The origins of the term are uncertain. According to one theory, it was first used as an acronym of "For Unlawful Carnal Knowledge." Other etymologists believe it derives from the *firk,* which means "a sharp thrust."

FUNCH. A quick sexual encounter performed at lunchtime.

GAG REFLEX TEST. During World War II, a study of gay patients in an Army hospital focused on techniques for identifying homosexual recruits. One key difference, according to the study, was that homosexuals did not gag when a tongue depressor was put down their throat. The *Gag Reflex Test* was thus recommended both for military use, and for civilian positions "where the sexual deviate must be eliminated."

GANYMEDE. A boy or youth kept for sexual purposes. In Greek myth, Ganymede was the Trojan youth whom Zeus made his cupbearer and bedmate. The term was used in this sense as early as 1603 by the writer Philemon Holland, and seems to have dropped from general use a few centuries later. In Roman mythology, Zeus is known as Jupiter and his cupbearer, Catamitus, is the equivalent of Ganymede. *See also Catamite.*

GAY. Homosexual. In the seventeenth century, *gay* expanded from its earlier meaning of cheerful and came to also refer to men with a reputation for being playboys; the phrase *gay Lothario* appeared by 1703. By the early 1800s, the meaning had further expanded to include prostitutes and women with a reputation for sexual promiscuity (*gay girls*), and then male prostitutes. It seems to have been adopted by gay people as a slang term referring to themselves early in the twentieth century. According to historian John Boswell, the first public use of the term in the U.S., outside of pornography, was probably in the 1939 film *Bringing Up Baby,* in which Cary Grant, appearing in a dress, exclaimed that he had "gone gay." But for many years it remained essentially an inside term: even in the early 1960s, *gay* still meant *cheerful* to most heterosexuals. Only since 1970 has it gradually gained acceptance as a standard, nonslang synonym for homosexual. In 1987, one of the last barriers to widespread usage of the term fell when the *New York Times* began using it as an adjective in their reporting.

GILLETTE BLADE. A bisexual woman.

GINGER. [*British slang*] Gay. Following the rules of British Cockney rhyming slang, *queer* was replaced with the rhyming *ginger beer,* which in turn was shortened to *ginger.*

GISM. Semen.

GIVE HEAD. To perform fellatio.

GLORY HOLE. A hole carved in the partition between stalls in a men's room, and used for sexual liaisons.

GO DOWN ON. To perform fellatio or cunnilingus on.

GOATSKIN. The foreskin of the penis.

GOAT'S MILK. Bitter-tasting semen.

GOLDEN SHOWER. A stream of urine, when used in a sexual context.

GOLF, SOFTBALL, and **BASKETBALL.** These terms are sometimes used by deaf lesbians and gay men as code words for sexual orientation. The first letters correspond to the first letter of the intended meaning: *Gay, Straight, and Bisexual.*

GOVERNMENT-INSPECTED MEAT. A gay man in the armed forces.

GREEK. To engage in anal intercourse. In its more common usage as an adjective, the term refers to a preference for anal sex. *See also French.*

GUNSEL. One who is, or is destined to be, a catamite. From the German/Yiddish word for "little goose."

GYNAEOTROPE. A lesbian. Kurt Hiller suggested this term in 1946 (and *androtrope* for a gay male), because of what he considered the negative connotations of "homosexual." Neither term caught on.

GYNANDER. A masculine-acting lesbian. The term (coined from the Greek words for *woman* and *man*) was used in a scientific context around the turn of the century; it did not have the pejorative connotations of much slang of the time. The comparable term for a gay man was *androgyne*.

HANDBALL. See *Fistfuck*.

HETAIRISTRIAI. A lesbian. This term was used by Plato, who apparently coined it himself, as a nonjudgmental alternative to *tribade*. It was never widely used.

HETEROSEXUAL. Primarily attracted to people of the opposite sex. The term seems to have been coined and first used by Karl Maria Kertbeny in 1868, and first appeared in a book in 1880.

HOLD A BOWLING BALL. To sexually stimulate another woman by rubbing the thumb and forefinger, simultaneously, on her clitoris and anus.

HOLLYWOOD UTERUS. [*Obsolete*] Anus. Bruce Rodgers reports this term being used in southern California in the late 1960s.

HOMOGENIC. Homosexual. Over the years, many synonyms for *homosexual* have been suggested; this one was proposed by Edward Carpenter, who objected to the fact that *homosexual* combined Greek and Latin roots. Others, such as Havelock Ellis, also objected to *homosexual,* but the objections never took hold, and Carpenter's creation died a natural death.

HOMOPHILE. Homosexual. *Philos* is the Greek word for "love." This alternative to *homosexual* gained currency in the U.S. in the 1950s, when some early gay leaders began using it because they felt that *homosexual* unduly emphasized *sex. Homophile* was widely used for several decades, but gradually fell from favor because gay activists of the early 1970s found it euphemistic.

HOMOPHOBIA. Irrational fear of gay people and of homosexuality. George Weinberg, author of *Society and the Healthy Homosexual,* popularized this word in the early 1970s. In just ten letters, it introduced the welcome idea that it was gay-bashers, not gays themselves, who had a problem. Unlike so many other consciously created words, *homophobia* filled a clear need and is widely used even outside the gay community. *Homophobic* (adj.) and *homophobe* (n.) are related forms.

HOMOSEXUAL. Attracted physically to people of the same sex. The term was coined in 1869 by Karl Maria Kertbeny, who used it in a pamphlet (which he published anonymously) arguing for the repeal of Prussia's sodomy laws. It first appeared in U.S. medical journals in the 1890s, and in general usage during the 1920s.

HOT-DOGGING. Having anal intercourse.

HUNDRED-AND-SEVENTY-FIVER. A homosexual. Paragraph 175 of the German Penal Code of 1872 outlawed homosexual practices; thus a 175er (*hundert-funf-und-siebziger*) in Germany was someone violating this law.

HUNG. Well endowed; having a large penis. The term can also be used more generally: "He was hung like a mouse" means "he had a small penis."

HUSTLER. A male prostitute.

IN-SISTERS. Two men, usually both effeminate, who have a close but not necessarily sexual relationship.

IN THE LIFE. Gay. Most common within the African-American community.

INTERMEDIATE SEX. Homosexual. The term was used by Edward Carpenter and others around the turn of the century, but soon fell into disfavor.

INTERSEXUALIST. Homosexual. The term was briefly in use around the turn of the century.

INVERSION. Homosexuality. This word, which seems to have first appeared in Italian (as *inversione*) in 1878, encompassed a philosophy of homosexuality as well as providing a new term for it, and for its practitioners (*inverts*). There is a natural order of things, this philosophy suggested — and it is to be contrasted with the unnatural state of homosexuality. The English translation was used late in the century by Edward Carpenter and others; in 1897 Havelock Ellis wrote that "Caesar was proud of his physical beauty, and like many modern inverts he was accustomed carefully to shave his skin." Despite its judgmental connotations, the term was often used by gay people even in the early 1900s.

IRISH CONFETTI. Semen.

ISOPHYL. A gay person. The term was coined by philosopher and mystic Gerald Heard, probably in the early 1950s, as he expounded his belief that gay people represented the next step in human evolution.

JACK OFF. To masturbate.

JAM. [*Obsolete*] This underground term of the 1930s and '40s generally meant *straight*. Author Clarkson Crane, in an unpublished 1946 novel, uses it as a slang term for heterosexual: "I hate jam parties," says a gay character. "There you are ... and you think of something you want to say and you can't say it because there's a jam person in the room." Occasionally it took a somewhat different nuance; Neel Bate, an artist popularly known at the time as Blade, later told *The Advocate* that *jam* meant "a gay boy who looks straight." Those in the know thus found unintended humor the popular 1930s song "It Must Be Jelly 'Cause Jam Don't Shake Like That."

JANEY. Vagina.

JASPER. A lesbian, usually one with a masculine bearing or appearance.

JERK OFF. To masturbate.

JISM, JIZZ, JIZZUM. *See Gism.*

JOHNSON BAR. A dildo.

JOY-STICK. Erect penis.

KEEP ONE'S HAIR UP. [*Obsolete*] To be homosexual. Early activist Harry Hay recalls this phrase, and the variation *keeping one's hair tightly pinned up,* from 1930s gay culture.

KIKI. 1940s slang for a lesbian comfortable with either a passive or aggressive partner.

KINSEY SIX. A person who is completely homosexual. The term comes from sex researcher Alfred Kinsey, who saw sexual orientation as a continuous spectrum, and used a scale of zero to six to quantify it as follows:

0. Exclusively heterosexual
1. Predominantly heterosexual, only incidentally homosexual
2. Predominantly heterosexual but more than incidentally homo-

sexual

3. Equally heterosexual and homosexual

4. Predominantly homosexual but more than incidentally heterosexual

5. Predominantly homosexual, only incidentally heterosexual

6. Exclusively homosexual

KISSING FISH. Lesbians.

KNITTING. Masturbating (in reference to a man).

KOROPHILIA. The sexual attraction of an adult woman for a girl. The term is rarely used.

KOSHER. Circumcised.

KY. A brand of water-soluble lubricant often used for sex.

LACE CURTAINS. The foreskin on an uncircumcised penis.

LESBIAN. A gay woman. The ancient Greek poet Sappho lived on the island of Lesbos. The use of lesbian to mean a woman-loving woman goes back as far as the sixteenth century, but such usage was rare until the nineteenth century. In the 1890s, as Sappho became known for her poems celebrating love between women, the term *lesbian* became more common, first as an adjective, then also as a noun.

LESBOCIOUS. A woman with particularly appealing lesbian qualities — according to "Susie Sexpert" Bright.

LILIES OF THE VALLEY. Hemorrhoids.

LIPSTICK LESBIAN. A lesbian who dresses in ways considered feminine, including the use of make-up, skirts, and related adornment that is stigmatized as "politically incorrect" in many circles.

LOLLIPOP STOP. A highway rest stop used by gay men for cruising.

LOVE JUICE. Semen.

LUCKY PIERRE. The middle man in three-way sex.

LUKE. The coital fluid in a woman.

MAKE A MILK RUN. To cruise a men's room.

MAKE SCISSORS OF SOMEONE. To masturbate a woman by simultaneously rubbing her clitoris with the thumb and her anus with the forefinger.

MARICON. A gay man. This is the Spanish equivalent of *faggot.*

MARIPOSA. This Spanish word for "butterfly" has come to also refer to a male homosexual.

MARY ANN. A gay man. The term was used in the late 1800s.

MEAT RACK. A gay male cruising area.

MILKING MACHINE. A vibratory device used by men to masturbate.

MISSIONARY WORK. An attempt by a gay man or lesbian to seduce a straight person of the same sex.

MOLLY. *[Obsolete]* An effeminate homosexual man. London police used this slang word during their raids of homosexual meeting places in the early eighteenth century. It most likely derived from the Latin word *mollis,* "soft." Other synonyms were *molly cull* and *mollycoddle.*

MOLLY DYKE. *[Obsolete]* The more passive woman in a lesbian relationship or liaison.

MOLLY HOUSE. *[Obsolete]* An eighteenth-century establishment where homosexual men gathered.

MONKEY. Vagina.

MONOSEXUAL. Attracted to only one sex (be it one's own sex, or the opposite sex) — as opposed to *bisexual,* attracted to both sexes.

MOONOLOGY. *[Obsolete]* Anarchist

Alexander Berkman, in recollecting a conversation with a prisoner that took place in about 1892, quotes the prisoner as referring to "moonology ... the truly Christian science of loving your neighbor, provided he be a nice little boy." The conversation is quoted by Jonathan Katz in his *Gay American History*.

MOTHER. The person who brings someone out.

MUFF or **MUFF-DIVE.** To lick a partner's vagina and clitoris. *Muff* and *muffet* can also refer to the vagina itself, in an erotic context.

MUFFER. A woman who muffs.

MUSICAL. [*Obsolete*] Homosexual. This was one of the code words used by gay people in the 1940s and 1950s to identify themselves; *temperamental* and *nervous* were others.

NANCE. [*British slang*] Effeminate.

NANCY. A gay man. This was a common slang term in the nineteenth century. In the 1830s, U.S. senator William Rufus de Vane King was referred to as "Miss Nancy" by those suggesting that he and James Buchanan were lovers, and historian Jonathan Katz documents its use in 1899 by a police captain referring to "Nancys and fairies ... degenerates."

NAPKIN RING. A cock ring.

NELLY or **NELLIE.** An effeminate gay man. In the 1940s, when this term gained popularity, it was often incorporated into the phrase *Nervous Nelly*. Also used as an adjective.

NERVOUS. [*Obsolete*] Homosexual. This was one of the code words used by gay people in the 1940s and 1950s to identify themselves; *temperamental* and *musical* were others.

NUMBER. A trick; a casual sex partner.

OLD FACEFUL. An erect penis, especially while ejaculating.

ONE-EYED CYCLOPS. [*French*] The head of the penis.

OUTING. The controversial practice of bringing someone out of the closet against their will. For years, nearly all gay people accepted the idea that coming out was strictly a personal decision, and that no one had the right to publicly identify another as gay. That began to change early in 1988, as AIDS activists argued that in matters of life and death, politicians had no right to hypocrisy. In June of 1989, U.S. representative Barney Frank threatened to expose gay Republican officeholders if GOP officials continued to gay-bait House Speaker Tom Foley. Only in that year did the practice become common enough to need a name.

PAEDOPHILIA. *See Pedophilia.*

PANSY. An effeminate gay man, usually used derogatorily. The term has been in use at least since the 1890s.

PANSY WITHOUT A STEM. A lesbian. This camp term came into use among gay men in the 1960s.

PARTHENOPHILIA. The attraction of a woman for a young but post-pubescent woman. The term is rarely used today, and was probably introduced early in the 1900s by sexologist Magnus Hirschfeld.

PEDERASTY. The sexual attraction of an adult man for a younger male, usually one in his teens. The term is most often used in connection with the relationships common in ancient Greece. Occasionally it is used in a broader sense, usually disparagingly, for male homosexuality involving any age groups.

PEDOPHILIA. The sexual attraction of an adult for a child.

PENIS BUTTER. Pre-ejaculate lubricatory fluid; pre-cum.

PICK UP THE SOAP. To be fucked.

PITCHER. [*Prison slang*] The active partner in anal intercourse.

PLAY BUGLE BOY. To perform fellatio on another man.

PLAY LEAP FROG. To engage in anal intercourse.

POCKET POOL. Male masturbation.

POOF or **POOFTER.** A gay man. This word, generally derogatory, is common in Australia and England.

POST-OP. A transsexual who has undergone a sex change operation.

PRE-OP. A transsexual who is contemplating a sex change operation (and may have begun hormone treatments), but has not yet undergone surgery.

PRINCETON RUB. Intercourse between two men in which one's penis rubs between the other's thighs, or between the two men's abdomens. Usually used humorously, this phrase has an uncertain history. It may have been coined in pride by Princeton undergraduates who thought they had discovered something new — or it could be strictly of Yale origin.

PRUSHUN. [*Obsolete*] The young (often in his early teens) companion of an adult male hobo. Jack London, in his memoir *The Road,* describes these relationships, in which the boy was often at the complete mercy of the older man.

PUNK. A young, often small, male who is forced into a sexually submissive role, usually in the context of prison. The term has also been used in hobo culture.

PUSSY. Female genitals. The first documented appearance of the term was in 1662, spelled *pusse.*

QUEEN. An effeminate gay man. Gay men who aspire to royalty will be disappointed to learn that this usage of the word *queen* is only a distant relative of the queen who sits on a throne. It is linguistically closer to *quean* — a disparaging word for an "unpleasant or promiscuous woman," dating to the sixteenth century. Because of its pejorative tone and implication of effeminacy, it was later applied to gay men. Countless compounds incorporate this word. *See also Bean Queen, Closet, Dangle, Dinge Queen, Drag Queen, Fan Queen, Frog Queen, Rubber Queen, Size Queen, Snow Queen.*

QUEER. Homosexual, usually with reference to men. Originally meaning "odd" or "counterfeit," the term seems to have acquired its sexual meaning early in the twentieth century. Oddly, the same people who complain that "using *gay* as a synonym for *homosexual* confuses the meaning of a perfectly good word" have never made the same complaint with regard to usage of *queer.* An alternative theory suggests that it derived from the old German word *quer,* meaning "crooked." Today, like other terms once used only pejoratively, it has been reclaimed by many of the people at whom it was once directed, in a highly politicized sense. A man or woman who identifies as *queer* isn't likely to care whether mainstream society approves of them or not.

RAINCOAT. A condom.

REVERSE MALINGERER. A World War II military recruit who was lesbian or gay but lied about it so as to be able to serve in the armed forces. Gay historian Allan Berube reports that the term was used by military officials during World War II.

RICE PUDDING. Semen, especially the semen of an Asian man.

RIM. To lick or tongue the anus of a sex partner.

ROUGH TRADE. A man who may become violent during or after engaging in gay sex. Typically the phrase refers to a young, straight-identified working-class man, often a hustler, who takes only the active role in sex, then threatens his partner with violence either to convince himself that he's still a man, or simply as part of a robbery. Some hustlers present a deliberate but false facade of "rough trade" merely to turn on their clients.

RUBBER QUEEN. Someone with a fetish for sheets, clothing, or other items made of rubber or latex.

RUBIES. Lips.

S&M, S/M. Sadism and masochism. S&M enthusiasts derive part of their pleasure from inflicting pain or humiliation (the sadist) or having pain inflicted upon them (the masochist) — but always within defined and mutually agreed limits.

SANTA FE, GONE. [*Obsolete*] To have become a lesbian. In the 1920s, many lesbians found a freer atmosphere in the southwestern towns of Santa Fe and Taos. Jeffrey Hogrefe, in his biography *O'Keeffe*, writes that a woman was said to have gone Santa Fe if she became involved with another woman.

SAPPHISTRY. Lesbian love; derived from *Sappho*, the lesbian poet of ancient Greece. *See also Lesbian.*

SEAFOOD. A gay sailor.

SEWING CIRCLE. A circle-jerk.

SHRIMPING. Toe-sucking.

SKIN FLUTE. Penis.

SIGNIFICANT OTHER. A partner in a serious relationship. In the early 1970s, unhappy with terms such as *lover, girlfriend,* and *boyfriend* for describing their same-sex partners, some gay men and lesbians began using the term *significant other.* It is now used by unmarried heterosexuals as well. An effort to shorten it to *sother* never met with wide acceptance.

SIMILSEXUALIST. Homosexual. This was one of several words coined late in the nineteenth century.

SISSY. A gay man, especially an effeminate one. Like other terms used derogatorily, this one is sometimes reclaimed by the individuals at whom it's directed. It probably began as a variation of *sister.*

SIX. *See Kinsey Six.*

SIXTY-NINE. Mutual and simultaneous fellatio or cunnilingus. The term comes from the resemblance of the position to the numerals 69, and is sometimes expressed in French: *soixante-neuf. See also Swaffonder.*

SIZE QUEEN. A gay man who is especially interested in partners with large penises.

SLACKS. [*Obsolete*] A lesbian.

SNOW QUEEN. A nonwhite gay man who is attracted to white men.

SODOMY. Sexual acts deemed unnatural by the person using the term. People have been harassed, imprisoned, and burned at the stake for the crime of sodomy, yet its opponents have never agreed on just what it is. The word is derived from the city of Sodom, on the Dead Sea; Sodom and Gomorrah are described in the Book of Genesis as being destroyed because of their inhabitants' evil ways, which according to some interpretations included homosexual practices.

Sodomy is variously used to mean any sex between two men; any sex between two men or two women; anal intercourse involving a man and a partner of either sex; or sexual acts involving a human and an animal. Alaska's sodomy statute defined the practice as "the actual penetration of the virile member into any orifice of the human body except the vaginal opening of a female." In the seventeenth century, the precise definition of the word gave rise to heated debate among jurists and clergy, as they sought to decide who should be punished under the sodomy laws of the time. One influential lawmaker defined sodomy as any penetrative act involving two men, or a male animal and a human partner of either sex. Another, smaller, faction defined it as any act of male ejaculation that did not include the possibility of procreation; masturbation was thus considered sodomy.

SOFTBALL. *See Golf, Softball, and Basketball.*

SOTHER. *See Significant Other.*

SOUL SAUCE. The semen of a black man (now considered dated).

SPITTER. A penis (referring to moment of ejaculation).

SPLIT. The vagina.

SPUNK. Semen.

STIRRING THE BEAN CURD. To engage in lesbian sex. Judy Grahn, in *Another Mother Tongue*, gives this as the rough translation of a Chinese term used to refer to the act of finger-fucking.

STOMP. To walk heavily, generally used in reference to butch lesbians.

STONE BUTCH. A lesbian who prefers not to be touched sexually during intercourse, but who may experience orgasm while making love to her companion.

SUGAR DADDY. An older man who provides funds to a younger sex partner or lover.

SWAFFONDER. Mutual oral sex. This term, sometimes used in the British navy, has a circuitous history. It began as *sixty-nine*. This was sometimes sweetened up by being expressed in French, as *soixante-neuf,* a phrase which eventually was changed back into English as *swaffonder* or *swassonder*.

SWEATER DYKE, SWEATER FAG. Someone with a preppy appearance, upscale aspirations, and a nonconfrontational approach to being gay. Usually derogatory, and most commonly used on the West Coast.

SWINGER. A bisexual man or woman. The term has a decidedly sixties connotation.

SWISH. To wiggle one's hips while walking, generally used in reference to gay men. Also a noun for an effeminate man.

SWORD SWALLOWER. Someone who enjoys, or is good at, performing oral sex on men.

TAKING CARE OF BUSINESS. *[Black slang]* Masturbating.

TEAROOM. A public lavatory that is often cruised by gay men.

TEMPERAMENTAL. [*Obsolete*] A euphemism for homosexual, documented by Jonathan Katz as being in use as early as 1927.

TIT KING. A lesbian attracted to women with large breasts.

TOOTSIE. A masculine-acting lesbian.

TRADE. A man, frequently straight-identified, who allows fellatio to be performed on him by another man (or, occasionally, who takes the active role in anal intercourse), but does not reciprocate. Often used to describe hustlers who adopt this attitude.

TRANSGENDER. Relating to transsexuals, transvestites, cross-dressers, and anyone else who tends to blur traditional gender boundaries.

TRANSSEXUAL. Someone with a deep-seated identification with the opposite sex, usually including a desire to actually be the opposite sex. Although transsexual feelings can be documented as far back as ancient Egypt, the medical knowledge and surgical skills to actually perform a sex-change operation have existed only since the 1930s. Transsexuality is different from, though often confused with, *transvestism*.

TRANSVESTITE. Someone who finds it sexually exciting to dress in clothes generally identified with the opposite sex. Although *transvestite* and *homosexual* have been used synonymously by ignorant writers, they are quite different. Many heterosexuals are transvestites, while most lesbians and homosexual men are not; the difference is that cross-dressing is more accepted and thus less hidden in the gay culture. Cross-dressing that does not include any sexual charge is usually referred to as *drag*.

TRIBADE. [*Obsolete*] A lesbian, particularly one taking a masculine role. The Greeks took their word *tribein*, "to rub," and used it as a root for *tribas*, "lesbian," on the grounds that a lesbian would rub another woman's genitals with her thigh or with a dildo. As *tribade*, it entered Europe in the sixteenth century. That term and *tribadism*, "lesbian sexual activity," remained in common use until the late nineteenth century. Today, they are archaic.

TRICK. A sex partner with whom there is no long-term or emotional involvement.

TROLL. An unattractive person. Also, to cruise; to look for a sex partner.

TRUCK DRIVER. A masculine person, usually a lesbian, but also sometimes used for gay men.

TS. A transsexual.

TURTLENECK SWEATER. The foreskin on an uncircumcised penis.

TV. A transvestite.

TWILIGHT. [*Obsolete*] Homosexual. This adjective gained prominence in the 1920s, producing such terms as *twilight men, twilight women,* and *twilight world.*

TWINKLE-TOES. An effeminate gay man, especially a young one.

TUNA. A young gay sailor. The usage is extrapolated from the tuna fish brand "Chicken of the Sea."

UNCUT. Uncircumcised.

URANIAN. *See Urning.*

URNING. [*Obsolete*] A homosexual male. This term was introduced by Karl Heinrich Ulrichs in 1864 as part of his theory of homosexuality. He derived it from Plato's *Symposium,* which refers to the goddess Urania as watching over the "heavenly" emotion of homosexual love.

Ulrichs, who was himself homosexual, was attempting to explain homosexuality in a positive light, but his work was done in a near-vacuum — few other scholars were even discussing the subject, much less trying to do so from a perspective free of prejudice. Extrapolating heavily from his own experience and feelings, Ulrichs hypothesized that only a female psyche could be attracted to a male body. Homosexuals, therefore, constituted a third sex — that of female souls in male bodies. He referred to such persons as Urnings. (In English, the term is translated as *Uranian*.) Ulrichs later recognized the existence of a counterpart in the opposite sex; his term for lesbians was *Urningin*. Ulrichs's theory is now discredited, and his terminology has not endured, but he laid the groundwork for much of the research that was done in the following decades.

In 1916, when the *New York Times* first used a word to refer to homosexuality, *Uranian* was the term it chose.

VANILLA SEX. Relatively conventional forms of sexual activity, usually used in contrast to S&M sex.

VARIANT. Homosexual. This usage was briefly popular in the 1940s and 1950s because it was less judgmental than most of the alternatives. Jeannette Foster used it in the title of her ground-breaking 1956 bibliography, *Sex Variant Women in Literature.*

VEGETARIAN. A gay man who does not perform fellatio (and thus does not "eat meat").

VICE ALLEMAND. [*French slang*] This nineteenth-century French term for homosexuality translates as "the German vice."

WANK. [*British slang*] To masturbate.

WARMER BRUEDER. [*German slang*] A German expression, literally translated as *warm brother*, referring to a male homosexual.

WARME SCHWESTER. [*German slang*] German for *warm sister* — a lesbian.

WATER CHESTNUT. A gay Japanese man.

WEAR BOXER SHORTS. To be the active or butch partner in a lesbian relationship.

WEARING THE MASK. To be gay. Early activist Harry Hay recalls this phrase as having been used in the 1930s.

WICK. [*British slang*] A lesbian.

WINK. To be uncircumcised.

THE BEST AND THE WORST

Rachel Pepper's Ten Best and Worst Lesbian Books

Rachel Pepper is a columnist, critic, and curmudgeon living in San Francisco.

THE BEST

THE PASSION by Jeannette Winterson. With this novel, a breathtakingly beautiful story about love, androgynous sexuality, and magic, Winterson has almost single-handedly rescued lesbian fiction from the literary doldrums. Other works of Winterson's, including the autobiographical *Oranges Are Not the Only Fruit*, are also well worth reading.

COMING TO POWER edited by Samois. This ground-breaking collection, compiled by a San Francisco S/M group, was the first to accurately capture the essence of what it means to be an S/M lesbian. The writing may stimulate, shock, stir, or soothe you, but there's no way you will emerge unchanged from reading it.

THE **DYKES TO WATCH OUT FOR** SERIES by Alison Bechdel. Cartoonist Bechdel is probably more widely syndicated — not to mention adored by lesbians — than any other gay writer or cartoonist living today. Her compelling cast of well-drawn characters, who range from the uptight, politically correct Mo to the playgirl Lois, are the perfect parable of the modern lesbian nation.

CURIOUS WINE by Katherine V. Forrest. The quintessential lesbian love story complete with a coming-out tale, first kisses, vanilla sex, and a happy ending, *Curious Wine* remains incredibly popular more than ten years after its original publication.

RUBYFRUIT JUNGLE by Rita Mae Brown. Everyone's favorite lesbian novel, this classic tale about the boisterous Molly Bolt and her utterly unself-conscious acceptance of herself and her life as a dyke has delighted and inspired readers since 1973.

TRASH by Dorothy Allison. Since writing *Trash,* Allison's become better known for *Bastard out of Carolina,* a beautiful and disturbing novel about struggle and survival that was nominated for a national book award. Nevertheless, it was Allison's earlier, more lesbian-specific collection of spicy, sexy short stories, *Trash,* that established her as a major dyke literary icon.

AFTER DELORES by Sarah Schulman. With the publication of *After Delores,* a gritty, darkly humorous tale set in the dyke underground of New York's East Village, Schulman simultaneously and successfully ac-

Myra Fourwinds

Sigrid Estrada

Colleen McKay

Three top writers (from left): Dorothy Allison, Rita Mae Brown, and Audre Lorde.

complished two amazing things: first, she catapulted the whole genre of lesbian fiction out of its formulaically romantic and whitebread girl-meets-girl doldrums by writing a quirky, punkish mystery that urban girls devoured in droves. Second, Schulman's tale was grabbed up by a major publishing house, giving hope to a whole generation of budding lesbian writers that there is life beyond the ghetto.

THIS BRIDGE CALLED MY BACK edited by Cherríe Moraga and Gloria Anzaldua. Anyone who has not read *This Bridge Called My Back* cannot claim to be a well-read lesbian, or to have any idea what it means to be a radical woman of color in today's misogynistic, white-run world. A standard of women's studies classes and a completely awe-inspiring collection.

ANNIE ON MY MIND by Nancy Garden. Dealing with teenage sexuality, especially young lesbian sexuality, is quite a thorny literary conundrum. Garden's tale of one girl's courageous perseverance of love in the face of homophobic adult intervention is an affirming read for teens and a powerful reminder for grown-ups that gay teenagers are capable of loving, too.

ZAMI: A new spelling of my name by Audre Lorde. This "biomythography" about the author's growing up and subsequent search for her place in the world as an African-American dyke is perhaps Lorde's most compelling work. Equally fine, however, is *Sister Outsider,* a collection of essays and personal writing.

THE WORST

THE WELL OF LONELINESS by Radclyffe Hall. Although beautifully written, Hall's book, the best-known lesbian novel in literature, has a disturbing and depressing message: that Stephen, its lesbian protagonist, is doomed to a life of sorrow after pushing away her true love into the arms of a man. Not exactly encouraging reading for someone just coming out. Read *Curious Wine* instead, okay?

WISH YOU WERE HERE by Rita Mae Brown. Rita Mae, who, you'll note, also graces our Best Book list, here plummets to a new literary low with this soggy mystery tale written by a cat. Perhaps it is time the author took up a new sport other than writing — like tennis, for example?

DYKE DETECTOR by Shelly Roberts. An amusing idea, but with its stereotypical depictions of lesbians as unattractive, short-haired, labrys-toting creatures, its exasperating emphasis on outdated cultural icons like Cris Williamson, and its complete denial of the true meaning of lesbian — and human — diversity, who needs the right wing?

NAIAD ROMANCES. Although Naiad does produce some good books, especially in the mystery department, its novels are notorious among discerning readers and booksellers for their poor cover design, lousy characterization, and weak plots. The fact that women around the world eat this stuff up in the name of literature makes you wonder if lesbians will pay $10 for gay garbage because of poor self-esteem or if they just have incredibly bad taste.

LESBIAN BEDTIME STORIES edited by Terry Woodrow. Probably the worst collection of lesbian fiction ever assembled, which was nonetheless popular because, as we all know, lesbians will basically buy anything written by other women that promises them sex and romance. The illustrations — mostly of flowers, rainbows, and cats — are even worse.

Richard Labonté's Ten Best and Five Worst Gay Books

Richard Labonté is a former Canadian journalist. He became a bookseller in 1979 when he helped start A Different Light bookstore in Los Angeles. He writes about books and publishing for *The Advocate, In Touch,* and other periodicals.

A BOY'S OWN STORY by Edmund White. The coming-out novel will always be a staple of gay fiction: *Better Angel* by Richard Meeker (Forman Brown) was published in 1933, and is among the best of the genre. But White's 1982 work sets the standard with its sexy meditation on the yearnings, confusions, and satisfactions of reconciling the emotional, physical, and intellectual selves — and all before the young narrator heads to college.

THE CELLULOID CLOSET by Vito Russo. Most of the books listed here are fiction. Film scholar Russo's accomplishment, however, is different. He has taken film, the American art form with the most appeal, and has detailed with saucy insight the undeniable presence of gay life both on the screen and behind the scenes. No community survives long without a sense of its history: Russo's 1981 survey (revised in 1987) is an invaluable exposition of one more aspect of a too-often-hidden gay past.

CITY OF NIGHT by John Rechy. Back before there were gay bookstores, gay best-seller lists, or gay publishers, there were of course gay writers writing books about gay life. None seized America's shocked, as-

Stephen Stewart

Lee Snider

(From left) Editor Ann Heron and authors Mark Thompson and Vito Russo appear on Richard Labonté's list of the best gay books.

tounded, or secretly thrilled imaginations as much as Rechy's 1963 first novel. A resonant depiction of pre-Stonewall sexual style, this book is part history and part sociology, and it is completely compelling in its raw honesty and unabashed lack of inhibition. There were youngmen then, there are youngmen now. Fiction is history, too.

FADEOUT by Joseph Hansen. Hansen, arguably one of the finest writers to consistently hit the top of gay bookstore best-seller lists, has done more than give good mystery in his ten-book (as of late 1988) Dave Brandstetter insurance-sleuth series; he's also satisfied the lust of readers for easy genre entertainment, with dry wit, intelligent style and, since the first book (1970), occasional attention to community politics. Better yet, he opened the way for the likes of Richard Stevenson, Nathan Aldyne, and Michael Nava.

GAY SPIRIT edited by Mark Thompson. Not many books kick-start the collective consciousness of a community: this 1987 collection of many essays (Harry Hay, Edward Carpenter, Malcolm Boyd, Dennis Altman, Gerald Heard, Christopher Isherwood, Mitch Walker, et al.), their theme of spiritual essence linked by Thompson's elegant introductions, ranks as the major anthology of the 1980s, charting a future while exploring our past and confronting the present. It's a book from which many others will be spun.

IN HEAT by Larry Mitchell. Not all best books are obvious and some are too diffident for their own good. It's time, then, to spotlight a tale of falling in love and of growing old with grace, set in a New York of hypnotic hues, peopled with men honest enough to fret and chat about the fearsome gulf between sex and love. Mitchell's 1985 novel quietly captures the post-Stonewall, pre-AIDS world of pretty common gay guys, neither closeted nor, ahem, flamboyant, and does so with gracious, gorgeous writing.

THE MALE MUSE edited by Ian Young. Culture is presence, culture is essence, culture is survival, and poetry is culture distilled. That's why Canadian poet Young's landmark 1973 anthology (see also *Son of the Male Muse*), while not the first and certainly not the last such collection, is a definite must on any discerning gay booklover's bookshelf. And, like any good pile of poetry, Young's choices have it all: coming out, falling in love, challenging norms, telling fictional tales, and exploring biographical fact.

ONE TEENAGER IN TEN edited by Ann Heron. Honesty about self is the only way to fight homophobia; the first thing that haters deny is that children, if left to learn and grow without hate and prejudice and fear stunting them, may be gay women-and-men-in-waiting. That's why this slim collection of young voices, a simple idea in itself, is among the most powerful political books of the decade. It gives form to the reality of gay generations and hope to every new generation of teenagers. Role models are rare, and they do make a difference.

A SINGLE MAN by Christopher Isherwood. Before the elegant snapshot of Andrew Holleran's *Dancer from the Dance*, or the slit-eyed reportage of Larry Kramer's *Faggots*, or the cultured romance of Mary Renault's *The Charioteers*, or the soap-opera aura of Marion Zimmer Bradley's *The Catch Trap*, there was this eloquent 1964 novel of the singular life of a gay man who had loved in his time. Each generation of gay writers crafts a masterpiece defined by its era. This one transcends.

TALES OF THE CITY by Armistead Maupin. Six books in one — a sneaky way of inflating a ten-best list, no? Maupin's decade-spanning account of life, friendship, laughter, love, and death started in the San Francisco of 1978 but has a generous universality to it, as characters deal with growing up and growing older. Best of all, they do so with wit through *Tales, More Tales, Further Tales, Babycakes, Significant Others*, and, finally, *Sure of You*.

THE WORST

THE CLOSET HANGING by Tony Fennelly. There is a danger in even the most well-meaning of straight women portraying the gay life. In this mystery set in New Orleans, the absorbing atmosphere and readable banter don't mask the fact that Fennelly's main character can't help but think he'd be better off if he were, well, more of a man. Who needs self-hatred masking as light entertainment? Not us.

THE FRONT RUNNER by Patricia Nell Warren. It's an eternal bestseller, nurturing the fevers and the fancies of thousands and thousands of pubescent boys and men. It's a book about a young homo athlete, hence a useful role model for the teen jock yearning to be himself. Why, then, is it one of my five worst? Because. Just because. It's the idiosyncratic flip side to my choice of *In Heat* as one of the best.

THE GREAT URGE DOWNWARD by Gordon Merrick. Only the self-loathing symbolism of the title makes this particular one of Merrick's too-many sucky romances stand out. Merrick's heroes, from *The Lord Won't Mind* to *Measure of Madness,* teach none too subtly that being gay is a horrible way to live a life. Warning: Reading Merrick will be hazardous to your development as a well-rounded gay person.

THE SMILE OF EROS by John Coriolan. Because many men define themselves only by sex, a lot of gay writing is about sex. Some (for example, the work of Samuel Steward, aka Phil Andros, or the sexy collections of Boyd McDonald) is raunchy fun. Most is a feckless bore. And Coriolan sets a sad standard here, with too many dozens of references to "dangling manthings" and no apparent self-parody in sight.

THE WORLD CAN BREAK YOUR HEART by Daniel Curzon. A boy is picked on by his snot-nosed peers, suffers miserable teen years, is ashamed of his sexual feelings, marries desperately, abandons his wife and kids, heads for Hollywood, finds no fame, fails again and again at love, rails against the world (it can break your heart, you know), and dies alone of AIDS. The author says it's reality, but it reads like a fundamentalist bigot's wet dream.

Terry Helbing's
Ten Best and Five Worst
Gay and Lesbian Plays

Terry Helbing has been active in gay theater in various capacities since he acted in the Boston and New England touring company of Jonathan Ned Katz's *Coming Out!* in 1973. He has worked as a producer, actor, and dramaturge for The Glines, was a co-founder and co-artistic director of Meridian Theatre, and was a co-founder of Gay Presses of New York. Currently his "theater news"

news and opinion column runs weekly in *Stonewall News*.

Read any critic's year-end ten-best list, and you know how hard it is to restrict such a compilation to just ten selections. The staggering proliferation of gay theater in the twenty years since Stonewall (the focus here) makes that especially true of a ten-best-gay-plays list. It seems logical to select works that are, first of all, excellent plays, but that also portray gays and lesbians with a positive, open attitude. Gay plays written before Stonewall were most often homophobic, largely because of the prevailing social climate which required that plays conform to popular morality. Some of the most homophobic plays are listed after my list of "best" plays.

Whole articles could be written on how to define a "gay" play, but for the purposes of this listing, I've chosen the straightforward definition of "having a major gay character or theme." This definition puts the emphasis on the play as literature, rather than as a production, and eliminates works that might be classified under the broader heading of "gay theatre," including the work of Charles Busch, the late Charles Ludlam, Ethyl Eichelberger, and the English troupe Bloolips. This list represents a very small sampling of the many worthwhile gay and lesbian plays of the past twenty years. It is therefore meant only to give a general idea of how gay men and lesbians have been depicted on the stage. Beyond that, I hope that it will arouse your interest enough to read other plays. My selections are listed in alphabetical order:

Terry Miller

In 1983 the Meridian Gay Theater produced Jane Chambers's *A Late Snow,* which Terry Helbing describes as reflecting the playwright's "warmth, genuineness, and a terrific sense of humor."

THE BEST

BENT by Martin Sherman. Not only does Sherman's play dramatize the little-known Nazi persecution of gays, but it also allows the two gay protagonists (who develop a relationship in a concentration camp and have orgasms while standing at attention and not touching each other) to demonstrate that "the joyous affirmation of the human spirit" is not strictly a heterosexual phenomenon.

COMING OUT! by Jonathan Ned Katz. Like his two gay history books that were published subsequently, Katz's play takes a documentary look at the history of gays and lesbians, with scenes about Walt Whitman, Willa Cather, Horatio Alger, female-to-male transvestism, and the early days of gay liberation. This truly co-sexual play, performed with a cast of five women and five men, played in New York City in 1972, and a separate cast played and toured New England in 1973.

JERKER by Robert Chesley. Part of what might be called the "second generation" of gay playwrights, Chesley tackles the subject of AIDS from as distinctive and liberating a viewpoint as the city he calls home, San Francisco. Two men meet and develop a "buddy" relationship entirely through a series of telephone calls — "many of them dirty," as his subtitle indicates — without ever meeting face-to-face.

LAST SUMMER AT BLUEFISH COVE and **A LATE SNOW** by Jane Chambers. Frequently described as "the breakthrough lesbian play," *Bluefish Cove* is about a tightly knit group of women who spend their summers together in a resort community. For one, dying of a brain tumor, it is her last summer there. (The play had been written and produced before playwright Chambers died of a brain tumor in 1983.) *A Late Snow* concerns, in the playwright's own words, "five women snowbound in an isolated cabin: Ellie and her first, last, current and next lover." Both plays — along with the handful of other plays and novels she wrote — reflect Chambers's warmth, genuineness, and terrific sense of humor.

THE NORMAL HEART by Larry Kramer. As the tragic AIDS epidemic continues to worsen, there might soon be reason to compile a separate list of "Best AIDS Plays" that would include such moving efforts as William M. Hoffman's *As Is.* But screenwriter–novelist Kramer's play, detailing the onset of AIDS and the New York City gay community's activist response to it, is included here because it is among the rare works of political theater that are as effective theatrically as they are politically.

STREET THEATER by Doric Wilson. Wilson's play, set on Christopher Street the two hours before the Stonewall riots, concerns the drag queens, bull dykes, leathermen, and closet cases who came together that fateful "full-moon Friday night" in 1969. Like his other plays — *A Perfect Relationship* and *Forever After* — *Street Theater* is full of witty one-liners, clever farce, and characters so right that they are archetypes rather than stereotypes.

THANKSGIVING by Loretta Lotman and **PATIENCE AND SARAH** by Isabel Miller. Both of these les-

bian plays are classified in the "coming out" genre, of which there are many examples, but their superior writing distinguishes them from the rest. *Thanksgiving,* the winner of the first Jane Chambers Memorial International Gay Playwriting Contest, features a pretty standard coming-out situation — lesbian reveals she's gay to her family at a major holiday (in this case, Thanksgiving) — while Miller's adaptation of her popular novel concerns two nineteenth-century New England farm women who discover their love for one another, reveal it to their respective families, and go off to make a life together.

TORCH SONG TRILOGY by Harvey Fierstein. Fierstein's three full-length plays, *The International Stud, Fugue in a Nursery,* and *Widows and Children First!* — originally performed separately at La Mama ETC — won two Tony Awards for the author–star when performed on Broadway in a slightly abridged form under this collective title. The plays chronicle the life of ex–drag queen Arnold Beckoff, and in their own way espouse "traditional family values," but in a most nontraditional and tolerant kind of extended family.

FALSETTOS by William Finn. Like *Torch Song Trilogy, Falsettos* was conceived as a trilogy, and also akin to *Torch Song Trilogy,* two-thirds of this work (*March of the Falsettos* and *Falsettoland*), took ten years and various productions in various combinations (*Torch Song Trilogy* had all three of its pieces included when it moved to Broadway, by the way), but the *Falsettos* piece did end up on Broadway, where it won two Tony Awards for author William Finn. Not surprisingly in gay shows, "family values" take on non-traditional meanings, as when central character Marvin's son actually has his *bar mitzvah* in a hospital room, where Marvin's one-time-lover-but-still-friend is a patient in the early 1980s, with an as yet unidentified disease, which we now know as AIDS.

THE SUM OF US by David Stevens. Author Stevens was nominated for an Oscar for his work on the screenplay of *Breaker Morant*, and with this play, which had a lengthy run off-Broadway in New York in 1991–92, he demonstrated his accomplishments can move acrosss the artistic ground to other formats. Set in Australia, this is essentially a coming-out play, as a son does so to his Archie Bunker–like father. While being honest about your sexual preference to your family has been addressed onstage many times, it's hard to quickly recall a work that does so with as much heart as Stevens's does.

THE WORST

Not surprisingly, most of these plays were written before Stonewall, when it seemed quite natural that the only logical conclusion for a play about a tortured faggot or dyke was for him or her to commit suicide. We've come a long way since then, but that doesn't mean that homophobic plays aren't still being written. Once again, the plays are listed in alphabetical order.

THE BOYS IN THE BAND by Mart Crowley. Some people might find it surprising that the very play that brought homosexuals to the attention of a wider theatrical audience is included on a list of homophobic plays. But with its self-loathing characters and its bitchy dialogue (one of the reasons why some people still like the play so much), the play was already a dated period piece when it was first performed in 1968, and it's surprising that anyone is still bothering to produce it today.

THE CHILDREN'S HOUR by Lillian Hellman. A malicious child's false accusation of a lesbian relationship between two teachers is enough to make one of the women wonder if, indeed, it might be true and feel so guilty that she must, of course, commit suicide.

THE KILLING OF SISTER GEORGE by Frank Marcus. Marcus wallows in some of the worst stereotypes about lesbians as he presents Sister George, a character in a BBC soap, whom he portrays as a cigar-smoking, gin-drinking, hard-cursing bull dyke who makes her lover wait on her hand and foot. A truly disgusting portrayal of gay women.

THE KNIFE by David Hare. Joseph Papp's Public Theatre was virtually silent on the subject of gay men and lesbians for many years, but has more than made up for it lately with productions of Larry Kramer's *The Normal Heart*, Albert Innaurato's *Coming of Age in Soho*, Harry Kondoleon's *Zero Positive*, and other plays. But Papp also produced this 1987 work, which is more implicitly than explicitly homophobic. In this musical about a male-to-female transsexual sex change, Hare refuses to allow his "new woman" to have a lesbian relationship with "his" former girlfriend. Seemingly such a relationship is impossible because "s/he" no longer has the requisite equipment. In addition, the musical contains a number by a group of gay waiters in which, to quote one critic, they are portrayed as "simpering, disagreeable fags."

TEA AND SYMPATHY by Robert Anderson. At a boys' school, the headmaster's wife "sacrifices" her marital fidelity and sleeps with a boy who is constantly being called a sissy, thus assuring him of his manhood. In the world of this play, gayness and manhood could not possibly be synonymous! This is the play that contains the dreaded line, "When you remember this years from now, and you will, be kind."

Vito Russo's Ten Best and Five Worst Gay Movies

Vito Russo was the author of *The Celluloid Closet: Homosexuality in the Movies.* His free-lance writing appeared in *Rolling Stone, The Advocate, The Village Voice,* and other national publications. A native New Yorker, he co-founded ACT-UP and was a tireless AIDS activist until his death in 1990 at age 44.

When listing the "best" of anything it is advisable to cite one's criteria for selection. Are we judging art or politics? Must the best gay films qualify as good cinema as well as good politics? Are the worst gay films those which are homophobic regardless of their value as art? As a rule I have chosen to list those films which I think have illuminated diverse aspects of the gay and lesbian experience in an exciting, personal, or unusual way. In doing so, I found that those listed among the best were generally good films and those on the worst list were usually not.

I have avoided obscure or inaccessible titles. Most of the films listed are available on videotape. Because of space limitations, I was forced to omit several worthy titles which came to mind or were suggested to me by friends. What remains is, I think, a valid primer for anyone wishing to sample the best and the worst ways in which the twentieth century's most popular art form has reflected lesbians and gay men.

THE BEST

ABUSE (1983), directed by Arthur J. Bressan, Jr. The story of a gay independent filmmaker and his relationship with a battered teenager. A daring and powerful exploration of the issues of child abuse and intergenerational sex.

LONGTIME COMPANION (1990), directed by Norman Rene. Originally shot for *American Playhouse,* this first feature film dealing with gay men and AIDS follows a group of friends through eight years in the epidemic. There's a lot of casual affection between men, they don't pander to straight expectations, and the writing is naturalistic and real.

MAURICE (1987), directed by James Ivory. A little too *Masterpiece Theatre* for some tastes, but an effective adaptation of the Forster novel that explores, perhaps for the first time onscreen, the fact that ho-

Daniel Day-Lewis (left) and Gordon Warnecke (right) provided the romance in Stephen Frears's *My Beautiful Laundrette.*

mosexuality is not a choice but a state of being.

MY BEAUTIFUL LAUNDRETTE (1986), directed by Stephen Frears. Pakistani playwright Hanif Kureishi's screenplay explores class, race, and sex in Thatcher's Britain. The central romantic relationship is quite incidentally — and charmingly — between two men.

PARTING GLANCES (1986), directed by Bill Sherwood. Superbly written, directed, and acted independent film about twenty-four hours in the lives of some gay New Yorkers in the age of AIDS.

SUNDAY BLOODY SUNDAY (1971), directed by John Schlesinger. Witty and literate original drama featuring a triangular relationship between Peter Finch, Murray Head, and Glenda Jackson. The first major film in which two men kissed on-screen.

TAXI ZUM KLO (1980), directed by Frank Ripploh. Intensely personal, funny, and controversial independent German film about the sexually promiscuous lifestyle of a high school teacher.

THE TIMES OF HARVEY MILK (1985), directed by Robert Epstein. Powerful, Oscar-winning documentary about the life of the San Francisco city supervisor who was assassinated along with Mayor George Moscone in 1977. Also won five Emmys and the New York Film Critics Award for best documentary.

TONGUES UNTIED (1989), directed by Marlon Riggs. A dazzling piece of filmmaking about black gay men. Poetic, political, and angry, this powerful film is the first to shatter the silence about gay people of color in a powerful and entertaining way.

VICTIM (1961), directed by Basil Dearden. Landmark blackmail thriller starring Dirk Bogarde as a London barrister who risks his marriage and career to change the laws that made homosexuality a criminal offense.

THE WORST

BUSTING (1974), directed by Peter Hyams. A slezoid look at the world of the vice squad with an emphasis on homosexual life in the ghetto.

CRUISING (1980), directed by William Friedkin. This murder mystery, based on Gerald Walker's homophobic novel, is set in New York's sex and S&M underground. Nasty, exploitative film which suggests that homosexuality can be acquired through contact.

PARTNERS (1982), directed by James Burrows. Ryan O'Neal and John Hurt, a straight and a gay police officer, pretend to live "as homosexuals" in order to trap a killer. Every neanderthal stereotype in the book.

THE SERGEANT (1968), directed by John Flynn. Rod Steiger as the officer in love with handsome young John Philip Law. A textbook case of the tortured, self-hating homosexual who commits suicide af-

ter giving in to his unnatural desires. The film implicitly approves of suicide as a solution to homosexuality.

STAIRCASE (1969), directed by Stanley Donen. Relentlessly grim portrait of two bitter, aging homosexual barbers facing a crisis when one is arrested for soliciting. The film and the play upon which it is based blame their misery not on their problems but on their sexuality.

Andrea Weiss's Ten Best and Five Worst Lesbian Movies

Andrea Weiss won an Emmy Award for her research for the television documentary *Before Stonewall*. With Greta Schiller, she produced and directed the films *International Sweethearts* and *Tiny and Ruby: Hell Divin' Women*. She is the author of *Vampires and Violets: Lesbians in Film* (Viking/Penguin, 1993).

MÄDCHEN IN UNIFORM (1931), directed by Leontine Sagan. West Germany. Distributed by Films, Inc. The recent emergence of lesbian independent cinema doesn't offer anything that can hold a candle to this classic story of a sensitive, defiant schoolgirl's passion for her teacher.

ENTRE NOUS (1984), directed by Diane Kurys. France. Although the jury is still out on whether this is a "lesbian film," the relationship between Madeleine (Miou-Miou) and Lena (Isabelle Huppert) is passionate, intellectual, dependable, and sensual, and provides the crucial tension which propels the film.

Helen Shaver (left) and Patricia Charbonneau in the 1986 film *Desert Hearts,* which Andrea Weiss calls "uncompromised in its representation of lesbians."

DAMNED IF YOU DON'T (1987), directed by Su Friedrich. United States. An experimental exploration of a nun's sexual desire which has been awakened by a beautiful stranger from outside of the convent.

I'VE HEARD THE MERMAIDS SINGING (1987), directed by Patricia Rozema. Canada. A funny, absurdist comedy about a "person Friday" in an art gallery who falls in love with her curator; weak on plot line but more than compensates by its resourcefulness and ingenuity.

QUEEN CHRISTINA (1933), directed by Rouben Mamoulian. Screenplay by Salka Viertal. United States. Never mind that Queen Christina falls in love with the Spanish ambassador in the snow. Greta Garbo as Queen Christina will always be remembered by lesbian viewers for her masculine attire, her refusal to marry, and her love for Countess Ebba.

DESERT HEARTS (1986), directed by Donna Deitch. United States. A great lesbian Western, this independently produced feature is conventional Hollywood in style but uncompromised in its representation of lesbians.

THE VIRGIN MACHINE (1988), directed by Monika Treut. West Germany. An ironic initiation of a young, naive West German researcher into the lesbian sexual underground of San Francisco, beautifully shot by cinematographer Elfi Mikesch.

DAUGHTERS OF DARKNESS (1970), directed by Harry Kumel. Belgium. Providing a feminist twist on the lesbian vampire genre, this film makes heterosexuality abnormal and violent, and offers a lesbian vampire (played by Delphine Seyrig) as its most sympathetic and likeable character. A "campy" lesbian classic.

THE GROUP (1966), directed by Sidney Lumet. United States. Based on the novel by Mary McCarthy. Perhaps the first Hollywood film to include an obviously lesbian character without exploitation and sensationalism. Candace Bergen plays the sophisticated, well-tailored Lakey who, when gay-baited, coolly and proudly proclaims her "Sapphism."

FORBIDDEN LOVE (1992), directed by Aerlyn Weissman and Lynn Fernie. Canada. A powerful piece of history, this documentary recalls the "twilight world" of lesbian romance and survival in the 1950s and '60s. The personal histories of nine women are set against the backdrop of colorful pulp novels and sensational tabloid headlines, suggesting an intricate relationship between truth and fiction, memory and fantasy, the individual and the collective imagination.

THE WORST

WAITING FOR THE MOON (1987), directed by Jill Godmilow. United States. Although this film is a portrait of the world's most famous lesbian couple, Gertrude Stein and Alice B. Toklas, it carefully avoids giving any sexual dimension to their lives or any intimacy to their interactions.

THE FOX (1968), directed by Mark Rydell. United States. The archetypal lesbian film in that it follows the bisexual triangle formula (man rescues woman from lesbian lover)

and ends with the obligatory death of the lover. A straight man's wet dream.

PERSONAL BEST (1982), directed by Robert Towne. United States. Lesbianism is an adolescent phase that Chris (Mariel Hemingway) passes through en route to a more mature relationship with a man. Three quotes: *New York Times,* "Undisguised voyeurism." New York *Daily News,* "According to this movie, lesbianism is something they catch in the locker room, like athlete's foot." Director's statement, "I like looking at [the athletes'] thighs. I adore them. I want to fuck the daylights out of them."

THE COLOR PURPLE (1985), directed by Steven Spielberg. United States. Spielberg isn't afraid of creatures from outer space, but a lesbian relationship is simply too threatening. His adaptation of Alice Walker's novel is classic Hollywood erasure of lesbian characters and themes (not to mention its objectionable treatment of race).

THREE OF HEARTS (1993), directed by Yurek Bogayevicz. United States. A more contemporary version of the same bisexual triangle formula we saw in *The Fox,* but here the lesbian relationship is essentially over before the film even begins. Twenty-five years and the women's and gay liberation movements have intervened between the making of the two films, and yet they both come down to the same point: Don't worry, guys, a woman will choose the first available man over a clinging, neurotic lesbian any day.

Adam Block's
Five Homo-Negative and
Ten Pro-Homo Pop Songs

Adam Block is a widely published San Francisco–based journalist, a columnist for the San Francisco *Sentinel,* and the pop music editor for *The Advocate.*

Growing up, listening to the radio, I heard all kinds of wonder and weirdness, freedom and delight pumping out of the local rock station. But in thousands of doomed romances, one subject never came up; homos and lesbians simply didn't exist. Nearly thirty years later the subject still makes the pop scene squeamish. Gay singers long believed that honesty would spell commercial suicide. Most still do. That fear has generally left it up to heteros to address the subject ... or to let it lie.

HOMO-NEGATIVE POP

The fact is that homophobic lyrics are a lot rarer than pop homophobia. Gays inspired by the songs of Donna Summer or Bob Marley would discover the artists' intolerant fundamentalism only from interviews. Fans of Neil Young and the Beastie Boys read their bigoted bile in magazines, not on lyric sheets. Metal morons like Sammy Hagar confined their queer-bashing to crowd-pleasing cracks in concert. The vinyl evidence is only the iceberg's tip.

"MONEY FOR NOTHING" and **"LES BOYS"** by Dire Straits. Songwriter Mark Knopfler insisted that the line "That little faggot has his own jet airplane" represented the voice of a blue-collar bigot with whom he had no sympathy. Anyone who had heard his earlier smug affront, "Les Boys," knew better.

"THE MESSAGE" by Grandmaster Flash & the Furious Five. This rap classic bit the bigot's hand, but took time out to level disdain on gays, sneering about a "fag hag" and evoking a prison rape that turns a man into that most horrible of all creatures: a limp-wristed queen.

"MACHO MAN" by the Village People. Originally a gay-concept-novelty (doing male drag to disco instead of female drag to showtunes, thereby portraying queers who would no longer live according to cherished stereotypes), crossover success sent the combo diving for their closets. With this song they celebrated the most moronic, narcissistic vision imaginable. Suddenly, the group became a eunuched family cartoon, neutering the spectre that had inspired them.

"I LOVE WOMEN" by Lou Reed. Of all the glitter gang, Reed was the only one to live openly with a male lover (even if it was a creature named Rachel), but this song marked his apostasy. It wasn't so much his marriage that galled — or the declaration, "I love women. I've always loved women" — but his insistence that "We all love women. We have always loved women." I figure Reed had the right to disown his own gay past, but I draw the line at his claim that the rest of us are simply deluding ourselves ... until the right woman comes along.

"ON ANY OTHER DAY" by the Police. Sting offered a litany of disasters: "My wife just burned the scrambled eggs, my daughter ran away, my son just said he's gay; it's been a terrible day." Later he would sing backup on the infamous "Money for Nothing," and release a film where his band slagged homos. Some suggest that his tribute to the distinctly old-school homo Quentin Crisp, "An Englishman in New York," was calculated to clear his name.

PRO-HOMO POP

This list doesn't pretend to be definitive. Many will miss the noble, if little-heard, independents like Steve Grossman, Blackberri, Charlie Murphy, Tom Wilson, Romanovsky & Phillips, Michael Callen, or any of the women on Redwood or Olivia. And where are such gay pop wonders as Sylvester, Boy George, and Marc Almond? As for "Lola" by the Kinks, endlessly cited by critics as "everybody's favorite," I never thought that old-school-homo singalong about a seduction by a drag queen had *any*thing to do with gay lib.

"REBEL REBEL" and **"QUEEN BITCH"** by David Bowie. A bitch with a boner, a boy on a tear: scary, sexy declarations of possibility as shameless as squealing tires and as hungry as true love.

"THIS CHARMING MAN" and **"DIAL A CLICHE"** by the Smiths. The great fey loner Morrissey's grandiose misery is illuminated by savage wit and erotic visions find the elegant outsider repeatedly betrayed by rough trade and still coming back for more. Boys flock to the vegan-celibate Morrissey with the

same fervor their big brothers brought to Bowie.

"SWIM TEAM" by Phranc. The brush-cut lesbian emerged from L.A.'s punk scene as a tough but disarming folksinger who enjoys using the "L" word. She won over young audiences when she opened for Husker Du and for the Smiths.

"GLAD TO BE GAY" and **"THE WEDDING"** by Tom Robinson. The first song, which he did with his band in 1978, was a black blast at gay apathy masquerading as an anthem. The second, a solo piece done nine years later, is a venomous, brilliant account of attending his boyfriend's wedding.

"JOHNNY ARE YOU QUEER?" by Josie Cotten. The Go Go's passed on this blast of pure pop which sweetly acknowledges that there *are* girls in high school who are confused by their gay boyfriends. Radical whimsy with a heart.

"THE ALTAR BOY AND THE THIEF" by Joan Baez. An astonishingly astute portrait of a 1970s gay bar, which climaxes with two youths dancing as Joan declares, "to me they will always remain: unclaimed, unchained, and unblamed — the altar boy and the thief — grabbing a little relief." Bravo.

"SMALLTOWN BOY" and **"WHY?"** by Bronski Beat. This unglamorous trio laid down a propulsive disco rhythm as Jimmy Somerville's falsetto soared on. A tale of a gay boy kicked out of his home in the industrial north of England and a toe-tapper assaulting gay-bashing and bigotry. The first gay socialist guerilas to top the dance charts.

"I AM WHAT I AM" by Gloria Gaynor. The lady who cut "Never Can Say Goodbye" and "I Will Survive" takes the climactic number from *La Cage Aux Folles* to the dance floor, and makes the coming-out anthem an endless celebration.

"GIMME, GIMME, GIMME (A MAN AFTER MIDNIGHT)" by Erasure. Andy Bell, the U.K. duo's brazen gay vocalist, turns Abba's confection into a glistening carousel with rugged studs in the place of ponies.

"CIRCLE JERK" and **"I WANNA FUCK YOUR DAD"** by the Impotent Sea Snakes. The Tampa, Florida, combo were on a tear when "13" wrote the lyrics to this unlikely LP. The music is generic speed/thrash, but the words are inspirational — like that of the boy so smitten with his girlfriend's pa that he rants, "I don't want your tits and cunt. Your fuckin' dad is all I want. I know your dad, he ain't no fool. He can't live without my love tool," and the paean to communal boy sex, which details a complex orgy, and then choruses, "Circle Jerk! Let's all: Circle Jerk! C'mon, c'mon and jack off with me. Whores cost money but friends are free!" are unparalleled in pop music's rocky relationship with queerdom.

PEOPLE

(with illustrations by Michael Willhoite)

The modern distinction between homosexual and heterosexual has not existed in most times and cultures. Many individuals listed here would not have considered themselves to be gay, or lesbian, or bisexual — for many, that terminology did not even exist. But in reclaiming a history that has generally been hidden, it's valuable to know how widespread same-sex relationships have been in human history.

The gay or bisexual orientation of most individuals listed here is well established. For a few, the evidence is circumstantial or open to question; these cases are indicated in the text.

ABBOTT, BERENICE. (July 17, 1898–Dec. 9, 1991), *U.S. photographer*. Berenice Abbott originally studied art and photography in New York, then moved to Paris where, throughout the 1920s, she worked in the lab of Man Ray. Her subjects included many writers and artists (James Joyce, Jean Cocteau, André Gide) and well-known lesbians (Sylvia Beach, Djuna Barnes, Margaret Anderson). She returned to New York in 1929 and began shooting the photos that would make up her famous book *Changing New York* — a record of the city's evolving architecture. Abbott settled in Maine in the 1950s, following the death of her longtime partner, essayist Elizabeth McCausland. Her later work included a book about U.S. Route 1, which stretches from Maine to Florida.

ABU NUWAS. (756?–810), *Arabian poet*. Abu Nuwas was born in Persia, and as a young adult moved to Baghdad, where he befriended the great Caliph Harun al-Rashid. In his lifetime he wrote some five thousand poems, establishing himself as the most widely quoted Arab poet of all time.

The poems of Abu Nuwas celebrate both heterosexual and homosexual love. His own homosexuality is graphically illustrated in the *Arabian Nights* story "Abu Nuwas and the Three Boys," and seems to have been cheerfully tolerated by the ruler. But Moslem society was not always so tolerant: only a few years earlier, upon finding two women attendants in a compromising position, the Caliph al-Hadi beheaded them on the spot.

ACKERLEY, J.R. (JOE RANDOLPH). (Nov. 4, 1896–Jun. 4, 1967), *British writer and editor*. Few people could write a book-length biography of their dog. Fewer still could get it published. That Joe Randolph Ackerley did both is one small measure of his unusual mind.

At the age of thirty-three, Ackerley got a shock that greatly shaped his future life and writings. His father died, and instead of the inheritance he had expected, Ackerley received only some startling news about himself: he was an illegitimate child, and he had a household of half-siblings sired secretly by his father.

Ackerley dedicated much of his time to discovering more about this mystery man who had been his father. The result appeared in his autobiography, *My Father and Myself.* Speculation about his father is interspersed with observations about his own homosexuality and his quest for the perfect lover — preferably a working-class uniformed soldier. He never found that; in later life, he settled into a comfortable niche as magazine editor and achieved a close companionship with his dog. He describes that relationship in *My Dog Tulip* and *We Think the World of You.*

AGATHON. (445?–400? B.C.), *Athenian dramatist.* None of Agathon's tragedies have survived, but the dramatist himself earned a place in literary history in 416 B.C. when a banquet at his home served as a basis for *The Symposium,* Plato's famous celebration of homosexual love. He is also noteworthy as history's first recorded example of a stereotypically effeminate homosexual; he was portrayed in that role in Aristophanes' comedy, *The Thesmophoriazusae.*

AKHENATEN. (ruled 1379?–1362? B.C.), *Egyptian Pharaoh.* Called "the world's first individual" by historian James Breasted, Pharaoh Akhenaten brought fresh and controversial ideas to ancient Egypt — a land that, in the fourteenth century before Christ, already had centuries-old traditions and beliefs. Akhenaten introduced the concept of internationalism to the ancient world. He also introduced monotheism — the idea of a single, omnipotent god, rather than the galaxy of greater and lesser gods worshipped by his predecessors. In doing so, he antagonized the powerful priesthood, but set the groundwork for modern religion.

Akhenaten married his mother and four other women. He also had a male lover, Smenkhkare. Their homosexuality does not seem to have bothered Akhenaten's contemporaries, but his challenge to traditional religion brought about his downfall. The priests joined forces with the army and assassinated Akhenaten and Smenkhkare, and his son Tutankhamen was made Pharaoh. Akhenaten and Smenkhkare were the first historically documented male couple in history but he is best remembered in another context: as the apparent basis for the myth of Oedipus.

ALBEE, EDWARD. (Mar. 12, 1928 –), *U.S. playwright.* A prolific and controversial dramatist, Edward Albee is known for such works as *The Zoo Story, The American Dream,* and *Who's Afraid of Virginia Woolf?* In his plays, Albee portrays a world where suffering is inevitable, but his vision is not truly pessimistic; although his characters confront pain, they are capable of growth and change. Forced to question their values, many take a more honest approach to life.

Albee was abandoned at birth by his natural parents and was adopted by millionaires Reed and Frances Albee. He was a rebellious child and was expelled from three prep schools and a military academy before graduating from Choate. In 1958 he wrote *The Zoo Story* as a "sort of a thirtieth birthday present to myself." With that, his writing career began in earnest. Since then, he has written more than twenty plays and has received two Pulitzer Prizes.

Albee rarely discusses his personal life in interviews, preferring to focus on his work, but he makes no secret of his homosexuality. Gay themes and characters find little place in his plays, although many critics feel that his homosexuality has influenced his portrayal of relations between the sexes.

Despite repeated speculation that Albee meant the squabbling couples in *Who's Afraid of Virginia Woolf?* to represent gay male couples, he has denied any such intent, and has on several occasions taken action to prevent the play from being staged with a cast of four men.

ALCIBIADES. (450?–404 B.C.), *Athenian general.* Born into a wealthy family and endowed with great beauty, Alcibiades gained a reputation early in life for arrogance and unruly behavior. As a teenager, he met Socrates, was captivated by the philosopher's questioning of accepted wisdom, fell in love, and attempted to seduce the older man. The seduction scene in Plato's *Symposium* is based on this incident.

In the ensuing years, Alcibiades became active in the political and military affairs of Athens, then switched allegiance to the rival city-state of Sparta. He was run out of Sparta by its king following rumors of an affair between Alcibiades and the queen, and transferred his loyalties to the Persians. A few years later he returned to Athens, where a right-wing coup had replaced his former enemies with allies, and was briefly made general and ruler of the city. He lost this position following a military defeat in 406 B.C., after which the Spartans and Persians, worried about where he might turn up next, had him murdered.

ALEXANDER I. (Dec. 23, 1777–Dec. 1, 1825), *Russian czar.* The friendly and handsome Alexander I became czar of Russia in 1801 at the age of twenty-three, following the murder of his father. His early hopes for domestic reform and international peace were quickly thwarted by the increasingly aggressive military actions of his neighbor, Napoleon.

In June of 1812, Napoleon invaded Russia with half a million soldiers. Rather than fight such an overwhelming force, Alexander's armies retreated, finally giving up Moscow to the French. Whether by genius or luck, this strategy worked. Short of supplies, and with a bitter winter approaching, Napoleon had to retreat; when he left Russia, eighty percent of his army had been wiped out.

Alexander's homosexual trysts were the subject of frequent comment during his lifetime. Napoleon referred to him as "the slyest and handsomest of all the Greeks."

ALEXANDER THE GREAT. (July 20?, 356–323 B.C.), *Macedonian king.* Alexander III became king of Macedonia at the age of twenty, and soon thereafter began his campaign to conquer the known world. He quickly subdued Greece, to the south of Macedonia, then began pursuit of the immense Persian army, which he overwhelmed in 330 B.C. By the time of his death seven years later, Alexander had taken his campaign as far as India, deliberately mixing Greek culture with Asian culture, and Greek blood with Asian blood, as he went.

For most of his life, Alexander's closest friend and colleague was Hephaestion, although there is no clear proof that their relationship was sexual. Alexander's sexual relationship with the young eunuch Bagoas is more clearly documented, and served as the basis for Mary Renault's engaging novel *The Persian Boy*.

ALGER, HORATIO. (Jan. 13, 1832–July 18, 1899), *U.S. writer.* Alger is best known for his stories of underprivileged boys who find great success in life through hard work and clean living. But before he became a writer, Alger had been a Unitarian pastor in the Cape Cod town of Brewster; there, he was run out of town for "the abominable and revolting crime of unnatural familiarity with boys."

Early in 1866 rumors began to fly about young Reverend Alger, particularly in regard to fifteen-year-old John Clark and his thirteen-year-old friend, Thomas Crocker. After the scandal broke, one townsman wrote: "On the sabbath after service, one of these boys called at his room to leave a book ... [Alger] bolted his door and then committed this unnatural crime, with the poor boy's sister waiting in the carriage in the cold."

Alger's family hushed up the scandal and Horatio left the ministry for New York, where his writing career began in earnest. Later, he "informally" adopted several young boys without any brouhaha.

ANACREON. (582?–485? B.C.), *Greek poet.* Anacreon was a prominent figure in ancient Greece, first in Samos, then in Athens. Little of his love poetry has survived, but it seems to have dealt mainly with boys. One fragment, that survived only because it was used in the Middle Ages to illustrate points of Greek grammar, contains the lines:

I love Cleobulus
I dote on Cleobulus
I gaze at Cleobulus.

The eighteenth century saw great interest in English imitations of Anacreon. One result was a popular song, "Anacreon in Heaven," which later supplied the tune for the American national anthem.

ANDERSEN, HANS CHRISTIAN. (Apr. 2, 1805–Aug. 4, 1875), *Danish storyteller.* Andersen wrote many plays and novels in his homeland of Denmark, but his international fame rests on his fairy tales, which have been translated into over a hundred languages. A lifelong bachelor, he perceived himself as having many female qualities and suffered through an unrequited love affair with his friend Edvard Collin.

ANDERSON, MARGARET. (1886–Oct. 18, 1973), *U.S. editor.* Anderson, with her friend and lover Jane Heap, founded and edited the legendary *Little Review,* a small but prominent literary magazine of the twenties. They adopted the editorial policy of "Making No Compromise with the Public Taste," a motto that was put to the test when they published James Joyce's *Ulysses* in installments, after other prospective U.S. publishers had all refused. The magazine was consequently prosecuted for obscenity, and the U.S. Post Office burned four issues of it.

ANNE. (Feb. 6, 1665–Aug. 1, 1714), *English queen.* At the age of eighteen, Anne was married to an undis-

tinguished Danish nobleman. They had seventeen children, all of whom died in childhood, and Anne's twelve years as queen, while prosperous ones for Britain, represented the last of the Stuart line.

But the true love of Anne's life was not her husband; it was Sarah Churchill, a duchess known for her intelligence and beauty. Churchill became Anne's attendant, and correspondence between the two women reveals an exceptionally passionate and close relationship.

ANTHONY, SUSAN B. (Feb. 15, 1820–March 13, 1906), *U.S. reformer.* A founder and leading inspiration of the nineteenth-century women's rights movement was Susan B. Anthony. Even as a teenager, she vehemently protested the inequities of marriage, an institution that she would later call "legalized prostitution."

In addition to her work for women's rights, Anthony supported the abolitionist movement. Through her anti-slavery work she met the beautiful Anna Dickinson, with whom she developed a close and probably sexual relationship.

Not all abolitionists saw a connection between their cause and that of women's suffrage. A prominent male abolitionist once told Anthony, "You are not married; you have no business discussing marriage." She replied, "And you are not a slave. Suppose you quit lecturing on slavery."

AUDEN, W.H. (Feb. 21, 1907–Sept. 29, 1973), *British poet.* Wystan Hugh Auden was a friend of Christopher Isherwood, and both were influenced by the early 1930s gay movement in Germany. During that period, he married cabaret performer Erika Mann so she could obtain a British passport and escape from Nazi Germany. Soon thereafter, a friend of Mann's found herself in the same predicament, and approached Auden for help. "What else are buggers for?" asked Auden, and he found a friend to oblige.

In 1937, Auden met fellow poet Chester Kallman, and within two years they developed a relationship that was to last a lifetime. Some of Auden's published poetry suggested his homosexuality, but his private verse was the most explicit. Dining with friends once, he summed up the most important elements of his nature by a bit of haiku he scribbled on the tablecloth:

My Epitaph—
A cocksucker. Yes.
A poet. I believe.
Good. And a Christian?

Auden received the 1948 Pulitzer Prize for poetry for his *Age of Anxiety.*

AUGUSTINE, Saint. (Nov. 13, 354–Aug. 28, 430), *Roman theologian.* The man who gave us the memorable epigram, "Lord, grant me chastity — but not yet!" practiced what he preached. Augustine was born in northern Africa. He was raised as a Christian by his mother, then experimented with the gloomy philosophy of Manichaeanism for a time, and at thirty-three finally converted back to Christianity. He is best remembered for his *Confessions,* in which he describes his passionate, youthful attachment to another young man: "I felt that his soul and mine were one soul in two bodies." Most authorities agree that this was a sexual as well as spiritual relationship. But the object of that affection died young. Augustine had later relationships with several women, and eventually did achieve his goal of celibacy.

BACON, Sir FRANCIS. (Jan. 22, 1561–April 9, 1626), *English jurist and scientist.* Born into a well-connected family, Bacon became active in politics early in life, and in 1618 became lord high chancellor — England's highest post except for the throne itself. Political opponents found evidence that he had accepted bribes while in this post, however, and after only four years Bacon's political career collapsed.

He then turned to scientific pursuits, which had long intrigued him. Bacon was among the first scholars to reject the traditional Aristotelian philosophy of science, preferring a more experimental approach. In the winter of 1626, to find out if cold foods would stay fresh longer,

Bacon filled a chicken carcass with snow. The chicken did fine, but Bacon got pneumonia and died three days later.

Bacon married at the age of forty-eight, but several of his contemporaries commented on his homosexuality. His mother chided him for "that bloody Percy" whom her son kept as "a bed companion," and biographer John Aubrey bluntly stated that Bacon "was a pederast."

His essay *On Beauty* focuses primarily on male beauty and Bacon coined the English language's first nonjudgmental term for gayness: *masculine love.* He did not actually come out, however, for the times discouraged such openness. Bacon's brother-in-law, the earl of Castlehaven, was executed in 1631 for engaging in homosexual acts.

BADEN-POWELL, Lord R.S.S. (Feb. 22, 1857–Jan. 8, 1941), *British civil servant.* Baden-Powell garnered worldwide recognition for creating the Boy Scouts in 1908, a youth movement credited with changing deprived, mostly middle-class boys into strong citizens ready to defend their country in World War I. Tim Jeal, in his biography *The Boy-Man,* concluded that Baden-Powell was a suppressed homosexual who warned his scouts against girls and masturbation, and who feared women and sex. Also in evidence were Baden-Powell's severe headaches that started after his marriage at age fifty-six, and wouldn't end until he stopped sleeping in the same bed with his wife.

BAEZ, JOAN. (Jan. 9, 1941–), *U.S. folksinger.* Baez began her career by singing in Boston coffeehouses, and was asked to perform at the Newport Jazz Festival in 1959. The following year her first album, *Joan Baez,* became an instant success. Baez's clear voice, accompanied only by her guitar, helped rekindle interest in folk music in the 1960s. Baez also became known for her political activism, working for civil rights organizations and in the antiwar effort. In 1972, Baez acknowledged her bisexuality, and received the support of her estranged husband at the time. "Everyone is more or less bisexual," she said. "People just don't want to admit it."

BAKER, JOSEPHINE. (Jun. 3, 1906–Apr. 12, 1975), *U.S. entertainer.* At the age of thirteen, Josephine Baker left home for the world of show business, soon landing in New York in the early  years of the Harlem Renaissance. When she substituted for a chorus girl in a show, the audience loved her comic antics so well that she quickly got better parts; by her twenty-first birthday, Baker had gone to Europe as part of an all-black show, and soon starred in the Folies Bergère. She eventually settled in France with her husband and a large, multiracial adopted family, but she had many lesbian affairs along the way.

In 1975, Baker celebrated a half-century onstage with a sensational farewell performance. She dropped off to sleep with the loud applause still ringing in her ears, and never woke up. Friends say that she died of joy.

BAKKER, JAMES. (1940–), *U.S. evangelist.* In March 1987, television evangelist James Bakker publicly confessed to a fifteen-minute sexual encounter with Jessica Hahn in 1980. What seemed at first like a small scandal quickly snowballed amidst stories of hush money, extravagant and illegal expense accounts, and prostitution. Homosexuality was among the charges: Chattanooga evangelist John Ankerberg testified that he knew a man who said he had been Bakker's lover. Another accuser reported that he had walked into Bakker's steam room "and there was Jim frolicking in the nude with three other men. They were dancing around and taking turns laying on a table, massaging each other. I wondered what the heck I had gotten into." Bakker denied these reports. "I am not a homosexual," he said at a press conference. But the next year the charges were back in the press, as former evangelist and fundraiser John Wesley Fletcher described past sexual escapades with Bakker in *Penthouse* magazine.

BALDWIN, JAMES. (Aug. 2, 1924–Dec. 1, 1987), *U.S. writer.* A leader in the black civil rights movement, James Baldwin was also a strong supporter of gay rights, although the *New York Times* and *Washington Post* scarcely mentioned his homosexuality in their obituaries.

Baldwin spent an unhappy

childhood with an abusive father in Harlem, where he honed his writing skills on paper bags because his family couldn't afford writing paper. After three years as a pentecostal preacher, he escaped to Paris in 1948, and spent much of his life there. A prolific writer, Baldwin left behind a collection of works impressive both for their number and their quality. These include *Go Tell It on the Mountain, Giovanni's Room, Another Country,* and the controversial *The Fire Next Time.*

Baldwin was primarily concerned with American society's need to discard many of its myths. He felt that Americans were "still trapped in a history they do not understand," and that they needed to break out of their false view of reality. The myth of white superiority was in Baldwin's mind the most important, and most destructive, of the many myths that informed American culture, and he saw it as closely related to the deep-seated homophobia prevalent in America.

BANNEKER, BENJAMIN. (Nov. 9, 1731–Oct. 25, 1806), *U.S. mathematician.* In the years following the American Revolution, Benjamin Banneker calculated the tables for one of the country's earliest almanacs, wrote anti-slavery tracts and other essays about political issues, and helped lay plans for the city of Washington, D.C.

Banneker was black, and the abolitionist movement often focused attention on him to emphasize the human potential that was suppressed by slavery. Banneker never married, and there is no evidence of his ever being romantically involved with a woman. From this, some historians have surmised that he may have been homosexual.

BARBER, SAMUEL. (Mar. 9, 1910–Jan. 23, 1981), *U.S. composer.* Samuel Barber began composing when he was seven, tried writing his first opera when he was ten, and entered the Curtis Institute of Music at thirteen. Throughout a career spanning more than fifty years, he created richly expressive, lyric music, including his Pulitzer Prize–winning opera *Vanessa* and the enormously popular *Adagio for Strings,* written when he was twenty-six. He remains today one of the most often performed of American composers in the international symphonic repertoire.

Barber's homosexuality was, throughout most of his adult life, an open secret in the music world. For many years he lived with and maintained a close personal and professional relationship with operatic composer Gian Carlo Menotti, who wrote the libretto for *Vanessa* and collaborated with Barber on a number of other works.

BARNES, DJUNA. (June 12, 1892–Jun. 19, 1982), *U.S. writer.* The last of the great generation of early-twentieth-century modernists in English literature, Djuna Barnes created such literary masterworks as *Nightwood,* in 1936. Funnier but less famous was her *Ladies Almanack,* which spoofed the Parisian lesbian circle that included Natalie Barney, Radclyffe Hall, and Dolly Wilde. Barnes also specialized in colorful interviews; her subjects included Alfred Stieglitz, Coco Chanel, and James Joyce.

Barnes had moved to Paris from Greenwich Village in 1919. After stays in Berlin and London, she returned to New York at the outbreak of World War II. A period of extreme poverty followed, during which she became so reclusive that e.e. cummings, who lived across from her in Greenwich Village, would occasionally call over to her, "Are you still alive, Djuna?"

Barnes had relationships with both women and men, but hesitated to call herself a lesbian. She once confided to a close friend, "I'm not a lesbian. I just loved Thelma."

BARNEY, NATALIE CLIFFORD. (Oct. 31, 1876–1972), *Parisian hostess.* "My only books/Were women's looks," Natalie Barney wrote of her schoolgirl days. "At twelve I knew exactly what I liked and I firmly decided not to let myself be diverted from my tastes." As a young adult, she fled her upper-class existence in Washington, D.C., to take up residence in Paris, where she became known as *l'Amazone,* and where her affairs with various famous women, including poet Renée Vivien and the spectacularly beautiful courtesan Liane de Pougy, aroused public curiosity and attention. Her weekly literary salons — held every Friday for more than sixty years — were also renowned as a meeting place for the cultural elite, and regularly attracted such notables as Anatole France, Ezra Pound, Gertrude Stein, and André Gide. Barney wrote numerous epigrams, memoirs, and poetry, but her fame rests primarily on her reputa-

tion as the most prominent and candid lesbian of her day. She served as the inspiration for several fictional characters, including one in *The Well of Loneliness. (See also Romaine Brooks, Renée Vivien.)*

BARNFIELD, RICHARD. (Jun. 13, 1574–Mar. 6, 1627), *British poet.* Mystery still shrouds the life of Shakespeare's friend Richard Barnfield, whose sonnets bear many similarities to those of the Bard. Barnfield's most famous verse appears in his first work, *The Affectionate Shepherd,* published anonymously when he was twenty:

> If it be sin to love a lovely lad,
> Oh, then sin I.

A year later, Barnfield published further sonnets with a homosexual theme, celebrating his love for a young man whose initials were J.U. — possibly the young actor John Underwood.

BARRIE, Sir JAMES M. (May 9, 1860–June 19, 1937), *British playwright and novelist.* The creator of Peter Pan, Barrie spent much of his life disillusioned with adulthood. This regret for his lost childhood shows up in his plays *The Admirable Crichton, The Will, Dear Brutus,* and, of course, *Peter Pan.*

In 1894, Barrie married actress Mary Ansell. But his real attraction was to boys, especially to the five boys of the Davies family, who provided models for *Peter Pan.* He revealed much of himself in these lines that he once wrote: "He was a boy only ... And boys cannot love. Oh, is it not cruel to ask a boy to love? ... He was a boy who could not grow up." No children resulted from his marriage, and it was probably unconsummated; he and his wife divorced in 1910.

Barrie once overheard a friend say to her young son, "You'll be sick tomorrow if you eat any more of those chocolates." The boy replied, "I'll be sick tonight." Barrie was so taken by the line that he paid the boy for it and included it in *Peter Pan*.

BEACH, SYLVIA. (Mar. 14, 1887–Oct. 5, 1962), *U.S. expatriate literary figure*. Beach moved to Paris permanently from the United States in 1919 and opened her renowned bookstore, Shakespeare and Company, that same year on the Left Bank. The store, which featured English and American literature, be-

came an important meeting place for such expatriate writers as Ernest Hemingway and James Joyce, and for French writers pursuing a newfound passion for American books. In 1922, Beach ventured briefly into publishing: She issued the first edition of James Joyce's *Ulysses* after other publishers rejected it for its sexual content.

For over thirty years, from the start of her permanent residency in Paris, Beach was in a relationship with French writer Adrienne Monnier, who also owned a bookstore, just across the street from Beach's, on the rue de l'Odeon.

BECKFORD, WILLIAM. (Oct. 1, 1760–May 2, 1844), *British writer*. Anyone can be an eccentric, but William Beckford had a special ad-

vantage. At the age of ten, he inherited from his father the largest fortune in England. At nineteen, Beckford fell in love with the eleven-year-old William Courtenay. To be near the boy, Beckford took Courtenay's aunt as his mistress. Despite its outward awkwardness, this arrangement lasted five years, until a visitor caught them in bed together; the newspaper reported the next day on "the rumor concerning a *Grammatical mistake* of Mr. B— and the Hon. Mr. C—, in regard to the genders." It was among England's earliest reported gay scandals.

Beckford moved to Switzerland and began writing. His best-known novel, *Vathek*, combined fantasy, satire, gothic horror, and a good dose of homoeroticism. With its publication in 1786, Beckford's notoriety soared.

After ten years abroad, Beckford returned to England and embarked on a new undertaking: he constructed a Gothic cathedral, with the tallest tower in London, on Fonthill Abbey estate. But at last, his ambition outstripped his means. The architect, faced with a tight schedule and inadequate funds, cut corners wherever possible. The resulting tower was impressive — until it collapsed of its own weight.

Beckford capped his peculiar career by serving in the House of

Commons, but it did little to restore his credibility. When he finally died, he was known as "The Fool of Fonthill."

BEECHER, HENRY WARD. (June 24, 1813–March 8, 1887), *U.S. lecturer and pastor.* Though not as famous as his sister, Harriet Beecher Stowe, Beecher became known in the nineteenth century for his eloquent and unconventional sermons. His favorite sermons, in the 1840s, dealt with the earthly vices, and his realistic descriptions of such sins often brought crowds of three thousand people to his Brooklyn church. When the Civil War broke out, Beecher put his oratorical skills to work in the cause of emancipation,

and after the war he sought to reconcile Christianity and the theory of evolution, thus inviting attack from fellow theologians.

Beecher was married, but he described the marriage as "hell on earth." His happiest relationship, he revealed to a biographer in his old age, took place as a student in Amherst. He had fallen in love with Constantine Fondolaik, a Greek student, and the two drew up a contract promising eternal devotion to one another. Constantine returned to Greece in 1842, where he died shortly thereafter. Beecher named one of his sons after the friend who had brought him the greatest happiness.

BEETHOVEN, LUDWIG. (baptized Dec. 17, 1770–Mar. 26, 1827), *German composer.* Beethoven's musi-

cal training began at the age of five, when his talent became apparent. He was encouraged by his father, an unstable alcoholic who saw the profit potential in the child prodigy.

Despite the pressures of his family life, the talents of the young musician flourished. At seventeen, he awed Mozart with his skills, and a few years later he studied under Haydn. Despite a hearing loss that began in his late twenties, Beethoven produced nine symphonies, two ballets, and dozens of other works.

Throughout his life, Beethoven developed a reputation for boorish behavior, which was only worsened by his embarrassment about his deafness. There is no evidence that he was ever in a relationship with a woman. There is unproven speculation that Beethoven's sexual energy focused on a young nephew named Karl, who did not return the affection and may have tried to blackmail Beethoven over the issue of his homosexuality.

BENEDICT IX. (1020–1056?), *pope.* One of several strong contenders for the title of history's worst pope, Benedict IX was appointed to the papal office in 1032, at the age of twelve, because the council responsible for making such appointments wished to keep the papacy under their control. Benedict is best remembered for the devotion he showed to homosexual orgies while serving as pope, and for his efforts to cash in on his position by selling the rights to the various titles he controlled. Finally, he ran out of lower offices and in 1045 sold the papacy itself to his godfather, Johannes Gratianus. He subsequently reclaimed the office for two brief periods, but was eventually deposed and run out of Rome. Benedict died in obscurity some years later.

BENEDICT, RUTH. (Jun. 5, 1887–Sep. 17, 1948), *U.S. anthropologist.* Benedict is best remembered for her influential study of Native American tribes, *Patterns of Culture*. In this popular book, she strove to demonstrate how greatly human behavior can vary in different cultures. Among the variances that she discusses nonjudgmentally is homosexuality.

Benedict was also a modernist poet and an early proponent of women's rights, calling for society to do away with the "dead rubbish of conventionalism" surrounding women. She was a mentor, and eventually lover, of fellow anthropologist Margaret Mead.

BENTLEY, GLADYS. (Aug. 12, 1907–Jan. 18, 1960), *U.S. entertainer.* Teased mercilessly by her family and classmates in Pennsylvania, Gladys Bentley ran away from home at the age of sixteen and headed for Harlem. There, as part of the Harlem Renaissance, she became a successful singer — but unlike so many others, Bentley used her success as an opportunity to come out, rather than as an excuse to stay closeted. Weighing in at four hundred pounds, she became known for dressing in tailor-made drag. She wore a white tuxedo when she married her girlfriend in a civil ceremony in Atlantic City.

BERNSTEIN, LEONARD. (Oct. 25, 1918–Oct. 14, 1990), *U.S. composer.* Bernstein, a Harvard graduate, began conducting the New York City Symphony in 1945, and went on to become the first American-born conductor of the New York Philharmonic in 1958. He composed constantly, writing for the stage (*West Side Story, Candide*), the movies (*On The Waterfront*), and his own symphony orchestra (the *Dybbuk*). Although Bernstein never explicitly came out during his lifetime, he actively supported gay causes, and his homosexuality was discussed by friends and associates after his death.

BEZA, THEODORE. (June 24, 1519–Oct. 13, 1605), *French theologian.* Theodore Beza was a close friend of theologian John Calvin and an outspoken supporter of Calvinism. He was also, at least in his youth, unmistakably homosexual. In his collection of Latin verse, *Juvenilia,* are love poems addressed to a young man named Audebert. In Beza's later life as a Calvinist, these poems provided considerable ammunition for rival Catholic polemicists, one of whom accused him of having been "tortured by a burning lust for his young Audebert." Another, the Catholic theologian De Sanctis, wrote that "Instead of your Audebert, now you have embraced Calvin, and so have substituted a spiritual male-whore for a carnal one; thus being still what you were — a sodomist."

BONHEUR, ROSA. (Mar. 16, 1822–May 25, 1899), *French artist.* By her early twenties, Rosa Bonheur had established herself, both in Europe and abroad, as a brilliant painter of animals. The most famous of her works, *The Horse Fair,* was purchased by Cornelius Vanderbilt in 1887 for a then-record sum of $55,000; it now hangs in New York's Metropolitan Museum of Art.

A forceful, strongly unconventional woman, Bonheur lived with her female companion, Nathalie Micas, for over forty years. Bonheur tried to discourage speculation that this was a lesbian relationship, but both contemporaries  (including early gay pioneer Magnus Hirschfeld) and modern historians believe otherwise. Bonheur was also involved with the American painter Anna Klumpke, whom she made her sole heir.

In 1857, the secretary general of France issued a permit allowing Bonheur to wear men's clothing — at a time when it was considered indecent for women to do so — ostensibly so that she could more conveniently wander through farms and slaughterhouses to research and sketch animal anatomy. Chided by a male acquaintance one evening for frequenting such places unchaperoned, Bonheur retorted, "Oh my dear sir, if you knew how little I care for your sex, you wouldn't get any ideas in your head. The fact is, in the way of males, I like only the bulls I paint."

BORDEN, LIZZIE. (July 19, 1860– Jun. 1, 1927), *U.S. celebrity.* On August 4, 1892, someone brutally murdered wealthy Abby and Andrew Borden of Fall River, Massachusetts. Andrew's daughter Lizzie was convicted of the crime in doggerel, but acquitted in court; she lived out a comfortable life on her inheritance.

Borden's guilt or innocence has been the subject of speculation (including at least fifteen books) since 1892. So has the question of her sexuality. As a 32-year-old single woman at the time of the murders, she was rumored even then to be a lesbian. According to one scenario, Lizzie's stepmother caught her in bed with the maid and was bludgeoned to death; her husband guessed the truth and met the same fate.

BOWLES, JANE. (Feb. 22, 1917– May 4, 1973), *U.S. writer.* From early childhood, Jane Bowles (née Jane Auer) was considered to be different, even odd. When she was twelve, she wrote in a friend's autograph book:

> You asked me to write in
>   youre book
> I scarcely know how to begin
> For there's nothing orriginal
>   about me
> But a little orriginal Sin.

As a young, unmarried woman, Bowles lived what at the time was considered an unconventional and highly adventurous lifestyle for a woman. She associated with bohemians and intellectuals and frequented Greenwich Village bars. She met writer–composer Paul Bowles in 1937 and went to Mexico with him; they were soon married. However, lesbianism seems to have always been a significant part of her life.

Though the quantity of her literary production was limited, Jane Bowles has been called "one of the finest writers of modern fiction in any language." She wrote one novel, *Two Serious Ladies;* one play, *In the Summer House;* and six short stories, all of which she completed by her early thirties.

BOYD, MALCOLM. (June 8, 1923 –), *U.S. theologian.* Boyd gave up a prominent career as a radio–television producer in 1951 to enter the seminary. He was ordained as an Episcopal priest in 1955 and became nationally renowned in the 1960s with his best-selling book *Are You Running With Me, Jesus?,* a collection of deeply personal prayers written in a modern idiom. He was also well known for his civil rights and anti-Vietnam activism.

In 1976, he publicly acknowledged that he was homosexual. He has since become outspoken as an advocate of gay rights.

BRADLEY, DAN. *U.S. politician.* In 1975, Dan Bradley helped found the Legal Services Corporation, a program that provides legal aid for the poor. He worked on the Carter presidential campaign, in the Carter administration, and then returned to Legal Services to help it survive the cutbacks of the Reagan era. After helplessly witnessing the bigotry of Anita Bryant's campaign to repeal a gay civil rights ordinance, and silently watching Congress debate the McDonald Amendment, which would have barred gay people from the use of Legal Services aid, Bradley publicly came out in 1982 and devoted himself to lobbying for gay rights issues. He was, at the time,

the highest-ranking official to have done so.

BRITTEN, Sir BENJAMIN. (Nov. 22, 1913–Dec. 4, 1976), *British composer.* Recognized as perhaps the greatest English composer since Purcell, Benjamin Britten's reputation rests primarily on his most famous operas *(The Turn of the Screw, Peter Grimes, Death in Venice),* his massive *War Requiem,* and numerous orchestral works, including the popular, often-performed *Young Person's Guide to the Orchestra.* He and British tenor Peter Pears were lovers for over forty years; in fact, it was for Pears's voice that Britten composed most of his solo vocal works and all of his major tenor roles. His relationship with Pears is chronicled in *Letters From a Life,* which reprints much of their correspondence. The two are buried side by side in Aldeburgh, England, the site of a music school and of an annual music festival they founded in 1947. *(See also Peter Pears.)*

BROOKS, ROMAINE. (1874–1970), *U.S. painter.* Brooks lived most of her life in Europe, where she gained recognition for her bold, stylized celebrity portraits. She probably had  her first romance as a teenager: in Paris to study voice, she became attracted to fellow student and future opera star Clara Butt, although it's unlikely that the attraction ever took physical form.

Early in life, for reasons that remain unclear, Romaine married gay poet John Brooks. Neither seems to have felt strongly about the affair: Romaine's diary entry for the wedding day consisted of a single word: "married." Her husband continued his affairs with young men; she persisted in asserting her independence; and they separated in 1904.

In 1915, Brooks met and became lovers with Parisian writer and salon hostess Natalie Barney. The relationship lasted for more than fifty years. It ended abruptly when both women were well into their nineties: Brooks, in a fit of jealousy over Barney's interest in the 69-year-old wife of a retired Romanian diplomat, vowed never to speak to her again. Maintaining her silence to the end, Brooks died a year and a half later; Barney survived her by barely thirteen months. *(See also Natalie Barney.)*

BROWN, MARGARET WISE. (May 23, 1910–Nov. 13, 1952), *U.S. writer.* Best known for her children's classic, *Goodnight Moon,* Margaret Wise Brown wrote at a time when the genre was being hotly debated by progressive educators, who favored a down-to-earth approach in children's books, and traditional librarians, who preferred fantasy. The bulk of Brown's work fell in the middle of these two extremes, and found favor with children and adults alike.

Brown's longest relationship was with a woman named Michael Strange, with whom she shared a living space in Manhattan. Their relationship was widely recognized among their contemporaries, and was discussed in print by Strange's daughter. At the time of her death, Brown was happily engaged to be married to a Rockefeller.

BUCHANAN, JAMES. (Apr. 23, 1791–Jun 1, 1868), *U.S. president.* Because he was the country's only bachelor president, James Buchanan's sexual orientation has often been the subject of speculation. There is no conclusive evidence on the subject, but writer Carl Sferrazza Anthony fueled the debate with his discovery of two letters to Buchanan by Alabama's Senator William Rufus King, with whom Buchanan shared rooms in Washington, D.C., for two decades. One reads that "I am selfish enough to hope you will not be able to procure an associate who will cause you to feel no regret at our separation."

Buchanan won the presidency as a compromise Democratic candidate, and spent a single, uneventful term in office. When he turned the White House keys over to his successor, Abraham Lincoln, Buchanan said, "If you are as happy on entering this house as I am in leaving it, you are the happiest man on earth." *(See also William Rufus King.)*

BURGESS, GUY. (1911–Aug. 30, 1963), *British defector.* In 1951, Guy Burgess and fellow British Foreign Service officer Donald Maclean defected to the Soviet Union. Both were gay, and their defection gave  new strength to the old prejudice that homosexuals were security risks. Though he never unearthed a single similar case in the U.S., Senator Joseph McCarthy made good use of the Burgess–Maclean case when he stirred up a mix of homophobia and anti-communism.

BURKE, GLENN. *U.S. athlete.* In 1978 Al Campanis, vice president of the Los Angeles Dodgers, called outfielder Glenn Burke into his office. "Everybody on the team is married but you, Glenn," he said. "When players get married on the Dodgers, we help them out financially. We can help you so you go out and have a real nice honeymoon." It was the first time the team management had recognized — even in an indirect way — that Glenn Burke was gay.

Burke had started playing for the Dodgers two years earlier. At the time, his potential seemed unlimited. "Frankly, we think he's going to be another Willie Mays," the Dodgers coach said. Burke's first small mark on sports history came a year later in a completely unexpected realm: in a burst of enthusiasm after a teammate hit a home run, he originated the high-five.

But during that period, the increasing rumors and the strain of a double life took their toll, and in 1978 Burke was traded to the Oakland A's. When he left professional baseball two years later, his career had not reached the heights he and others had hoped it might — but he was soon the star of San Francisco's gay softball league.

BURROUGHS, WILLIAM S. (Feb. 5, 1914–), *U.S. novelist.* Called the "writer and oracle of the Beat Generation," William S. Burroughs rebelled against his upper-class background, depicting it in his novels as lifeless and oppressive. Throughout his early adulthood, he sought an alternative to that empty existence, and found it in morphine in 1944. Burroughs saw in drugs the possibility of breaking free of social conditioning and of expanding his consciousness, and he made addiction a way of life for the next fifteen years.

In the late 1950s Burroughs gave up his drug habit and devoted himself to writing. His works include *Naked Lunch,* which a Boston court declared to be obscene in 1965, *Queer,* and many others. In his revolt against bourgeois convention, Burroughs created a new novel form known as the pop-art novel, which includes elements of popular culture usually ignored by literary writers.

Although he was married twice, Burroughs has lived in New York since 1974 with James Grauerholz, who acts as his companion, secretary, and agent.

BURTON, Sir RICHARD. (Mar. 19, 1821–Oct. 20, 1890), *British explorer and scholar.* Burton was best known during his lifetime for his extensive explorations of Asia, Africa, and South America. He learned twenty-five languages and fifteen additional dialects, always seeking to examine other cultures on their own terms.

At the age of twenty-four, Burton undertook a study of the male brothels in the Moslem city of Karachi. Later research included an 1853 visit to Mecca — a perilous destination, since non-Moslems discovered there were likely to be executed. As part of his disguise, he had himself circumcised. A story later circulated in London that while on his trip, Burton once failed to crouch while urinating, thus giving himself away to an Arab youth, whom he murdered to protect his own life. Burton at one point suggested that the story was true, but later swore otherwise. He and John Speke were among the earliest British explorers of Africa.

Burton's fifty books include many reports of his journeys. He was also the first English translator of *The Arabian Nights* to faithfully include its homoerotic passages.

Burton married the strong-willed Isabel Arundell. But his continuing interest in homosexuality, and his open appreciation of male beauty, led to speculation that his knowledge of homosexuality was not always secondhand. Probably it wasn't, but after his death Isabel burned her husband's journals and diaries, thus destroying whatever evidence he might have left.

BYRON, Lord (GEORGE GORDON). (Jan. 22, 1788–Apr. 19, 1824), *British poet.* Byron was the leading poet of the Romantic period. His epic satire *Don Juan* is considered his masterpiece; but he is also known for his *Childe Harold* and *Manfred.*

Byron's life was filled with lovers of both sexes. As a seventeen-year-old student at Trinity College, he fell in love with John Eddleston, a choirboy of the same age. Byron wrote that "I certainly love him more than any human being." Some biographers have dismissed this as a platonic infatuation, but there is less uncertainty surrounding Byron's 1811 relationship with Nicolo Giraud, a youth of mixed French-Greek blood whom Byron described as "the most beautiful being

I have ever beheld." They were inseparable for a time, and Byron consulted a doctor about a relaxation of the sphincter muscle that was giving Giraud trouble.

Byron's many other liaisons included one with his half-sister Augusta; when this relationship was criticized as incestuous, he explained, "I could love anything on earth that appeared to wish it." He married in 1815 but separated a year later; relationships with a beautiful Italian noblewoman, then with another handsome Greek youth, followed. Parts of Byron's life will remain unknown; although he wrote his memoirs and entrusted them to his friend Thomas Moore, they were considered too scandalous for publication after his death and were burned.

CADMUS, PAUL. (Dec. 17, 1904–), *U.S. artist.* Born to parents who were both artists, Paul Cadmus became a full-time art student at the age of fourteen. Fame arrived unexpectedly: In 1934, his painting *The Fleet's In!* was to be displayed at Washington's Corcoran Gallery. A retired admiral saw it and raised a furor about what he called "a representation of a disgraceful, sordid, disreputable, drunken brawl with a number of enlisted men consorting with a party of street walkers." The painting was removed; other artists, publishers, and politicians protested its removal; and Cadmus's career took off.

Cadmus is best known for his male nudes, drawn in a style

uniquely his own, and he has long been open about his homosexuality, while not dwelling on it. "The word *gay* doesn't please me," he told an *Advocate* interviewer in 1976. "It sounds too frivolous. Think of calling Socrates *gay* or Michelangelo *gay*. It sounds as though that were the whole aim in life, as though it were a career in itself. That depresses me a bit." But, he added, "I haven't thought of a substitute."

CAESAR, JULIUS. (July 12 or 13, 100 B.C.–Mar. 15, 44 B.C.), *Roman statesman*. Gaius Julius Caesar was born to a great patrician family, but early in life he adopted the ideology of the democratic leader Marius. As a young man he became a military tribune, and played a key role in the defeat of the slave uprising organized by Spartacus in 73 B.C. Blessed with great personal charm, as well as military skill and a shrewd political mind, Caesar consolidated his power and in 49 B.C. was appointed dictator for life. But despite his many reforms, Caesar's display of imperial airs and his decision to dissolve the trade unions antagonized many former supporters. On March 15, 44 B.C., he was assassinated by dissatisfied Romans.

Caesar kept up a full and varied sex life. He had three wives, as well as his famous relationship with Cleopatra, and several male lovers, thus earning the epithet "Husband to every woman and wife to every man." The best-known male lover was Nicomedes, king of Bithynia. The two young men met during the course of the Second Methridatic War, and their liaison became something of a scandal. When Ni-

comedes died eight years later, at the age of thirty-six, he left his kingdom to the Romans.

CAMBACÉRÈS, JEAN JACQUES RÉGIS DE. (Oct. 18, 1753–Mar. 8, 1824), *French lawmaker*. Born into a family of jurists and trained for the law, Cambacérès put his legal skills to use against the state during the French Revolution in 1789. He survived the feuds and bloodletting that followed, and served as president of the infamous Committee of Public Safety in 1795.  When Napoleon took power in 1799, Cambacérès won his trust and became the primary architect of the new Napoleonic Code.

Cambacérès was apparently discreet, but not secretive, about his homosexuality. It was through his influence that the Napoleonic Code — and the many later laws throughout Europe that were based on it — legalized private consenting homosexual acts between adults.

CAPOTE, TRUMAN. (Sept. 30, 1924–Aug. 25, 1984), *U.S. personality*. As a young writer, Capote gained a following for his haunting *New Yorker* stories; he then achieved national prominence with his first novel, *Other Voices, Other Rooms* (1948), which made no secret of his homosexuality. In the decade that followed, the unconventional Capote fulfilled and perhaps enforced the stereotype of the androgynous, high-voiced, and gossipy homosexual. His later writing never lived up to the promise of his earlier work, and toward the end of his life he was better known for his connections with the rich and famous than for his own accomplishments.

CARPENTER, EDWARD. (Aug. 29, 1844–June 28, 1929), *English reformer.* At the age of thirty, Edward Carpenter left his conventional job as a Church of England curator and became active in the working-class movement of the time. He combined Fabian Socialism with his own radical views on sex.

Carpenter's first work on homosexuality, *Homogenic Love and Its Place in a Free Society,* appeared in 1894. Further books followed. In his most widely read book, *Love's Coming of Age* (1897), Carpenter proposed equality between the sexes, and included a gay-positive chapter titled "The Intermediate Sex." This chapter was expanded into a full book a decade later, under the same title, and it became (with Havelock Ellis's *Sexual Inversion*) one of the most widely read books on the subject in the English language.

Even that did not exhaust Carpenter. In *Iolaus: An Anthology of Friendship* (1902), he collected homoerotic poetry from both ancient and contemporary sources. His 1914 book *Intermediate Types among Primitive Folk* showed that in primitive societies — held up by anthropologists as reflecting pure human behavior — homosexual behavior was often considered normal, or was even exalted. He himself had a lifelong lover, George Merrill.

CARSWELL, G. HAROLD. (Dec. 12, 1919–), *U.S. jurist.* In 1970, Richard Nixon nominated Harold Carswell to the U.S. Supreme Court, but Carswell was rejected by the Senate because, among other things, he was regarded as an advocate of racial segregation. In 1976, Carswell was arrested for soliciting a plainclothes police officer outside a shopping mall men's room in Tallahassee, Florida; he was convicted and fined $100. After his arrest, Carswell checked himself into a local psychiatric hospital.

CASEMENT, Sir ROGER. (Sept. 1, 1864–Aug. 3, 1916), *Irish patriot.* Born in Ireland, Roger Casement grew up in a family that ardently supported the cause of Irish independence. At age twenty, working as a ship's purser, he traveled to the Belgian Congo, where he was horrified at the treatment the native Africans received from European colonists. For the next twenty-six years, Casement fought against these inhuman conditions, and in 1911, he was knighted for his work.

Casement then turned his energies to the Irish nationalist cause. When war broke out between Britain and Germany, Casement urged his Irish compatriots to support the Germans, on the grounds that England was their common enemy. He arranged for Germany to ship arms to Ireland for use against the British. Word of this reached England, and Casement was arrested for treason. He argued that he was Irish, not British, and that his acts were therefore not treasonable, but his reasoning fell on deaf ears and he was sentenced to death.

Many prominent world leaders sympathized with Casement and urged the Crown to commute his sentence. That probably would have happened except for one twist of fate: the discovery of Casement's personal diaries, in which he graphically detailed numerous homosexual liaisons over the preceding dozen years. Copies of the diaries were distributed by the British government, and sympathy for Casement evaporated. He was hanged on August 3, 1916.

CATHER, WILLA. (Dec. 7, 1873–Apr. 24, 1947), *U.S. novelist.* A free spirit from a young age, as a teenager Willa Cather got a crew cut, dressed like a boy, and called herself William. At college in Lincoln, Nebraska, she discovered her love of writing, and upon graduating she moved to Pittsburgh, which she thought would  provide a more stimulating environment. There she developed a close relationship with Isabelle McClung. In 1905 Cather moved to New York, leaving Isabelle behind, and met Edith Lewis, who became Cather's lifetime companion. Cather's best-known novels include *O Pioneers!* and *My Antonia.* She won a 1923 Pulitzer Prize for *One of Ours.*

Before her death, Cather took pains to see that details of her lesbianism were destroyed, but it was an impossible job. Today there seems no real doubt on the subject.

CAVAFY, CONSTANTINE. (Apr. 17, 1863–Apr. 29, 1933), *Greek poet.* By developing his own individualistic style of poetry, Cavafy became one of the West's most important  poets. Most of his best work, however, was written after he turned forty — and published only after his death.

Though he was Greek, Cavafy never actually lived in Greece. He was born, and died, in the Egyptian city of Alexandria. As a young man there, he often visited male houses of prostitution. He bribed his servants to ruffle up his sheets at night so his mother would not realize he had not been home.

CHAMBERS, JANE. (Mar. 27, 1937–Feb. 15, 1983), *U.S. playwright.* Jane Chambers began her professional theatrical career in 1955 as an off-Broadway actress. She at first had to supplement her income by writing soap opera scripts, but by the early sixties she had become a successful free-lance writer and broadcast journalist. She was an ardent supporter of equal rights for minorities; her many organizational affiliations included the East End Gay Organization for Human Rights.

Chambers is known for her off-Broadway stage plays, particularly those set in the lesbian subculture. One of those plays, *Last Summer at Bluefish Cove,* won her a Drama-Logue Critics Circle Award. She once commented, "I write from my experience and interests. I do not consciously create my characters — I just look up one day and notice that they are standing in front of my typewriter."

CHEEVER, JOHN. (May 27, 1912–June 18, 1982), *U.S. writer.* Called "the most graceful American fiction writer after F. Scott Fitzgerald," John Cheever was noted for his masterful short stories, which portrayed middle-class, suburban America in an ironic and often comedic light, and for his five novels, including *Bullet Park* and *Falconer,* the latter of which incorporated homosexuality as a central theme. In 1979, a collection of Cheever's short stories won the Pulitzer Prize.

Two years after Cheever's death, his daughter published a memoir in which she disclosed that her father had struggled all his life with homosexual desires. She also revealed — based on material in his private, unpublished journals — that he finally allowed himself to have a love affair with another man.

CHRISTINA. (Dec. 8, 1626–Apr. 19, 1689), *Swedish queen.* When Christina was born, the midwives thought she was a boy. Contemporaries often referred to her as having a masculine appearance, and there is speculation that she was a pseudo-hermaphrodite, with superficial male organs. She became queen at the age of six, upon the death of her father. As a young woman, she was rumored to have love affairs with suitors of both sexes, but it was her open relationship with Ebba Sparre, her lady-in-waiting, that caused the most concern among the court. Christina gave little attention to pleas that she be less open, however, and publicly referred to Sparre as her "bedfellow."

Christina encouraged the growth of science and industry in Sweden, but her aloofness from the people, a desire to travel, and the jealousy of her advisers contributed to her frustration with her position as monarch. In 1654 she abdicated and traveled throughout Europe, often dressed as a man. Ultimately, she converted to Catholicism and lived off papal charity in Rome until her death.

CHURCHILL, Sir WINSTON. (Nov. 30, 1874–Jan. 24, 1965), *British statesman and author.* Following a successful career as a writer and a mixed career in politics, Churchill became Britain's prime minister in 1940, and led the country through World War II. There is no reason to believe Churchill was  homosexual, but his lifelong friend Somerset Maugham once recalled a conversation they had:

"Winston, your mother often indicated that you had affairs in your youth with men."

"Not true," Churchill replied. "But I once went to bed with a man to see what it was like."

"Who was it?"

"Ivor Novello." [Novello was a popular writer of musical comedies in the 1920s.]

"And what was it like?"

"Musical."

CLAIBORNE, CRAIG. (Sep. 4, 1920–), *U.S. chef.* Craig Claiborne's name has long been associated with fine food. Born into a poor Mississippi family, he received a solid grounding in classical cuisine at a Swiss hotel school. After a stint at *Gourmet* magazine, Claiborne became food editor at the *New York Times.* In his combination cookbook and memoir *A Feast Made for Laughter,* he writes openly about his homosexuality.

CLIFT, MONTGOMERY. (Oct. 17, 1920–July 24, 1966), *U.S. actor.* Clift began his professional acting career when he was fourteen and he made his screen debut in 1948 in Fred Zinnemann's *The Search,* for which he received the first of his four Oscar nominations. Shortly thereafter, he was arrested in New York City for soliciting sex from a young hustler; his lawyers kept the incident out of the newspapers.

After a disfiguring automobile accident in 1957, Clift relied heavily on drugs and alcohol; that, along with escalating emotional problems, sent his career into decline. John Huston, who directed Clift in *The Misfits* in 1961, later speculated that, "The combination of drugs, drink and being homosexual was a soup that was just too much for him." Clift appeared in only two more major films, and died of a heart attack at the age of forty-five.

COCTEAU, JEAN. (July 5, 1889– Oct. 11, 1963), *French artist.* Cocteau grew up in Paris and spent most of his life there. In his speech, education, ideas, and habits, he was in many ways the quintessential Parisian.

One major influence on Cocteau's work was his lover, Raymond Radiguet, whom he met in 1918. Radiguet was then a sixteen-year-old literary prodigy whose writing stressed a simplicity that came to characterize Cocteau's later work. Radiguet's death in 1923 left Cocteau devastated.

Cocteau's talents extended to a wide variety of areas, including literature, the visual arts, and the cinema. He has been called "the most versatile artist of the twentieth century," and the range and quality of his work attest to the truth of this claim. His works include the play *Orphee,* the novels *Les Enfants terribles* and *La Machine infernale,* and the film *La Belle et la bete.*

COHN, ROY. (Feb. 20, 1927–Aug. 2, 1986), *U.S. attorney.* Well before his thirtieth birthday, Roy Cohn had established his reputation as the flamboyant sidekick of Senator Joseph McCarthy in the 1950s. As the arrogant but incisive inquisitor of McCarthy's Communist-hunting committee, Cohn destroyed hundreds of careers and reputations through skilled use of innuendo or guilt by association.

In 1954, Cohn inadvertently triggered McCarthy's downfall when a friend was drafted into the army. Cohn tried to get special privileges for his friend; when that failed, he allegedly threatened to wreck the army with an investigation. In the ensuing, televised Army-McCarthy hearings, McCarthy came across as a fulminating demagogue and never recovered his credibility.

Cohn, however, survived the hearings and became a lawyer. Rich clients flocked to him, despite his notoriety. "I'd rather have him inside pissing out than outside pissing in," explained one. But even being Cohn's friend wasn't always a successful strategy. Six weeks before his death, Cohn was disbarred in New York after being found guilty of dishonesty, fraud, deceit, and misrepresentation. Among the many accusations upheld by the court was the charge that in 1976, Cohn had gone into the hospital room of a dying friend and tricked him into signing over control of a multimillion-dollar estate.

Only at the end did Cohn's dishonesty catch up with him. His homosexuality, a closely guarded secret in the fifties, was widely known when he finally succumbed to AIDS.

COLE, JACK. (Apr. 27, 1911–Feb. 17, 1974), *U.S. choreographer*. Jack Cole is the legendary choreographer of such stage hits as *A Funny Thing Happened on the Way to the Forum, Man of La Mancha,* and *Kismet*. He worked with Rita Hayworth, Marilyn Monroe, Jane Russell, Betty Grable, and Mitzi Gaynor. His innovative approach to dance blended the styles of Harlem jazz with East Indian and South American dances, and paved the way for future choreographers like Jerome Robbins and Bob Fosse. His style and talent were apparently matched by his temper; he was rumored once to have punched a female dancer when she proudly announced that she had been cast in a Broadway show. Cole lived with his partner, John David Gray, for over thirty years; those who knew the couple had a great respect for their loyalty and commitment.

COLETTE. (Jan. 28, 1873–Aug. 3, 1954), *French novelist*. An outstanding French writer of the twentieth century, Sidonie Colette Goudeket wrote novels and short stories largely concerned with the pleasures, pains, and ironies of love. Her work is often remembered for its evocative sensuality — it was said she could describe a vegetable as if it were a love object — and for its unbridled love of life.

Although she married three times, Colette enjoyed numerous lesbian affairs, and left her first husband for another woman. In her life, and in her work, she refused to make what she saw as an artificial distinction between "normal" and "abnormal" sexuality.

CONRADIN. (Mar. 25, 1252–Oct. 29, 1268), *Titular king of Jerusalem and Sicily*. Conradin, the son of Hohenstaufen ruler Conrad IV, was born in Bavaria and spent most of his short life there. His father died when he was only two, and while Conradin was still a child, his guardians assumed for him the titles of king of Jerusalem and king of Sicily. At the age of fourteen, he was approached by several Italian cities to help free Italy from its French invaders. Conradin agreed; his army crossed the Alps and joined with Italian patriots to march against the French. Despite several early victories, Conradin was ultimately defeated by the French army and forced to retreat.

The young king was captured. The French tried him for treason, and at the age of sixteen, he was beheaded. His lover, Frederick of Baden, titular duke of Austria, voluntarily accompanied Conradin to the block. Their remains rest in the monastery of Santa Maria del Carmine at Naples.

COPLAND, AARON. (Nov. 14, 1900–Dec. 2, 1990), *U.S. composer*. Some critics have called Aaron Copland America's greatest composer. His works include the Pulitzer

Prize–winning *Appalachian Spring,
Rodeo,* and *Fanfare for the Common
Man,* which was played at Ronald
Reagan's presidential inauguration.
Copland's lifelong homosexuality
was well known among his friends
during his lifetime, though he didn't
discuss it in his memoirs. After his
death, several friends (including
Paul Moor, in an obituary he wrote
for *The Advocate*) commented on it
publicly.

COWARD, Sir NOEL. (Dec. 16,
1899–Mar. 26, 1973), *British playwright.* Noel Coward is best known
for his light and intricate comedies
of manners. Although primarily a
playwright, he also acted, produced, directed, danced, and sang.
His work was greatly appreciated
both in the United States and Britain,
and Queen Elizabeth knighted him
in 1970.

Coward came out publicly in
1966, although his homosexuality
was already known in theater circles. He once met writer Edna Fer-
ber when she was wearing a suit
similar to his. "You look almost like
a man," he told her lightheartedly.
"So do you," she replied.

CRANE, HART. (July 21, 1899–Apr.
27, 1932), *U.S. poet.* A leading figure
in the 1920s literary renaissance,
Hart Crane was an experimental
poet and an outspoken admirer of
Walt Whitman. He is best known for
his collection of poems titled *The
Bridge,* in which the Brooklyn
Bridge becomes a symbol of his
belief in America's spiritual destiny.
Homoeroticism permeates several
of Crane's works, and he was especially partial to portrayals of virile
sailors.

Crane was lonely most of his
life. A sailor he met in 1929 provided one of his life's few romantic
interludes, though probably not a
sexual one. In 1932, while aboard
ship, Crane called, "Good-bye,
everybody," jumped overboard,
and drowned.

CUKOR, GEORGE. (July 7, 1899–
Jan. 24, 1983), *U.S. film director.*
Cukor's Hollywood career spanned
more than fifty years and included
such classics as *The Women, The
Philadelphia Story,* the 1954 version
of *A Star Is Born,* and *My Fair Lady,*
which won him the 1964 Oscar for
Best Director. He was often labeled
a "woman's director," because of his
ability to draw bravura performances from such great actresses as
Greta Garbo, Judy Garland, and
Katherine Hepburn. In an interview
shortly before his death, he said of
his homosexuality, "I didn't put on
any big act. You know, a lot of
people are so funny. They go out
with girls and all that, and that's
absolutely ridiculous. I didn't pretend."

CULLEN, COUNTEE (PORTER).
(May 30, 1903–Jan. 9, 1946), *U.S.
poet.* With the 1927 publication of
The Ballad of the Brown Girl and
Copper Sun, Cullen was briefly considered Harlem's poet laureate. In a
spectacular 1928 ceremony, he married the daughter of W.E.B. DuBois.
Two months later, Cullen sailed off
to Europe with Harold Jackman —
his best man at the wedding. Their
close friendship had already been
known to friends, who referred to
the two men as David and Jonathan,
and Cullen's marriage to DuBois
dissolved.

His popularity as a poet was likewise short-lived. He tried to write in the romantic tradition of John Keats, a style not always  suited to the subjects (such as lynching) about which he wrote. Cullen himself expressed the problem in his 1925 sonnet, "Yet Do I Marvel," writing that God had done a "curious thing: To make a poet black, and bid him sing."

In 1940, Cullen was again married, with apparently more success. But his earlier relationship was not forgotten. When Harold Jackman died in 1960, a collection of papers on African-Americans that he donated to Atlanta University was named the Countee Cullen–Harold Jackman Memorial Collection.

CUSHMAN, CHARLOTTE. (July 23, 1816–Feb. 18 1876), *U.S. actress.* Cushman began her stage career as an opera singer, then switched to drama. She played a superb Lady Macbeth, but also took on male roles (including Romeo and Hamlet), and was called the greatest actress of her day. Her diaries detail many affairs with women; the main one was a nineteen-year relationship with Emma Stebbins.

DAVID. (1035?–960? B.C.), *Israeli king.* Born into a rural peasant family, David earned his place in history when he killed the Philistine warrior Goliath with his slingshot. This helped establish his position in the court of King Saul, where he became a military leader and also a close friend of Saul's son Jonathan.

Jonathan and Saul died in the battle of Gilboa (1013 B.C.), and David was grief stricken. "My brother Jonathan," he wrote, "thy love to me was wonderful, surpassing the love of women."

After Saul's death, David became the king of Israel, beginning a lineage that lasted four centuries. The exact nature of his friendship with Jonathan is subject to speculation, but its intensity is not; it is recounted in the book of I Samuel of the Bible.

DAY, F. HOLLAND. (July 23, 1864–1933), *U.S. photographer.* Day was a daring and homoerotic photographer whose depictions of idyllic Greek tableaux, the Crucifixion (with himself as Christ), and the death of St. Sebastian stirred up quite a controversy in his chosen home of Boston. He was immersed in the art world, founding a literary-occult society, The Visionists, and publishing a weekly art journal, *The Mahogany Tree.*

Day's homosexuality was expressed in many of his photographic series, especially in the eroticizing of St. Sebastian, and the pastoral youths that populated his Greek tableaux. He also knew, and published, a great number of other artists whose homosexuality was reflected in their works, including Oscar Wilde, Willa Cather, Walter Pater, and Aubrey Beardsley. In his correspondence with Wilde and Beardsley, Day confirmed his sexual orientation.

DEAN, JAMES. (Feb. 8, 1931–Sept. 30, 1955), *U.S. actor.* In his first two films, *Rebel without a Cause* and *East of Eden,* James Dean became the idol of the post-war generation with his portrayals of a sensitive and tormented teenager searching desperately for love. This screen portrayal was not much different from the real-life James Dean, who identified himself as bisexual but whose main emotional and physical bonds were with men. Dean's third film — *Giant,* with Rock Hudson and Elizabeth Taylor — was his last. Before its release, he died in a high-speed car crash.

DELANY, SAMUEL. (Apr. 1, 1942 –), *U.S. writer.* One of America's most popular and critically acclaimed writers of science fiction, Samuel Delany is also one of relatively few black writers in the genre. His highly original writing style developed as the result of his struggle to overcome dyslexia.

Delany was born in Harlem into a successful professional family. He married poet Marilyn Hacker — who was aware of his gayness — in 1961; they separated after thirteen years and shared custody of their one daughter. His impetus for writing science fiction came in 1962, when Hacker came home from her job at Ace books and expressed frustration that the women characters in the books she edited were "crazed bitches or dottering simps with nothing in between." Delany wrote his first science fiction novel, *The Jewels of Aptor,* in response to that complaint. He stayed with the genre, and his novels ever since have been noteworthy for the three-dimensionality and variety of their characters. Delany's early life is documented in his candid memoirs, *The Motion of Light in Water.*

DEMOSTHENES. (384 B.C.–Oct. 12, 322 B.C.), *Athenian orator.* The leading orator of the ancient world began his career with a speech against his guardian, who had attempted to steal his inheritance. Success in that case encouraged Demosthenes to pursue public speaking, and he is best remembered for  his orations against Philip of Macedonia, which gave birth to the word *philippic.*

According to legend, Demosthenes was bothered by a stammer in his youth. To cure it, he practiced speaking on the beach with pebbles in his mouth, and to gain lung power, he rehearsed poetry while running uphill. Although married, Demosthenes was reported to have had several male lovers.

DEMUTH, CHARLES. (Nov. 8, 1883–Oct. 23, 1935), *U.S. painter.* The work of Charles Demuth was long unknown except to specialists. One of the many artists who emigrated to Europe in the pre–World War I era, he did much to introduce modernist styles and a greater sexual openness in art. But his choice of subjects — flowers, gay baths, bars, and sailors — prevented his paintings from being received with much enthusiasm in a puritanical United States.

Demuth was intensely private about his personal life; scholars have found few letters or other writings to shed light on his innermost feelings. Many works that he did not exhibit during his lifetime have explicitly gay sexual imagery, and he was clearly familiar with gay bars and baths. Demuth exhibited at the gallery of the influential Manhattan dealer Alfred Stieglitz, but because of his homosexuality he was never truly accepted by Stieglitz's circle.

DIAGHILEV, SERGEI. (Mar. 31, 1872–Aug. 19, 1929), *Russian impresario.* Diaghilev began his career organizing art exhibitions in Russia, then switched his interests to ballet. His imperious and domineering personality earned him the title "Tsar of the Arts."

In 1909, he arranged a Parisian tour of Russian ballet. This brought him in touch with Vaslav Nijinsky, who even as a teenager was already Russia's most promising ballet dancer. Nijinsky was captivated by Diaghilev's strong personality, referring to him as "a genius, a great discoverer of talents, and the only man I could compare to Leonardo da Vinci." The two became lovers.

In 1911, Diaghilev was named director of the new Parisian company, the *Ballets Russes,* which flourished thanks to his ability to discover and bring together talented choreographers and musicians. For two years, Diaghilev's genius as an impresario combined with Nijinsky's dazzling talent to create performances that became the talk of Europe.

Diaghilev, however, was a difficult employer and a possessive lover. Nijinsky eventually began to chafe, and a rift developed between the two men. Diaghilev continued as director of the *Ballets Russes* until his death three decades later. During his lifetime, he collaborated with such geniuses as Picasso, Stravinsky, and Cocteau.

DICKINSON, EMILY. (Dec. 10, 1830–May 15, 1886), *U.S. poet.* Much of Emily Dickinson's private life remains a mystery. Her sister, Lavinia, burned most of the correspondence she had received from Dickinson, as did other friends and family members. But in 1951, critic Rebecca Patterson dug through what was still available and published her findings in a book, *The Riddle of Emily Dickinson.*

In 1852, Dickinson had written passionate love letters to her friend  Susan Gilbert: "Susie, forgive me darling, for every word I say — my heart is full of you, none other than you in my thoughts." A later love affair, with Kate Scott, commenced in 1859 and was even more serious; Dickinson wrote that "I had been hungry all the years."

Dickinson had strong emotional ties with men, as well. Whether it is accurate to consider her a lesbian, given what is known of her life, depends mainly on definitions. Her biographer was convinced that she was. Shortly before her death, Patterson said that "The most unconventional thing I have done is to blunder onto the tragedy of Dickinson's life and to insist hard-headedly over the years that that is the explanation and the only basis on which her poetry makes sense."

DIDRIKSON ZAHARIAS, BABE. (June 26, 1914–Sep. 27, 1956), *U.S. athlete.* Didrikson started her athletic career on an insurance company's basketball and baseball teams; by 1932, she had set world records in the javelin throw and the 80-meter hurdles in the Olympic Games. In 1938, she married professional wrestler George Zaharias, and she turned her athletic efforts toward golf, where she won every women's title. She was voted Outstanding Female Athlete of the first half of the twentieth century by the Associated Press in 1950. Just three years later, Didrikson was diagnosed with the cancer that killed her.

In 1950, Didrikson cofounded the Ladies Professional Golf Association; she also started a long-term affair with one of the other female founders. Her affairs with women she met through the golf circuit were common knowledge among her contemporaries.

DIETRICH, MARLENE. (Dec. 27, 1901–May 6, 1992), *German actress.* Marlene Dietrich was born in Berlin and studied acting under Max Reinhardt, an innovative theater director. With the advent of film, she played bit parts until she was given her first starring role, in *The Blue Angel.* She went on to star in many other films, including *Blonde Venus, Shanghai Express,* and *A Touch of Evil.* She also performed for Allied troops during World War II, and sang extensively in night clubs. Pre-Nazi Berlin was an active gay and lesbian community and Dietrich — a product of that culture — was always open about her bisexuality.

DOLAN, TERRY. (1950–1986), *U.S. conservative activist.* John Terrence Dolan was one of several gay New Right activists in the early 1980s who suffered from the very homophobia they helped stir up. Dolan was most prominent as the founder (in 1975) and head of the National Conservative Political Action Committee (NCPAC), a leading New Right group. It pumped two million dollars into Ronald Reagan's 1980 campaign while sponsoring vicious — and often inaccurate — television ads against liberal senators that it targeted for defeat.

But Dolan's approach soon grew counterproductive, and even fellow conservatives questioned NCPAC's effectiveness. In 1982, Dolan put together a "hit list" of twenty senators; nineteen won re-election anyway.

Frustrated by NCPAC limitations, and by the militantly anti-gay posturing of his fellow conservatives, Dolan cofounded Concerned Americans for Individual Rights (CAIR) in 1981. CAIR was to be a gay Republican organization, combining a conservative economic philosophy, strong support for military spending, and a libertarian approach to gay rights. Dolan opposed gay civil rights legislation, for example — he considered it government intrusion — but felt that the government should not discriminate against gays in the military and in other hiring.

In 1982, Perry Young chronicled the growth of the New Right in his book *God's Bullies.* Young charged that Dolan was gay, and included an account by a man who claimed to have had an affair with him. Dolan denied the affair, but refused to discuss his sexual orientation.

Dolan's death in 1986, at the age of thirty-six, was reported by the Washington *Post* to be the result of

AIDS; his doctor denied that story. His brother responded with a two-page ad in the Washington *Times* denouncing the "malicious falsehood ... that my brother lived and died a homosexual." Anthony Dolan claimed that his brother had repudiated his homosexuality before his death.

DOOLITTLE, HILDA (H.D.). (Sep. 10, 1886–Sep. 27, 1961), *U.S.-born poet.* Although born in the U.S., Hilda Doolitle moved to Europe in 1911, befriended Ezra Pound, and began writing under the name "H.D." She married British writer Richard Aldington soon thereafter, but in 1918 she fell in love with the novelist Bryher. Their relationship lasted a lifetime. Bryher was already married to Robert McAlmon, a bisexual writer and publisher. Fully aware of what was going on, he became H.D.'s publisher, and the two women lived out most of their years in Switzerland.

DUNCAN, ROBERT. (Jan. 7, 1919–Feb. 3, 1988), *U.S. poet.* Robert Duncan is widely regarded as the most influential writer of his generation. His own body of work, his involvement in a number of literary movements, his support of younger poets, and his championing of female writers (like Gertrude Stein) combine to show his great dedication to and love for his work.

Duncan holds the distinction of being the first American writer to use homosexuality as his main topic, in his 1944 essay "The Homosexual in Society." His literary influence and stature spilled over into his dedication to the gay liberation movement, though he claimed individual rights — not gay rights — was his goal.

DUQUESNOY, JEROME. (1602–1654), *Flemish sculptor.* Although less famous than his brother Francois (whose works include Brussel's *Mannekin Pis*), Jerome Duquesnoy was the official court sculptor in Flanders. While in that position, he was accused of sodomy with two church acolytes who had served as his models. Upon being found guilty, Duquesnoy was strangled, then burned at the stake.

EAKINS, THOMAS. (Jul. 25, 1844–Jun. 25, 1916), *U.S. painter.* A good friend of the poet Walt Whitman, Eakins taught at the Philadelphia Academy of Fine Arts from the late 1870s until 1886, when he was forced to resign over his insistence on using live nude models in class. His paintings showed a love of the male body — one favorite scene depicted a group of boys skinny-dipping — and disturbed his Victorian contemporaries because of their stark, realistic portrayal of everyday life. Eakins's appreciation of the male form has led many critics to assume he was gay, but clear proof is still lacking.

EARHART, AMELIA. (July 24, 1897–July 2?, 1937), *U.S. aviator.* Earhart was the first woman to fly alone over the Atlantic, a feat that won her the nickname "Lady Lindy." This was soon followed by other aviation milestones: she was the first person to fly alone from California to Hawaii (a longer distance than the trans-Atlantic flight), and the first to solo from Mexico City to the east coast of the U.S. In the summer of 1937, she and navigator Frederick

Noonan were attempting to fly around the world when their plane mysteriously disappeared near the

Marshall Islands in the South Pacific.

The frequent speculation that Amelia Earhart was a lesbian is based on strong but circumstantial evidence that includes her masculine dress and appearance, her fierce independence, her friendship with lesbians, and a letter in which she expressed reluctance to marry her eventual husband, publisher George Putnam.

EDWARD II. (Apr. 25, 1284–Sept. ?, 1327), *English king.* Although his father, Edward I, was famous for his wartime exploits, Edward II showed little interest in military affairs. He showed more interest in Piers Gaveston, the orphaned son of a French knight who became his companion when Edward was fourteen and Gaveston sixteen. Rumors about their relationship circulated throughout the castle. In 1307, Edward's father banished Gaveston from the kingdom and arranged for his son's marriage to Princess Isabel of France. But the king died soon afterward, and as the new king, Edward II invited Gaveston back before proceeding with the marriage.

In the years that followed, Edward's devotion to Gaveston did not go unnoticed by Isabel. She conspired with the country's powerful barons to again have Gaveston banished. When he returned from that exile, at Edward's urging, Isabel and the barons approached the

French king for support in a rebellion. It succeeded, and the barons executed Gaveston in 1312.

The conflict between Edward and the barons continued over the next decade. Edward found a new lover. But his wife likewise began an affair; with support from the French and from many barons, she and her lover eventually defeated Edward and forced him to abdicate. Edward was then killed by having a red-hot poker thrust into his rectum,

a method which satisfied his executioners that he was being punished for his sins, but that left no marks on his body.

EPSTEIN, BRIAN. (Sep. 13, 1934–Oct. 25, 1967), *British businessman.* The first manager of the Beatles, Epstein was homosexual, and was undoubtedly in love with John Lennon. The extent to which Lennon returned that love physically is open to dispute; certainly, it was reciprocated less than Epstein would have wished.

ERASMUS, DESIDERIUS. (Oct. 27, 1466?–July 12, 1536), *Dutch theologian.* Erasmus, the illegitimate son of an educated priest, is often considered the greatest scholar of the Reformation. Among his achievements were definitive editions of many classics, including the Greek New Testament.

Shortly after joining the monastery in 1488, Erasmus became enamoured of Servatius Roger, who spurned his attentions. His most enduring relationship was a platonic one with William Blount, Fourth Lord Mountjoy.

ERTÉ (Romain de Tirtoff). (1893–Apr. 22, 1990), *Russian fashion designer.* Born in St. Petersburg, Erté worked in Paris, designing dresses for everyone from Mata Hari to the Ziegfeld Follies. His stylish designs of thin women with long, flowing clothing graced the covers of hundreds of *Harper's Bazaar* magazines, and enjoyed a resurgence of popularity in the 1970s.

In his biography *My Life/My Art,* Erté claims that the most important relationship in his life was with Nicolas Ouroussoff, an older, distant cousin. They lived together for nearly twenty years.

FASHANU, JUSTIN. (1959–), *British athlete.* In the late 1980s, Nigerian-born Justin Fashanu was the highest paid and most prominent black athlete in Great Britain. He served as a role model for the entire black community.

In October of 1990, Fashanu revealed his homosexuality in the British tabloid *The Sun,* setting off a storm of controversy and homophobia in the British press and its black community. Fashanu was the first professional British sports figure to come out, although he mentioned in the interview that he knew of other gay professional soccer players. Publicly rejected by his equally famous, soccer-playing brother, the rest of his family, and the Nigerian High Commission, Fashanu disappeared from public view for a

while, then reappeared as a soccer manager.

FASSBINDER, RAINER WERNER. (May 31, 1945–June 10, 1982), *German cinematographer.* In just thirteen years, Rainer Werner Fassbinder produced forty-one full-length films, including *Fox and His Friends, Querelle de Brest,* and *The Marriage of Maria Braun.* He was openly gay, and dealt with gay themes in many of his films, though his gay characters regularly suffered sad fates. Fassbinder died at the age of thirty-six, apparently from simultaneously ingesting cocaine and sleeping pills.

FAYE, FRANCES. (1912–Nov. 8, 1991), *U.S. entertainer.* Frances Faye recorded her first hit, "No Regrets," in 1936, and became a popular nightclub singer in the 1940s and 1950s. Like many other entertainers of her era, she was a lesbian. Unlike many others, she was open about it. Faye continued to perform until 1981.

FLYNN, ERROL. (Jun. 20, 1909–Oct. 14, 1959), *U.S. actor.* During his lifetime, Errol Flynn was surrounded by an aura of romantic mystery that he deliberately fostered. Little is known of his origins; he claimed on different occasions to have been born in Tasmania and in Ireland. After spending much of his youth in New Guinea where he prospected for gold, sailed a schooner, and wrote stories for the *Sydney Bulletin,* Flynn headed to Hollywood and achieved instant stardom in *Captain Blood.* A string of swashbuckling roles followed in films such as *The Adventures of Robin Hood, The Sea Hawk,* and *Gentle-*

man Jim. In 1942, he was tried for statutory rape, and despite his acquittal, his popularity dropped. Flynn was notorious for his romantic adventures and was considered to be a ladies' man; only after his death did his homosexual affairs become widely known outside of Hollywood circles.

FORBES, MALCOLM. (Aug. 18, 1919–Feb. 24, 1990), *U.S. publisher.* The flamboyant publisher of *Forbes* magazine was best known for his wealth, his style, his hobbies (motorcycling and hot-air ballooning among them), and his non-affair with Elizabeth Taylor (which the press played up, although reporters knew there was no romance involved). He was divorced in 1985 after thirty-nine years of marriage and five children, and soon the rumors of his homosexuality were abundant. After his death, the talk started appearing in print, and there is little doubt now that at least in his latter years, Forbes identified as gay.

FORSTER, E.M. (Jan. 1, 1879–June 8, 1970), *British writer.* Although in his lifetime he was a prominent essayist and critic, Forster's fame rests primarily on the novels *Howard's End* and *A Passage to India.* Forster made sure that his novel of homosexual love, *Maurice,* was not published until 1971 — the year after his death — although he had finished it in 1914. The work was revolutionary in its treatment of homosexuality as an inherent trait of a person, rather than simply a type of behavior.

Forster discarded the intricate descriptions and elaborations so common in the nineteenth-century novel, and instead favored a simpler style. He was keenly interested in Mediterranean culture, which he considered more spontaneous and closer to nature than the culture of Britain and other countries of Northern Europe.

FOSTER, STEPHEN. (Jul. 4, 1826–Jan. 13, 1864), *U.S. composer.* Foster was the most popular American composer in the years before the Civil War. His better-known tunes include "De Camptown Races," "Beautiful Dreamer," and "Jeannie with the Light Brown Hair."

Foster's early family life was unsettled and he spent most of his childhood with his older brother William. After marrying and fathering a daughter, Foster spent more and more time in New York City, away from his wife and family, finally making the separation permanent in 1860. From that time until his death his closest relationship was with a poet named George Cooper, fifteen years his junior. They collaborated on more than twenty of Foster's songs. It was Cooper who cared for Foster in the days after the accident that eventually claimed the composer's life.

FOUCAULT, MICHEL. (Oct. 15, 1926–Jun. 25, 1984), *French philosopher.* Foucault is considered to be among the most important thinkers of the twentieth century; he is known particularly for his analyses of the concepts and codes by which societies operate. In his *History of Sexuality,* a three-volume examination of Western attitudes, he challenged the traditional belief that Victorian society was characterized by a repressive silence surrounding sexuality; in reality, he maintained, sexual issues were discussed then with a greater frequency than ever before. Foucault died in 1984 of an AIDS-related illness.

FRANK, ANNE. (Jun. 12, 1929– March, 1945), *German diarist*. Anne Frank, who from 1942 to 1945 hid from the Nazis with her family in an Amsterdam attic, gained posthumous fame when her diary was published. Until recently, only edited versions of the diary have been available, as many publishers found the original version too sexually explicit. Particularly problematic were those passages in which the young girl described urges and fantasies that centered on women. In January 1944, for example, she wrote, "I become ecstatic every time I see a naked figure of a woman, such as Venus, in my art history book. Sometimes I find it so wondrous and beautiful that I have to hold myself in, so that I do not begin to cry."

FRANK, BARNEY. (Mar. 31, 1940 –), *U.S. congressman*. For years, Frank established a reputation as one of Massachusetts's wittiest and most liberal politicians, first in the state legislature, then in the U.S. Congress. In 1987, Frank gave an interview to the *Boston Globe* in which he became the first member of the U.S. House of Representatives to come out completely voluntarily. It was a point he had been moving toward steadily for several years, as he had come out to an increasing number of friends and acquaintances.

FREDERICK II (THE GREAT). (Jan. 24, 1712–Aug. 17, 1786), *Prussian king*. Born to the iron-willed military ruler Frederick William I, the young Frederick II often found himself at odds with his father. Unlike his father, Frederick was absorbed by the arts and literature, and developed an effeminate air. Most galling to the king was his son's passionate friendship with the 25-year-old Hans von Katte, a lieutenant in the Prussian army. As his father grew increasingly abusive, Frederick made plans at the age of eighteen to flee to England with Katte. They were caught and imprisoned, and Frederick was forced to watch as his father had Katte beheaded.

Upon the death of his father ten years later, Frederick became king. His reign was marked by a number of reforms, including the abolition of torture and increased religious tolerance. A ho-mosexual subculture thrived in Berlin during Frederick's reign, relatively unpersecuted by the authorities. Voltaire, his confidant for many decades, believed that Frederick was homosexual, and historical evidence strongly supports that belief.

GARCIA LORCA, FEDERICO. (June 5, 1898–Aug. 19/20, 1936), *Spanish poet*. Lorca is one of Spain's most highly regarded dramatists and poets, best known for the poems collected in *Gypsy Ballads,* and the play trilogy of *Blood Wedding, Yerma,* and *The House of Bernarda Alba.* He formed an intellectual relationship with other European artists of his generation, like Salvador Dali and Luis Buñuel, and influenced many others, like Jean Genet.

The exact nature of Lorca's relationship with Dali remains unclear, though the artist said that they attempted sexual relations. There is no doubt of Lorca's homosexuality. Much of his poetry deals with the different kinds of love between men, or descriptions of beautiful young men. On a trip to America, Lorca was introduced to poet Hart Crane, and the two men cruised the streets for sailors. In 1936 the fascist Falangists seized power in Spain and purged the country of left-wing sympathizers. Lorca, found hiding in the home of poet Luis Rosales, was taken to an olive grove and shot.

GEFFEN, DAVID. (Feb. 21, 1943–), *U.S. film producer.* David Geffen, called Hollywood's richest man by *Forbes* magazine, started in the music business in the late sixties. His first success was in signing singer Laura Nyro in 1969, and he went on to sign Joni Mitchell, Jackson Browne, Linda Rondstadt, and the Eagles. After a brief, disastrous alliance with Warner Brothers on the box-office failure, *Personal Best,* Geffen started his own record company, Geffen Records, in 1980, and courted such artists as Aerosmith, Donna Summer, and Elton John. Not one to admit defeat, he then dove into the movie business again, this time striking gold with movies like *Risky Business* and *Beetlejuice.* In 1990, MCA bought out Geffen's film and record business, and made him one of the richest men in the country.

Although Hollywood friends and business associates knew that Geffen was bisexual, his silence on the subject infuriated activists. Finally, in 1991, Geffen came out in *Vanity Fair* magazine: "I date men and I date women. What Woody Allen said was true. Say what you will about bisexuality, you have a 50% better chance of finding a date on Saturday night." Geffen has been generous in his support of gay rights issues, and made a large donation to the 1993 March on Washington.

GENET, JEAN. (Dec. 19, 1910–Apr. 15, 1986), *French writer.* Genet spent most of his adolescence and young adulthood in prison for robbery. Although he didn't begin writing until the age of thirty-two, he became one of the most prolific French writers of the century. His works include poetry; the plays *The Balcony* and *The Maids;* and the novel *Our Lady of the Flowers.* From the beginning of his writing career, Genet's work was distinguished by a rigorous, pure, and highly original style. This is particularly remarkable in that for most of his life, he had been exposed only to slang and literature of poor quality.

Genet was aware even at a young age of his attraction to boys. In fact, he recalled later, he was happy for the first time in his life when he was sent to reform school, because it gave him the chance to express his homosexual desires. During the Great Depression, he earned a living as a male prostitute, and he was involved in relationships with men throughout his life, most of them short-lived.

Genet was "a cat's cradle of contradictions," says his biographer, Edmund White. "He was a homosexual whose closest friends were women, a world celebrity who lived in crummy railway hotels, the author of a handful of the most sumptuously stylish novels of this century who, after the age of ten, received all of his education in reform schools." He died in a Paris hotel in 1986 after falling and hitting his head. His death followed that of Simone de Beauvoir, his old friend and ally, by just a few hours.

GERNREICH, RUDI. (1922–1985), *Austrian-born U.S. fashion designer.* By his early thirties, fashion designer Rudi Gernreich was designing swimsuits for Marilyn Monroe and his work was featured in magazines ranging from *Life* on down. His fame grew with his introduction of the topless bathing suit, the unisex look, and other innovations. In 1967, *Time* featured him on its cover.

Gernreich had a previous history every bit as revolutionary as his fashions, but it was never mentioned in the media coverage. Gernreich came to the U.S. from Vienna in 1938, and quickly grew active in leftist politics. In 1950 he met another leftist, Harry Hay, who for two years had been searching for someone who shared the dream that gay people could organize and fight for their rights. Gernreich was that person. They became lovers, and organized the Mattachine Society, forerunner of today's gay movement.

Gernreich dropped out of political activism in 1953, when the red-baiting attitudes of the McCarthy era infiltrated even the Mattachine Society. He devoted his time to his career and his new lover, UCLA professor Oreste Pucciani, and his homosexuality was carefully kept from the public eye. Only with his death did he come out. The wealth that he and Pucciani had accumulated was bequeathed to the American Civil Liberties Union to pursue gay civil rights cases.

GIDE, ANDRÉ. (Nov. 22, 1869–Feb. 19, 1951), *French writer.* Among the most prolific and distinguished French writers of the twentieth century, Gide did much to further the cause of gay people. His works include novels, plays, and essays. He shocked his contemporaries in 1924 with his autobiographical *Si le grain ne meurt* (*If It Die*), which discussed his homosexual experiences. But the controversy surrounding his life didn't keep Gide from winning the Nobel Prize in Literature in 1947.

Gide's homosexuality had been evident even in childhood. At the age of eight, he went to a costume party and fell wildly in love with a boy dressed in black tights. That attraction set a pattern, and throughout his life, Gide was enamored of boys and young men. His first gay relationship came at twenty-three, with a fourteen-year-old Arab boy in Tunisia. Gide tried marriage, although his relationship with his wife was probably purely platonic, and had a heterosexual affair that resulted in a daughter, but his homosexuality would not go away. At the age of forty-seven Gide began a relationship with Marc Allegret, then sixteen, who later became a well-known film producer. Gide also had a long-standing friendship with Oscar Wilde.

GIELGUD, Sir JOHN. (Apr. 14, 1904–), *British actor.* One of few major actors to come out, Gielgud didn't take his first step willingly: He was arrested in the early sixties on a morals charge in a London lavatory. A reporter recognized him at the trial and the next day the *London Daily Mail* was calling for him to give up the knighthood that had recently been bestowed on him. But the fuss soon died down. According to legend, as he returned to rehearsal following the arrest (he was appearing in Wilde's *The Importance of Being Ernest*), Dame Edith Evans admonished him, "Now, John, we know you've been a naughty boy, but let's get on with it."

GILLES DE RAIS. (1404–1440), *French general.* Born into a noble French family, Gilles de Rais grew up surrounded by the finest books, art, and music. At the age of twenty-two, he personally organized and funded a small army to help France in its fight against the English. His combat abilities brought him fame, and he became a close friend and bodyguard to Joan of Arc.

Ending his military career, Gilles set up his own castle in Brittany, rivaling even the palace of the French king in its pomp and splendor. When his massive fortune was depleted, an assistant persuaded him that through alchemy Gilles could create new wealth for himself, though doing so would require the sacrifice of human children, mostly boys, to appease the devil. In the years that followed, some two hundred peasant boys are believed to have been lured into his castle, where they were raped, tortured, and murdered. Gilles's high position at first protected him from the growing suspicions of the local population, but his luck finally ran out. In 1440 he was arrested by the bishop of Nantes; he made a full confession under the threat of torture, and was promptly hanged.

GINSBERG, ALLEN. (June 3, 1926–), *U.S. poet.* While attending Columbia University, Allen Ginsberg met Jack Kerouac and William Burroughs, and the three became the central figures of the Beat movement. Ginsberg's epic poem *Howl* (1956) is considered one of the most significant poems of the latter half of this century.

Ginsberg's homosexuality is widely known; indeed, *Howl* incorporates elements of his sexual orientation, drug use, and Buddhism, as well as his critique of the senseless materialism of post–World War II America. He served as a father figure to the late-1960s bohemian society, and has remained outspoken and active in the gay liberation movement since then.

GLUCK (Hannah Gluckstein). (Aug. 13, 1895–Jan. 10, 1978), *British artist.* Hannah Gluckstein adopted the name Gluck to thumb her nose at both her wealthy family and the society that barely recognized female artists. Because she spent many years engaged in a battle to make the paint industry standardize its products, her actual body of work is rather small. Gluck was openly lesbian and insisted on dressing in men's clothing — probably another way to affront her family and society. Her affairs were tumultuous and her lovers suffered at her harsh treatment; she persuaded her last lover, the writer Edith Heald, to sell her home to

Gluck's family, and then scoffed at Edith's horror of becoming dependent on charity.

GOODMAN, PAUL. (Sep. 9, 1911–Aug. 2, 1972), *U.S. writer.* A leading anarchist influence of his time, Paul Goodman represented a voice of dissent in the early gay liberation movement. While many took a single-minded approach to gay rights, Goodman advocated alliances with other progressive causes.

His book *Growing Up Absurd* brought him fame in 1960, and he soon became known as "the Father Figure of the New Left." Goodman's ideological anarchism was reflected in his life. He was married twice and fathered three children, yet he made no secret of his homosexual desires. In the early 1950s he was denied tenure at the avant garde Black Mountain College in North Carolina, in part because of his open bisexuality — but also because he aggressively fondled his male students.

GRIMKÉ, ANGELINA WELD. (February 27, 1880–June 10, 1958), *U.S. poet.* In 1868, former abolitionist  leader Angelina learned about Archibald Henry Grimké, a black man who was eloquently arguing and working against racism. Because he shared her uncommon name, she wrote to him, and they soon established that he was her nephew. Angelina and her sister Sarah had been prominent abolitionists, but their brother John was a slaveholder. He had become sexually involved with a slave, and Ar-

chibald Henry Grimké was their child. Yet only because of their common work did Angelina and Archibald learn of one another's existence.

Archibald named his only child after his aunt. The younger Angelina was born in Boston; she became a poet and writer and was a part of the Harlem Renaissance along with black writers Georgia Johnson and Alice Dunbar-Nelson. At the age of sixteen she fell in love with her friend Mamie Burrill. "If you only knew how my heart overflows with love for you," Grimké wrote to Burrill; their relationship lasted seven years.

As an adult, her poems were strongly woman-identified and often included verses of love to other women:

> My sweetheart walks down
> laughing ways
> Mid dancing glancing sun-
> kissed ways
> And she is all in white...

HADRIAN. (Jan. 24?, 76–Jul. 10, 138), *Roman emperor.* Orphaned at the age of ten, Publius Aelius Hadrianus was adopted by the future Emperor Trajan, whose wife Plotina became especially fond of the boy and took responsibility for his personal development. In 98, Trajan became emperor and designated Hadrian as his heir. Upon Trajan's death in 117, Hadrian was crowned emperor.

Hadrian proved to be one of Rome's better emperors. He instituted welfare payments for poor children, reduced taxes, codified the laws, and enacted legislation against the mistreatment of slaves. In about the year 124, Hadrian met and fell in love with Antinous, a Greek youth of great beauty. For six years the two were inseparable. In 130, on a trip to Egypt, Antinous drowned in the Nile. According to one widely believed account, an oracle had foreseen Hadrian's death, and Antinous deliberately sacrificed himself to let Hadrian survive in his place. The grief-stricken Hadrian deified Antinous, but never fully adjusted to the loss. Hadrian deteriorated, both physically and mentally, until his own death eight years later.

HALL, RADCLYFFE. (Aug. 12, 1880–Oct. 7, 1943), *British writer.* Even in childhood, Radclyffe Hall was different: she adopted the nickname "John," and began her lifelong preference for masculine dress and appearance. This identification with masculinity prompted her to readily adopt the theory of "sexual inversion" as an explanation for lesbianism.

Although she wrote poetry and achieved some success with her 1926 novel *Adam's Breed,* it was The Well of Loneliness, two years later, that thrust her into the spotlight. Although it seems apologetic by today's standards, in 1928 the novel shocked the English-speaking world with Hall's open portrayal of lesbianism and her plea for sympathy and tolerance for "inverts." A British court found the book to be an "obscene libel" and ordered all copies destroyed; the ban was not overturned until Hall's death. The novel was also tried in an American court, which allowed its publication.

When she was twenty-seven, Hall fell in love with the fifty-year-old Mabel Batten. Eight years later,

she became involved with Una, Lady Troubridge, who was an admiral's wife. Batten died of a heart attack after arguing with Hall about this new liaison, and the Hall-Troubridge relationship lasted thirty years. Their circle of friends included Romaine Brooks, Colette, Dolly Wilde, and Natalie Barney.

HALLIBURTON, RICHARD. (Jan. 9, 1900–March 23?, 1939), *U.S. adventurer.* He swam the Panama Canal (lengthwise), consorted with headhunters in Borneo, flew all over the world in the early days of early aviation — then, in 1939, Richard Halliburton set sail from Hong Kong in a custom-made Chinese junk and was lost at sea. Although he is largely forgotten today, Halliburton's colorful books and lectures made him a household name in his lifetime. What the public didn't know was that, when not on an adventure, Halliburton lived in Laguna Beach with his lover Paul Mooney.

HAMILTON, ALEXANDER. (Jan. 11, 1757–Jul. 12, 1804), *U.S. statesman.* In 1774, while still in his teens, Alexander Hamilton wrote the first of three eloquent anti-British pamphlets. He fought in the Revolutionary War as a trusted confidant of George Washington, and afterward became a leading proponent of a strong central government.

Over the years, there has been recurring speculation that Hamilton was romantically involved with his friend and fellow soldier John Laurens. In 1779, Hamilton wrote to Laurens, "I wish, my dear Laurens, it might be in my power, by action rather than words, [to] convince you that I love you." But letters in that era were often more florid than they are today, and it is unclear just how this should be interpreted. Reaching even further, though with less factual basis, some gay historians have also suggested a relationship between Hamilton and George Washington.

HAMMARSKJÖLD, DAG. (July 29, 1905–Sept. 18, 1961), *Swedish statesman*. Dag Hammarskjöld, whose father was the Swedish prime minister during World War I, gained national prominence as chairman of the Bank of Sweden. In 1953, he was elected secretary-general of the United Nations, and was re-elected in 1957. As one of its earliest leaders, Hammarskjöld greatly enhanced the prestige and influence of the U.N., and he was awarded the 1961 Nobel Prize for his peacekeeping efforts. He died that year in an airplane crash in Northern Rhodesia, while negotiating a cease-fire between U.N. troops and Katanga forces.

Hammarskjöld never married, and there was considerable specu-lation about his sexuality when Hammarskjöld became a candidate for the office of U.N. secretary-general; he flatly denied them. It is clear, however, that throughout his life Hammarskjöld's closest emotional ties were always to men. In *Markings,* a record of his spiritual life that was published posthumously, several passages suggest feelings for other men that went beyond what one would expect in a heterosexual.

HANSBERRY, LORRAINE. (May 19, 1930–Jan. 12, 1965), *U.S. playwright*. With the production of *A Raisin in the Sun,* Lorraine Hansberry became the first black woman to have a drama produced on the Broadway stage. The play met with tremendous success and won the New York Drama Critics' Circle Award.

As a child, Hansberry lived with her family in a white neighborhood of Chicago and encountered open hostility in her walks to and from school. This experience had a profound impact on her writings.

She moved to New York City in 1950 and worked at several jobs, while at the same time she perfected her writing style. Hansberry became politically active and outspoken on behalf of civil rights and freedom of sexual expression. In a 1957 letter published anonymously in the early lesbian magazine *The Ladder,* Hansberry wrote, "I'm glad as heck that you exist." She expressed her belief that "homosexual persecution and condemnation has at its roots not only social ignorance, but ... anti-feminist dogma." In one of her last plays, *The Sign in Sidney Brustein's Window,* Hansberry presented a homosexual character with sympathy and insight, making him one of the best adjusted members of the cast. Her promising career was cut short by her death from cancer at the age of thirty-five.

To Be Young, Gifted and Black, an adaptation of her writings prepared by her ex-husband Robert Nemiroff, was produced off-Broadway in 1969. The lesbian aspect of Hansberry's life has been discussed by Adrienne Rich in *Freedomways* magazine.

HARMODIUS. (532?–514 B.C.), *Athenian patriot.* In 527 B.C., after the death of their father, Hippias and Hipparchus jointly became tyrants of Athens. They lacked their father's political talents, however, and public sentiment gradually turned against them. Their downfall came when Hipparchus sought the attention of the handsome Harmodius. Harmodius rebuffed him and Hipparchus, out of spite, publicly insulted Harmodius's sister.

This event triggered a long-simmering democratic uprising. It was led by Harmodius and his lover Aristogeiton, who conspired to assassinate the cotyrants. The plan succeeded only partially. Hipparchus was killed, but Hippias escaped and briefly put down the uprising after having the two lovers executed. Other patriots, however, continued the battle, and in 510 B.C., Hippias was driven from Athens. Meanwhile, Harmodius and Aristogeiton had achieved the status of folk heroes, whose legends elevated the status of homosexuality in Athens.

HARTLEY, MARSDEN. (Jan. 4, 1877–Sep. 2, 1943), *U.S. artist.* Marsden Hartley, now best known for capturing the coast of Maine on canvas, spent time in the cafes of pre–World War I Paris and Berlin, gathering knowledge, experience, and inspiration from the likes of Picasso, Kandinsky, and Braque. His bold, intense style and images made him a favorite with critics and students.

When in Europe, Hartley underwent an intellectual and sexual awakening. A soldier he met in Berlin inspired Hartley's "Portrait of a German Officer," and his tragic love affair with a Nova Scotia fisherman who drowned at sea profoundly influenced his later work. Unfortunately, most of Hartley's mildly erotic sketches of muscular fishermen and soldiers are seldom shown, while his Maine landscapes still enjoy popularity.

H.D. *See Hilda Doolittle.*

HENRY III. (Sep. 19, 1551–Aug. 2, 1589), *French king.* Soon after taking the French throne at the age of twenty-three, Henry III found himself at odds with the Catholic Church for refusing to persecute Protestants with sufficient vigor. At the age of thirty-eight, he was assassinated by a fanatical Dominican monk.

But during the years in between, Henry had fun. He appeared in drag at public events, earned a reputation for effeminate behavior, and surrounded himself with handsome young men. The best available evidence suggests that Henry slept freely with both men and women.

HENRY. (1726–1802), *Prussian prince and general.* The younger brother of Frederick the Great, Henry is remembered chiefly as the prince who might have been the first American king.

In 1786, many influential Americans were dissatisfied with the weakness of their new country under the Articles of Confederation. One solution they seriously contemplated was to install a liberal-minded European monarch as king. A group that included Alexander Hamilton and James Monroe expressed their support of Henry for such a position. But the telegraph arrived a century too late for Henry. By the time he got the message and could send a reply, the Constitutional Convention had already convened in Philadelphia. A monarchy was no longer being considered.

Had events turned out otherwise, America's first king would soon have been embroiled in scandal. Henry had never made much effort to hide his interest in young men, and an exposé published in 1789 was explicit, referring to Henry's "passion for pederasty," and noting that "The aristocracy of the army knows that with Prince Henry, the Ganymedes shall always be in control."

HIGGINS, COLIN. (1941–Aug. 5, 1988), *U.S. film director.* Colin Higgins, who died in 1988 as a result of AIDS, was one of Hollywood's few openly gay producers and directors. Born in New Caledonia to an American father and an Australian mother, he enrolled at the UCLA film school in 1967, beginning his successful career as a filmmaker. His master's thesis there was a screenplay about a 20-year-old man who falls in love with a 79-year-old woman; it was produced as the film *Harold and Maude,* which launched his career as screenwriter and director. Among Higgins's other credits are *The Devil's Daughter, Silver Streak,* and *Foul Play.*

HINSON, JON. (Mar. 16, 1942–), *U.S. politician.* Jon Hinson was elected to Congress from the state of Mississippi; he remained there until 1981, when he was arrested for having sex with another man in an office building restroom. Hinson had just been re-elected to his seat in 1980, despite a previous arrest at a cruising spot, and his surviving a fire at an all-male cinema in 1977. During the 1980 election, Hinson assured his followers that his time of "spiritual crisis" had passed, and he was happily living with his wife and his church; he said he was not gay. His next arrest proved too much for the voters, however, and Hinson resigned.

Hinson now lives in Virginia and works with several gay political organizations, including Virginians for Justice. He is divorced and openly gay. He has spoken about the horrors of living in the political closet, and the need for voters to know exactly where candidates stand on gay rights issues.

HIRSCHFELD, MAGNUS. (May 14, 1868–May 14, 1935), *German sexologist.* Hirschfeld began his career as a general practitioner, but the trial of Oscar Wilde and the suicide of a patient who was about to be married sparked his long-standing interest in homosexuality and sexology.

In 1897 Hirschfeld founded the Scientific-Humanitarian Committee, an early gay-advocacy organization, and drew up a petition to the Reichstag for the repeal of Germany's sodomy laws. In a landmark 1900 study, he prepared a questionnaire on a range of sex-related topics that was ultimately filled out by ten thousand men and women. After publishing a number of studies on sexuality, Hirschfeld gained the reputation of being Germany's leading expert on homosexuality and its first avowed specialist in psychosexual studies. With the Nazis' rise to power, Hirschfeld was forced to leave Germany. He died in Nice on his sixty-seventh birthday.

Besides being homosexual, Hirschfeld was a transvestite, and many gay men of the time referred to him as "Auntie Magnesia." In spite of his exhaustive work, Hirschfeld's homosexuality led many to question his objectivity.

HOOVER, J. EDGAR. (Jan 1, 1895–May 2, 1972), *U.S. criminologist.* The man who had secrets on everyone else was often rumored to have a secret of his own — but he was careful that no one ever got tangible proof. It is well documented that longtime FBI director Hoover and Clyde Tolson (1900–1975) were unusually close friends for forty-four years. Hoover's biographer, Richard Gid Powers, writes that "the relationship was so close, so enduring, and so affection-ate that it took the place of marriage for both bachelors ... An indication of the intimacy of the relationship is the collection of hundreds of candid photographs Hoover took of Tolson (who was strikingly handsome as a young man.)" Powers concludes that the relationship between the two men was "spousal." A more recent biography has him gallivanting at gay parties in drag.

Whatever secrets Hoover had about his private life, he was quite public about his own homophobia.

HOSMER, HARRIET. (Oct. 9, 1830–Feb. 21, 1908), *U.S. sculptor.* Hosmer was a bold neoclassical sculptor whose subjects included women raised up and out of the realm of male sexuality, such as Medusa and Daphne; or women oppressed by men, such as the queen Zenobia, captured by the Romans, and Beatrice Cenci, executed for killing her abusive father. Hosmer developed a pure, detailed style that brought both physical and intellectual life to her subjects.

Hosmer's letters reveal that her relationships were largely with women. She commonly dressed in male clothing, and used this to her advantage; she and her friend Robert Browning visited monasteries closed to women, to see the various art collections held there.

HOUSMAN, A.E. (Mar. 26, 1859–Apr. 30, 1936), *British poet and educator.* Housman was born into a distinguished and close-knit Worcestershire family. He showed an early talent for scholarship and poetry and studied at Oxford, then taught at Trinity College in Cambridge, and elsewhere. In 1896, Housman published, at his own expense, five hundred copies of *A Shropshire Lad,* the work for which he is best known. This book consists of a loosely connected series of poems and is notable for its directness of wording and its reflections on life and death. Although the critics' reactions were mixed, the volume had an enormous influence on modern English poetry.

Housman's romantic experience was probably limited to one unsatisfying affair with Moses J. Jackson, a roommate at Oxford.

Housman fell deeply in love with Jackson, who, although he reciprocated with friendship, had little interest in sex. Apparently Housman later persuaded Jackson to engage in sexual relations of some kind. But when Jackson accepted a post at Sind College in India, the affair ended, as did Housman's sex life.

Housman's siblings, both noted in their fields, were both gay. His brother Laurence was a book illustrator, and his sister Clemence a wood engraver.

HOWARD, ROBERT ERVIN. (Jan. 22, 1906–1936), *U.S. writer.* The 1982 film *Conan the Barbarian,* starring muscleman Arnold Schwarzenegger in the title role, brought to life a figure who was half a century old and very heterosexual. But the character's original creator, Robert Howard, is believed to have been homosexual. As a boy, Howard was exceptionally close to his mother and tended to be reclusive. Bullied by older boys, he turned to exercise, and developed the body that he admired in other men. When Howard's mother lapsed into a coma, he promptly blew his own brains out with a borrowed pistol, and the Texas town of Cross Plains had a double funeral. Howard was only thirty, but he had written twenty-one Conan stories.

HUDSON, ROCK. (Nov. 17, 1925–Oct. 2, 1985), *U.S. actor.* Born Roy Scherer, Jr., in Winnetka, Illinois, Hudson served in the navy during World War II before going to Hollywood in 1946 to seek employment. There he was discovered by agent Henry Wilson. Through careful grooming and well-orchestrated publicity, Wilson transformed Hudson into a leading star on the Universal Studios lot. "He's wholesome," said *Look* magazine, when they chose Hudson as their Star of the Year in 1958. "He doesn't perspire. He has no pimples. He smells of milk. His whole appeal is cleanliness and respectability — this boy is pure." By the late 1950s, Hudson was one of Hollywood's most successful leading men, thanks to his performances in such popular films as *Magnificent Obsession, Giant* (for which he received an Oscar nomination in 1956), and *Pillow Talk,* the first of several light bedroom comedies costarring Hudson's friend Doris Day.

Throughout his later career, Hudson repeatedly denied rumors that he was homosexual. However, in 1984, with the announcement he had AIDS, his sex life became a matter of open speculation and, finally, public certainty. The announcement also gave a public face to a disease that until then had received scant coverage in the national media. Shortly after Hudson's death, *Time* magazine praised the actor for his courage in announcing his condition and said that it "may have been the best and most dramatic gesture in his long career."

HUGHES, LANGSTON. (Feb. 1, 1902–May 22, 1967), *U.S. poet and writer.* Langston Hughes was elected class poet of his grammar school at the age of thirteen; it was only the start of an illustrious career as poet, biogra-

pher, translator, and dramatist.

Despite his upbringing in all-white neighborhoods, Hughes was a deeply black-identified writer. His works incorporate black themes and the rhythms of black music; they include a collection of poetry, *Fine Clothes to the Jew;* a short-story collection, *The Ways of White Folks;* and the novel *Not without Laughter.*

In the summer of 1924 — in a move designed to help his career — some historians believe that Hughes had an affair with Alain Locke, the Howard University professor Hughes described as midwife of the Harlem Renaissance. Locke, in return, arranged a great deal of valuable patronage for Hughes, including a "blank check" from the wealthy, eccentric Mrs. Charlotte Osgood. Throughout his life, Hughes remained extremely closeted. He often said, "There are some things I don't tell nobody, not even God. He might know about them, but it certainly ain't because I told him." *(See also Alain Locke.)*

HUNTER, ALBERTA. (Apr. 1, 1895–Oct. 17, 1984), *U.S. vocalist.* Alberta Hunter was the last of America's great African-American blues stars, and she performed right up until the end of her 89-year life.

Hunter ran away from home at the age of eleven, working first in Chicago, then in New York. In 1919 she met Lottie Tyler; they fell in love and their relationship lasted many years. Hunter also worked with the great Louis Armstrong, and with several other lesbian or bisexual vocalists, including Billie Holliday, Bessie Smith, and Ethel Waters.

Hunter retired from music in 1956 and became a nurse, but resumed singing when she lost her job on account of her age. She once again became a sensation, singing at the Carter White House several times, and was among the first performers in the Kennedy Center Honors awards program in 1978.

HYDE, EDWARD (Lord CORNBURY). (Nov. 28, 1661–Mar. 31, 1723), *British colonial governor.* Lord Cornbury, who became the colonial governor of New York and New Jersey in 1702, spent each afternoon walking about in public dressed as a woman. He explained that this was a tribute to his cousin, Queen Anne — an explanation that did not satisfy the townspeople, who complained to the queen about her cousin's behavior. She ignored these complaints, but in 1708 recalled him for his financial shenanigans, including the misuse of public funds and extortion of bribes from wealthy landowners. Although his cross-dressing is well documented, and gave rise to speculation that he was gay, there is no good evidence either way.

INGE, WILLIAM. (May 3, 1913–Jun. 10, 1973), *U.S. playwright.* Inge created many moving plays and screenplays, usually focusing on life in the midwestern United States. It took the strong support of Tennessee Williams to get his first play produced, but he went on to win a Pulitzer Prize for *Picnic* and an Academy Award for the screenplay of *Splendor in the Grass.* His other works included *Come Back, Little Sheba, Bus Stop,* and *The Dark at the Top of the Stairs.*

Of the suicide in *The Dark at the Top of the Stairs,* he said, "Some people felt upon reading the play, and others upon first seeing it, that the announcement of the suicide came as too much of a shock; but every suicide I ever heard of came to me in the same way, with no preparation. I have never heard of a suicide that I expected."

When Inge died, he left several short unproduced playscripts. One was a monolog titled *The Love Death*. It depicts an aging homosexual novelist, alone one evening, making a few phone calls as he prepares to end his life. The first call goes to his psychiatrist. Pretending to be researching his next book, the novelist asks how many sleeping pills are needed to commit suicide. He takes the prescribed dosage, then makes calls to his mother, a close friend, and his agent. Finally the pills take effect. *The Love Death* would seem overly sentimental except for one fact: it was probably written shortly before Inge's own suicide.

ISHERWOOD, CHRISTOPHER. (Aug. 26, 1904–Jan. 4, 1986), *English-born U.S. writer.* Considered by many to be a prophet of the gay rights movement, Isherwood is best known in literary circles for his novels set in the Berlin of the early 1930s. These novels, which inspired the musical *Cabaret,* were based on his own experiences there.

Isherwood came out while still young. "I told my mother quite early on," he said in a 1975 interview for *The Advocate.* "She provoked me. She didn't believe in any sexual relation that didn't involve a woman. She could have respected a lesbian relationship, perhaps. But she didn't believe men *did* anything together."

Having witnessed the decay of the Weimar Republic and the rise to power of the Nazis, Isherwood left Germany and in 1939 moved to the United States, choosing to settle in southern California. Upon his arrival in the United States Isherwood embraced pacifism and Hinduism.

Many of Isherwood's works explored the issue of homosexuality. *A Single Man,* perhaps the most highly regarded of these, portrays one day in the life of a lonely, middle-aged gay man.

From 1953 until his death, Isherwood lived with his lover, the artist Don Bachardy; both were involved in the gay rights movement and in gay circles of southern California.

JAMES I. (June 19, 1566–Mar. 27, 1625), *English king.* James, the son of Mary, Queen of Scots, was born in Edinburgh Castle and became the titular king of Scotland the year after his birth. Although he married at the age of twenty-three and had several children, there was frequent gossip of his many liaisons with male lovers, beginning with his cousin Esmé Stuart, when James was thirteen. The rumors were to continue for the rest of his life.

The ambitious James allied himself with Queen Elizabeth of England, and succeeded her in 1603. Already, however, he was unpopular with his subjects, and as he took the throne the quip circulated that "Elizabeth was king, now James is queen." His twenty-two years as king were marked by the beginning of work on the King James Version of the Bible and by his constant feuds with Parliament, which he usually ended by dissolving that body.

James's dalliances with male lovers continued while he was king. Among them was the handsome Robert Carr, who was made a Gentleman of the Bedchamber. When Carr later married, James wrote to him complaining of Carr's "withdrawing yourself from lying in my chamber, notwithstanding my many hundred times earnestly soliciting  you to the contrary." Of a later favorite, George Villiers, the earl of Buckingham, James said: "You may be sure that I love the earl of Buckingham more than anyone else. Christ had his John and I have my George."

JENKINS, WALTER. (Mar. 23, 1918–Nov. 23, 1985), *U.S. political aide.* A longtime aide and close personal friend of Lyndon Johnson, Jenkins was forced to resign from his position as Special Assistant to the President after he was arrested in 1964 for committing homosexual acts in a YMCA two blocks from the White House. It was later revealed that Jenkins had been arrested five years earlier on similar charges at the same YMCA. His resignation caused a scandal for Lyndon Johnson and was used by Barry Goldwater's 1964 presidential campaign to imply that the nation's security might have been breached under Johnson's administration.

JESUS. (4 B.C?–A.D. 29), *Religious leader.* In 1958, historian Morton Smith discovered an ancient manuscript in a Judean desert monastery that led him to believe that Jesus was a magician rather than a religious leader. Furthermore, Smith asserted that after raising Lazarus from a state that resembled death, Jesus had spent a night with him in both spiritual and physical communion.

These conclusions, not surprisingly, were ignored or denounced by most church authorities. But Smith was hardly a crackpot. He was a history professor at Columbia University, and his book on this subject, *Clement of Alexandria and a Secret Gospel of Mark,* was published by the reputable Harvard University Press.

Other researchers have suggested that Jesus had a homoerotic relationship with the Apostle John. The Bible offers some evidence of a special relationship between the two, in passages such as John 13:23. But like most theories about little-documented events of two thousand years ago, this one seems unlikely to be conclusively proven or disproven today.

JOHNSON, PHILIP. (July 8, 1906 –), *U.S. architect.* In 1932, Johnson became the first director of the Department of Architecture and Design at New York's Museum of Modern Art, a position that he held on and off until 1954. Johnson's first designs — like his own home, the "Glass House" — define the International style of architecture, but he eventually went on to work with the Postmodern style, which can be seen in the New York State Theatre at Lincoln Center (1964) and the AT&T Building in New York City (1982). In 1993, the news broke that a forthcoming autobiography will discuss both Johnson's homosexuality and his early interest in fascism. Johnson said of the latter interests, "I have no excuse [for] such utter, unbelievable stupidity."

JONATHAN. (1045?–1013 B.C.), *Israeli crown prince.* In 1028 B.C., Saul became the first king of Israel. His son Jonathan, first in line for the throne, was among his chief military aides. When the young shepherd David appeared in the court, eager to help the new ruler, the Bible reports that "the soul of Jonathan was knit with the soul of David, and Jonathan loved him as his own soul."

Eventually, however, King Saul feared that David was plotting to capture his throne, and he made plans to have David killed. When Jonathan learned of this plot, he was torn between loyalty to his father and his love for David; he chose to help David hide, and later to escape.

Jonathan and Saul both perished in the Battle of Mt. Gilboa, in which the Israeli army was crushed by the Philistines. It was left to David, in the years to come, to reunite the kingdom. *(See also David.)*

JULIUS III. (Sep. 10, 1487–Mar. 23 1555), *pope.* Julius III's short five-year reign as pope was an uneventful one, during which he devoted more time to boys than to religion. While still a cardinal, Julius made no secret of his preferences. One teen-aged boyfriend, nicknamed the Prevostino, accompanied him to meetings; when other cardinals objected, he told them, "The Prevostino is worth more than the whole lot of you."

Upon his election as pope in 1550, Julius made cardinals out of the Prevostino and several other teenagers. His orgies were well known to his colleagues, and when the archbishop of Benevento wrote "In Praise of Sodomy," it was dedicated to Julius III — to Julius's amusement.

KAHLO, FRIDA. (1907–1954), *Mexican artist.* Married to artist Diego Rivera, and overshadowed by him during her lifetime, Frida Kahlo was a surrealist who specialized in self-portraits. She and Rivera shared an intense passion for their country; she even misrepresented the year of her birth as 1910, to coincide with the year of the Mexican Revolution. In the early 1990s, Kahlo's work received a tremendous amount of attention, and the painter became a feminist icon — a symbol of great female talent eclipsed by a more popular male.

Kahlo was bisexual. She stood up to her philandering and possibly abusive husband by having her own affairs with men and women — including some of Rivera's mistresses. Her love for women is reflected in some of her paintings, such as *Two Nudes in a Forest* (1939).

KEYNES, JOHN MAYNARD. (June 5, 1883–Apr. 21, 1946), *British economist.* Widely regarded as the greatest economist of the twentieth century, John Maynard Keynes extended his influence well beyond that field. He was a strong supporter of the arts, a respected  teacher, and a central member of the Bloomsbury group.

Six years after the death of Keynes, a biographer managed to completely omit any mention of his interest in men. But in reality, despite his 1926 marriage to ballerina Lydia Lopokova, Keynes was essentially homosexual. He had an affair with painter Duncan Grant early in life, and later carried on a long correspondence with Lytton Strachey, in which they openly discussed their homosexuality.

KING, BILLIE JEAN. (Nov. 22, 1943–), *U.S. athlete.* King was a four-time winner at the U.S. Open Championships between 1967 and 1974, and took the women's crown at Wimbledon four times from 1968 to 1975. During that period, King and Rosemary Casals split off from the men's tennis circuit, found a sponsor in Virginia Slims, and worked to get better prize money and recognition for women tennis players. King mused in her autobiography, "The best men players were better than the best women, but I do wonder what would happen if we played against men on equal terms right from birth."

In 1981, King shocked the sports world when, as the result of a palimony suit (it became "galimony" in tabloidese) brought against her, she publicly acknowledged a lesbian affair with her former hairdresser and secretary, Marilyn Barnett. However, King resisted being classified as a lesbian. "If you have one gay experience, does that mean you're gay?" she asked an interviewer. "If you have one heterosexual experience, does that mean you're straight? Life doesn't work quite so cut and dried." The lawsuit was ultimately thrown out of court.

KING, WILLIAM RUFUS. (Apr. 7, 1786–Apr. 18, 1853), *U.S. vice president.* After graduating from college in 1803, King began a long political career that included serving in the North Carolina legislature, the U.S. House of Representatives, the U.S. delegation to Russia, as minister to France, and as a U.S. senator from Alabama. Former president Andrew Jackson dubbed the lifelong bachelor "little Miss Nancy" after King took fellow politician James Buchanan as a roommate — an arrangement that lasted over twenty years. Speculation that they were more than roommates began then, and still continues.

After Buchanan lost the presidential nomination in 1852 to Franklin Pierce, party bosses offered the vice presidential spot to King, hoping to placate Buchanan supporters. The Pierce-King ticket won the election but King's victory was short-lived. In Cuba seeking relief from tuberculosis, he died only twenty-nine days after taking office. *(See also James Buchanan.)*

KITCHENER, HORATIO HERBERT. (June 24, 1850–June 5, 1916), *British general.* In 1892 Horatio Herbert Kitchener became commander-in-chief of the British army in Egypt, and four years later he became a major-general. His role in the Boer War, in which he ruth-  lessly destroyed Boer farms and herded 120,000 women and children into concentration camps, secured his reputation as England's greatest military hero since Wellington. After serving as field marshal and war secretary, Kitchener was killed in 1916 while on a secret mission to Russia, when his ship struck a mine.

Kitchener had a reputation as both a woman-hater and an active homosexual. His most notable homosexual liaison was with his military secretary, an affair that lasted many years.

KOPAY, DAVID. (June 28, 1942–), *U.S. athlete.* David Kopay seemed to have everything going for him. He was a professional athlete — intelligent, charming, and handsome. Then, in December of 1975, he publicly announced that he was gay, sending shock waves through the world of sports.

Raised in a devoutly Catholic household, Kopay entered a junior seminary that prepared boys for the priesthood. He left after eighteen months, and in 1961 he entered the University of Washington on a football scholarship.  Following a successful college football career, he signed on as a professional with the San Francisco Forty-Niners. Over the next decade, he played for a number of teams, including the Detroit Lions, the Washington Redskins, and the Green Bay Packers.

After a serious depression, Kopay began psychotherapy. His doctor convinced him to get married, but the marriage eventually ended in divorce. In 1975, after ten years as a professional football player, Kopay ended his athletic career and came out in a series on homosexuality that appeared in the *Washington Star*. He elaborated on it in his autobiography, *The David Kopay Story.*

KRUPP, FRIEDRICH ALFRED. (1854–1902), *German industrialist.* Krupp's father was "the cannon king," who made a fortune through innovative new uses of cast steel. Friedrich Alfred Krupp expanded his father's empire, and became a major supplier of ships for the expanding German navy.

Krupp invested part of his fortune in building an elaborate pleasure palace on the island of Capri, where he entertained Italian youths. When his wife learned what was going on, she went straight to the Kaiser — who promptly had her committed to an insane asylum. The Krupp empire was too valuable to be destroyed by such stories. Eventually, however, the truth came out, and Krupp committed suicide.

KUZMIN, MIKHAIL. (1875–1936), *Russian poet.* The first noted Russian author to make homosexuality a central theme in his work, Kuzmin scandalized the literary high circles of prerevolutionary Russia with an explicitly homoerotic autobiographical novel, *Wings* (published in 1906), and with a number of sonnets and poems that explored homosexual desire. Not long after the Revolution, the poet fell into disfavor with the ruling Stalinist regime. Kuzmin's lover was executed during a purge in the 1930s, and Kuzmin himself was apparently marked for deportation to a labor camp just before he died in Leningrad in 1936.

LAUGHTON, CHARLES. (Jul. 1, 1899–Dec. 15, 1962), *British actor*. A critically acclaimed character actor, Laughton gave memorable performances in more than fifty motion pictures, including *Mutiny on the Bounty, The Private Life of Henry VIII* (for which he won an Oscar), and *Witness for the Prosecution*. He married actress Elsa Lanchester in 1929. Two years later he revealed to her that he was homosexual but they remained married, as close friends, for over three decades.

Laughton's homosexuality is discussed at length in Charles Higham's biography of the actor and in Elsa Lanchester's own memoir, *Charles Laughton and I*.

LAWRENCE, T.E. (LAWRENCE OF ARABIA). (Aug. 15, 1888–May 19, 1935), *British soldier*. Lawrence was one of the most colorful figures to emerge from World War I. His lifelong interest in Arabia began in his youth; he studied archaeology and the Near East at Oxford. When the war broke out, the British government sent him to Cairo, where he worked first in the map department, then in military intelligence.

Lawrence was instrumental in the efforts to incite an Arab revolution against the Turks. During a raid he was captured by the Turks, who tortured and raped him in a well-publicized incident at Deraa. The event had a special significance for Lawrence who realized, to his horror, that on a deep level he had *enjoyed* the torture.

Lowell Thomas, an American journalist looking for a scoop, saw it in Lawrence. With his subject's ready cooperation, Thomas made the Englishman into a military hero — and the focus of a popular newspaper series. Lawrence's memoirs, *The Seven Pillars of Wisdom,* were published in 1926.

There is general agreement that Lawrence was a repressed homosexual. In his book, he writes about Arab homosexuality as "pure" and "clean" — and even "sexless." There is no agreement as to whether he was ever sexually involved with anyone, though he certainly had passionate feelings for the handsome Arab youth Dahoum. Dahoum, whom Lawrence called "Sheik Ahmed," died during the war, and Lawrence dedicated *The Seven Pillars of Wisdom* "to S.A."

LEONARDO DA VINCI. (Apr. 15, 1452–May 2, 1519), *Italian renaissance man*. Often considered the greatest genius of all time, Leonardo da Vinci is best remembered for such paintings as the *Mona Lisa* and  *The Last Supper*. But his genius went far beyond that. He earned a reputation in his own life as an architect and engineer, and his notebooks show that he was experimenting with scientific ideas far ahead of his time, including a plan for a helicopter. His other interests included anatomy, meteorology, and mathematics.

At twenty-four, Da Vinci and four other Florentines were arrested for sodomy with a seventeen-year-old boy, and he was imprisoned for two months. He left Florence for the more liberal climate of Milan, where he acquired an apprentice, Andrea Salaino, a graceful and curly-haired youth whom he described as "a thieving, lying glutton"; nonetheless, they were inseparable for twenty-five years. Salaino was eventually succeeded by Francesco Melzi, who remained with Leonardo until Leonardo's death and inherited many of his drawings and writings.

LEWIS, EDMONIA. (1844?–1911?), *U.S. artist.* Lewis, who was born to a Chippewa mother and an African father, entered Oberlin College in 1859, where she was accused of poisoning two white female boarders. Although the charges were dismissed, Lewis was beaten by a group of white vigilantes and retreated to Boston. She studied clay modeling with Edward Brackett, and soon opened her own studio. Her sculpting style challenged the traditional conception of black art as passive and jolly, and she turned to such prominent black subjects as Col. Robert Gould Shaw. Lewis soon employed twenty workers in her studio.

Lewis liked to dress in men's clothes and fell in with a group of lesbian artists — Harriet Hosmer, Anne Whitney, and Emma Stebbins. Hosmer greatly influenced Lewis's work, and Lewis's involvement with the liberated, free-thinking group helped shape her own ambitions. Lewis sank into obscurity, and little is known of her later life.

LEYENDECKER, J.C. (Mar. 23, 1874–Jul. 25, 1951), *U.S. artist.* Along with Norman Rockwell, J.C. Leyendecker was one of the country's leading commercial artists. His work often graced the cover of the *Saturday Evening Post,* and he is especially remembered for creating the original Arrow Collar Man, a ubiquitous symbol of manhood in the early decades of the century.

The model for the Arrow shirt man, it was later revealed, was Charles Beach; he and Leyendecker were lovers for half a century.

LIBERACE, WLADZIU VALENTINO. (May 16, 1919–Feb. 4, 1987), *U.S. showman.* Both fans and critics would agree that Liberace was a reasonably talented pianist who put showmanship ahead of music. His abbreviated versions of musical classics, combined with his extravagant presentations and glittery costumes, won him legions of fans. Liberace was considerably less popular with critics; to one he retorted, "What you said hurt me very much. I cried all the way to the bank."

Many of Liberace's fans were middle-aged women, and he walked a fine line between being a flamboyant and sometimes even effeminate showman, while at the same time keeping his homosexuality a secret. In the 1950s, at the height of his fame, he successfully sued a London tabloid that suggested he was gay. Years later, when a young man sued him for palimony, he could no longer keep the rumors at bay. But right up until his death from AIDS in 1987, Liberace and his family tried to cover up his gayness.

In the end, the truth didn't hurt his celebritydom. At the auction of his estate in 1988, nearly all of Liberace's possessions brought far more than their estimated value, as eager fans bid for souvenirs. His Nevada driver's license, expected to bring under $100, commanded a price of $4250.

LIEBMAN, MARVIN. (July 21, 1923–), *U.S. politician.* In 1990, Marvin Liebman wrote a coming-out letter to a friend; that friend happened to be arch-conservative William F. Buckley, Jr., and the letter was published in Buckley's *National Review.* Liebman caused quite a controversy, because for the past thirty-five years he has worked as a staunchly conservative Republican, helping Ronald Reagan, Barry Goldwater, and Buckley himself with their careers. Liebman came out to show his colleagues that gay people did indeed exist among their own ranks, and to show gay groups that gay Republicans are necessary to the success of the rights movement.

In his book *Coming Out Conservative,* he defined conservatism as placing the rights of the individual over those of the state, thus keeping the government out of the bedroom. By his definition, the religious right has no claim to the conservative Republican party. Liebman expressed hopes that his book and his public coming out would make the public aware that both conservatives and gays are important elements of society.

LOCKE, ALAIN. (Sept. 13, 1886–June 9, 1954), *U.S. writer.* Born into one of Philadelphia's elite families, Alain Locke concluded an outstanding academic career by becoming the first black American Rhodes scholar. He became a professor of philosophy at Howard University in Washington, D.C., where he remained on the faculty

for forty years. With his writings and criticism, he became a leader and chief interpreter of the Harlem Renaissance.

Locke also used his connections to secure patronage for young, male writers he felt deserved such assistance — often after they had shown their appreciation in the bedroom. Writers Countee Cullen and Langston Hughes were rewarded in this way. Others in Locke's circle of gay associates were black writers Richard Bruce Nugent and Claude McKay, and white literary critic Carl Van Vechten.

Locke was less generous to women writers, regardless of their talent. He was said to have dismissed women students on the first day of his class with an automatic "C." Even writer Zora Neale Hurston, whom Locke liked and recommended, described him as "a malicious, spiteful little snot."

LORCA, FEDERICO GARCIA. *See Garcia Lorca, Federico*

LORDE, AUDRE. (Feb. 18, 1934–Nov. 17, 1992), *U.S. writer.* One of the most inspiring contemporary writers of both poetry and prose, Audre Lorde grew up poor in Harlem. Her work is both deeply personal and intensely political, always incorporating her radical view of the world. Far from adopting an "art for art's sake" stance, her poetry was always intimately connected to real-life experience, which often included her lesbianism. In *The Cancer Journals* (1980), Lorde combined a personal account of her battle with breast cancer with an angry political look at her treatment, as an African-American lesbian, by the medical establishment. In *Zami: A New Spelling of My Name,* which she described as a biomythography, one passage in her dedication reads, "To the first woman I ever courted and left. She taught me that women who want without needing are expensive and sometimes wasteful, but women who need without wanting are dangerous — they suck you in and pretend not to notice."

LOUIS XIII. (Sept. 27, 1601–May 14, 1643), *French king.* Backward, reserved, and withdrawn, King Louis XIII nevertheless enjoyed a triumphant reign largely due to the efforts of master politician Cardinal Richelieu. One of Louis's early romantic attachments was with Baradas, a beautiful but simple-minded page, who was made First Gentleman of the Chamber. But Baradas, who engaged in affairs with other nobles, eventually found himself in the king's disfavor and was replaced.

In about 1637, for reasons that remain obscure, Richelieu introduced Louis to the handsome young Marquis de Cinq-Mars. Some historians believe Richelieu arranged, with Louis's permission, to have Cinq-Mars impregnate the king's long-neglected wife, Queen Anne, so as to produce an heir to the throne. For several years, Cinq-Mars was the king's favorite, but in 1641, angry that Richelieu would not give him an important military post, Cinq-Mars entered into a conspiracy with Louis's renegade brother, the duke of Or-

leans. Faced with proof of this treachery, Louis condemned his lover to death. The episode left Louis heartbroken, and less than a year later, the collapse of his reign was complete with the deaths of both Richelieu and Louis.

LOWELL, AMY. (Feb. 9, 1874–May 12, 1925), *U.S. poet.* Born to a prominent New England family, Amy Lowell did little in her early adulthood to set herself apart from other well-off Boston women of her time. In 1912, however, two events radically changed Lowell's life: she discovered poetry, and she got to know Ada Dwyer Russell. Russell was a professional actress who provided the emotional support Lowell needed to write — and who would inspire many of Lowell's love poems.

From the time she began to write, Lowell's life was filled with constant activity. She gave frequent speaking engagements in Europe and the United States and was involved in Ezra Pound's Imagist movement. She exuded an independence and defiance of the norm that her contemporaries found unnerving, right down to her love of a good cigar.

Lowell and Ada Russell lived together from 1914 until Lowell's death in 1925; by then, Lowell was among the best known and most controversial figures in American poetry. She was awarded a posthumous Pulitzer Prize for her collection *What's O'Clock.*

LUDLAM, CHARLES. (Apr. 12, 1943–May 20, 1987), *U.S. theater producer.* In 1967 Charles Ludlam was fired from the Playhouse of the Ridiculous; most of his fellow company members left with him, and they founded the Ridiculous Theatrical Company, with Ludlam presiding as the writer, producer, director, actor, designer, and teacher. Ludlam reigned at his company for twenty years, slowly creeping toward mainstream popularity with over thirty increasingly successful plays — among them, *When Queens Collide, Whores of Babylon, Camille, Galas, Salammbo, Bluebeard,* and, his most popular, *The Mystery of Irma Vep.*

Ludlam's plays are eclectic mixes of operatic camp, classical drama, and a gay worldview that he never compromised for his audience. Many of the plays have all-male casts, with female roles performed by men in drag. Ludlam enjoyed his growing audience but resisted the mainstream; in the mid-eighties, as AIDS awareness heightened and after the *New York Times* praised *Irma Vep,* Ludlam responded with the lurid sexuality of *Salammbo,* which made critics and audiences squirm. His last play, *Whodini, A Piece of Pure Escapism,* was unfinished when Ludlam died from AIDS-related pneumonia.

LUDWIG II. (Aug. 25, 1845–June 13, 1886), *Bavarian king.* Ludwig is best known for his insanity and his fairy-tale castles, which nearly bankrupted the Bavarian state. Ludwig was obsessed, moreover, with the work of Richard Wagner; in addition to backing extravagant productions of Wagner's works, he paid the composer's debts and provided him with a large subsidy. He showed no interest in women and carried on affairs with a succession of men, showing a marked preference for muscular young farmers.

Ludwig's behavior grew increasingly eccentric and led him to neglect his duties as king. Eventually, he was forced to abdicate. A few days later, Ludwig persuaded his doctor to accompany him for a walk on the shore of Starnberger Lake. Within hours, the drowned bodies of the two men were found. The exact circumstances of their deaths were never determined.

MABLEY, JACKIE "MOMS." (1897–May 23, 1975), *U.S. comedian.* Born to a poor black North Carolina family, Moms Mabley ran away from home at the age of fourteen. She worked her way into show business, performing at Harlem's legendary Cotton Club and the Apollo Theater in the twenties and thirties. Onstage, she made fun of the war between the sexes; offstage, she seems to have been comfortable with her identity as a lesbian.

Only much later did Mabley reach a mass audience. In 1960, *Moms Mabley at the U.N.* sold over a million albums, and she appeared at Carnegie Hall in 1962. She made her first television appearance in 1967, and toward the end of her life, she appeared with Merv Griffin, Bill Cosby, and Johnny Carson.

MACKAY, JOHN HENRY. (1864–1933), *German writer.* Mackay was born in Scotland, but was only nineteen months old when his Scottish father died; his German mother returned with him to Germany, where he grew up. Having spent a year in 1887–1888 among political exiles in London, Mackay described his experience in *Die Anarchisten* (*The Anarchists*, 1891); the book made him famous overnight and was translated into eight languages. He also wrote lyric poetry (some set to music by Richard Strauss and others), early naturalist prose, and one of the first literary sports novels, *Der Schwimmer* (*The Swimmer*, 1901).

In the following years little was heard of Mackay, for under the pseudonym Sagitta he was waging a fight for the recognition of man/boy love. His struggle was crushed by the German state in 1909 when his Sagitta writings were declared "immoral" and ordered destroyed. He later printed his "Books of the Nameless Love," however and sold them underground. They include the autobiographical novel *Fenny Skaller*, which a friend called his "confessions of life and love." A final novel, *Der Puppenjunge* (*The Hustler*), appeared in 1926.

During his lifetime Mackay was best known as the leading German exponent of individualist anarchism. He never publicly revealed that he was also Sagitta, but he specified in his will that his true name was to appear on any posthumous publications.

MANN, THOMAS. (June 6, 1875– Aug. 12, 1955), *German novelist.* Widely acclaimed as the greatest German novelist of the twentieth century, Mann won the Nobel Prize for Literature in 1929 for his early novels *Buddenbrooks, Death in Venice,* and *The Magic Mountain,* the second and third of which contain homosexual themes.

With the outbreak of World War I, Mann espoused the German war effort and defended German authoritarianism and militarism. After the establishment of the Weimar Republic, however, his views changed drastically. He openly opposed the Nazis and urged a common front of the cultured bourgeoisie and the Socialist working class to oppose the Nazis. When Hitler became chancellor in 1933, Mann was on holiday in Switzerland and was warned by his son and daughter not to return to Germany. He spent much of the rest of his life in the United States, becoming a citizen in 1944. His correspondence reveals affairs with several young men.

Mann's eldest son, Klaus Mann (1906–1949), was openly homosexual and portrayed gay characters in several of his works. His daughter Erika, in a marriage of mutual convenience, escaped Nazi Germany by wedding gay poet W.H. Auden.

MAPPLETHORPE, ROBERT. (Nov. 4, 1946–Mar. 9, 1989), *U.S. artist.* Robert Mapplethorpe studied in Pratt Institute in Brooklyn from 1963 to 1970, then became a filmmaker, sculptor, and finally a photographer. His subject matter ranged from flowers to nudes to S/M; he was especially interested in portraying black males. Mapplethorpe was diagnosed with AIDS in September 1986, and his photographic self-portraits provide a vivid chronicle of the disease's toll. His greatest fame came only after his death, when an exhibit of his artwork was cancelled by Washington's Corcoran Gallery because of its explicit homoerotic content.

MARLOWE, CHRISTOPHER. (Baptized Feb. 26, 1564–May 30, 1593), *English dramatist and poet.* Marlowe is said to have been the originator of truly effective English blank verse, and his influence appears in many Shakespearean works. He himself wrote several successful dramatic pieces, including *Edward II* with its explicitly homosexual theme, and *Dr. Faustus.*

Marlowe is famous for his homosexual tastes as well as his unrestrained lifestyle, both summarized by his epigram that "All they that love not tobacco and boys are fools." He was stabbed to death by a drinking companion, apparently in a quarrel over a boy.

MAUGHAM, W. SOMERSET. (Jan. 25, 1874–Dec. 16, 1965), *British writer.* Somerset Maugham's work is characterized by a clear, straightforward style that presents keen psychological analyses of people living in cosmopolitan settings. He was a prolific writer, best known for four novels: *Of Human Bondage, The Moon and Sixpence, Cakes and Ale,* and *The Razor's Edge.* The cynical Maugham held to a resigned atheism and general skepticism regard-ing the extent of humanity's innate goodness and intelligence. Although he was involved sexually with both women and men at various times, Maugham summed up his situation late in life: "I was a quarter normal and three-quarters queer, but I tried to persuade myself it was the other way 'round. That was my greatest mistake."

Maugham's inclinations were known to his friends during much of his life. On one occasion, a friend encouraged him to stay longer at a party. Maugham, who believed that early nights would keep him young, declined, saying, "I want to keep my youth." The friend retorted, "Then why didn't you bring him with you? I should be delighted to meet him."

Maugham's nephew Robin Maugham (1916–1981) was openly gay. His book *The Servant* and his memoirs of his uncle are still read occasionally, but whatever talents he had were mostly dissipated in a lifelong bout with alcoholism.

McDONALD, RONALD (? –), *Hamburger clown.* No, not really. But the man behind the clown smile, Bob Brandon, came out in 1977. McDonald's threatened legal action if he ever put on the costume again, or suggested that Ronald was gay. Speculation about Ronald himself will just have to continue.

McKINNEY, STEWART B. (Jan. 30, 1931–May 7, 1987), *U.S. congressman.* As a liberal Republican from Connecticut, Stewart McKinney was a supporter of gay civil rights and a strong advocate for the poor — shortly before his death, he spent a cold night demonstrating on behalf of Washington's homeless.

Until he died from AIDS, however, few people knew that McKinney was gay. He had a wife in Connecticut, but maintained a second home in Washington. Next door, in an apparently separate dwelling that actually had an inside doorway to McKinney's home, lived his lover, Arnold R. Denson.

After McKinney's death, his doctor suggested that the congressman had contracted AIDS from a blood transfusion, thus highlighting an ethical question for the medical community: Is a doctor justified in implying that someone was infected with AIDS from a transfusion, thus fueling public fears about the blood supply, when gay sex was the probable route of infection?

McKUEN, ROD. (Apr. 29, 1933–), *U.S. poet.* Called by the *New York Times* "America's only native *chansonnier,*" Rod McKuen has produced a vast body of work. His poems are noted for the simplicity of their images and style and by their accessibility. Although McKuen acknowledges having had affairs with men as well as with women, he hesitates to call himself gay. He asks, "I have had sex with men; does that make me gay? I have a son who's fifteen; does that make me bi?"

MEAD, MARGARET. (Dec. 16, 1901–Nov. 15, 1978), *U.S. anthropologist.* Margaret Mead was born in Philadelphia in an academic and woman-oriented household. One of the closest relationships of her life began when she was a student at Barnard College — with her instructor, Ruth Fulton Benedict. Benedict's enthusiasm for anthropology rubbed off on Mead. After the publication of her famous *Coming of Age in Samoa,* Mead became permanently linked with the study of guilt-free sex and love.

One of Mead's closest friends, describing Mead's three marriages and involvements with women, said that she "fell in love with women's souls and men's bodies. She was spiritually homosexual, psychologically bisexual, and physically heterosexual." Mead herself, when asked what she thought of homosexuals, replied, "They make the best companions in the world."

MELVILLE, HERMAN. (Aug. 1, 1819–Sept. 28, 1891), *U.S. novelist.* The creator of such American classics as *Moby Dick, Billy Budd,* and *White-Jacket,* Herman Melville was well versed in the technical aspects of writing. Unlike American novelists before him, he made extensive use of symbolism, and greatly influenced literary trends to follow.

Although he married and fathered children, his closest relationship seems to have been with fellow writer Nathaniel Hawthorne. The two men met in 1850 in Pittsfield, Massachusetts, and quickly became friends. Melville wrote that "this Hawthorne has dropped germinous seeds into my soul. He expands and deepens ... and further, shoots his strong New England roots into the hot soil of my Southern soul."

MENOTTI, GIAN CARLO. *See Samuel Barber.*

MEW, CHARLOTTE. (Nov. 15, 1869–Mar. 24, 1928), *British poet.* Mew is often ranked as one of the top British poets of the twentieth century. Although her lesbianism was discussed as early as 1956, in Jeannette Foster's *Sex Variant Women in Literature,* it received little attention until recently. Penelope Fitzgerald discusses Mew's unrequited love affairs in her biography *Charlotte Mew and Her Friends.*

MICHELANGELO BUONARROTI. (Mar. 6, 1475–Feb. 18, 1564), *Italian artist.* The painter of the Sistine Chapel ceiling, and creator of such timeless pieces of homoerotica as the statue *David,* Michelangelo possessed a complex and often difficult personality. His relationships with several of his male models, including the beautiful young Gherardo Perini, caused much gossip at the

time. In his later years, Michelangelo added poetry to his list of achievements, and wrote several sonnets to the young aristocrat Tommasso Cavalieri, who is believed to have been his great love.

Toward the end of Michelangelo's life, the liberal cultural climate of the Renaissance began to change, and Pope Paul IV ordered loincloths painted on the male nudes of *The Last Judgment.* Worse, following his death, Michelangelo's poems and sonnets were altered to suggest that they were addressed to women. Not until 1960 were the original texts restored and published.

MILK, HARVEY. (May 22, 1930–Nov. 27, 1978), *U.S. politician.* Harvey Milk grew up on Long Island, an average child and teenager in almost every respect. After serving in the Navy, he returned to Long Island, where he taught high school and met Joe Campbell. The two settled into a marriage-type relationship.

As a young adult, Milk was a political conservative; he worked hard and spent his free time creating a stable home life. But then he moved to San Francisco and his conservatism gradually gave way to an ardent liberalism. He went to anti-war demonstrations and associated with flower children.

In 1977, after several unsuccessful campaigns for public office, Milk was elected to the San Francisco Board of Supervisors. When a state senator sponsored an electoral initiative to ban gay people from teaching, Harvey Milk was at the forefront of the opposition. A few weeks after that initiative was defeated, both Harvey Milk and Mayor George Moscone were shot and killed by former city supervisor Dan White, a rabid opponent of gay rights. A jury from which gay people were excluded convicted White only of manslaughter. The leniency of the sentence enraged the gay community, and a riot followed in which 120 people were injured. White later committed suicide.

MILLAY, EDNA ST. VINCENT. (Feb. 22, 1892–Oct. 19, 1950), *U.S. poet.* In 1912, with the publication of her poem "Renascence," twenty-

year-old Millay became an overnight literary celebrity. Eleven years later, she received a Pulitzer Prize — the first woman ever to get the prestigious award. During the 1920s, her poetry was seen as the embodiment of romantic rebellion and bravado, as illustrated by the famous line "My candle burns at both ends," from her 1920 work *A Few Figs from Thistles.* Today, she is regarded as one of the greatest love poets of the English language.

Throughout her life, Millay — who was known to friends as "Vincent" — remained unabashed about her bisexuality. She once wrote, "For surely, one must be either undiscerning, or frightened, to love only one person, when the world is so full of gracious and noble spirits."

MILLER, MERLE. (May 17, 1919–Jun. 10, 1986), *U.S. writer.* Merle Miller was among the first prominent Americans to come out in the early days of the modern gay movement. In 1972 he announced his homosexuality in a *New York Times Magazine* essay, then went further in his book *On Being Different: What It Means to be a Homosexual.*

Miller's best-known books were portraits of recent presidents: *Plain Speaking* was based on several years of interviews with Harry Truman, and *Lyndon: An Oral Biography,* portrayed the life of Lyndon Johnson. Miller wrote over a dozen books in all, including a gay novel titled *What Happened.* When he died at the age of sixty-seven, he was survived by his companion of twenty-two years, David Elliott.

MISHIMA, YUKIO. (Jan. 14, 1925–Nov. 25, 1970), *Japanese writer.* Virtually all of Mishima's many works reveal his preoccupation with the conflict between Westernization and traditional Japanese values. Yet although he raged continually against Japan's imitation of the West, he himself maintained an essentially Western lifestyle and possessed a wide knowledge of Western culture.

In his first novel, *Confessions of a Mask,* the bisexual Mishima intro-

duced the theme of homosexuality that recurs throughout his work. The novel met with both critical and commercial success, and Mishima devoted his full energies to writing.

On November 25, 1970, Mishima and four companions seized control of the commanding general's office at the military headquarters in downtown Tokyo. He gave a ten-minute speech in which he attacked the weakness of Japan's postwar constitution; then, in a ritual suicide, Mishima disemboweled himself before the eyes of his audience and was decapitated by a youthful disciple — who promptly followed suit. Mishima's handsome partner in this double-suicide was also his lover.

MOLIERE. (Jan. 15, 1622–Feb 17, 1673), *French dramatist.* Moliere was born in Paris, the son of an upholsterer to the king. He received a good education, and, after studying law for a short time, pursued a dramatic career. He joined the Bejard family troupe and toured the provinces with them. The success of Moliere's comedies established him as one of the most popular of French playwrights, a reputation that still endures.

Throughout his life, Moliere was surrounded by intrigue and controversy regarding both his writings and his personal life. There was much speculation that his wife was actually his own daughter, and his long-standing relationship with the young actor Michel Baron led to rumors of another kind. This relationship eventually resulted in the estrangement of Moliere from his wife; he and Baron then lived together from 1670 until Moliere's death in 1673.

NAVRATILOVA, MARTINA. (Oct. 18, 1956–), *Czech-born U.S. athlete.* Navratilova was already a tennis champion in her homeland of Czechoslovakia when, as a teenager, she came to the U.S. in 1973. Two years later, she defected to the U.S.

In 1978, lesbian novelist Rita Mae Brown was writing a novel with a Czech character. She arranged to meet Navratilova, and soon they were in love. "She was the first person I ever met that I could really talk to," recalled Navratilova. But the relationship was sensationalized by the media, and plagued by the different interests of the two women. In 1981, it came to a well-publicized end, and Navratilova explained that "I guess I'm bi. I like both. I just have a better time with women, straight or gay." She also voiced concern that if she continued talking about her sexuality, Avon Products might stop sponsoring women's tennis, and her application for U.S. citizenship could run into trouble.

As a result of publicity about her liaison with Brown, Navratilova was forced to resign as head of the Women's Tennis Association. Her replacement was Billie Jean King. *(See also Billie Jean King.)*

NICOLSON, HAROLD. *See Vita Sackville-West.*

NIGHTINGALE, FLORENCE. (May 12, 1820–Aug. 13, 1910), *British nurse.* Called the "Lady of the Lamp" for her tireless work among sick and wounded British soldiers, Florence Nightingale was not only responsible for the reform of conditions in military hospitals, but was also the founder of trained nursing as a profession. After serving in Turkey during the Crimean War, she returned to England where she set herself to the tasks of improving conditions for British soldiers and of training nurses for the profession. From 1857 to her death, she  lived as an invalid, mainly in London, and from there carried on an enormous correspondence and received countless visitors. In 1907, the king conferred on her the Order of Merit, making her the first woman thus honored.

Though Nightingale never married and lived in many ways a highly unconventional lifestyle for a woman of her time, her notions of sexual morality seemed conventionally Victorian. Nevertheless, late in life she wrote, "I have lived and slept in the same bed with English countesses and Prussian farm women ... no woman has excited passions among women more than I have."

NIJINSKY, VASLAV. (Mar. 12, 1890–Apr. 8, 1950), *Russian dancer.* The child of Polish dancers, Nijinsky was already considered a phenomenon at the Imperial Ballet School when he met the great impresario, Sergei Diaghilev. Backward and uneducated, Nijinsky at first let his life and his career be formed by Diaghilev's strong personality; as Diaghilev's lover and protégé, Nijinsky became one of the greatest dancers of the century.

For several years, the team of Diaghilev and Nijinsky produced many spectacular shows. Their success was amplified on some occasions, and threatened at other times, by Nijinsky's delight in adding unexpected sexual overtones to his performances, either in the choreography or in the costumes.

By the time he was twenty-three, Nijinsky was feeling suffocated by the highly possessive and misogynous personality of Diaghilev, who forbade his male dancers to associate with women. Separated from Diaghilev while on a South American tour, Nijinsky met and fell in love with Romola Markus, a Hungarian dancer, and they married. When news of this reached Diaghilev, he promptly fired Nijinsky. The dancer continued to perform for several years, but by 1920 both his mental and physical health were in decay. He spent most of his last thirty years in institutions for the insane.

NOVARRO, RAMON. (Feb. 6, 1899–Oct. 31, 1968), *Mexican-born American actor.* Descended from conquistadores and Aztec nobility, Novarro arrived in Hollywood at the age of seventeen with ten dollars in his pocket, and a determination to succeed in show business. He appeared in over a hundred films by 1922, then got his big break when a producer decided to push him as a rival to Rudolph Valentino. Novarro's biggest film was the 1926 silent version of *Ben Hur*. After Rudolph Valentino's death, Novarro carried on the role of the Latin lover.

With the end of the silent film era, the career of Novarro went downhill. He remained a well-liked member of the film community, however, known for his generosity and kindness. In his later life, he performed occasional bit parts on TV.

On October 31, 1968, Novarro's secretary found Novarro's nude body, battered, tied, and bloody, on his bed. Two brothers, ages seventeen and twenty-two, were arrested for the murder; they apparently had been hired by Novarro as hustlers, and beat him to death while trying to learn where he hid $5000 they believed he had.

O'KEEFFE, GEORGIA. (Nov. 15, 1887–Mar. 6, 1986), *U.S. artist.* Georgia O'Keeffe and her husband, the photographer and arts patron Alfred Stieglitz, were central figures in American art in the early part of the century. Her famous landscapes and giant floral shapes — which were easily transferred to posters and prints — enjoyed a resurgence of popularity in the 1970s. O'Keeffe, who outlived her older husband by forty years, enjoyed the business of selling her art. She frequented many lesbian and bisexual circles of wealthy society women and art collectors.

O'Keeffe was bisexual. Before Stieglitz's death, both he and O'Keeffe had many affairs, sometimes with the same women. One such woman was Rebecca Strand, a married woman whose relationship with O'Keeffe outlasted both their marriages. O'Keeffe later took up with Maria Chabot, who became her housekeeper, personal assistant, and house-builder, as well as lover. Benita Eisler, in her biography of O'Keeffe and Stieglitz, quoted Chabot as saying, "I was the second of O'Keeffe's slaves. Rebecca Strand was the first."

OLIVIER, Sir LAURENCE. (May 22, 1907–July 11, 1989), *British actor.* Olivier's legendary achievements on stage and in film spanned decades and left their mark on the art of acting. Olivier rejected method acting, instead basing his characters on details from real life, and on the characters' own experiences. He revolutionized Shakespearean acting by changing the traditional enunciation of the text, and bringing a psychological background to the characters. His film versions of *Hamlet, Henry V, Richard III, Othello,* and *King Lear* set new standards for classical acting and film interpretation.

Olivier was married three times, to Jill Esmond (a lesbian), Vivien Leigh, and Joan Plowright; all three ended in divorce. After his death, it became known that the actor also had a ten-year love affair with comedian Danny Kaye. One story from their relationship had Olivier passing through customs in a New York airport, en route to Los Angeles. A customs clerk pulled Olivier into a nearby cubicle and strip-searched the confused actor in minute detail. After Olivier had suffered through these indignities, the clerk stood back, pulled off a rubber mask, and revealed that he was Danny Kaye. The two, who were lovers at the time, spent the night in a New York hotel before proceeding on to L.A. the next morning.

ORTON, JOE. (Jan 1, 1933–Aug. 9, 1967), *British playwright.* Orton rocketed to fame in 1964 with his first play, *Entertaining Mr. Sloane,* a brilliant black comedy that crystallized Orton's own belief that people "are profoundly bad, but irresistibly funny." He followed it in 1965 with another success, *Loot,* which satirized police corruption, the Church of England, and English notions of justice.

Orton was supported in his work by his lover Kenneth Halliwell; they had been lovers since 1951, when Orton was eighteen. Orton acknowledged his lover's help privately, but not publicly. In 1967, years of frustration and jealousy exploded: Halliwell drove a hammer into Orton's skull, then immediately killed himself. Orton's career had just reached its peak.

PARADZHANOV, SERGEI. (Mar. 18, 1924–1990), *Russian film director.* Paradzhanov won sixteen international prizes for his 1965 film, *Shadows of Forgotten Ancestors.* But in 1974 he was convicted of homosexuality and spent six years in a prison labor camp. His incarceration was reported with approval in the U.S. by the ultraconservative *Manchester Union-Leader.* "This is one of the reasons why the Soviet Union is presently stronger than the United States. The Soviets understand that permissiveness in regards to homosexuality has always resulted in the downfall of a nation," said the paper in a 1974 editorial, in what was probably their first and only pro-Soviet editorial.

PASOLINI, PIER PAOLO. (Mar. 5, 1922–Nov. 2, 1975), *Italian film di-*

rector. Among the most controversial of modern-day directors, Pasolini frequently clashed with government and church authorities over his graphic portrayals of sex and violence in such films as *The Canterbury Tales, The Decameron,* and *Salo — The 120 Days of Sodom.* He was an avowed Marxist with a deep but highly mystical belief in Christianity, who also generated storms of controversy with his articles espousing unorthodox political and religious reforms.

Even in the 1950s, Pasolini depicted homosexuality in his film scripts, and as a young director he made no effort to conceal his gayness. After producing his own version of *Oedipus Rex,* he was asked at a press conference, "Signor Pasolini, did *you* ever want to sleep with your mother?" He thought, then replied, "No ... but perhaps sometimes with my brother."

In 1975, Pasolini was murdered by a seventeen-year-old hustler known as Pino the Frog, who bludgeoned the director with a nail-encrusted board, then ran over him with a sports car. The boy later claimed that Pasolini had picked him up, driven him to a vacant lot, and tried to seduce him.

PAUL, Saint. Episcopal bishop John Spong suggested in his 1991 book, *Rescuing the Bible from Fundamentalism,* that St. Paul was a "self-loathing and repressed gay male." Paul's "self-judging rhetoric, his negative feeling toward his own body," closely resemble the feelings of closeted gay men today, wrote Spong, who himself is heterosexual but had taken controversial pro-gay positions in the past. Other biblical scholars disagree with these conclusions, and accurate historical information about the apostle is so scarce that Spong's conjecture will remain just that.

PEARS, Lord PETER. (Jun. 22, 1910–Apr. 3, 1986), *British tenor.* Pears began his musical training at the age of five, later studied at Oxford, and in 1938 met composer Benjamin Britten, who was his lover for the next forty years. The 1945 premiere of Britten's opera *Peter Grimes,* in which Pears sang a leading role, brought world attention to both composer and tenor. Their successful personal and professional collaboration continued through the next three decades. When Britten died in 1976, it was said that Queen Elizabeth II, in a rare departure from custom, accorded Pears the same formal courtesies usually reserved for the surviving mate of a heterosexual marriage. Pears was knighted by the queen in 1977 and died ten years after Britten. *(See also Benjamin Britten.)*

PLATO. (427?–347 B.C.), *Athenian philosopher.* The most famous student of Socrates, Plato founded his own school, The Academy, where he taught philosophy and mathe-  matics. It became the first university in Europe, and provided a basis for Plato's vast influence through the ages.

As a youth, Plato was actively homosexual and had a number of male lovers. In the *Symposium,* to illustrate the highest kind of love,

Plato drew his examples solely from homosexual love.

POPES.

Leo X. (1475–1521). Became a patron of the arts.

John XII. (938–964). Elected to the papacy at age eighteen, he initiated a tradition of homosexual orgies in the palace.

Julius II. (1443–1513). Patron to Michelangelo, he was attacked by French and German officials as a sodomite.

Paul II. (1417–1471). He was so vain he tried to take the name Formosus, meaning "beautiful."

Sixtus IV. (1414–1482). Many handsome young men became cardinals during his reign.

Alexander VI. (1431–1503). Fathered a number of children, but believed to have engaged in homosexual liaisons as well.

(See also Julius III; Benedict IX.)

PORTER, COLE. (Jun. 9, 1892–Oct. 16, 1964), *U.S. songwriter.* Working with Ira Gershwin and Lorenz Hart, Cole Porter enriched American theater with such songs as "I've Got You under My Skin" and "I Get a Kick out of You," and Broadway shows that included *Kiss Me Kate, Anything Goes,* and *The Gay Divorcee.*

Other songs, like "My Heart Belongs to Daddy," got less air time. Porter married in 1919, but that only made him slightly more discreet about his interest in men. Throughout his life, he dropped hints to the public of this dual identity; in his 1929 song "I'm a Gigolo," a character confesses to having "just a dash" of lavender.

PROUST, MARCEL. (July 10, 1871–Nov. 18, 1922), *French writer.* Proust is best remembered today for his eleven-volume novel *Remembrance of Things Past,* an extensive and realistic study of French society. Born into a wealthy family, the young Proust made every attempt to associate himself with the fashionable and intellectual circles of Paris. At twenty-two, he met his first male lover, the Venezuelan composer Reynaldo Hahn. Their relationship lasted two years; Proust then began a series of short affairs with younger working-class men. He became increasingly reclusive as he grew older and, after the deaths of his parents, withdrew from society almost completely.

Although Proust did much to demystify homosexuality in Western literature, his own attitudes on the subject were ambivalent. He had relationships with a number of men, but he expressed negative ideas about homosexuality in his short piece, *A Race Accursed.* The major homosexual character in his novels, the Baron de Charlus, is a pathetic stereotype.

PRZHEVALSKY, NIKOLAI. (Apr. 6, 1839–Nov. 1, 1888), *Russian explorer.* Often called the Russian counterpart of David Livingston, Przhevalsky traveled through much of central and far eastern Asia and pioneered the mapping of Siberia  and eastern Russia. His explorations, and the plant and animal collections he brought back, opened up to European eyes a forbidding region previously shrouded in mystery.

Przhevalsky perplexed his academic acquaintances by his habit of choosing handsome, submissive, teenaged boys as assistants on his long journeys. He was also renowned for an isolated country estate, named Svoboda ("Freedom"), where only one woman was allowed to set foot: his beloved nanny, Olga. It was Olga who introduced Przhevalsky to the eighteen-year-old Pyotr Kozlov. The two were perfectly suited for one another both physically and temperamentally; when Przhevalsky died a few years later, Kozlov carried on his explorations.

PU YI. (Feb. 7, 1906–Oct. 17, 1967), *Chinese emperor.* The last imperial emperor of China, Pu Yi is portrayed in the film *The Last Emperor* and in a book of the same name by *Newsweek* correspondent Edward Behr. The film ignores the subject, but Behr is quite clear: "There is no doubt in my own mind that Pu Yi was bisexual," he wrote. Pu Yi's Japanese sister-in-law wrote in her diary that "the Emperor had an unnatural love for a pageboy. He was referred to as 'the male concubine.'"

RAINEY, MA. (Apr. 26, 1886–Dec. 22, 1939), *U.S. vocalist.* In 1904, a young black woman named Gertrude Pridgett married traveling comedian Pa Rainey, and thus a rising young vocalist got a new name. Pridgett had just begun adapting black spirituals and folk music into a new style of music that became known as "the blues"; she toured the South and Midwest from 1904 until she retired in 1935. At the

height of her success in the 1920s, she had recorded over ninety of her songs and was traveling with her own troupe, which at times included singer Bessie Smith.

Pa Rainey disappeared from her life at some point, but Ma didn't seem to miss him. She was arrested in 1925 at a party in Chicago with a group of young women — most of them undressed. It fell to Bessie Smith to bail her out the following morning. Later in her career, Ma wrote and recorded the openly lesbian "Prove It on Me Blues," that included the lines: "Went out last night with a crowd of my friends, They must've been women, 'cause I don't like no men." *(See also Bessie Smith.)*

RENAULT, MARY. (Sep. 4, 1905–Dec. 13, 1983), *French writer.* Renault — who was born Mary Challans — began her writing career while serving as a nurse during World War II. Though she was to become known for her historical novels, set in ancient Greece, her earliest books were all contemporary romances.

In the 1950s, Renault began exploring gay themes. Her first effort, which won her wide recognition, was *The Charioteer.* Written in 1953, it portrayed an injured young soldier in World War II as he realizes that he is homosexual. Many readers still believe this to be Renault's most eloquent work, but the honest treatment of a taboo subject didn't appeal to publishers, and not until six years after its original British publication did the book appear in the U.S.

Perhaps because of that reaction, Renault chose a new approach: she set her novels in ancient Greece, where same-sex relationships were less threatening to modern editors. With books such as *The Last of the Wine* and *The King Must Die,* she established her reputation as a pre-eminent writer of historical fiction.

One unanswered question about Renault's life is why she chose to portray gay male relationships so often, and lesbian ones so rarely. She wrote only one lesbian novel: *The Friendly Young Ladies,* published in the U.S. as *The Middle Mist.* Renault herself lived with a companion, Julie Mullard, for the last fifty years of her life.

RICHARD I (RICHARD THE LION-HEARTED). (Sep. 8, 1157–Apr. 6, 1199), *English king.* More warrior than ruler, Richard became king of England in 1189 but spent less than a year of his ten-year reign in England. Soon after taking the throne, he left his kingdom in the hands of his brother John and embarked on the Third Crusade, hoping to liberate Jerusalem from the Moslem forces of Saladin. Instead, he met Saladin and the two established an amicable relationship, signing a treaty that allowed access to Jerusalem by both sides.

On his return trip to England, Richard was taken prisoner as he passed through Austria. According to some accounts, it was the great love of his life, his troubadour Blondel, who helped free him. A legend that circulated in the thirteenth century recounts how Blondel traveled from one castle to another singing the first lines of a song that he and Richard had composed in happier times. When Richard sang back the answering refrain, Blondel knew with certainty that he had found his king.

RIMBAUD, ARTHUR. (Oct. 20, 1854–Nov. 10, 1891), *French poet.* Famous for his tempestuous affair with fellow poet Paul Verlaine, Rimbaud was a child prodigy, already showing brilliant intellectual gifts at age ten. By fifteen, he had produced some of his finest poems. In 1871 he wrote the great symbolist poem *Le bateau ivre* and sent it to Verlaine, who was  already an established poet. Verlaine invited Rimbaud to his home in Paris and, upon meeting him, immediately fell in love. The two men traveled in France, England, and Belgium, but Verlaine's alcoholism and Rimbaud's infidelity led to quarrels, which climaxed when Verlaine shot and seriously wounded Rimbaud.

At the age of nineteen, Rimbaud abandoned both poetry and France. He spent most of the rest of his life pursuing adventures in the East Indies, Cyprus, the Middle East, and Africa. He died in a Marseilles hospital after the amputation of one of his legs, but his poems lived on and have greatly influenced the development of modern poetry throughout the Western world. *(See also Paul Verlaine.)*

ROBESPIERRE, MAXIMILIEN DE. (May 6, 1758–July 28, 1794), *French statesman.* Robespierre, a leading figure in the French Revolution, was a young idealist who eventually became a ruthless fanatic and tyrant, eliminating almost all of his friends and colleagues. When the National Assembly was formed after the French Revolution, Robespierre  joined the radical left. Largely through his association with the Jacobin Club, he gained influence in the government and accelerated the revolutionary tempo. In July 1793, Robespierre initiated his famous Reign of Terror and began executing his political opponents. This only served to increase the number of his enemies, and Robespierre himself ended up on the guillotine.

Although Robespierre may never have acted on his homosexual feelings, his strong attraction to members of his own sex is indisputable. His attachment to the handsome Saint-Just, known as "The Archangel of the Revolution," led to frequent rumors.

RÖHM, ERNST. (Nov. 28, 1887– Jun. 30, 1934), *German militarist.* After Germany's defeat in World War I, Röhm became associated with the ultranationalist, militaristic movement that was gaining strength in Germany. He was the guiding spirit in building up a secret army later known as the S.A., or Brown Shirts. They made their first attempt at revolution in the Munich *Putsch* in which they tried and failed to overthrow the Bavarian government. Adolf Hitler, with whom Röhm by this time was closely associated, was imprisoned. Röhm broke with Hitler shortly thereafter and spent several years in Berlin where he was active in homosexual circles.

In 1928 Röhm and Hitler were reconciled, and two years later Hitler invited Röhm to take command again of the Brown Shirts; Röhm accepted. The relationship quickly grew tense, however, as Röhm filled many top posts with homosexuals.

By June 1934, Hitler was convinced that Röhm was conspiring against him. Röhm was arrested and given an opportunity to shoot himself; when he refused, he was executed in his cell at Stadelheim Prison. The formal charges against Röhm were for his homosexuality, although Hitler had known about it for at least fifteen years and had until then chosen to overlook it.

ROOSEVELT, ELEANOR. (Oct. 11, 1884–Nov. 7, 1962), *U.S. humanitarian.* Often surrounded by controversy during her long lifetime, Eleanor Roosevelt continued that tradition after her death when letters were discovered that revealed an intense love affair between her and reporter Lorena Hickok.

Roosevelt entered the public eye as the wife of Franklin Delano Roosevelt. During the earlier years of their marriage, from 1905 to 1918, she filled the traditional role that was expected of her, although not with much relish; she once confided to her eldest daughter that marital sex "is an ordeal to be borne."

Then she discovered her husband's love affair with his secretary,

Lucy Mercer. The discovery changed her life. Eleanor and Franklin remained married — his political career could not have survived a divorce. But their relationship evolved from that of husband and wife to that of colleagues, emotionally independent of one another.

During FDR's 1932 campaign for the presidency, the Associated Press assigned reporter Lorena Hickok to cover the Roosevelts. A relationship developed that, whatever its physical manifestations, was undoubtedly the major love affair of Eleanor Roosevelt's life. Hickok and Roosevelt exchanged sapphire rings, and when they were separated Eleanor wrote to Hickok, "Your ring is a great comfort. I look at it and think she loves me or I wouldn't be wearing it." On another occasion, she wrote, "All day I've thought of you. Oh! I want to put my arms around you; I ache to hold you close."

ROREM, NED. (Oct. 23, 1923–), *U.S. composer. Time* magazine has called Ned Rorem "the greatest living composer of art songs," and in a forty-year career he has written numerous symphonies, concertos, and operas, as well as the hundreds of songs and song cycles that have established his reputation. He won a 1976 Pulitzer Prize for his *Air Music.*

Rorem's reputation is further embellished by his four published diaries, whose candor has been described as "refreshing" by one critic and "tedious" by another. A sample entry: "During the year 1962 I had 205 orgasms, 85 of them with people I know (not 85 different people, however). Of the remaining 120 about one-fourth was masturbation and the rest anonymous."

Although completely open about his homosexuality, Rorem's attitude toward the subject is perhaps best summarized by his often-quoted remark that "Anyone can be gay — it's no accomplishment — but only I can be me."

RUSS, JOANNA. (Feb. 22, 1937–), *U.S. writer.* Joanna Russ recalls that she wrote her first lesbian science fiction in high school; it was a story "about a tall, dark woman (me) who falls in love with a short, blond one (my friend Madeleine, whom I was crazy about in summer camp)." Seventeen years later, she came back to that theme with her widely praised short story, "When It Changed."

In 1975, she shook up the science fiction world with her third novel, *The Female Man.* Its open discussion of sex-role reversals and lesbian sex was followed by such later works as *On Strike against God,* which took up the theme of lesbian awakening. She is open about being a lesbian.

RUSTIN, BAYARD. (Mar. 17, 1910– Aug. 24, 1987), *U.S. civil rights activist.* Born to a poor immigrant from the West Indies, Bayard Rustin became politically active at an early age. After two years in prison as a conscientious objector during World War II, he served as head of the War Resisters League. In 1955, he began a long affiliation with Martin Luther King, Jr. That association culminated with his central role in organizing the giant 1963 civil rights march on Washington. But although Rustin was the chief organizer, black leaders asked A. Philip Randolph to be the march's official head. They were afraid opponents would exploit Rustin's homosexuality to discredit the march.

Segregationists tried to do so anyway. Rustin had been arrested on a morals charge in 1953, and he later told his civil rights colleages that he was gay. Shortly before the march, Senator Strom Thurmond told the press about the 1953 arrest, but march organizers rallied behind Rustin, and the march was a tremendous success.

Rustin often spoke to gay organizations in the 1980s, and a common theme was his encouragement that young people come out. "Although it's going to make problems, those problems are not so dangerous as the problems of lying to yourself, to your friends, and missing many opportunities," he said.

SACKVILLE-WEST, VITA. (Mar. 9, 1892–Jun. 2, 1962), *British writer.* Her marriage to Harold Nicolson produced two children, but both she and he discovered the truth about their own orientations, and about each other, and soon each was having outside affairs with their own sex. Yet the marriage grew stronger, despite all this, and when Vita died in 1962, Harold's zest for life also died and he soon followed her to the grave. It's all described in their son Nigel Nicolson's book *Portrait of a Marriage.* Sackville-West herself is best summed up by novelist Jane Rule's remark: "For her life, one is grateful. For her fiction, one is not." *(See also Virginia Woolf.)*

SADE, Count DONATIEN ALPHONSE FRANCOIS DE (Marquis de SADE). (Jun. 2, 1740–Dec. 2, 1814), *French writer.* Although he was a count for most of his life, the man whose name provided the root for *sadism* is best known as the Marquis de Sade. His father forced him to marry Renée de Montreuil, a woman he greatly disliked. In reaction, Sade threw himself into a life of debauchery and gained fame for his ability to devise new and refined vices. He presided over orgies conducted at one of his wife's estates in Provence and was involved in one scandal after another.

Sade wrote a number of highly successful novels in which he contrasted the happy fortunes of the amoral Juliette with the tragic fate of her priggish sister Justine. In 1800 he published a pornographic novel, *Zoloe and her Two Acolytes,* with characters clearly based on Napoleon and Josephine. As a result, he was put in prison and later sent to an insane asylum, where he died at the age of seventy-four. Although he had many affairs with women, his novels are filled with references to homosexual relations, and he even went so far as to preach the superiority of male attractions.

SAPPHO. (610–580 B.C.), *Greek poet.* The first person in the Western world known to depict romantic love was the poet Sappho. Her beautiful poetry won praise both from her contemporaries and from later generations; Plato called her the "Tenth Muse." Most of her poetry was destroyed centuries later by church authorities, and only an estimated one-twentieth of her total output remains.

Sappho spent most of her life on the Greek island of Lesbos, where she ran a girls' school that taught poetry and writing. She drew lovers from both sexes, and had a child, but from her own time onward, Sappho was especially remembered for romances with her students. Today, two words synonymous with love between women — sapphism and lesbian — are derived from her name and that of her island.

SARTON, MAY. (May 3, 1912–), *Belgian-born U.S. writer.* May Sarton began writing while still in her teens, and achieved success in many forms: poetry, fiction, memoirs, and journals. She came out in 1965 with the publication of *Mrs. Stevens Hears the Mermaids Singing,* in which the title character finally concludes that "We have to be ourselves, however frightening or strange that may be." Following that advice cost Sarton her teaching job in 1965, but her reputation and following have only grown.

SCHUBERT, FRANZ. (Jan. 31, 1797–Nov. 19, 1828), *Austrian composer.* Schubert bridged the gap between the Classical and Romantic periods with poetic, revolutionary music cast in formal, Classical modes. In his short life he produced a remarkable body of work — including his masterpieces the *Great Symphony, The Magic Harp,* and the *Fantasy in F Minor* — and even enjoyed some popularity during his lifetime. In 1817 a friend introduced Schubert to noted baritone Johann Michael Vogl. A collaboration ensued, and Vogl's singing of Schubert's work became a drawing room staple in Vienna. The two moved in together during this time. Schubert

returned to his teaching duties, and then moved in with poet Johann Mayrhofer.

Scholars have recently found clear evidence of Schubert's homosexuality, and continue to debate whether it influenced his work. It does, however, cast a new light on his relationships with Vogl, Mayrhofer, and the artists who formed his clique.

SHAKESPEARE, WILLIAM. (baptized Apr. 26, 1564–Apr. 23, 1616), *English playwright.* The greatest dramatist of the English language was born in Stratford-on-Avon into a leading family of the town. Little is known of his actual life. He was married to Anne Hathaway in 1582 and had three children.  The marriage proved unhappy, and Shakespeare eventually left his wife.

Although there is no proof that Shakespeare was actively homosexual, same-sex themes and imagery abound in his work. This is especially true of the *Sonnets,* in which Shakespeare writes of his intense feelings for a handsome young man.

SHAWN, TED. (Oct. 21, 1891–Jan. 9, 1972), *U.S. dancer.* After an illness early in life, Ted Shawn took up dance as therapy, thus starting his career as dancer, teacher, and choreographer. He married Ruth St. Denis in 1914, and the two started the Denishawn dance school and company. Shawn's choreography drew from ethnic dances, theater, and laborers' movements, blending them into a strong, masculine style that, for the first time, opened up the field of dance to men. Though they never divorced, Shawn and St. Denis ended their marriage and their professional association in 1931. Shawn went on to form the Men Dancers, a group that evolved into the internationally renowned Jacob's Pillow Dance Festival in Lee, Massachusetts.

Despite Shawn's homosexuality and his great interest in male dances, his choreography was non-erotic; he seemed most interested in establishing respect and appreciation of male dance. Though he was careful not to blend his homosexuality with his choreography or his troupe, Shawn embarked on a fifteen-year relationship with Men Dancers member Barton Mumaw.

SMITH, BESSIE. (Apr. 15, 1894–Sep. 26, 1937), *U.S. vocalist.* Regarded by many as the greatest blues singer in history, Smith was renowned for her violent temper, her bouts with alcoholism, and her lusty, pleasure-seeking lifestyle. Her 200-pound frame gave expression to a tough inner core: she once stood off a Ku Klux Klan gang single-handedly.

Smith was married twice, and enjoyed sex with both men and women. She told one chorus girl in her show, after the girl publicly rebuffed her advances, "The hell with you, bitch. I got twelve women on this show and I can have one every night if I want it."

Smith made her first recording, "Down-Hearted Blues," in 1924; to Columbia Records' surprise, it sold 780,000 discs in less than six months. She died following a car accident in 1937. According to stories that have circulated since then, but have never been documented, she might have lived except that the first hospital where she was taken turned her away because she was black.

SOCRATES. (469?–399 B.C.), *Athenian philosopher.* Although he received only a limited education in his youth, Socrates taught himself geometry, astronomy, and philosophy. At one point he claimed to have received a divine commission to expose ignorance and promote intellectual and moral improvement, and he eventually earned a reputation as the wisest man in Greece. In 399 B.C., charges were brought against Socrates for "denying the gods recognized by the state" and "corrupting the young." He was found guilty, and sentenced to death.

Socrates' passion for beautiful boys became proverbial after his death; for many years the term "Socratic love" served as a euphemism for homosexuality. His most famous lover was the Athenian statesman and general Alcibiades.

STEIN, GERTRUDE. (Feb. 3, 1874–Jul. 27, 1946), *U.S. writer.* Through her famous salon and her patronage of the arts in Paris during the early part of this century, Stein influenced and inspired many writers and artists, among them Pablo Picasso, Henri Matisse, Guillaume Apollinaire, Ernest Hemingway, and Jean Cocteau. Stein herself wrote stories, poems, novels, art criticism, drama, and several memoirs, all in her distinctively repetitious, impressionistic style; she has often been labeled by critics a "cubist writer."

In 1907, while living with her brother Leo in Paris, Stein first met Alice B. Toklas, a young American visiting Europe from her home in San Francisco. Toklas soon became a lover, secretary, cook extraordinaire, and inseparable companion to Stein. Their enduring relationship as history's best-known lesbian couple lasted nearly forty years, until Stein's death from cancer in 1946.

Although she has come to symbolize lesbianism, Stein's views on male homosexuality would make many modern-day activists shudder. "The act male homosexuals commit is ugly and repugnant and afterwards they are disgusted with themselves," she once told Ernest Hemingway. "They are disgusted with the act and they are always changing partners and cannot be happy. In women, it is the opposite. They do nothing that they are disgusted by and nothing that is repulsive and afterwards they are happy and they can lead happy lives together."

STEUBEN, Baron FRIEDRICH WILLIAM VON. (Sep. 17, 1730–Nov. 28, 1794), *Prussian-born U.S. patriot.* Originally an aide to Frederick the Great, von Steuben lost that position, according to some reports, because he became overly fond of the young men around him. He joined George Washington and the new Continental army in Valley Forge. There's ample reason to believe that his seventeen-year-old French interpreter helped von Steuben stay warm during the bitter winter nights of 1777–1778. During the daytime, he brought discipline to his ragtag troops, then went on to lead them in battle. Congress recognized his contributions by voting him a pension and land in his retirement. In his ever-entertaining *Gay Book of Days,* Martin Greif reports that von Steuben legally adopted two handsome young American patriots, Ben Walker and William North, as he entered retirement.

STODDARD, CHARLES WARREN. (Aug. 7, 1843–Apr. 23, 1909), *U.S. writer.* Stoddard was born in Rochester, N.Y., but at age twelve he moved with his family to San Francisco, a mostly male city of gold prospectors, sailors, and adventurers. Stoddard later wrote about San Francisco as a vibrant city filled with colorful characters. He traveled to Hawaii and Tahiti, which inspired his *South-Sea Idyls,* then on to Europe as a reporter for the *San Francisco Chronicle.* Stoddard eventually returned to California and wrote *For the Pleasure of His Company,* a novel with homosexual overtones that are notably vague, as was necessary to get published at the time.

Both the travelog *South-Sea Idyls* and the novel *For the Pleasure...* clearly demonstrate that Stoddard was interested in men who loved other men. While in the islands, Stoddard wrote to Walt Whitman, "For the first time I act as my nature prompts me. It would not answer in America, as a general principle, not even in California, where men are tolerably bold. This is my mode of life."

STRACHEY, LYTTON. (Mar. 1, 1880–Jan. 21, 1932), *British biographer and critic.* Strachey adopted an irreverent attitude to the past and wrote biographies and biographical essays — such as his *Eminent Victorians* and *Queen Victoria* — that emphasized personality over achievement, and personal relationships over affairs of state. He is credited with revolutionizing the art of biography, by working from the position that a biographical subject should be depicted "warts and all." He was a leading figure in the Bloomsbury group, a circle of brilliant writers, artists, and intellectuals that included Virginia Woolf, E.M. Forster, and John Maynard Keynes.

Strachey's homosexuality was known to his contemporaries, as was his ironic and often acerbic wit. Questioned by a tribunal investigating his stance as a conscientious objector in World War I, he was asked how he would respond if he discovered his sister being raped by a foreign soldier. Strachey dryly replied, "I'd do my best to get between them."

STUDDS, GERRY EASTMAN. (May 12, 1937–), *U.S. congressman.* Elected to Congress as an anti-war candidate in 1972, Gerry Studds was the first Democrat in two generations to represent the Cape Cod district of Massachusetts in Congress. His 1972 victory came with a margin of only a fraction of a percentage point, but by staunchly protecting the interests of the local fishing industry, Studds was soon being returned to office by landslide votes, despite his controversial stance on foreign affairs.

In 1983, Studds was censured by Congress for having engaged in sexual activity with a seventeen-year-old House page ten years ear-

lier. Rather than deny the incident, or plead that he was drunk, as others in similar circumstances had done in the past, Studds chose to come out publicly in a speech to the House. While not excusing his actions of a decade earlier, he discussed the difficulties of combining the pressures of a public life with being gay. Studds won re-election sixteen months later by a comfortable margin, thus becoming the first openly gay person elected to the U.S. Congress.

SULLIVAN, Sir ARTHUR. (May 13, 1842–Nov. 22, 1900), *British composer.* Sullivan is best known for his collaborative work with William S. Gilbert. Together, they created some of the best-loved musical comedies in the history of the theater, including *H.M.S. Pinafore, Pirates of Penzance, Iolanthe,* and *The Mikado.*

Sullivan made no secret of his homosexuality, and it seems to have been widely tolerated. Some scholars believe the quarrel that led to the breakup of Gilbert and Sullivan was due, at least in part, to Gilbert's discomfort with his partner's sexual orientation.

SWINBURNE, ALGERNON. (Apr. 5, 1837–Apr. 10, 1909), *British poet.* Although he once was considered the liberator of a generation, Algernon Swinburne has been largely neglected by critics. In his time, he was well known for  his innovative, unconventional approach to poetry. His correspondence with friends clearly reveals Swinburne's homosexuality and his S/M inclinations.

SYLVESTER. (1948–1988), *U.S. entertainer.* Most gay celebrities have spent considerable energy trying to keep the closet door shut. Sylvester James Hurd put his energy into his performances. His stage debut came in 1970, with the infamous drag group, the Cockettes. His first album, *Lights Out,* appeared in 1972, and in 1977 his album *Step II* went gold. Success continued with several Top-40 hits, an officially proclaimed "Sylvester Day" in San Francisco, and sell-out tours of Europe.

By his own account, Sylvester had his first gay sex at age seven, when he was seduced in church by a local evangelist. "He really did a number on me," the singer recalled later, "but I was a queen even back then, so it didn't bother me." He was openly gay throughout his career, and performed at many AIDS benefits in the later years of his life.

SYMONDS, JOHN ADDINGTON. (Oct. 5, 1840–Apr. 19, 1893), *British essayist.* Symonds gained prominence as a historian of the Italian Renaissance, a poet, and an essayist. An outspoken proponent of sexual freedom, Symonds reached his position circuitously. His father, a strict doctor, taught the boy that the love of men was evil. Despite that warning, Symonds became infatuated with one choirboy after another as a fellow at Magdalen College — and suffered several nervous breakdowns as a result. He married and fathered four daughters, but his efforts to suppress his homosexuality were unsuccessful and finally Sy-

monds arrived at a liberal understanding with his wife that allowed him the sexual freedom he craved.

Symonds was the first person to explore many aspects of gay psychology and history. It was Symonds who, after months of research, brought to light poetry and correspondence from Michelangelo that revealed the famous artist's homosexuality. His 1891 book *A Problem in Modern Ethics* proposed some of the first theories as to the causes of homosexuality. And it was Symonds, in 1890, who asked Walt Whitman point-blank if Whitman's *Leaves of Grass* was really a celebration of homosexuality. Whitman angrily denied it, but neither Symonds nor future historians were convinced.

Only recently has the full extent of Symonds's writing on gay issues come to light. Hoping that his own story might help others who were struggling to emerge from the then-unnamed closet, Symonds carefully recorded his thoughts and worries and experiences as he came to an understanding of his gayness. But his effort was largely wasted. Symonds's literary executor placed his autobiography and other writings in the London Library with the stipulation that they could not be quoted or published until 1976.

TCHAIKOVSKY, PETER I. (May 7, 1840–Nov. 6, 1893), *Russian composer.* Peter Tchaikovsky was as well known for his high-strung temperament as for his legendary works *The Nutcracker Suite* and *The 1812 Overture.* His homosexuality is clearly documented in his correspondence. In an 1876 letter to his brother he wrote that "I am aware that my inclinations are the greatest and most unconquerable obstacle to happiness; I must fight my nature with all my strength. I shall do everything possible to marry this year." The next year he did marry, but the union was doomed and his wife, frustrated by his lack of interest in her, took a lover; she later was institutionalized.

Tchaikovsky's many homosexual affairs included one with his student Vladimir Shilovsky. Toward the end of his life, he became devoted to his nephew, Bobyk, to whom he dedicated his famous *Pathétique* Symphony.

TEASDALE, SARA. (Aug. 8, 1884–Jan. 29, 1933), *U.S. poet.* Although neglected by modern critics, Sara Teasdale was America's best-loved poet in the 1920s. From a conventional St. Louis background, she struggled all her life to express herself despite the Victorian standards that dominated her upbringing.

Teasdale focused on issues of interest to women and explored questions of female passion in her verses. In *Sonnets to Duse,* she addressed Eleanora Duse, a well-known actress at the time. For Teasdale, Duse represented a woman who, despite the constraints of her society, refused to hide her feelings. Teasdale herself found the struggle for self-expression far more difficult; throughout her life, she suffered from nervous conditions and was admitted to sanitariums on several occasions. During the last few years of her life she grew particularly despondent, and she finally ended her life with an overdose of sleeping pills.

Teasdale married, but her strongest feelings were reserved for other women. In 1926 she fell in love with college student Margaret Conklin; their relationship lasted until Teasdale's death.

THOMPSON, DOROTHY. (Jul. 9, 1893–Jan. 30, 1961), *U.S. journalist.* Dorothy Thompson was a journalist who wrote with passion about the issues of the day; in 1939, *Time* magazine called her one of the most influential women in the United States.

Thompson's career began in New York, where she wrote for various magazines and newspapers. In 1920 she went to Europe as a foreign correspondent; four years later, in Berlin, she became the first woman to be a foreign correspondent for a major news bureau. She interviewed Adolf Hitler for *Cosmopolitan* in 1931, but was later ordered by the führer to leave. Thompson returned to the United States a celebrity, and for two decades she wrote a highly successful and influential newspaper column.

Although thrice married, Thompson had several affairs with women, about which she felt decidedly ambivalent. After her divorce from Josef Bard, her first husband, she blamed him for "throwing me back into ... an adolescent homosexuality..." In 1932, when Thompson and her second husband, novelist Sinclair Lewis, were in Austria, she met Christa Winsloe, with whom she fell deeply in love. Thompson and Winsloe lived together as a couple until Winsloe went to France in 1935.

TILDEN, WILLIAM (BIG BILL).
(Feb. 20, 1893–Jun. 5, 1953), *U.S. athlete*. During the 1920s, "Big Bill" Tilden became the best-known tennis player in history; he dominated tennis as few athletes have ever dominated any sport. From his first Wimbledon victory in 1920 to his last, a decade later, he drew huge crowds as he toured Europe and the U.S.

During his years as an active player, Tilden seems to have put his greatest energy into his tennis game, suppressing his sexuality. But in later years, that changed. He took on a succession of young men as protégés, apparently in a confused search for companionship. In 1946, Tilden was arrested for making advances to a fourteen-year-old boy and served seven months in prison. Three years later, he was arrested again on similar charges, and again spent time in prison.

During his earlier career, Tilden had been known for his outspokenness. On at least one occasion he had been quick to stand up against what he saw as unfair discrimination: when a Latino player was barred from playing on a tennis court in Los Angeles, Tilden protested and the ban was lifted. But when his own life took a turn for the worse, Tilden found that his friends deserted him and he was no longer welcome at tournaments. He died a few years later.

TRIFONOV, GENNADY. (June 3, 1945–), *Soviet poet and dissident*.
The Soviet Union's most prominent openly gay writer has been fighting with authorities since 1965, when at the age of twenty he was drafted into the Red Army. There, the KGB tried to blackmail him to spy on other soldiers. In the 1970s, as a young poet, Trifonov introduced the ideas of the American youth movement into the Soviet Union, and wrote gay poetry that he circulated privately. He has been repeatedly arrested and imprisoned — either specifically for being gay, or on trumped-up charges — since 1976.

TSVETAEVA, MARINA IVANOVNA. (Oct. 8, 1892–Aug. 31, 1941), *Russian poet*.
A leading Russian poet of this century, Marina Tsvetaeva led an active and tragic life. Separated from her husband and one remaining daughter, she left Russia in 1922, traveling to Berlin, Prague, and finally Paris, where she fell in with the salon-art crowd. In Paris, Tsvetaeva met poet Sophia Parnok, and they embarked on an eighteen-month relationship. Tsvetaeva wrote of Parnok:

> My heart told me instantly:
>   'There she is!'
> I forgave you everything in
>   advance
> not yet knowing your name,
>   knowing nothing...

Parnok also inspired "The Woman Friend," a seventeen-poem cycle collected in Tsvetaeva's *Juvenilia*.

In 1939 Tsvetaeva returned to Russia to be with her daughter and husband, only to find her daughter imprisoned and her husband shot. During Moscow's evacuation in World War II, she was sent to a small town where she knew no one. Filled with loneliness and despair, she committed suicide.

TUKE, HENRY SCOTT. (1858–1929), *British painter.* Born to Quaker parents, Henry Scott Tuke showed an aptitude for drawing at an early age. After some formal training in the field, Tuke began painting what interested him. He painted nude boys on the beach, nude boys aboard boats, and nude boys in the water. A theme was emerging.

Many of Tuke's contemporaries specialized in depictions of nude girls, and his work raised fewer eyebrows than might have been expected in Victorian England. But it did nothing to enhance his career. One critic complained that Tuke was "the strongest artist outside the Academy circle, and there can be no doubt that had he confined himself to the canons of modern art ... he would have been admitted as an Associate of the Royal Academy years ago." Nude boys notwithstanding, the prestigious Academy admitted Tuke anyway in 1900; a host of other honors followed.

Even in his own diaries, Tuke was careful to leave few clues about his own sexuality. In one passage, he refers to his model Bertie White with the Greek word *kalos,* which refers to a sexual beauty. And in his thirties, Tuke associated regularly with homosexual men. The strongest clue as to his feelings, however, comes not from his diaries, or those who knew him, but from the paintings he left behind.

TURING, ALAN M. (Jun. 23, 1912–Jun. 7, 1954), *British mathematician.* The man who played an instrumental role in the defeat of Hitler was utterly destroyed by the country he helped to save, only six years after the führer's fall.

A prodigy obsessed with the concepts that paved the way for the modern computer, Turing joined the British intelligence project at Bletchley Castle at the age of thirty and masterminded the cracking of Enigma, the German secret code. Thanks to his genius, the Allies obtained access to Hitler's most secret communications, significantly shortening the war.

After his first love, Christopher Morcom, died of tuberculosis, Turing spent the rest of his life seeking to replace him. One of his later lovers was Arnold Murray, a working-class youth whom Turing later suspected of burglary and reported to the police. Turing naively revealed his sexual relationship with Murray and found himself on trial, charged with twelve counts of "gross indecency." The classified status of his wartime activities made it impossible to use this information to save him, and he was forced to choose between prison and "organotherapy," hormone treatments that caused him to grow breasts and to develop a chemical depression. Turing died of cyanide poisoning in 1954, an apparent suicide.

ULRICHS, KARL HEINRICH. (Aug. 28, 1825–July 14, 1895), *Prussian-German lawyer and early gay rights advocate.* Karl Ulrichs became the first person in modern history to publicly acknowledge his homosexuality when he announced at a convention of jurists that he was an "Uming." Two years before, he had written a defense of a young Frankfurt lawyer who was caught with a boy in a park and sent to prison. Other articles and pamphlets in favor of homosexual rights followed. Not surprisingly, Ulrichs was violently opposed by members of both the legal and medical establishments; ultimately, he was forced to leave Germany and he spent his last years in Italy.

Although Ulrichs failed to gain legitimacy and respectability for homosexuals, his work paved the way for later liberationists. The German sexologist Magnus Hirschfeld acknowledged his debt to Ulrichs and called him a pioneer in the study of homosexuality.

VALENTINO, RUDOLPH. (May 6, 1895–Aug. 23, 1926), *Italian-U.S. actor.* A landscape gardener by training, Valentino went to Hollywood in 1917, and landed various bit parts in films before achieving instant stardom in the lead role of *The Four Horsemen of the Apocalypse* in 1921. He became a national phenomenon, with women fainting in the aisles during screenings of his films. Because of

his screen image as a lithe love god with foppish manners, he was lambasted in the national press as the "Pink Powder Puff," and his influence on popular culture was lamented by journalists. "When will we be rid of all these effeminate youths?" grumbled one columnist, "powdered, bejeweled, and bedizened, in the image of Rudy — that painted pansy?" Nonetheless, his sudden death from

a perforated ulcer, at the age of thirty-one, provoked a national wave of hysteria in 1926.

Although he was married twice (once to lesbian set designer Natasha Rambova), Valentino wrote explicitly of at least one homosexual experience in his private journal.

VAN VECHTEN, CARL. (Jun. 17, 1880–Dec. 21, 1964), *U.S. writer and*

photographer. A leading supporter, chief photographer, and unofficial archivist of the Harlem Renaissance was a tall, blond, white man from Cedar Rapids, Iowa: Carl Van Vechten. His best-known novel, *Nigger Heaven* (1926), depicted the lustier side of Harlem cabaret life, and was praised by some black activists but condemned by most.

It was Van Vecten's book *The Blind Bow-Boy,* however, that contains his best-remembered line: the stationery of one character includes the motto "A thing of beauty is a boy forever."

VERLAINE, PAUL. (Mar. 30, 1844–Jan. 8, 1896), *French poet.* Verlaine decided early in life to be a poet; he joined the anti-Romantic Parnassian group and became a leading symbolist poet. In 1871 he met the sixteen-year-old poet Arthur Rimbaud. The two fell in love, and Verlaine left his wife for a stormy relationship with Rimbaud. Verlaine was an alcoholic, Rimbaud was temperamental, and they both used drugs and quarreled violently. In 1873, Verlaine shot Rimbaud and wounded him in the wrist. The police discovered the nature of the relationship and imprisoned Verlaine for two years. His relationship with Verlaine disintegrated soon after his release. Although their names are forever linked, their tempestuous relationship had lasted only two years. *(See also Arthur Rimbaud.)*

VIDAL, GORE. (Oct. 3, 1925–), *U.S. writer.* Vidal is a celebrated, outspoken man-of-letters known for his historical novels and for his intelligent, biting wit. In 1948 he wrote *The City and the Pillar,* a frank, honest portrait of a homosexual that shocked critical and commercial audiences and kept them away from his next five novels. Vidal turned to television, stage, and film writing, scoring great successes with *The Best Man, Ben-Hur, The Scapegoat,* and the film version of *Suddenly Last Summer.* He returned to controversial ground with *Myra Breckinridge,* the comic story of a transsexual, and the more recent *Live from Golgotha,* in which NBC-TV travels back in time to provide live coverage of the crucifixion.

Vidal's wit and geniality have made him a popular and enduring celebrity in America. He is outspoken in his criticism of the American government and his support of gay rights, though he has made great efforts to keep from being pigeonholed as a gay rights activist. Vidal is also a distant cousin of Vice President Al Gore.

VISCONTI, LUCHINO. (Nov. 2, 1906–Mar. 17, 1976), *Italian film director.* Luchino Visconti's film style ranged from the stark, trendsetting neo-realism of *Obsessione,*

to the garish operatics of *The Damned,* to the haunting lyricism of *Death in Venice.* An aristocrat by birth (he once proudly proclaimed, "I myself belong to the times of Mann, Proust, Mahler"), he was obsessed by form and dignity in his work, and was exceedingly circumspect in his personal life.

In his seventies, when asked by some younger friends if he wanted to go to a gay bar, he indignantly replied, "A gay bar? When I was young, homosexuality was a forbidden fruit, a fruit to be gathered with care, not what it is today — hundreds of homosexuals showing off, dancing together in a gay bar. What do you want to go there for?"

VIVIEN, RENÉE. (1877–1909), *French writer.* With Natalie Barney, Renée Vivien laid the groundwork for a new lesbian consciousness. They hoped to reclaim the powerful female figures of myth by retelling their stories from a nonpatriarchal perspective.

Born in London of Scottish and American ancestry, Vivien (originally Pauline Mary Tarn) was the more literary of the two women. She wrote nine volumes of poetry, two volumes of short stories, and two novels. In *The Woman of the Wolf,* she tells the story of chaste women who choose to die rather than yield to the cravings of men. She also translated Sappho's poetry in *The Women of Kithara.*

Throughout her life, Vivien was obsessed with death. She suffered from ill health, and may well have been anorexic, alcoholic, or both. She committed suicide at the age of thirty-two. The story of Vivien and Barney's love is vividly recounted in

Karla Jay's book, *The Amazon and the Page. (See also Natalie Barney.)*

WALPOLE, HORACE. (Sep. 24, 1717–Mar. 2, 1797), *British writer.* Walpole, a member of the House of Commons, is best remembered for popularizing the Gothic style in both architecture and literature. In 1754, he began altering his villa on the Thames, called Strawberry Hill, creating from it a unique Gothic castle that greatly influenced subsequent architecture. With the 1764 publication of his novel *The Castle of Otranto,* Walpole also introduced the gothic novel, from which are descended both gothic and detective novels of modern times.

Walpole's letters document his strong attraction to his cousin, the military general Seymour Conway. Conway was heterosexual, however, and Walpole's love went unrequited.

WARHOL, ANDY. (Aug. 6, 1927 ... or 1928 ... or 1929 ... or 1930–Feb. 22, 1987), *U.S. artist.* Born Andrew Warhola in McKeesport, Pennsylvania, the son of Czech immigrants, Andy Warhol had three nervous breakdowns by the age of ten. As a young man, he left Pennsylvania for New York, and worked his way up from illustrator and commercial artist to become one of the most influential pop artists of our times. Fascinated with the rich and famous, he gained entry to their circles with his portraits of such celebrities as Elizabeth Taylor and Mick Jagger.

Always cultivating a highly ambiguous sexual image, Warhol was told early in his career that he was "too swish" to be a major artist. Although he never actually identified himself with the gay movement, Warhol made no secret of his homosexuality. In 1986 he donated a painting to the Philadelphia gay and lesbian art show; characteristically, however, the work did not portray a gay theme.

WASHINGTON, GEORGE. (1732–1799), *U.S. president.* The Father of His Country never fathered anything else; from this slim thread of evidence, some have inferred more than others.

Throughout his life, George Washington showed little interest in women. As a young single man, he told friends that there was only one woman that he would ever consider marrying and that she had already wedded his friend George William Fairfax. He did eventually marry Martha Dandridge Custis after being persuaded that it was unseemly for a public figure to remain single.

Nevertheless, his closest attachments were always to men, particularly Alexander Hamilton. Throughout the Revolution, Hamilton served as Washington's aide-de-camp, personal secretary, and closest companion. During Washington's term of office, Treasury Secretary Hamilton was the guiding force of the administration and wrote Washington's famous "Farewell Address." There has been speculation, but no hard evidence, that the relationship went further.

WHALE, JAMES. (Jul. 22, 1896–May 29, 1957), *U.S. film director.* Whale is best remembered for the quartet of successful horror classics he directed in the 1930s: *Frankenstein, The Old Dark House, The Invisible Man,* and *The Bride of Frankenstein.*

To each, he brought sophistication, a fluid camera style, and unmistakable wit. He was a perfectionist and eccentric in an industry more comfortable with compromise and predictability; he was also openly gay and, according to some sources, entertained guests at his home by reading extracts from his own explicitly homoerotic diary. For many years he and Hollywood producer David Lewis were lovers.

Four years after a bitter artistic dispute with Universal Studios, Whale retired. Following a disastrous attempt at a comeback in 1949 and a series of debilitating strokes, he committed suicide in 1957.

WHITE, PATRICK. (May 28, 1912– Sep. 30, 1990), *Australian novelist.* Although born in London, White spent much of his life in Australia, which figures prominently in his dense and heavily symbolic novels. White, who was open about his homosexuality, won a Nobel Prize in 1973 for his novel *Eye of the Storm.*

WHITMAN, WALT. (May 31, 1819– Mar. 26, 1892), *U.S. poet.* Best known for his ambitious collection of poems, *Leaves of Grass,* Whitman has greatly influenced the development of modern poetry, and even the modern gay movement. Although his own homosexuality has been the subject of great debate, his verses actually leave little room for doubt on the subject. The most clearly homosexual of his poems are in the *Calamus* sec-

tion of *Leaves of Grass,* in which he dealt with the "institution of the dear love of comrades." In the poem "When I Heard at the Close of Day," the poet describes his truly happiest moment as being when "the one I loved most lay sleeping by me under the same cover in the cool night ... And his arm lay lightly around my breast — and that night I was happy."

Whitman apparently formed a number of close attachments with men in his life, but only one is clearly documented. This was with Peter Doyle, a trolley-car conductor to whom Whitman wrote many letters between 1868 and 1880. In these letters Whitman expressed intense feelings for Doyle, and closed with such phrases as "Many, many loving kisses to you."

At one point, the English poet and sexologist John Addington Symonds, with whom Whitman carried on a long-standing correspondence, inquired outright about Whitman's sexual orientation. Whitman hotly denied any homosexual tendencies and as evidence claimed to have fathered six illegitimate children. Those scholars who have rejected the idea that Whitman was homosexual have depended largely on this letter to bolster their argument — but they've never been able to produce the children. That Whitman was homosexual is now accepted by most scholars.

WILDE, DOLLY. (1899–1941), *British wit.* The niece of playwright Oscar Wilde, Dolly shared many traits with her famous uncle, including an extravagant wit, a literary talent expressed in brilliant conversation — and a taste for members of the same sex. "I am more Oscar-like than he was like himself," she once declared. According to contemporaries, she even looked like her uncle. "Her face," wrote Bettine Bergery, "is exactly like Aubrey Beardsley's drawing of Oscar Wilde." Dolly became known as part of Natalie Barney's circle in Paris in the 1930s, and for more than a decade she maintained a tumultuous, on-again, off-again love affair with Barney; their unhappy relationship drove Dolly to two suicide attempts. Eventually, she abandoned Paris and returned to London, where she died in obscurity of cancer at the age of forty-one. Summing up her short and tragic life, Gertrude Stein eulogized, "Well, she certainly hadn't a fair run for her money."

WILDE, OSCAR. (Oct. 16, 1854– Nov. 30, 1900), *Irish wit.* The legendary Irish playwright (*The Importance of Being Earnest*) and novelist (*The Portrait of Dorian Gray*) achieved fame more for his wit and flamboyance than for his writing. Even at college, he talked of "art for art's sake," decorated his room with peacock feathers, sported long hair, and took up the affectations that later made him a caricaturist's delight. In 1882, he boarded a ship to begin a tour in the United States, announcing to customs upon his arrival, "I have nothing to declare except my genius."

Oscar Wilde married in 1884, and fathered several children. But his homosexual nature kept surfacing. He became involved first with Robert Ross — later to serve as Wilde's literary executor — then with the young, pretty Lord Alfred Douglas. Douglas's father, the mar-

quis of Queensbury, was furious that his son should be associated with such a man; he tried to break up the relationship, and charged Wilde with being a degenerate.

Wilde responded by bringing libel charges against the marquis. During the first day of the trial, he used the witness box as a forum for his own ostentation. When the opposing lawyer complained at one point that "I cannot bear fools," Wilde retorted, "But your mother did." The next day, however, it grew clear that the marquis could marshall numerous witnesses to Wilde's homosexuality. Wilde withdrew his suit. The marquis then pressed the government to prosecute Wilde for sodomy. He was convicted and imprisoned. Five years later, an alcoholic and a physical wreck, Oscar Wilde died.

WILDER, THORNTON. (Apr. 17, 1897–Dec. 7, 1975), *U.S. writers.* Thornton Wilder was a popular playwright and novelist who used an innovative style to explore traditional themes. Plays like *Our Town* and *The Skin of Our Teeth,* which both won Pulitzer prizes, celebrate small-town America and strong family relationships, while challenging the audience to imagine the props and scenery, as characters address the audience directly. Wilder also wrote *The Matchmaker* (later adapted into the musical *Hello, Dolly!*) and *The Bridge of San Luis Rey.*

As his plays and novels attest, Wilder was uncomfortable discussing sex in any way, though his homosexuality was known in the artistic community. In 1937 Gertrude Stein sent writer Samuel Steward to visit Wilder in Zurich; Steward later reported that he and Wilder struck up a casual friendship and sexual relationship that lasted a number of years.

WILLIAM II (WILLIAM RUFUS). (1060?–Aug. 2, 1100), *English king.* One of the earliest kings of England, William Rufus was nominally a Christian, but actually practiced pagan rites that incorporated sex and sex-magic. As a result, he was constantly in conflict with the archbishop of Canterbury, and eventually Pope Urban threatened to excommunicate the king. Among the accusations directed at the monarch was that of "the crime not spoken of between Christians." Gay historian John Boswell, however, suggests that most of William's enemies were out to besmirch him any way they could; imputations of homosexuality could have been based in fact, but may simply have represented the worst insult the critic could think of at the time.

William was killed by an arrow in the back while on a hunting expedition. Some historians believe this to have been an assassination orchestrated by his brother, who immediately seized the throne as Henry I. Another theory was that the arrow came from his lover's bow as a part of an ancient ritual in which a man was killed by his homosexual lover.

WILLIAMS, TENNESSE. (Mar. 26, 1911–Feb. 25, 1983), *U.S. playwright.* Born Thomas Lanier Williams in Columbus, Mississippi, Williams achieved his first success with the production of *The Glass Menagerie* in 1945 and followed it two years later with his most-acclaimed play, *A Streetcar Named Desire; Streetcar* won both the Pulitzer Prize and the Critics' Circle Award for that year. His later plays included *Summer and Smoke, Cat on a Hot Tin Roof,* and *Suddenly Last Summer,* which aroused considerable controversy for its treatment of such subjects as lobotomy, homosexuality, and cannibalism. After the early 1960s, critics were generally disappointed with his work, and he never again wrote anything to compare with his earlier critical triumphs. Williams also wrote numerous short stories, poems, and two novels.

Williams had been open about his homosexuality for years, but the 1975 publication of his explicitly candid *Memoirs* — in which he discussed his career, his love affairs, and his one-night stands — brought his sexuality to the attention of the general public, and created even more attention for an already controversial author.

WITTGENSTEIN, LUDWIG. (Apr. 26, 1889–Apr. 29, 1951), *Austrian philosopher.* Among the most original philosophical thinkers of the early twentieth century was Ludwig Wittgenstein; it is said that he was so brilliant he nearly drove Bertrand Russell out of the field. Although he attended Cambridge and spent much of his time in England, Wittgenstein was born in Vienna, to a wealthy Jewish family.

In his youth, the handsome Wittgenstein often cruised Vienna for what one biographer calls "rough young men [who] were ready to cater to him sexually"; he later lived with a lover in England. His homosexuality probably had little influence on his philosophical thinking, and his family and estate did their best to keep it secret. "There are certain stories which it would be foul to relate or tell about somebody even if they were true," complained an executor of his estate after a biographer touched on this aspect of Wittgenstein's life.

WOLLSTONECRAFT, MARY. (Apr. 27, 1759–Sep. 10, 1797), *British writer.* An early advocate of equality for women, Wollstonecraft led an unorthodox and controversial life. In 1774, she met Frances "Fanny" Blood, two years her senior, and they began an intense affair. Wollstonecraft wrote to her sister, "The roses will bloom when there's peace in the breast, and the prospect of living with Fanny gladdens my heart: — You know not how I love her." They did live together for a time, but Fanny married Hugh Skeys in 1784, ending Wollstonecraft's dream of a permanent relationship. Fanny died in childbirth the next year.

Wollstonecraft published two books with feminist themes: *A Vindication of the Rights of Women* and *Thoughts on the Education of Daughters.* She became involved in radical politics, and bore two daughters. One she named after Fanny Blood; the other eventually married poet Percy Shelley and became famous as Mary Shelley, the author of *Frankenstein.*

WOOLF, VIRGINIA. (Jan. 25, 1882–Mar. 28, 1941), *British writer.* A leading figure of the Bloomsbury group and one of the most original writers of the twentieth century, Woolf created such landmark works as *Mrs. Dalloway, Jacob's Room,* and *The Waves.* Woolf suffered bouts of insanity throughout her life, and in 1941 she drowned herself.

Although Virginia Woolf's sexual orientation remains open to debate, the greatest love of her life seems to have been Vita Sackville-West. The two women may never  actually have had a physical relationship, but Virginia Woolf's deep feelings of esteem and affection for Sackville-West are undeniable. It was in honor of Sackville-West that she wrote the novel *Orlando,* in which the main character starts out as a man and becomes a woman.

WOOLLCOTT, ALEXANDER. (Jan. 19, 1887–Jan. 23, 1943), *U.S. journalist and critic.* An acerbic theater critic, journalist, and radio commentator from the 1920s to the early 1940s, Woollcott was variously described by other prominent figures as "a butterfly in heat," "a New Jersey Nero who mistakes his pina-  fore for a toga," and "a fat duchess holding out her dirty rings to be kissed." He was renowned (and sometimes despised) for his scathing reviews and his devastating wit, as when he wrote of pianist and writer Oscar Levant, "There's nothing wrong with Oscar Levant — nothing that a miracle couldn't fix."

Woollcott, who enjoyed dressing as a woman in college and who handed out calling cards introducing himself as "Alexandra Woollcott," was apparently tormented much of his life by ambiguous sexual feelings. Even after he achieved fame, he sobbingly confessed to playwright Anita Loos that all of his life he had wanted to be a woman. Whether he was ever actively homosexual, however, remains a matter of speculation.

YOURCENAR, MARGUERITE. (Jun. 8, 1903–Dec. 17, 1987), *French writer.* Although born in Belgium (as Marguerite de Crayencour), and a French national, Yourcenar lived much of her life in the  United States. In 1981 she received France's highest intellectual honor when she was named to the Academie Francaise — the first woman ever so honored.

Yourcenar was a translator, critic, and scholar, but she is best known for her novels. The most famous is *Memoirs of Hadrian,* published in 1951. This fictional account portrays a passionate romance between the Roman emperor Hadrian and his lover Antinous.

When she was about twenty-four, Yourcenar met an American named Grace Frick. They bought a house together on Maine's Mt. Desert Island, and lived together until Frick's death in 1979. Although she refused to categorize herself as a lesbian, Yourcenar's feelings toward Frick were summed up in her author's note to *Hadrian.* The book "ought to have been dedicated to G.F.," she wrote, "but even the longest dedication is too short and too commonplace to honor a friendship so uncommon ... [with someone] who leaves us ideally free, but who nevertheless obliges us to be fully what we are."

ADVICE FOR EVERYDAY LIFE

The skills and knowledge that we gain while growing up — from family and friends, school and church — don't always meet our later needs as lesbians and gay men. Some of the articles in this chapter were written specifically from a gay male or a lesbian perspective. We hope you'll read them all, however, and that you'll agree with us that the similaries between lesbians and gay men in these situations are greater than the differences.

FINANCIAL PLANNING FOR LESBIANS AND GAY MEN
by Harold Gunn

Few people realize how much the financial planning and insurance concerns of gay people differ from those of straight people. While homosexuals *and* heterosexuals are concerned with saving on taxes, making the right investments, and planning for a secure future, gay people often need to use different techniques to achieve these goals.

For example, when a man and woman marry, the laws of the state in which they live do some benevolent financial planning for them. Though the couple may choose to arrange things otherwise, the state dictates how property acquired during their marriage is owned and how it will be distributed after one of them dies. This intervention by the state is designed to protect each party and encourage the institution of marriage. A gay couple, however,

Harold Gunn is an attorney in New York City specializing in wills and trusts.

must actively construct this framework for themselves, yet few know how to go about it.

Similarly, insurance coverage is structured to favor married couples. As the number of AIDS cases increases, life, health, and disability insurance are becoming harder to get, just at the very time they are more crucial to our financial security. There *are* ways around these obstacles.

Another often overlooked part of planning for a secure future involves executing a will. Without such a safeguard, your lover or friends would almost certainly get nothing from your estate. Even with a will, disgruntled relatives can thwart the wishes of the deceased by contesting the document's validity. Taking precautions now can eliminate these problems.

Planning for a life together

The delights of living together can mask some of the financial complications caused by the legal system's bias toward heterosexual couples. The financial advantages that our laws grant to married couples include the right to financial support from a spouse, the right to inherit from a spouse without a will, and the right to recover damages for a spouse's wrongful death. Without these protections gay couples are at a disadvantage, but there are alternative ways to secure the financial benefits associated with marriage.

First, the couple should work out the money details of their relationship before they move in together. Gay lovers tend to live together with only an ambiguous understanding about how they will share expenses. The wise couple will sit down together, discuss their financial concerns and expectations, and come to an agreement in the form of a living-together contract.

Recent litigation might make such a contract legally enforceable, although that cannot be taken for granted. In any case, consider such an agreement a useful tool to avoid or help resolve disputes.

In addition to living-together contracts, gay couples should seriously consider the advantages and disadvantages of joint savings, checking, and credit card accounts. The primary advantage of joint accounts are their convenience. However, a joint account means that each person is responsible for the debts incurred on that account by the other. A disgruntled lover could charge thousands of dollars on a joint credit card or withdraw everything from a joint checking account and skip town. One solution: Hold credit cards and bank accounts separately, but open a joint checking account in which only a moderate amount is maintained to cover joint expenses.

Gay couples should know that leases obligating both of them to pay the rent, or loan agreements obligating both of them to pay the amounts due, offer both risk and legal protection. These are called "joint and several" obligations, which means that the creditor can choose to sue both partners — or either of them alone — for the full amount owed. If the creditor collects from only one partner, however, the lover who paid the joint obligation would generally have the right to look to her partner for a share of the debt.

Purchasing a home with a lover also requires careful planning. Ownership by two persons may take several forms, each with its own financial consequences:

• *Joint tenants* each own an equal, undivided interest in the whole property during their lives. Upon the death of a joint tenant, his interest will automatically pass to the survivor, even overriding a provision in his will to the contrary. If a joint tenant sells his interest to someone else, the new owners automatically become "tenants in common."

• *Tenants in common* each own a separate, undivided interest in the property. "Tenants in common" can own property in unequal shares and can bequeath their interests to whomever they specify in their wills.

• *Tenants by the entirety* are married joint owners. (Essentially, this is the same as a joint tenancy, except it is more difficult to sever the ties of joint ownership.)

Unless you specify which type of ownership you are taking when purchasing, the form will be determined by the law of the state in which the property is located. In many states the law presumes that unmarried joint property owners are "tenants in common" — unless you explicitly indicate otherwise.

Planning for the unexpected: Health, life, and disability insurance

A person without health insurance courts financial ruin. Though Medicaid can help pay medical expenses, the patient must first exhaust practically all other personal resources. Group health insurance plans provide coverage for employees of most larger businesses, but all other individuals should purchase their own policy.

Purchasing a new policy, or making a claim on an existing one may present difficulties. "Pre-existing conditions" are the most common problem. An insurance company may refuse to pay a claim if, at the time she purchased the policy, the claimant knew or should have known that she had the condition which gave rise to the claim. Most health insurance contracts provide a period of time after which claims on pre-existing conditions must be honored — usually eleven months, although some are as long as two years.

An insurance company may also deny a claim if the claimant made a "material misrepresentation" on his application. For this move to succeed, the misrepresentation must be serious and sufficiently related to the illness that, if the company had known, it would not have issued the policy. In most states, however, an insurance company has two years from the time the policy is issued to raise an objection to the misrepresentation. After that time, a claim must be paid.

These issues take on a new significance in light of the AIDS epidemic. Some insurers have expanded their definition of a pre-existing condition so as to withhold benefits from policyholders with AIDS who exhibited certain ailments prior to their diagnosis. The best advice would be to answer the questions on the insurance application honestly and completely, but without volunteering any unrequested information. For example, you would not want to disclose that you have tested positive for the HIV antibody. (A number of states currently forbid insurers from asking this question, although the industry would like that changed.)

As you change jobs, be sure your health coverage follows you. In many states you can convert group health insurance to an individual policy with the same company without having to provide new proof of insurability. Though an individual policy is more expensive and provides less coverage, at least the coverage continues.

Congress has also passed COBRA (Consolidated Omnibus Reconciliation Act) which allows any employee leaving a job to stay on the company's group insurance plan by paying the group premium. Though this option is less expensive than converting to an individual policy, an ex-employee may only continue with the group coverage under COBRA for a period of eighteen months.

Health insurance, though essential, is not helpful if, through disease or workplace accident, you should lose the ability to work. This kind of protection is provided by disability insurance. For the single gay person, disability insurance is far more important than life insurance. According to insurance industry statistics, if your age is between thirty-five and sixty-five, you have a fifty percent chance of becoming disabled for at least ninety days prior to your sixty-fifth birthday. Make certain that your disability coverage is adequate.

If others depend on your income, purchase enough life insurance to be sure that they will not face a serious financial setback in the event of your death. This is becoming trickier than it sounds. In response to the AIDS crisis, insurance companies are making special efforts to identify those applicants believed to be at high risk for contracting the disease, then requiring them to take the HIV antibody test. Those who test positive are denied life insurance. This is completely legal in most states.

Insurance companies examine a number of factors to determine a high-risk applicant, including marital status, occupation, history of sexually transmitted diseases, and naming an unrelated person of the same sex as a beneficiary. Again, while you should answer all of the questions on the application honestly, do not volunteer information. Avoid naming your lover as a beneficiary: Name your estate instead, and make a will that leaves your estate to him or her.

Finally, any information that you supply to an insurance company may be made available to other insurance companies through the Medical Information Bureau, Inc. (MIB). MIB attempts to reduce underwriting costs by uncovering dishonest applicants. MIB maintains files of personal medical information, and other "nonmedical information of a very restricted nature regarding insurability."

The Fair Credit Reporting Act of 1970 assures your access to the file MIB may be keeping on you. You may request this information by filling out a special form, which can be obtained by writing M.I.B., P.O. Box 105, Essex Station, Boston, MA 02112. The records, once released, may only be sent to a "licensing medical professional" which you designate. After reviewing the file with your doctor, you may submit corrections to MIB.

Planning for your estate

By failing to draft a will, you agree to let the state dispose of your earthly possessions. Since state laws are based on the assumption that your family is the natural object of your affection, your estate would go to your closest blood relative. Lovers and close friends would receive nothing.

It is possible to direct the disposition of property by means other than a will: recall that property held as joint tenants passes to the survivor automatically. However, for assets that are not held jointly, there is no reliable substitute for a carefully drafted will.

Contrary to popular belief, there is no law *requiring* that a certain portion of your estate go to your relatives. If you do leave them little or nothing, they can initiate legal proceedings in an attempt to have the will declared invalid. This can be successfully argued by proving that (1) the will was improperly executed, (2) someone used undue influence to coerce you into executing the will, (3) you were mentally incompetent to execute a will, or (4) someone deceived you as to how the will would dispose of your property. A careful will and estate plan can thwart such arguments ahead of time. Another device that can avoid will contests is the *in terrorem* clause. When put in a will, this clause disinherits anyone who contests the legality of the document.

As you plan your estate, seriously consider making a bequest to charitable or political organizations that promote the health, civil rights, and vital interests of the gay community. There are dozens of worthwhile groups that depend on our contributions for their survival. A generous bequest would help ensure that they have the resources to continue with their important work.

Gay men and women can generally achieve their financial planning goals, but it takes advance information and thought, a bit more work, and a little ingenuity. The key is to plan ahead, before calamity strikes.

FINDING A GAY-AFFIRMATIVE THERAPIST
by Marny Hall

Perhaps the most important quality that lesbians and gay men shop for in a therapist — an affirmative attitude toward our sexuality — is also the most difficult to find. After all, "gay" or "lesbian" is not a single kind of behavior. Each represents a whole cluster of styles, sexual practices, tastes, social environments, and political networks. Obviously, there can be no single, monolithic attitude toward such a behavioral mix on the part of any therapist.

Likewise, there is no single profile of a gay-affirmative therapist. Such therapists, like any other counselors, run the gamut of experience and training. "Gay-affirming" simply represents an additional layer on top of their particular therapy orientation. Such therapists share a determination not to reinforce in gay and lesbian clients the devaluing messages issuing from the culture. Instead, they offer clients the view that being lesbian or gay is a positive choice.

Not all these therapists are themselves lesbian or gay. In some parts of the country, lesbian or gay therapists may be difficult, even impossible, to find. There's no rule that says a heterosexual therapist can't be helpful to us — and none that promises competence and nurturing from a therapist who is gay.

How to check
a counselor's attitude

Obviously, a referral is the fastest — and least risky — way to meet a gay-affirmative therapist. When

Marny Hall is a practicing psychotherapist in the San Francisco Bay Area. This essay is excerpted from her book THE LAVENDER COUCH: A CONSUMER'S GUIDE TO PSYCHOTHERAPY FOR LESBIANS AND GAY MEN.

there's no such referral, and no other evidence is forthcoming — no gay periodicals in the waiting room and no clearly affirmative statements from the counselor — you need to look for subtler clues.

How does the therapist say your lover's name? What expressions and body language do you notice when you describe something sexually explicit? How does the counselor react to words like "dyke" and "faggot?" How does the counselor respond when you discuss AIDS or becoming a gay or lesbian parent?

If your therapist is not affirmative about lesbian and gay experiences, it will be difficult to help the client become and remain so. The focus of work with gay clients is to flush out the old, demeaning standards and hold them up for examination. It means helping the client realize the irrelevance of many non-gay values. A therapist who has any doubt or ambivalence about this is probably the wrong one for you; such a therapist may only reinforce the homophobia that is inside and around you. In the absence of any clear-cut statements by your therapist, your intuition is probably your best guide. Use it.

Shopping for a bi-focal approach

Gay affirmation is an indispensable part of effective therapy with lesbians and gay men. Good therapy, however, is not limited to lesbian and gay issues. Plenty of problems, although they may be indirectly related to sexual orientation, have a reality independent of lesbianism or gayness. Such problems, which must be dealt with

separately, include: drug or alcohol abuse; parenting or career issues; aging; and illness.

A gay or lesbian counselor, to be most effective, must have a bi-focal approach, an ability to move easily from a gay perspective to one where homosexuality is incidental. A therapist without this ability can do limited good. Such a therapist may overidentify with a client, flatten the differences among clients, rob each client of her or his uniqueness, and provide too limiting or too comforting an environment.

How to find a gay-affirmative therapist

• *Bookstores, Coffeehouses, Newspapers.* These will often provide leads through bulletin boards, conversations, or advertisements.

Ads are a legitimate way to find a therapist. Some offer initial consultations free — a good way to start the shopping process. Many therapists who don't advertise free first sessions will offer one if you ask.

• *Switchboards.* Operating in many urban areas, switchboards provide a source of lesbian and gay counselors. They are usually listed in the phone book under "Feminist," "Gay," "Lesbian," or "Women." In areas without visible gay or feminist communities, switchboards for crisis intervention, substance abuse support, or even peace groups may offer the information you need.

• *Lesbian and Gay Directories.* The professional organizations to which psychotherapists belong frequently have lesbian and gay caucuses, which offer, upon request, listings of lesbian and gay therapists across the country. Several other directories for lesbians and gay men also list lesbian and gay mental health resources.

• *Sleuthing*. The difficulty of finding a gay-affirmative therapist is compounded by closetry — the conviction on the part of some therapists (particularly those who work in agencies or clinics) that they dare not come out at work.

If you get the name of someone in a clinic, call the person directly. If the person is lesbian or gay and closeted, a comment like "you've been recommended to me as a therapist and I want to know if I can arrange for you to see me," is a nonthreatening introduction. Approached in this way, therapists will often either arrange to see you, or alert the intake worker to assign you to him or her.

Country ways

The task for rural gay people seeking therapy is different from their urban counterparts. Some rural lesbians and gay men have located therapists in nearby cities whom they drive to see.

If driving long distances for therapy is not feasible, country dwellers may elect, instead, to have telephone therapy. Some therapists who live in urban areas are open to negotiating regular telephone sessions with clients who don't have access to their offices.

Social contact with other lesbians and gay men who are not necessarily counselors may be especially important for rural lesbians and gay men.

How do you find someone who — even if not lesbian or gay — is sympathetic, warm, and supportive?

Such a search means getting involved in aspects of local community work which reflect shared values, and cultivating friendships with people who have the qualities you would seek in any therapist. Such people are "natural helpers": those whose listening ability and empathy make them sought-out "counselors" within their communities.

The search for the right therapist may be quick and direct, or arduous and time-consuming. The search will be facilitated by drawing on available resources such as referrals and national publications, by assertive interview techniques, and most importantly, by your own creativity and intuition.

Anyone may receive referral information from the Association of Gay and Lesbian Psychiatrists by contacting: AGLP Referral Service, c/o Phillip Cushman, 2830 N.W. 41st St., Suite B, Gainesville, FL 32606, (904) 372-0387.

Finding a Gay-Affirmative Doctor or Lawyer
by Wayne Curtis

There is no assurance that a gay doctor or lawyer is, by definition, better than a straight one, but there are compelling reasons for searching out gay-identified, or at least gay-affirmative, legal and health care professionals. In some urban areas this is as simple as turning to your local gay community publication's service guide. But for many of America's gay men and lesbians, no

Wayne Curtis is the editor of REVELA-TIONS: A COLLECTION OF GAY MALE COMING-OUT STORIES.

such community listing is readily available.

Why should I bother to look for a gay doctor or lawyer?

While many medical and legal situations have nothing to do with sexual preference, you won't get the best possible service from a doctor or lawyer if you don't feel free to talk about any aspect of your life. Also, as a consumer, you have the right to expect treatment unclouded by the professional's personal prejudices.

From a health care standpoint, this means a thorough understanding of your special needs as a gay man or lesbian, whether single or coupled. A doctor or health care worker should not only understand whatever physical health problems you may have, but also need to be sensitive to the types of "legal" discrimination that can be based on a gay individual's medical history. If you have a lover, your doctor should respect your visitation rights if one of you becomes seriously ill.

Similarly, your legal needs are influenced by the generally heterosexist bias of our legal system. Nontraditional family units do not get the legal status or prerogatives of a married couple, and gay people must construct a more elaborate protective framework to make up for that disadvantage. A sympathetic lawyer can also provide the best defense of your rights should you be victimized by anti-gay discrimination or violence.

Where can I look to find a gay-affirmative lawyer or doctor?

The recommendation of a trusted friend is often the easiest, and best, place to start. Another option is to use a locally produced gay or lesbian paper or guide. Keep in mind, however, that advertising in a local gay publication says more about a doctor's or lawyer's attitudes on gay issues than about their professional qualifications.

Several national organizations can also provide you with recommendations. Gay and Lesbian Advocates and Defenders (GLAD), a nonprofit law firm, publishes the *National Attorney Directory for Lesbian and Gay Rights,* now in its fourth edition. It's available for $12 (postpaid) from GLAD, P.O. Box 218, Boston, MA 02112.

A good source for finding a gay-affirmative doctor or clinic is the American Association of Physicians for Human Rights (AAPHR), which can refer you to one of its members. Write the AAPHR at 2940 16th St., #105, San Francisco, CA 94103.

THE FIVE STAGES OF A RELATIONSHIP
Larry Uhrig

The joy of a relationship is discovered only with time. As we live together and pursue our vocations, something wonderful happens. We begin to develop our corporate identities. This happens as lives merge into shared goals, property, feelings, hopes, and friends. An extended family may develop to in-

Larry Uhrig is the pastor of the Metropolitan Community Church in Washington, D.C. This essay is from his book THE TWO OF US: AFFIRMING, CELEBRATING AND SYMBOLIZING GAY AND LESBIAN RELATIONSHIPS.

clude the relatives and parents of the couple as well as close intimate friends.

This bonding process unfolds in what can be viewed as five stages.

Discovery

The discovery stage includes the initial meeting of two people and incorporates all of the courting and dating customs of our culture. It is the stage most filled with passion and wonder, the stage most often exploited by the Hollywood myth. Here is the phase where so many of us get stuck. It is in the discovery period that infatuation is strong and love not yet defined. While this stage is filled with energy, joy, and excitement, it is also filled with ambiguity and confusion.

Disappointment

Stage two is the point at which many couples decide not to continue the relationship. In this stage, the two people encounter reality. The shortcomings of the other become more focused and for a time these shortcomings dominate the horizon. Here, the conflict usually occurs between the myth of a "shopping-list lover" and the real qualities of the person at hand. The temptation is to get rid of the one at hand and go out to find the personification of the myth. It is essential to know that this process will repeat itself again and again. Discovery is always followed by disappointment and it sometimes appears easier to leave the relationship than to stay.

Decision

Disappointment always brings both people to the point of deci-

sion. At this intersection, each must evaluate their goals. Clear communication is required to perceive accurately where the other person is. This is a time to take "inventory" as to what you each have invested in the other. Are your assumptions about the relationship open and shared, or is one or both operating on the basis of assumptions not disclosed to the other? Decision is an essential stage in establishing a long-term commitment. The way you encounter this decision will set the pattern for how you resolve future conflicts.

Disappointment and decision are recurring cycles in any relationship. We must realize that this is not a sad reality to escape but an inevitable human process which can enrich each person's life as each accepts the other partner and grants the other the freedom to grow and change.

Development

Development is the term I choose to refer to the often extensive period following the decision to continue the relationship. This is a period of nitty-gritty living, change, and growth. It is often characterized by higher levels of security and the growth of trust between two people. The choice to stay carries with it a mutual acknowledgment of each other as persons of worth, persons who are loved.

The development stage of the relationship is often the time when the couple begins to publicly acknowledge their pair-bonding to friends, co-workers, and families. The time between the discovery and the development stage of a relationship is about six months to one year. Understanding that this is a natural process which takes time to develop will ease pressure.

Destiny

The final stage — which may follow a series of decision stages — I am calling "destiny." This is the stage of mutual trust and honesty. At this point in a relationship there will be regular and clear communication, a developing ability to face conflict and resolve it, an absence of jealousy and possessiveness, and a mutual independence and freedom. This is a stage of "good health" which allows the future to be a blessing and challenges to be faced together.

This stage of a relationship does not occur until after an extensive period, usually not until the third year or later.

A major problem in gay relationships is our impatience to hurry the process along. We cannot leapfrog any stage nor even greatly shorten it. Each must unfold naturally. Sometimes, however, the process can be enhanced, when two people begin the process at the discovery stage with maturity and high levels of trust. This often results from the successful resolution and completion of former relationships. Moreover, one's present relationship, when based on honesty, greatly helps heal the pain and hurt carried over from a previous relationship.

Destiny is the intention to spend a life together in a relationship bonded through time, testing, trust, and honesty.

A GAY MAN'S GUIDE TO COMING OUT
by Wes Muchmore and William Hanson

First you come out to yourself. You admit that erotically your primary interest is in other men.

Men new to their gayness sometimes believe that if they have sex with a male, or even think about it, some terrible Jekyll-Hyde change will come over them. The truth is that nothing special will happen. You will not turn into anything, develop a sudden, unconquerable yen to wear dresses, jewelry, or makeup, or become a woman. You will not now lust for little boys, turn girlish, or begin to talk in a lisping manner. You will not start to hate females, lose your sense of morality, or go wild over the colors purple, lavender, pink, or green. That's all nonsense. If nobody could tell about you before, nobody can tell about you after.

Coming out is not always pleasant even under the best of circumstances, and it can be an extremely difficult process. Very often a man has to completely reassess and restructure his whole existence.

Along with the strains of adjustment several problems may arise from within. Difficulties frequently have two sources. First, in American society where virtually everyone is raised to be heterosexual, we all

---

Wes Muchmore and William Hanson are the authors of Coming Out Right: A handbook for the gay male *(from which this is excerpted) and of* Coming Along Fine: Today's gay man and his world.

learn as children that homosexuality is a sickness or a sin. At the least we are led to view it as a faintly amusing misfortune. When a man realizes that he is one of them, a certain degree of self-hatred is almost inevitable.

Second, many gays feel that they have had very much less than idyllic upbringings. Anyone who has grown up in an atmosphere of unusual conflict and hostility is more apt to have unresolved tensions that can affect his adult relationships.

With all the negative emotions it can raise, the discovery of oneself as gay usually brings to an end months or even years of doubts, confusion, and anguish. A dizzying sense of elation may take their place. Remember that other people in your life may find it difficult or impossible to share whatever feelings of release you may have.

Coming out to friends

Be prepared for some surprises. The friend you've regarded as the most liberal may turn out to be the one who can't handle the idea that you're gay. Others may accept it intellectually but will become uneasy when confronted by tangible evidence of your sex life, such as your lover.

Roughly speaking, your straight male friends who do not feel secure about their own sexual identification are likely to reject you. Even those straight men who are not hung up about gayness may fear guilt by association if they are known to be friends with someone who is gay.

The problem is that few hetero males are self-confident sexually.

Many fear their own quite normal homosexual impulses; their role stereotypes, being few and difficult to live up to, inspire self-doubts and anxiety. Thus gay men become useful to them as scapegoats and also to highlight their masculinity: "Maybe I'm not Superstud, but at least I'm no goddamned faggot."

All this said, let us point out that some heterosexual males will not be bothered by your sexual orientation, so don't write off all of them.

Straight female friends are far more likely to take your news without getting upset. You can expect a nasty reaction in only a few cases. The first, again, is the woman who is not confident of her sexuality. This type is a small minority among females. The second is the woman who, although you may not know it, happens to be in love with you. Naturally she is going to be disappointed. Finally, if you've been dating a female merely to pass yourself off as Mr. Macho, she's not going to enjoy learning that she has been used.

Coming out to your family

For the young man, these are the most usual reactions:

1. Your parents will accept you as you are. This is not common, and with the best intentions in the world they may take a long time to come to terms with your situation.

2. Your parents will try to understand, but the news will make them feel guilty, as if your gayness is their fault. They probably will think your life is headed for ruin if you persist in your homosexuality, and therefore will pressure you to change.

3. Your parents will not react. They will refuse to believe you, and the subject will never be brought up again.

4. Your parents will reject you. Melodramatic as this may seem, gay people do get thrown out of their family home, disowned, and told never to come back.

If you are an older man, living on your own and perhaps located at some distance from your parents, you don't have the problems a younger man has — it is easier to leave well enough alone.

At any age, the parents you tell may want you to keep your gayness a dark secret. Remember, that is for you alone to decide; it's your life and nobody else's.

Brothers and sisters can be very unpredictable at any time. Homophobia, often in the form of exaggerated fears for their children's safety in your presence, or sibling rivalry, or the fear that if you are, maybe they could be, can affect their reaction.

On all sides the potential for hurt is great. Whatever you decide to do, tread very carefully and consider what is to be gained by your revelation and what lost.

Where to come out

Valuing the friendship and warmth of straight friends and family but not wanting to live in the closet, many gay men leave their community and settle in some usually distant city that has a large gay population. New York, Chicago, New Orleans, Los Angeles, and San Francisco are common choices, and each of them has one or more gay neighborhoods or districts.

For some men this works well and gives a sense of freedom. For others, especially those with close attachments to family and straight friends, this alternative is more an exile than a liberation.

The etiquette of coming out

There are gay men that everybody can spot, that nobody can spot, and that only other gay men can spot. Some of us are up-front all the time by choice, some of us are deeply closeted, and a lot of us range somewhere in between. Every gay man has the right to decide for himself just how open he will be about his gayness, and this may vary with time, place, and situation.

Do not identify anybody as homosexual to any person who is heterosexual. This may sound like a needless warning, but it is easy to screw up, uncloseting a man who will not appreciate the favor.

Just how open you want to be is a decision to make only after carefully considering your own feelings and personal circumstances. Some men choose the closet, others refuse to hide at all, still others don't want to make a big fuss about it, and effeminate men may feel they have no choice in the matter.

Certainly for most men, the less strain and play-acting, the better. And on a larger scale, the more men who come out publicly as gay, the greater the benefit to all gay men. However many of us there are, we can't defend ourselves and maintain our rights if each of us is hiding alone.

THE LESBIAN EX-LOVER TRANSITION

by Carol Becker

It is our inward journey that leads us through time — forward or back, seldom in a straight line, most often spiraling. Each of us is moving, changing, with respect to others. As we discover, we remember; remembering, we discover; and most intensely do we experience this when our separate journeys converge.

—Eudora Welty

To varying degrees, lesbian ex-lovers retain their ties to one another after their breakup and use these bonds to rebuild their lives. An ex-lover remains an important part of a woman's evolving identity: as a woman, as a lesbian, and as a participant in intimate relationships.

The bond of lesbianism: Because lesbians are a stigmatized minority group, lesbian ex-lovers are united to one another by a bond of sisterhood. As lovers, they have fought for acceptance and understanding from their nuclear families, their children, their colleagues, and their neighbors. Having grown up in a homophobic environment, they have shared a battle against internalized homophobia as well.

When both women remain lesbian-identified after their breakup, they share the cultural experience of recovering from the ending of a stigmatized relationship. Despite the unresolvable differences that resulted in their breakup, lesbian ex-lovers remain connected by an overriding common cause — that of combating negative stereotypes of themselves, their relationships, and their lifestyle.

When her lover relationship ends, a lesbian loses a major source of validation for her identity as a lesbian — the intimate relationship that was a central expression of her sexual orientation. In leaving or in being left by her lover, a woman's evolving identity as a lesbian is disrupted. To sustain herself in the face of homophobia, it is important for her to strengthen her relationships with other lesbians and nonhomophobic family members and friends. Because they had shared a common struggle against society's negations and had validated each other's positive lesbian identities, lesbian ex-lovers remain connected by this bond of sisterhood.

Most often, a woman's family of friends help her through the ending of a partnership and its aftermath. Lesbian friends model and mirror a woman's life choices and give social validity to her personal experiences. Ex-lovers, who have known one another more intimately than other friends, are important sources of validation for one another. Because former partners have lived through many aspects of their lives together, they provide an inclusive reference point in each other's histories.

Relationships between lesbian ex-lovers provide a context within which a woman can weave together the broken pieces of her

---

Carol Becker practices psychotherapy in San Francisco and Berkeley, and is the author of UNBROKEN TIES: LESBIAN EX-LOVERS, in which she explores various aspects of the breakup of lesbian relationships. This essay is excerpted from her book.

intimate relationships and her identity. A woman's relationship with an ex-lover provides an important touchstone that adds continuity to her changing life. When a casual or a close friendship with an ex-lover is possible, a woman can integrate the important aspects of her past into her present and future life. When a relationship with an ex-lover is fictitious or absent, a woman has to find other sources of validation with which to mend her lesbian identity.

In addition to the personal support systems that tie lesbian ex-lovers to one another, these women share an involvement in their wider gay and lesbian communities. Extending their support systems into cultural and political realms is an important way they strengthen their lives as a depreciated minority. For many lesbians, building friendships with ex-lovers is an important part of building a wider community. A woman's sense of belonging is cultivated by this legitimating social world; it provides her a realm within which she can celebrate her relationships and her lifestyle.

Breakups as catalysts for growth: When a woman is ending a lover relationship, she often experiences the breakup as a death: of the relationship, of aspects of her lover, and of parts of herself. She sees her dreams shatter; she feels herself torn from the safe place where she belonged in the world. She witnesses the depths of her disappointment, pain, and longing. At first she can think only of how she might have saved the relationship or of how she or her lover could have been different.

As time passes and her emotional wounds heal she is able to see that she has grown and changed in desired ways by experiencing these losses. As her involvement with a lover is stripped away, she is left facing herself. She becomes aware of aspects of herself that she had forgotten while in the partnership — the hopes behind her disappointments, and the old wounds that were reopened by the new pain.

As a woman recovers from the ending of a relationship, she finds that she has increased her understanding of herself and her interpersonal needs and desires. In sifting through the rubble of the breakup, she has to clarify who she had been in the relationship and who she wants to be in subsequent relationships. She has to decide what she wants to salvage and what she wants to leave behind. In retrospect, she can see the errors she has made: how she had tried to make her lover into who she wished her to be; how she had not known what she wanted when she entered the relationship; how she had been unaware of her ambivalences and fears and dissatisfactions.

A woman acquires a better understanding of her emotional strengths and weaknesses by going through the ex-lover transition. In becoming aware of her own interpersonal habits and problems, she improves her ability to realistically assess her own, and her partner's, limitations and capabilities. A woman also gains knowledge of some of the fundamental issues in intimate relationships and improves her ability to prioritize her needs and preferences. This reconciliation of old issues increases her self-awareness, enriches her life experience, and enables her to develop stronger and more satisfying relationships in the future.

In the resolution of the ex-lover transition, lesbians discover that what they once thought of as a tragedy was an important catalyst for their evolution.

HEALTH

There is no such thing as a "gay disease." Lesbians and gay men are subject to infection by the same bacteria, viruses, and parasites as are heterosexuals.

Many sexually transmitted diseases, however, have been more prevalent among gay men than in the general population. There are several reasons for the difference: Gay men have the opportunity to engage in sex with more people than do most heterosexuals, and some practices that have been common in the gay community — especially rimming (anal-oral contact) and anal intercourse — are highly efficient ways of transmitting disease. In addition, closeted gay people are often reluctant to get prompt medical attention for sexually transmitted diseases. Fortunately, the increasing acceptance of safer sex, as a way of preventing AIDS, has also reduced the spread of other sexually transmitted diseases.

Lesbians have a lower incidence of most sexually transmitted diseases than does the general population. But this is a mixed blessing. Many women with AIDS have been diagnosed later than necessary, by doctors who perceived AIDS as primarily a male concern. And some diseases, such as gonorrhea, show symptoms less readily in women than they do in men; women who may have been exposed, then, must make it a point to be tested for it even if they are asymptomatic. In addition, some health experts believe that lesbians face a higher risk of getting breast cancer than do heterosexual women.

AIDS

What it is: AIDS is a condition that weakens the immune system and thus greatly reduces the body's ability to fight off infection. It is believed by most medical specialists to be caused by a virus, known as the Human Immunodeficiency Virus (HIV).

Cause and Prevention: HIV is most often transmitted when fluids — especially semen and blood — from an infected individual enter the body of another. The risk of contracting the virus can be significantly reduced by limiting sexual activity to less risky practices ("safer sex") and by using condoms, latex gloves, or dental dams when engaging in activities that could spread the virus.

Symptoms: The symptoms of AIDS can vary greatly, but generally include one or more of the following: swollen glands; unexplained, prolonged fever; weight loss; diarrhea; and purple lesions known as Kaposi's sarcoma.

Treatment: There is currently no known way to eliminate HIV from the body, but many of the infections and conditions associated with AIDS can be treated with a number of approved and experimental drugs.

AMEBIASIS

What it is: Amebiasis is caused by a small parasite — an ameba — that lives in the large intestine. Until the 1970s, this ameba was little known in the United States. In the 1970s, however, it spread rapidly through sexual contact, and amebiasis is now recognized as a sexually transmitted disease.

Cause and Prevention: The amebas causing this disease are usually transmitted through oral-anal contact. But any other activity, such as anal intercourse, that allows one person's fecal matter to eventually come into contact with a partner's mouth, can transmit it.

Symptoms: It is possible to have amebiasis for years without showing any symptoms. However, once the amebas begin invading the actual wall of the bowel, symptoms are likely to appear. These may include a change in bowel habits; bloody diarrhea; and abdominal cramps.

Treatment: Amebiasis is difficult to diagnose. Usually several stool specimens are examined under a microscope for signs of infection; however, this method does not always detect infections. Nor is the treatment sure to be successful; none of the drugs available for amebiasis is always effective, and frequently two or three treatments are required.

BREAST CANCER

What it is: While many other types of cancer seem to be in decline, incidences of breast cancer have been rising about 2% a year since the early 1970s. It is not sexually transmitted, but is included here because some experts believe that lesbians are at a substantially higher risk for it.

Cause and prevention: Breast cancer, like other forms of cancer, is still not thoroughly understood. Many factors influence an individual's cancer risk. Epidemiologist Susan Haynes of the National Cancer Institute reported four factors that seem to create a higher risk for lesbians: never having been pregnant, obesity, high alcohol consumption, and not having regular health checkups. In 1993, Haynes estimated that lesbians may be three times as likely to get breast cancer as straight women. Haynes stressed that her findings are still tentative and that further studies must be done. Although some of these factors can be changed, this is no guarantee of health; breast cancer is all too common even in women with no identifiable risk factors. Early detection is therefore vital. Experts recommend a mammogram once a year for women over 50, and every year or two for those 40 to 50. These recommendations are being re-evaluated, however; for women under 50, there is some doubt about whether mammograms are useful. While not all researchers agree on the value of breast self-exams, there's certainly no danger in doing them, provided they aren't used as a substitute for mammograms.

Symptoms: Mammograms remain the best form of detection.

Treatment: Early treatment is vital. Among women for whom the cancer is caught before it spreads beyond the breast, over 90% are still alive after five years. That figure drops to under 20% for those in whom it has spread widely.

CHLAMYDIA

What it is: Chlamydia is a family of organisms that cause several different diseases, including lymphogranuloma venereum (LGV), nongonococcal urethritis (discussed below as NGU/NSU), and trachoma eye infections. It's believed to be the most common sexually transmitted disease in the U.S. Untreated, it can lead to sterility in women.

Cause and prevention: The various diseases associated with the chlamydia organisms are usually contracted through sexual contact. The best means of prevention is to avoid contact with sexual partners who are infected. Condoms are protective.

Symptoms: Symptoms can be quite varied, but men usually experience burning on urination and a discharge from the penis. Women may experience painful urination and vaginal discharges, or a general pain in the lower abdomen, but often have no symptoms at all until advanced stages of the disease. At least half the women who are infected, and one-quarter of the men, show no initial symptoms of the disease, so anyone with multiple sex partners should be tested annually.

Treatment: Testing and treatment with antibiotics are necessary.

CRAB LICE

What it is: Known as "crabs," pubic lice are closely related to head and body lice, but they cannot infect the scalp, because their living habits require hairs that are relatively far apart.

Cause and Prevention: Crabs are usually caught from sex partners and are said to be the most highly contagious sexually transmitted disease. They can also be spread through shared towels, clothing, or even toilet seats.

Symptoms: The main symptom of crab lice is intense itching in the pubic area, starting three to four weeks after infection. The itching is frequently worse at night. It is often possible to see the lice and their eggs (nits) in the pubic hair.

Treatment: The usual prescription medication is gamma benzene hexachloride (sold under the name Kwell), which is available as a shampoo, cream, or lotion. The nits may have to be removed with a fine-tooth comb. Over-the-counter remedies are available, but are not always as effective.

CYSTITIS

What it is: Cystitis is an inflammation of the female urinary tract that can lead to a more serious kidney infection if not treated.

Cause and Prevention: Cystitis is most often caused by friction from intercourse, and is more common in heterosexual women than in lesbians. However, it can be caused by any continuous irritation to the urinary opening, and women with a low resistance due to poor health are more susceptible to it.

Symptoms: A frequent desire to urinate, and a burning sensation while urinating, are the usual symptoms of cystitis.

Treatment: Some women have reported successful home treatment by drinking large quantities of cranberry juice and water, taking vitamin C supplements, and avoiding caffeine and alcohol. Sulfa drugs and antibiotics are the usual medical treatments. Before using sulfa drugs, black women must be sure they are tested for an inherited blood deficiency of the enzyme G6PD; this occurs in about one-eighth of the black population in the U.S., and for anyone with this deficiency, use of sulfa drugs can be fatal.

GIARDIASIS

What it is: Giardiasis is similar to amebiasis, but is caused by a protozoan — *Giardia lamblia* — that lives in the small intestine. It is responsible for what is often known as "traveler's diarrhea," and in the past decade, has become common in gay men as well.

Cause and Prevention: The same anal-oral contact that transmits amebas (see *Amebiasis*) will transmit giardia.

Symptoms: Symptoms are often not present. Diarrhea (without blood present), nausea, and cramps are among the most common symptoms.

Treatment: Giardia, like amebas, is usually detected through a stool examination, although even then the disease is not always detectable. Several relatively effective drugs have been found for it.

GONORRHEA

What it is: Gonorrhea, known colloquially as the "clap," the "drip," or "GC," is caused by a bacterium that can infect the urethra, the rectum, the throat, or the eye. It may also appear as a generalized infection.

Cause and Prevention: Sexual contact with an infected partner is the usual cause of gonorrhea. It can also be contracted by infants as they pass through the birth canal. The only way to avoid gonorrhea is by avoiding sexual contact with someone who is infected; safer sex techniques used to prevent AIDS can also greatly reduce the likelihood of transmitting gonorrhea. Urinating after sexual contact may decrease the likelihood of developing urethral gonorrhea.

Symptoms: Because the bacterium can infect many different parts of the body, the symptoms vary. In men, the primary symptoms are a burning sensation when urinating, a penile discharge, and sometimes a sore throat or diarrhea. Vaginal and anal gonorrhea may result in a discharge, but usually do not. In women, there are often no symptoms until pelvic inflammatory disease (PID) develops. Many people never develop symptoms, though they are still infected and contagious, especially when gonorrhea occurs in the throat or rectum.

Symptoms can first appear from 1 to 30 days after exposure; the average time is 3 to 5 days.

Treatment: Patients must be treated with the appropriate antibiotic, depending on where the infection is located.

HEPATITIS-A

What it is: Hepatitis-A is caused by a virus that multiplies within the liver and causes inflammation of that organ. Hepatitis-A is considered the least harmful type of hepatitis because it does not cause permanent damage to the liver. A person who has had hepatitis-A will develop an immunity to future exposure, and will not be contagious after the initial bout is over.

Cause and Prevention: The hepatitis-A virus is found in fecal matter, and is commonly transmitted when even a small amount of feces is ingested. Oral-anal sex is a common route of transmission, as is anal intercourse. (The use of a condom does not necessarily protect against this disease, since a person's hands may come into contact with fecal matter on the rubber while removing it, and it can then be easily transmitted to his partner's mouth.) Hepatitis-A is also sometimes caught from contaminated water, from food that is not prepared under sanitary conditions, or from contaminated raw shellfish.

Symptoms: In its early stages, hepatitis-A can cause symptoms such as fever, headache, and loss of appetite. Then come the more distinctive symptoms: jaundice (a yellow tint to the eyes and skin); dark urine; and light, chalk-colored stools.

Treatment: Only in rare cases does hepatitis-A require hospitalization. Usually bed rest at home is adequate, and some people continue their daily routines while recovering from hepatitis-A. A person who suffers from hepatitis should not drink alcohol, as it will place a further burden on an already strained liver. Drugs or medications should be used only after consulting with a doctor.

HEPATITIS-B

What it is: Like hepatitis-A, hepatitis-B is an inflammation of the liver. However, it is much more serious. It sometimes causes permanent liver damage and cancer, and persons infected with this virus can become permanent carriers, able to infect others for the rest of their lives. It is estimated that about five percent of gay men are chronic carriers.

Cause and Prevention: The hepatitis-B virus, like the AIDS virus, is carried in many bodily fluids, most notably blood and semen, and it is transmitted in many of the same ways as the AIDS virus. Anal intercourse and needle-sharing are especially effective ways to transmit hepatitis-B. However, hepatitis-B is transmitted much more easily than the AIDS virus; you can become infected with hepatitis-B by sharing a toothbrush or drinking glass; through oral sex; or from any other activity in which you are exposed to the blood, semen, saliva, or urine of another person.

If you believe you have recently been infected with hepatitis-B, you can get an inexpensive gamma globulin shot, which helps your body's short-term defenses against the disease. For the longer term, a hepatitis-B vaccine is now available. Although relatively expensive ($100 to $200), most doctors recommend it for sexually active gay men who have not yet been infected. Many gay men are already immune.

Symptoms: About half of the people with hepatitis-B show no visible symptoms. When symptoms do appear, they may include fever or headache, joint aches, loss of appetite, or a rash. As with hepatitis-A, the best-known symptoms, which take slightly longer to appear, are jaundice (a yellow tint to the eyes and skin), dark urine, and light stools.

Treatment: Hepatitis-B is best diagnosed through blood tests. It usually does not require hospitalization, but adequate rest at home is important in fighting off the infection. Anyone still infected after about six months is considered to have chronic hepatitis.

HERPES SIMPLEX

What it is: Herpes simplex is a virus that causes cold sores and genital infections. It belongs to a family of four DNA viruses that cannot be completely eradicated by the immune system. Once infection occurs, the virus remains in the body, even if no symptoms are present.

Cause and Prevention: Herpes is spread only through close physical contact. It is transmitted through the mucous membranes of the mouth, genitals, rectum, or eyes. As with other sexually transmitted diseases, the best prevention is to avoid sexual contact with infected persons. Although it is possible to get herpes from asymptomatic partners, most people catch herpes from partners with visible lesions.

Symptoms: The primary symptoms are clusters of painful blisters or ulcers in the mouth or throat or vagina, on the penis, near or in the rectum, or on the buttocks. There may be itching or burning in the genital or rectal area. Generalized symptoms such as fever, headache, and vomiting may also occur.

Treatment: There is no cure for herpes. Daily doses of acyclovir, an antiviral drug, can reduce the severity and duration of outbreaks in some cases.

NGU/NSU

What it is: Nongonococcal urethritis (NGU) or nonspecific urethritis (NSU) is an infection caused by any one of several bacteria-like organisms, the most common being *Chlamydia trachomatis* and *Ureaplasma urealyticum.*

Cause and Prevention: NGU/NSU is transmitted primarily through sexual contact.

Symptoms: The usual symptoms in men are a burning sensation when urinating and more frequent urination. A penile discharge often accompanies NGU. Because these symptoms are similar to those for gonorrhea — but will not respond to penicillin as gonorrhea usually does — it is important that neither you, nor your doctor, assume that a penile discharge automatically indicates gonorrhea.

Women may also experience this burning sensation, but usually have no symptoms.

The first symptoms appear after 1 to 3 weeks.

Treatment: NGU is usually treated with tetracycline. If NGU is accompanied by gonorrhea, other drugs may also be required.

PELVIC INFLAMMATORY DISEASE (PID)

What it is: Pelvic inflammatory disease is estimated to afflict about one out of every ten American women of child-bearing age. PID causes scarring of the fallopian tubes; in severe cases, fertilized eggs can become trapped in the fallopian wall, endangering the woman's life.

Cause and Prevention: Both chlamydia and gonorrhea can lead to pelvic inflammatory disease.

Symptoms: Swelling of the uterus and cervix, detected during a routine exam, are often the first signs of PID, although a clear diagnosis sometimes requires a minor surgical procedure.

Treatment: PID can be stopped with antibiotics. At the same time, women with PID should try to track down the source of the responsible bacteria, to prevent reinfection.

SCABIES

What it is: Scabies is caused by a mite too small to be seen with the naked eye. It belongs to the Arachnida class of insects, along with spiders and scorpions. Unlike the pubic crabs, which stay on the surface of the skin, the female scabies mite burrows under the skin, where she lays her eggs.

Cause and Prevention: Scabies is transmitted primarily through close physical contact. Since the mite can survive on sheets and towels for two or three days, it is also possible to catch it from them.

Symptoms: Itching begins about a month after infestation. It becomes especially severe at night.

Treatment: Like crabs, scabies is treated with Kwell. The cream or lotion must be applied to the entire body from the neck down, left on for eight to twenty-four hours, and then washed off. A second applica-

tion is necessary a week to ten days later to kill newly hatched organisms. Itching may persist for weeks, even after successful therapy.

SHIGELLOSIS

What it is: Shigellosis is caused by the *Shigella* bacteria. Like other sexually transmitted intestinal diseases, it has spread rapidly in the last couple of decades.

Cause and Prevention: The same anal-oral contact that transmits amebas (see *amebiasis*) will transmit shigella.

Symptoms: Shigellosis may be asymptomatic. Often, however, it is characterized by a violent and sudden onset of cramps, diarrhea, and fever within three days of exposure.

Treatment: A stool culture can detect the presence of shigella; however, this process takes one or two days. Although drugs are available for the disease, most people with shigellosis recover on their own after about a week. During this period, it is important to drink enough fluids to replace those being lost because of the diarrhea. Anti-diarrheal medications are generally not advisable unless recommended by a doctor.

SYPHILIS

What it is: Syphilis is caused by an organism known as a spirochete. In 1983, gay and bisexual men accounted for fifty percent of reported new cases, although that percentage dropped as safe sex practices became widespread. It is a serious disease that, if untreated, can many years later lead to brain damage, paralysis, heart disease, and death.

Cause and Prevention: The vast majority of syphilis cases are sexually transmitted. The spirochete enters the body through broken skin or mucous membranes. The only way to prevent syphilis is by avoiding sexual contact with infected partners.

Symptoms: The symptoms of syphilis vary according to how long a person has been infected. In the primary stage, there is often a painless ulcer or chancre at the point of contact, usually the penile shaft or anus for men, and around the vaginal opening for women. These chancres heal naturally, but the disease continues to spread.

In the secondary stage, typically at about twelve weeks, rashes, flulike symptoms, hair loss, swollen lymph nodes, and mouth sores are common. Eventually, the disease attacks the brain, eyes, heart, and other organs.

Symptoms may appear 10 to 90 days after exposure; the average period is 3 weeks.

Treatment: Persons infected with syphilis must be treated with antibiotics, usually penicillin. If treated too late, however, the disease can do permanent damage.

TRICHOMONIASIS

What it is: Often just called trich, trichomoniasis is a vaginal infection caused by a one-celled protozoan called a trichomonad. If not treated, it sometimes leads to more serious problems.

Cause and Prevention: The parasite that causes trich is common, and easily spread. Women can pass it to one another through sexual contact, and by sharing clothing, towels, or toilet seats. Heterosexual and bisexual women can get it through vaginal intercourse with a man. (Men can carry the infection, though they do not show symptoms.)

Symptoms: Trich is characterized by a foul-smelling greenish or greenish-yellow vaginal discharge, appearing 4 to 28 days after infection. Vaginal itching and irritation may also occur.

Treatment: The most effective treatment for this persistent infection is a potent drug called Flagyl, which must be used under a doctor's supervision.

VENEREAL WARTS

What they are: Warts are skin tumors caused by a virus. Although unpleasant, they are not considered dangerous in themselves. However, experts suspect they may be linked to cervical and penile cancers.

Cause and Prevention: Venereal warts are almost always sexually transmitted, and the only sure protection is to avoid any sexual contact with infected partners. Even the hand-to-genital contact of mutual masturbation can spread them. Once you are infected warts can be "self-seeding" and easily spread beyond the point of initial infection.

Symptoms: Warts are painless growths usually around the vaginal opening, the anus, or on the shaft of the penis. On women, they may also appear in the vagina or cervix, where they will be detected only during a medical exam. They may make their first appearance several months after exposure. Anal warts can cause itching and bleeding with anal intercourse or after bowel movements.

Treatment: Several forms of treatment are possible. Podophyllin is the most common. It is applied directly to the warts and washed off several hours later. Other treatments include liquid nitrogen, lasers, and surgery. Repeated treatments are often necessary.

YEAST INFECTION

What it is: Also called monilia, monilial vaginitis, or candiasis, a yeast infection is a vaginal infection usually caused by the body's reaction to an unwelcome change in a woman's diet, medication, or clothing. When it appears in the throat, the infection is called thrush.

Cause and Prevention: This infection may be triggered by such diverse factors as too much sugar in the diet; wearing tight or non-cotton underwear; high stress; pregnancy; vaginal deodorants; frequent douching; and certain medications. It may be spread from one woman to another through sexual contact, and by sharing clothing or towels; it can also be transmitted via toilet seats.

Symptoms: Yeast infections are characterized by a thick white discharge from the vagina, which resembles cottage cheese and smells like yeast. Vaginal itching may also occur.

Treatment: A common home treatment for yeast infection consists of inserting several spoonfuls of unflavored, unsweetened yogurt into the vagina twice a day. This will not work in all cases, and medical treatments, involving vaginal suppositories, are also available.

SAFER SEX

by Laurie Sherman

The AIDS epidemic has illuminated a host of national concerns: a failing health care system, the ineffectiveness of the government's efforts to fight drug addiction, and an alarming spread of sexually transmitted diseases. The crisis has also prompted discussion specifically *within* our gay and lesbian communities, pushing us to re-examine our own attitudes about sexuality, addiction, and other concerns.

Many gay men and lesbians involved in AIDS work are beginning to discuss how our socialization about sex influences safer-sex guidelines for avoiding HIV transmission. For example, judgments about "promiscuity" are conveyed in some safer-sex information produced by the gay community. We still read that reducing the number of sexual partners is the simplest way to play it safe. It is true that as the number of partners increases, so does the likelihood of *encountering* one who is HIV-positive; however, the single most important factor is clearly what *behavior* you engage in. Unsafe sex with a single infected lover can put someone at higher risk than practicing safe sex with a multitude of partners.

Laurie Sherman served as the managing editor of GAY COMMUNITY NEWS, *and more recently she has supervised fifty volunteer AIDS educators at the AIDS Action Committee of Massachusetts.*

Pamphlets produced within our community still warn against a number of sexual activities that do not transmit HIV, such as "water sports" — urinating on a partner as part of sex play. Since infection only occurs when an HIV-positive person's *blood, semen,* or *vaginal fluids* get into a partner's bloodstream, water sports do not put either partner at risk. The U.S. Centers for Disease Control has concluded that saliva, tears, sweat, and urine are among those body fluids that *do not* transmit HIV.

Similarly, rimming and fisting remain on the "high risk" list in many pamphlets circulating among gay men, and yet neither activity creates a direct risk for HIV infection. Rimming can result in intestinal viruses which can lead to health problems, especially for people who are already HIV-positive. However, in the absence of open sores, it is unlikely that a person would get enough blood in their mouth from licking in or around someone's anus — and then have that blood get directly into their bloodstream — to be infected with HIV. However, as of this writing, a new theory is developing that suggests Kaposi's sarcoma may exist independently of HIV, and can be transmitted by rimming.

Brochures fail to explain that the problem with *fisting* comes when a man puts his hand in someone's anus, and causes some tearing in the lining; if he then inserts his

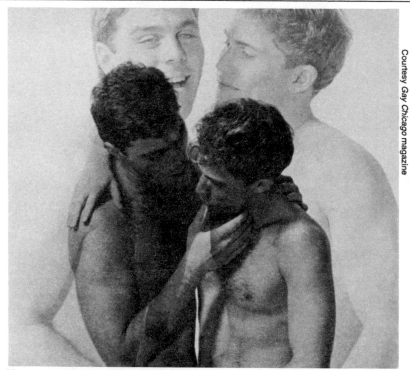

Courtesy *Gay Chicago* magazine

Many organizations have responded to the need for educational materials that promote safer sex. *Gay Chicago* magazine's "Safe Sex is Great Sex..." calendar uses erotic images to get the message across.

penis and ejaculates, HIV can pass through the injured lining into his partner's bloodstream. Fisting alone is not a high risk behavior for HIV transmission.

The risk of oral sex is not as clear, and much debate has developed in the past year about oral sex — for both gay men and lesbians. At least two cases of HIV infection have been documented from men swallowing the semen of infected partners. In response to this, some AIDS educators advocate the use of condoms for oral sex on a man.

Other AIDS educators believe we have enough information about the mouth's ability to fight off infection to assert that oral sex — going down on a man or woman — will never be a common route of infection. A small number of organizations in the U.S. and abroad have even begun "suck don't fuck" campaigns aimed at gay men.

The majority of educators seem to fall somewhere in between, urging men not to take semen into their mouths, and leaving other ways of having oral sex up to the individual's judgment. Options include: (1) go down on a partner until he is about to ejaculate, taking pre-cum but not semen into your mouth (researchers have not yet determined the concentration of HIV in pre-cum but avoiding semen would lower your risk); or, even safer, (2) lick the head of the penis only if there is little or no pre-cum; or, to be safest, (3) use the "harmonica" method and lick only the shaft of the penis and the testicles, without putting your mouth on the head of the penis.

Some gay men are willing to take a partner's pre-cum or semen into their mouths only until they find out the partner is infected. Because of the high infection rate among gay men, it is advisable to assume a male partner is infected — unless you are certain he is not — and then decide what risks you are comfortable taking. "Know your partner" is a common phrase used in the media that may be unhelpful to people trying to decide when and with whom to use safer sex practices. A new partner may not always be honest about his or her past, and your partners will not always know the sexual and drug use history of their former lovers.

For lesbians, the risks of oral sex are also under debate. Theoretically someone could get infected by going down on an HIV-positive woman — through her menstrual blood or vaginal fluids, and this seems to have happened in a few cases, although researchers aren't yet certain.

In response, some educators suggest lesbians use dental dams or cut open a condom and place it over a partner's vulva as a barrier; this would certainly be the safest way to perform oral sex on a woman. Other educators believe transmission from going down on a woman is highly unlikely and suggest we refrain from it only if there are sores in our mouth, and our partner is menstruating or has a vaginal infection.

Many people discuss AIDS in terms of eliminating any risk, and look for 100% guarantees of never contracting HIV. However, we have no guarantees about most activities we engage in, and we take risks every day. We know we face the risk of gay-bashing when we leave our community bars, and sometimes when we simply walk down the street, but we refuse to let that fear keep us at home. We constantly must decide whether to come out at work — and possibly risk our paycheck — and whether to come out to family.

Women regularly balance the risk of sexual assault with the reality that we need to walk somewhere alone at night. Many people take the risk of getting into a car with a driver who's had "just a few" drinks. We know that getting into a car at all carries some risk. While many lesbians have become fearful of sexual transmission of HIV, few of us check our breasts monthly for lumps. Yet such a simple precaution would allow for early detection of the type of cancer that attacks 140,000 women every year in the U.S. — many more than we expect to ever face AIDS.

It may be helpful to put HIV into the realm of the other choices we make and to think less about risk elimination and more about *risk management* — making thoughtful choices about what levels of risk are acceptable to us and comfortable for us.

The AIDS epidemic is bringing to light for our community concerns other than sexuality and sexual decision making. The diversity of gay men and lesbians seeking AIDS ser-

HIGH-RISK BEHAVIORS

1. Sharing IV needles that have not been bleached clean
2. Anal intercourse without a condom
3. Vaginal intercourse without a condom. In both anal and vaginal intercourse, the receptive partner (the partner receiving the semen) is at higher risk. Insertive partners have also been infected with HIV through both anal and vaginal intercourse, and should use a condom for their protection as well. It is especially risky to receive semen in the anus or vagina after being fisted.

ADDITIONAL INFORMATION

1. It is becoming more apparent that re-infection with HIV can hasten the development of AIDS. HIV-positive men and women are urged to continue practicing safer sex and not to share IV needles or works.
2. Condoms are not 100% effective. They are much less likely to break if used correctly. Call your local AIDS hotline for detailed instructions.
3. It is recommended that you do not take semen into your mouth. Researchers have not studied the vaginal fluids of HIV-positive women enough to know whether taking them into your mouth can lead to HIV infection. Call your local hotline to stay updated on new developments.
4. Sharing sex toys may be risky if you get your partner's blood, semen, or vaginal fluids on them, then insert them immediately into your own vagina or rectum. You can clean them in between, or use only your own.

LOTS OF SEXUAL ACTIVITIES ARE SAFE AND FUN!
Call your local AIDS hotline to talk.

vices are forcing our organizations to redefine who comprises "the gay community." For example, the majority of lesbians who have AIDS — and there are many more than feel comfortable coming out publicly — have been infected through IV needle use. This is true for some HIV-positive gay men as well. And many of us are beginning to look at the role of noninjected drugs — alcohol, cocaine, poppers — in lessening inhibition and increasing the likelihood of unsafe sex.

Taboos on discussion of bisexuality leave many in our community without life-saving information. Lesbians who have sex with men may be at risk for HIV infection; the heterosexual female partners of bisexual men may be at risk as well. At the Sixth International Conference on AIDS in June 1990, one study demonstrated that HIV is up to fourteen times more likely to be transmitted from men to women during intercourse, than from women to men. Hence the reminder that regardless of one's sexual identity, the relevant factor is the *behaviors* in which we engage.

As we grapple with grave losses to AIDS, we continue learning about our community, re-examining definitions of who we are and who our community agencies serve. More gay men and lesbians are working together in the AIDS epidemic, breaking ground for these discussions about sexuality, addiction, and much more, across gender lines.

THE NAMES PROJECT AND THE AIDS MEMORIAL QUILT

Cleve Jones was devastated when his best friend died of AIDS in the fall of 1986. For months afterwards, he found himself on the edge of despair. The memory of his friend was so painful that he found it difficult to carry on in his everyday life. Then, one day Cleve and a friend spread fabric across his back patio and began painting names and designs with paint they had found in the garage. While doing so, they talked, laughed, and reminisced about the friends they had lost to AIDS. Cleve found the experience so therapeutic that he asked friends to join him in creating a giant quilt to commemorate those who had died of AIDS. Thus began the NAMES Project.

The NAMES Project has become a national AIDS memorial, taking the form of a huge quilt, made up of individual three-foot by six-foot panels, each bearing the name of a person lost to AIDS.

The Quilt was first displayed on the Capitol Mall in Washington, D.C., in October 1987. The memorial is an ongoing project, and panels continue to be added. As the toll on lives of men, women, and children rises, the Quilt is offered as a compassionate response to the epidemic.

The goals of the Quilt are:
• To illustrate the impact of the AIDS epidemic by showing the humanity behind the statistics;
• To provide a positive and creative means of expression for those whose lives have been touched by the epidemic; and
• To raise vital funds and encourage support for people with AIDS and their loved ones.

The NAMES Project is now taking these messages to every corner of America. It has already been displayed in over a hundred cities in the U.S. and abroad. Hundreds of thousands of people have visited the Quilt, and hundreds of thousands of dollars have been raised for direct care services for people with AIDS. These funds remain in the local communities where the Quilt is displayed and are distributed through local AIDS organizations.

Doug Hinckle/The Washington Blade

HOW TO CREATE A MEMORIAL PANEL:

1. Select a durable, lightweight fabric for the background. Cut and hem the fabric to 3' by 6'. (The NAMES Project staff will hem it for you if you leave three inches extra fabric on each side.)

2. Design the letters. Some suggestions:
   - Appliqué: sew letter to background fabric
   - Painting: brush letters on with paint, dye, or ink
   - Stencil: spray-paint cut-out letters
   - Collage: glue on material with fabric glue
   - Embroider: sew on beads, sequins, or rhinestones

3. When the panel is complete, write a one- or two-page description of the person you have memorialized. Enclose a photograph of the person if you're willing to part with it.

4. Wrap the panel securely before mailing it to: The NAMES Project, P.O. Box 14573, San Francisco, CA 94114.

5. Please include as generous a contribution as possible.

Have any questions? Call The NAMES Project at (415) 863-5511.

CHURCH POLICIES ON GAY CONCERNS

BAPTIST CHURCH

The 26 million members of the Baptist church in North America have divided into four conventions, with distinct approaches to gay issues.

Of all mainline denominations, the **Southern Baptist Church** takes the most conservative view. In 1987, the Southern Baptist Convention condemned homosexuality as "a manifestation of a depraved nature" and "a perversion of divine standards." Furthermore, the Convention linked homosexuality to a general problem of moral decline in modern society. Unlike other churches which, though unbending in their condemnation of homosexual acts, make a distinction between homosexual orientation and homosexual acts, the Southern Baptist Church fails even to go this far, declaring that "homosexuals like all sinners can receive forgiveness and victory" through faith in Jesus. At its 1992 convention, the church voted to expel two congregations — one for recognizing a gay holy union, the other for licensing an openly gay pastor. In 1993, it voted to refuse membership to any congregation that condoned homosexuality.

At the other end of the spectrum are the **American Baptists**. The most liberal of the Baptist sects, they have generally supported the rights of minorities. In 1974, church president Peter Armacost broached the subject with the guardedly supportive statement that "The church is open to any individual, regardless of whether some people think he's sick or not, regardless of whether he's sinned or not. We are all to some extent sinners, and no church ought to be closed to someone just because he's a homosexual."

BUDDHISM

Alone among the major world religions, Buddhism does not condemn homosexuality or premarital sex. The emphasis in Buddhism is on achieving a state of enlightenment, but the religion provides only guidelines, not strict commandments, as to how individuals should strive for this. Rape and adultery are considered misconduct, but an individual is free to engage in consenting sexual acts that do not violate marital or monastic commitments.

Buddhist countries tend to have few social and legal prohibitions against homosexuality. Some, such as Thailand, are surprisingly free of homophobia.

CHRISTIAN SCIENCE

On many levels, the Christian Science movement has succeeded in moving beyond the narrow concepts of heaven and hell and a vengeful God toward an emphasis on God as love. But on the question of how that love can be expressed by humans, church officials have remained on the same plane as the most conservative religions. Sex exists only for procreation, according to church officials; homosexuality thus has no place in the life of a proper Christian Scientist. The church has fired employees for being gay.

EPISCOPAL CHURCH

For the past century, the Episcopal Church has been more receptive to gay worshippers than have most other Christian denominations, without ever quite making up its mind about just how warmly to extend its welcome. It was the first mainstream U.S. denomination to ordain a woman who was openly lesbian. Many gay people, in turn, have been attracted to the elaborate rituals of Episcopalian ceremonies.

At its triennial convention in 1976, the U.S. Episcopal Church passed a resolution that "Homosexual persons are children of God who have full and equal claim with all other persons upon the love, acceptance, pastoral concern and care of the Church. Homosexual persons are entitled to equal protection under the law with all other citizens and [the Church] calls upon society to see that such protection is provided in actuality." At the same convention, the church voted to approve ordination of women.

At its next General Convention, three years later, the church backpedaled. The House of Bishops approved a resolution barring the ordination of practicing homosexuals and reaffirmed "the traditional teaching of the Church on marriage,

marital fidelity and sexual chastity."

In 1988, the House of Bishops voted to forbid discrimination in the church on the grounds of sexual orientation, but the House of Deputies, made up of clergy and laity, narrowly voted the proposal down. A 1991 resolution stressed that sex should be confined to the marital relationship, noted that not everyone would buy this philosophy, and called for three more years of study. Meanwhile, however, bishops are allowed to ordain openly gay, sexually active lesbians and gay men.

In England, where Episcopalianism (generally termed Anglicanism in that country) is the state religion, the church has been less supportive on gay issues.

ISLAM

The Moslem religion has a long tradition of severely proscribing homosexuality in theory, but winking at it in practice. Islamic law distinguishes strongly between public and private acts. Muslims are expected to marry, and both homosexuality and adultery are condemned. But in actual practice, it is only public homosexual acts that are punished; four adult male witnesses must testify against an offender before he or she can be punished. Islam culture also differentiates between the active and passive partner in gay male sex, ascribing much more dishonor to the latter.

JUDAISM

Because Jewish congregations vary so widely in questions of doctrine and policy, there is no single definitive Jewish policy regarding homosexuality. Orthodox synagogues have generally taken a dim view of homosexuality. The Conservative branch of the church for many years held back from dealing with gay issues, but in 1990 it voted to recognize the equality of congregation members, regardless of their sexual orientation.

Reform Judaism, which is the largest branch of American Judaism, has also been the most progressive. In 1979, the main association of Reformed congregations in the United States adopted a resolution that homosexual persons were "entitled to equal protection under the law," and congregations were encouraged to "conduct appropriate educational programming ... to provide greater understanding of the relation of Jewish values to the range of human sexuality." The Central Conference of American Rabbis has also encouraged "legislation which decriminalizes homosexual acts between consenting adults, and prohibits discrimination against them as persons."

In 1990, Reform Judaism went even further, officially voting to accept sexually active homosexuals as rabbis.

LUTHERAN CHURCH

On July 2, 1970, the Lutheran Church in America "liberalized" its policy on homosexuality, adopting the position that "the sexual behavior of consenting adults is not an acceptable subject for legislation or police action." At the same time, however, it noted that "homosexuality is viewed biblically as a departure from the heterosexual structure of God's creation. Persons who en-

gage in homosexual behavior are sinners only as are all other persons — alienated from God and neighbor. However, they are often the special and undeserving victims of prejudice and discrimination in law, law enforcement, cultural mores, and congregational life."

In 1988 the Lutheran Church in America merged with the American Lutheran Church and the Association of Evangelical Lutheran Churches, forming the Evangelical Lutheran Church in America (ELCA). The new organization quickly showed what it was made of in 1990, when it suspended two San Francisco churches for ordaining openly gay and lesbian ministers.

MORMONS
(CHURCH OF JESUS CHRIST OF LATTER-DAY SAINTS)

The Mormon Church has the most anti-gay policies of any religion widely practiced in the U.S. today. Like the Victorians, the Mormons focus their denunciations on male homosexuality, while ignoring lesbianism as much as possible.

This homophobia is not confined to the church itself. The Mormon-run Brigham Young University has regularly persecuted gay students. A 1965 witch-hunt, in which gay students were pressured to confess their own "sins" and to give names of others who might be gay, resulted in five suicides. A decade later, BYU president Spencer Kimball referred to homosexuality as "the ugly sin." To those who suggested they were born homosexual, he responded that "This is as untrue as any other of the diabolical lies

Satan has concocted. Man is made in the image of God. Does the pervert think God to be 'that way'?" He offered counseling and shock therapy for Mormons who wanted to change, and wrote: "To those who say that homosexuality is incurable, I respond: 'How can you say the door cannot be opened until your knuckles are bloody, till your head is bruised, till your muscles are sore?' It can be done."

PRESBYTERIAN CHURCH—USA

If the Presbyterian Church still seems undecided on the issue of homosexuality, it's not for lack of discussion.

In 1970 the General Assembly of the United Presbyterian Church created an uproar within the church when it accepted for church study — but not as policy — a report that urged reconsideration of attitudes toward homosexuality, extramarital sex, and abortion. Two years later, church head Lois Stair called for the church "to extend a warm hand of welcome" to gay people. The summer 1973, issue of *Trends,* an official Presbyterian church publication, was devoted to articles by gay people about their role within the church. This caused further controversy; the church's conservative wing demanded the replacement of responsible staff members.

In 1976, the General Assembly reaffirmed a previous resolution that stated that the "practice of homosexuality is a sin," and voted that it would be "injudicious if not improper" to ordain homosexuals to the ministry.

Two years of further study followed, after which the church's Task Force to Study Homosexuality issued its findings. They were essentially an exercise in fence-sitting, stating that "some forms of homosexuality truly express sin" while "some forms do express a responsible, self-giving love." The task force found no intrinsic reason gay people should not be ordained within the church, and said individual congregations should set their own policies on the matter.

In 1979, before the merger by which they became the Presbyterian Church (U.S.A.), the northern and southern Presbyterian churches jointly adopted a policy opposing the ordination of gay people. That is still being followed. Delegates at the 1991 conference refused to discuss a controversial concept termed "justice-love," under which nonmarital sexual relationships would have been sanctioned. Instead, they issued a letter stating that homosexuality was "not God's wish for humanity," rejected any sanctioning of same-sex unions, and forbade the ordination of openly gay clergy. The following year, a church court revoked the appointment of the Reverend Jane Spahr, a lesbian co-pastor in Rochester, N.Y.

In 1993, the church reaffirmed that sexually active gay people could not be ordained. Lest anyone be offended, however, church officials took a further step: They agreed to keep studying the issue.

ROMAN CATHOLIC CHURCH

The Catholic Church has consistently condemned all homosexual activity as inherently sinful. It has at the same time, however, distinguished between a homosexual orientation, which in itself is considered to be morally neutral, and homosexual practices, which are considered to be sinful in every case.

In 1976, the Sacred Congregation of the Faith issued a "Declaration on Certain Questions Concerning Sexual Ethics," which addressed a number of questions related to sexual morality, including homosexuality. The Declaration reaffirmed the Church's traditional stance on homosexuality, stating that "homosexual acts are intrinsically disordered and can in no case be approved of." Further, the Vatican issued a letter on homosexuality in October of 1986, now known as the "Halloween letter," which called homosexuality "behavior to which no one has any conceivable right."

As for the officials who are supposed to enforce Vatican doctrine: In 1982 a task force convened by the San Francisco Archdiocese concluded that 30% of Roman Catholic nuns, priests, and brothers were gay or lesbian. Others have suggested that the figure is much higher.

RELIGIOUS SOCIETY OF FRIENDS (QUAKERS)

As far back as 1682, when William Penn founded the colony of Pennsylvania along Quaker principles, this group has shown an openness to homosexuality. A 1963 statement by English Quakers states that "One should no more deplore homosexuality than left-handedness." Twenty-one years later, U.S. Quakers wrote that "We affirm the power and joy of nonexploitive, loving relationships. As a society and as individuals we oppose arbitrary social, economic or legal abridgement of the right to share this love."

However, many decisions in this nonhierarchical church are made locally. When it has actually come to recognizing same-sex marriages, the issue has often caused deep divisions. Local meetings operate by consensus rather than by vote, and a few strong opponents of such marriages are enough to block a resolution in their favor.

SEVENTH-DAY ADVENTISTS

This small sect has been vocal in its condemnation of homosexuality, calling same-sex practices "obvious perversions of God's original plan."

UNITARIAN UNIVERSALIST ASSOCIATION

The Unitarian Universalist Association has gone further than any other denomination to defend the rights of gay men and lesbians. On July 4, 1970, the Unitarian General Assembly approved a resolution upholding the rights of gay men and lesbians, and calling for an end to discrimination against gay and lesbian candidates for the ministry. The church later affirmed the practice of conducting services of union for gay and lesbian couples, and funded an Office of Gay Concerns.

UNITED CHURCH OF CHRIST

In 1972, the United Church of Christ became the first Christian denomination to ordain an openly gay person to the ministry. Three years later, it affirmed the civil liberties of gay and bisexual persons. While carefully avoiding a position on "the rightness or wrongness of same-gender relationships," it stated that the church "must bear a measure of responsibility for the suffering visited upon same-gender-oriented persons." At its biennial General Synod in 1983, UCC delegates voted overwhelmingly in favor of a statement that sexual orientation should not be grounds for barring a person from being ordained; it was the first major denomination to take such a stand.

UNITED METHODIST CHURCH

In 1972, the United Methodist Church issued a "Statement of Social Principles" in which the church declared that homosexuality was "incompatible with Christian teaching," although it supported the civil rights of homosexuals. This position has characterized the Methodist position in succeeding years, and was formally reaffirmed in 1992.

In 1973, the United Methodist Council of Bishops unanimously approved a statement declaring that the bishops did not "advocate or support ordination for practicing homosexuals," a policy that was reiterated in 1984 and 1988 at a General Conference meeting.

A Boulder, Colorado, minister brought the issue to the forefront in 1982. The Reverend Julian Rush confided to his senior pastor that he had become involved in a local gay organization. In the resulting controversy, Bishop Melvin E. Wheatley defended Rush, arguing that nothing in UMC doctrine prohibited a gay person from being a minister. The church court agreed, but in 1984, the church changed its policy so that gay ministers could be banned.

LAWS AND ATTITUDES, BY COUNTRY

Maintaining up-to-date information about more than a hundred countries is difficult. In these brief paragraphs, we have done our best to synthesize information from a number of sources; countries for which we could not obtain reliable information are not included. We welcome reports from people who have traveled to these countries, for use in future editions.

ALBANIA: Homosexuality is not illegal; in 1977 the government set a common age of consent, for both gay and straight sex, at 14. But legal does not mean welcome. Albanian life is rigidly controlled by the communist government. There is no gay and lesbian movement. If there is any gay and lesbian culture, it is well hidden.

ALGERIA: Homosexual activity is illegal, punishable with fines or jail sentences of up to two years (three years for sex with someone under 18). Gay people are very discreet.

ARGENTINA: Although there are no laws against homosexuality, long-entrenched prejudices are only slowly giving way to more enlightened attitudes. Conditions improved after an elected government replaced the former dictatorship in 1983. More recently, however, members of the Comunidad Homosexual Argentina (CHA) have protested that the growing gay population of Buenos Aires faces regular police harassment, and that gays are sometimes denied the right to vote on grounds of "unworthiness." There have been confirmed reports of men murdered for being gay. In 1991, Argentine president Carlos Menem was dogged whenever he traveled abroad by gay protesters advocating reforms. The next year, CHA was finally granted legal standing, but the oppression continued. Later that year, Canada took the unusual step of granting political asylum to an Argentine man who faced anti-gay persecution at home.

AUSTRALIA: Australia was ruled by British law in the 1800s, and "buggery" was a capital offense until 1861, when the penalty was reduced to life imprisonment. Under the constitution of 1990, each state sets its own laws about matters such as sodomy laws and the age of consent. The southeastern part of the country, where most of the population is concentrated, took the lead in abolishing sodomy laws for those over age 18, and most other states followed suit. Today only the conservative island state of Tasmania still prohibits gay sex. Melbourne and Sydney boast vibrant and highly visible lesbian and gay communities; Sydney is famous for its annual gay and lesbian Mardi

Gras, which draws half a million people. On November 23, 1992, Prime Minister Paul Keating announced that he was dropping the ban on allowing gay people in the military, effective immediately.

AUSTRIA: In 1787 Austria reduced the penalty for male homosexuality from death to life imprisonment. In 1852, the penalty was further reduced, but lesbianism was made illegal. Not until 1971 were these laws abolished. However, evidence of anti-gay attitudes continues in Austria's odd ages of consent: 18 for gay male sex; 14 for lesbian and heterosexual sex. The penal code also forbids advocacy of homosexuality, although this law is not enforced and several gay organizations are active in the larger cities. In smaller towns, however, there is little sign of a gay community. Homosexuals are allowed in the armed forces.

BAHAMAS: Homosexual activity is illegal, and the laws are enforced: in 1992, gay men from Britain and Trinidad were arrested on charges of public homosexual sex, and spent two months in prison. The gay community is still undeveloped.

BARBADOS: Homosexuality is illegal here, but the law is rarely enforced against discreet private behavior.

BELARUS: Gay sex is legal in this former Soviet republic, although there is still considerable prejudice against gay people.

BELGIUM: Lesbian sex was never illegal here, and gay male sex has been legal since 1795. The age of consent is 16, the same as for het-

erosexuals. The general atmosphere is one of tolerance, but falls short of the total acceptance found in the adjacent Netherlands. Homosexuals are allowed in the armed forces.

BELIZE: Homosexual activity is legal between consenting adults, but gay life remains discreet.

BERMUDA: Homosexuality is illegal in Bermuda, which is a British colony but has an independent criminal code. Sex between men can be punished by up to ten years in prison. There is no visible gay culture, and the 1992–1993 edition of the gay guide *Spartacus* reports that "upon inquiring, we were told by the Bermudan Police Headquarters that homosexuality 'is the type of crime that is not tolerated in Bermuda.'"

BRAZIL: Brazil's penal code, which was written under the influence of the Napoleonic Code, has never forbidden homosexual activity for consenting adults (over 18), but police harassment is not uncommon, usually under the guise of protecting the public morals. Brazil has had a small gay movement since the mid-1970s, often affiliated with leftist political movements. The festive Rio de Janeiro Carnival, in February or early March each year, attracts gay people from around the world.

BULGARIA: Both lesbian and gay male sex were illegal until 1968, when the restrictions were lifted but were replaced with a discriminatory age of consent: 18 for lesbians and gay men, 14 for heterosexuals. But even with legalization, the authorities find ways to make life tough for anyone suspected of being gay.

Consequently, lesbians and gay men are virtually invisible. The first known gay organization (Gemini) appeared in 1990 and was officially recognized in 1993; the first gay and lesbian magazine (*Flamingo*) made its appearance in 1992. Progress is likely to continue, but not quickly.

CANADA: Homosexual activity has been legal here since 1969. The age of consent is generally 14, but rises to 18 if prostitution or anal intercourse are involved, or if one partner is a dependent of the other. Gay civil rights legislation has passed in the provinces of Ontario, Montreal, Manitoba, and Yukon, and in 1992 Ontario extended spousal benefits to the same-sex partners of government workers. Overall, there is a slightly stronger climate of acceptance of lesbians and gay men than in the U.S. On October 27, 1992, in light of an unfavorable court ruling, the Canadian government dropped its ban on allowing gays in the military.

CHILE: Homosexuality is still illegal here, punishable by up to twenty years in prison. Although the law is rarely if ever enforced, it provides an excuse for frequent police raids of bars and other gathering spots. Chile remains an uncomfortable — and sometimes dangerous — place to be openly gay.

CHINA: Although open same-sex relationships have been well documented in earlier Chinese cultures, British colonialists brought anti-gay attitudes that persist today. The official line for many years portrayed homosexuality as a bourgeois sickness that did not exist in China. Homosexuality is not explicitly for-bidden under Chinese law, but is prosecuted under a statute that outlaws "revolting behaviors." Public disapproval runs so strong that it is difficult for gay people to meet one another, and has been virtually impossible for any sort of political movement to form. Only the threat of AIDS has forced officialdom to reconsider its head-in-the-sand position.

In April 1992, the government allowed lesbians to continue living together, a gesture considered so significant that it was reported in the official media. Later that year, authorities allowed the formation of China's first open gay organization, Men's World, in Beijing, apparently in hopes that it will help prevent the spread of AIDS. A year later, without explanation, they shut it down.

COLUMBIA: Homosexuality is not specifically illegal here for people over 18, but police harassment is common, as is gay-bashing. Gay men, especially transvestites and young hustlers, have repeatedly been found murdered in the hills outside Bogotá. Despite all this, a gay underground can be found in the larger cities.

COSTA RICA: In its attitudes about homosexuality, as in so many other respects, Costa Rica stands apart from its Central and South American neighbors. Homosexuality is legal for those 17 and over. Although there are occasional reports of police harassment, the population tends to be tolerant and friendly.

CUBA: Fidel Castro, supposed liberator of Cuba, filled its jails with homosexuals in the 1960s and 1970s. Although the law is no longer quite as rigid, public displays of same-sex affection are still punishable by a jail sentence. In addition, AIDS has brought out the worst in the Cuban government. HIV testing is mandatory for many groups, including gay men, and anyone who tests positive can be institutionalized for life.

CYPRUS: Male homosexuality is illegal here, and punishable by up to five years in prison; lesbian sex is not mentioned in the law. In 1993 the European Court of Human Rights ruled that Cyprus must repeal this law; it remains up to the Cyprus government, however, to actually do so. Gays are banned from the military on "health" grounds, and the church has threatened to excommunicate not only gay people, but homosexual sympathizers, as well. Not surprisingly, there's no gay movement or community.

CZECHOSLOVAKIA: Czechoslovakia dropped its laws against lesbian and gay sex in 1961, and at the time of Czechoslovakia's dissolution, the age of consent was 15 for heterosexuals and homosexuals alike. A gay movement was just starting to form when the country divided. It is too early to predict the climate in the two new countries, but early reports are not promising. Although homosexual activity is legal in the Czech Republic, anti-gay hate crimes are common, and in mid-1993 officials banned a music video with the lyrics, "love is love/boys with girls/boys with boys/girls with girls."

DENMARK: Denmark, which boasts one of world's most liberal social codes, abolished its sodomy laws in 1930; previously male homosexuality had been illegal while lesbianism was not mentioned by the law. Today the age of consent is 15 for everybody, and anti-discrimination laws protect lesbians and gay men. In 1989, the country went a step further and legalized same-sex marriages. Even in the countryside the people tend to be tolerant and friendly, and anti-gay discrimination is rare. Homosexuals have been allowed in the armed forces since 1979.

DOMINICAN REPUBLIC: Homosexuality is illegal here, and the laws can be sternly enforced against residents. Tourists are generally not bothered as long as they show reasonable discretion.

ECUADOR: This highly Roman Catholic country is highly intolerant of homosexuality, which can be punished with substantial prison terms. Although the law is not often enforced, it serves as a pretext for harassment and extortion. The publisher of a gay newsletter folded it because of threats after two issues, and with good reason. According to local activists, at least twenty people were murdered in the last five months of 1991, merely for being gay; most of the deaths were miscategorized as crimes of passion or of revenge. There is little visible gay life.

EGYPT: Homosexuality is legal, and the social code does not make the rigid gay-straight division common in the U.S. Married and straight-identified men often think nothing of having sex with another man, and gay male sex is less secretive than in other Arab countries.

Although they are less visible, there seem to also be a considerable number of women in same-sex relationships. There are strong social pressures to marry, however. Few Egyptians seem to think of themselves as gay or lesbian in the Western sense, and only a handful — mostly in Alexandria and Cairo — openly identify themselves as such.

ENGLAND: *See United Kingdom*

ESTONIA: This former Soviet republic abolished its sodomy laws in 1992; until then, as in the former Soviet Union, gay male sex was illegal while the law ignored lesbian sex. However, Estonia is socially more progressive than the rest of the former Soviet Union. According to Peter Tatchell in *Europe in the Pink*, it was gay and lesbian Estonian activists who organized the Soviet Union's first conference on homosexual issues. A lesbian organization was reported to have over 100 members in 1992.

ETHIOPIA: Homosexual activity is illegal, and punishable with up to five years imprisonment. There is no visible gay and lesbian community or movement.

FINLAND: Finland has lagged behind the rest of Scandinavia in accepting gay people. For many years, it had some of Europe's most repressive anti-gay laws. Homosexual activity was legalized in 1971, but the age of consent was set at 18 for same-sex couples but only 16 for heterosexuals, and age-of-consent violations are punished more harshly for same-sex offenders. Anti-gay discrimination is illegal, yet the law itself discriminates by for-

bidding "encouragement of homosexuality" — which has been interpreted to keep gay programs off television. Homosexuals are allowed in the armed forces.

FRANCE: Lesbian sex has never been specifically banned in France. Prohibitions against male homosexuality were dropped when a new criminal code was issued in 1791, in the wake of the French Revolution. The Napoleonic Code of 1810 institutionalized this concept that private homosexual activity should not be illegal, and provided a model that was soon followed by other Catholic nations.

Today, the age of consent is 15 for everybody, and since 1985 employers have not been allowed to discriminate on the basis of sexual orientation. A domestic partners law recognizes gay couples for purposes of state health insurance. Paris has a large, visible, and exciting lesbian and gay community, and many other cities have a few gay-identified establishments. Homosexuals are allowed in the armed forces.

Several overseas French departments are governed by the same laws as France itself. They include St. Barthelemy and St. Martin (which are part of the department of Guadeloupe) and Martinique, all in the Caribbean.

GERMANY: Male homosexual activity was outlawed in Germany in 1871, under the notorious Paragraph 175; lesbian activity has never been specifically outlawed. Some of the earliest sodomy law repeal campaigns took place in Germany in the first decades of this century, but without success. Instead, in 1935, the Hitler regime carried the law even further, making it illegal to even have homosexual thoughts. Countless thousands of homosexuals were marked for extermination in the Nazi concentration camps.

East Germany legalized gay sex in 1968, and West Germany in 1969, though both had discriminatorily high ages of consent. In 1986, well before German unification, East Germany took a surprising leadership position on gay issues. It's still a matter of debate whether this change came about from a genuine conviction that lesbians and gay men constituted an oppressed minority, or merely because the regime was desperately trying to find a base of support somewhere, or because it was proving impossible to stop the spread of AIDS while forcing gay people underground.

Many details of German unification are still being worked out. It looks as if homosexuality will be legal throughout Germany, with an age of consent of 16 or 18. Homosexuals are allowed in the armed forces — but not as officers. Berlin had a thriving gay subculture as early as the 1920s, which was wiped out under Hitler, but re-established itself in the 1970s. Attitudes in Berlin and other larger cities are quite accepting; in rural and southern areas, there is still open hostility to gay people.

GHANA: Homosexual activity is legal here, and the country is relatively open-minded about sex.

GIBRALTAR: Although it is a British territory, Gibraltar makes its own laws. For many years, it was the only part of the United Kingdom to still outlaw gay sex. In 1993, however, pressure from British officials finally prevailed on the legislature to repeal its sodomy laws. The age of consent, however, is two years higher than for heterosexual activity.

GREAT BRITAIN: *See United Kingdom*

GREECE: Homosexual activity is legal. Since 1987 the age of consent has been 15 — the same as for heterosexuals — although seducing someone under 17 to engage in anal intercourse is a crime. But despite Greece's great historical significance for both lesbians and gay men, there are heavy social pressures to be straight, or at least to act straight. Gay sex is common, but the visible gay community, while growing, remains small. The beautiful Greek island of Mykonos, a six-hour boat ride from the mainland, is decidedly gay-friendly, though it draws more gay men than lesbians.

GUATEMALA: Homosexual activity is legal, with the age of consent set at 18, but social intolerance runs high. There is no gay culture or movement.

GUYANA: Not the best place for a gay vacation, Guyana punishes "buggery" with a maximum sentence of life imprisonment.

HAITI: Homosexual activity is legal; the age of consent is 18. Although it was once a popular vacation spot for gay travelers, AIDS and political turmoil have changed that. Any gay men who do go there, if they are sexually active, will not find themselves particularly welcome.

HONDURAS: Homosexual activity is legal in Honduras, which vies with Costa Rica for the title of the most gay-friendly country in Latin America. The constitution guarantees civil rights for all; there is no government persecution, and the *Spartacus* guide reports that "bisexuality is widely accepted here." The visible gay and lesbian community remains very small, however.

HONG KONG: Gay male sex was punishable by life imprisonment until 1991; lesbian sex was not mentioned in the law. In July of that year, Hong Kong repealed its sodomy law for consenting adults in private. However, rather than setting the age of consent at 16, as it is for heterosexual activity, Hong Kong fixed it at 21 to protect younger males who "may be curious about and inclined to experiment with new activities and thus be led into homosexual practices." There is a small but quite visible gay community. Hong Kong will pass from British to Chinese control in 1997, and residents fear that their limited progress will erode at that point. The colony's first gay newspaper, *Hong Kong Connection,* appeared in 1993.

HUNGARY: Homosexual activity has been legal since 1962; until then, both gay male and lesbian sex were illegal. Vestiges of the old attitudes remain in the age of consent, which is set at 18 for gay and lesbian sex, at 14 for heterosexual activity. The climate is improving; Peter Tatchell, in *Europe in the Pink,* reports that the gay rights organization Homeros Lambda, formed in 1988, was the first officially approved lesbian and gay organization in Eastern Europe, and Budapest has a magazine named *Mások (Another).* But openly gay men and lesbians face tremendous hostility, and even official harassment.

ICELAND: Iceland is slowly catching up with its Scandinavian neighbors on this issue. Gay male sex is legal at age 18; heterosexual and lesbian sex at 16. Much social animosity remains toward lesbians and gay men, but this is gradually changing. Reykjavik, the island's only real city, has an active gay organization, and the government is increasingly supportive of gay-rights efforts.

INDIA: Gay male sex is forbidden by law, punishable with a maximum sentence of life imprisonment, and activists accuse the police of using the law to harass them and to extort money from closeted gay men. Lesbian sex is not mentioned in the law, but both genders face strong social and family pressures to be straight. Consequently, India has little visible gay and lesbian life. Bombay got its first lesbian and gay organization only in 1990.

INDONESIA: Indonesia has a long history of accepting homosexuality. There are no laws or social proscriptions against it, same-sex households are common, and even married men, if so inclined, are casual about engaging in sex with men. The only cloud on the horizon is that as the country becomes more westernized, anti-gay attitudes are becoming more prevalent.

IRAN: Under Islamic law, homosexuality is illegal, and authorities have called for the extermination of homosexuals. For many years, male homosexuality was explicitly forbidden, while lesbian sex was punished under vague laws against "prohibited acts." In 1991, in perhaps the only step it had ever taken toward sexual equality, the Iranian government decreed that same-sex acts were prohibited for both men and women. Violators were to be flogged for their first three offenses, and executed for the fourth. While it is difficult to get accurate information from Iran, these laws do seem to be enforced. Columnist Jack Anderson reported in early 1990 that "the medieval government of Iran celebrated the New Year" by beheading three gay men and stoning two lesbians to death. Over the years, other reports have reached the West of both men and women being executed for same-sex offenses. Whether these people were all gay is unclear; it is quite clear, however, that lesbians and gay men are unwelcome here.

And yet, as in other Moslem countries, sex between Iranian men is still extremely common, but is merely considered a sexual outlet that has nothing to do with homosexuality, and it isn't talked about. Moslem law requires four male witnesses before someone can be convicted of sodomy — suggesting that such liaisons are considered okay, as long as you keep them private. Reports of sex between women are scarce, due to the invisibility of women and women's sexuality.

IRAQ: Unlike most of its neighbors, Iraq does not explicitly outlaw homosexuality, but in other respects it follows the usual Moslem tradition: Same-sex activity is common, but not discussed, and there is no organized gay or lesbian community.

IRELAND: Following the Victorian tradition (*see United Kingdom*), Irish law long criminalized sex between men, prescribing life imprisonment for anal intercourse. Lesbian sex was not illegal. In 1988, the European Court of Human Rights ordered the country to abolish its sodomy law, but not until 1993 did the Irish parliament finally repeal the law.

Ireland is one of only three European countries where "incitement to hatred" on the grounds of sexual orientation is illegal; this law was passed even before the sodomy laws were repealed. It still isn't Denmark, but Ireland today is a far more accepting place for lesbians and gay men than it was a decade ago.

ISRAEL: Homosexual activity between men was legalized by the Knesset in 1988; for women, it had been strongly discouraged, but not illegal. Military service is universal but for many years, although lesbians and gay men served openly in the armed forces, they were barred from some positions; those barriers were dropped in 1993. Israel is gradually coming to accept lesbians and gay men, but in a country where national-security concerns take precedence over practically everything else, many political and religious leaders are reluctant to take up such a potentially divisive issue.

ITALY: Homosexual activity became legal in some Italian principalities as early as 1792, and it has been legal throughout Italy since 1889. The age of consent is 14 for both homosexuals and heterosexuals, but an adult can be accused of corrupting a partner aged 14 or 15 who has never before had intercourse. In the south, especially, openly gay people are likely to meet with hostility, but Italian culture is generally tolerant of homosexuality as long as it's discreet. Italy has had an active (and highly political) gay movement since the early 1970s. In 1992, for the first time, an openly gay man was elected to the Italian parliament on the Communist Party ticket.

JAMAICA: Homosexual activity is illegal, and attitudes are generally intolerant. A small gay movement and community is just beginning to form in Kingston.

JAPAN: The law makes no distinction between homosexual and heterosexual activity. The age of consent for males ranges by locale from 13 to 17. There is a large lesbian and gay community; Tokyo has one of Asia's only lesbian community centers.

JORDAN: Homosexual activity is common, but illegal, in Jordan.

KENYA: Homosexual activity is strictly forbidden here, punishable by up to fourteen years in prison. Gay people are virtually invisible in the media and in society, and would face considerable hostility if they came out. An incident at the 1985 U.N. Women's Decade Conference, held in Kenya, summarizes the situation clearly. Sylvia Borren, a Dutch participant, recalls that "a number of times during the workshop [about lesbians] a Kenyan woman would get up and say, 'In our country it does not exist.' Then a whole group

of Kenyan women would yell out, 'Yes it does! Yes it does!'"

KOREA: See South Korea. We have no information about the very closed society of North Korea, but there is no reason to suppose that anyone would want to be gay there.

KUWAIT: In Kuwait, as in most Islamic countries of the region, male homosexuality can be punished with death. Lesbian sex, while not explicitly prohibited, can be punished under vaguely worded statutes.

LATVIA: When the Soviet Union annexed Latvia in 1940, anal sex between men became illegal, just as it was in the Soviet Union; lesbian sex was not mentioned in the law. In 1992, soon after Latvia again became independent, gay sex was legalized, with the age of consent set at 18 — two years higher than for heterosexuals. The Latvian Association for Sexual Equality provides support for lesbians and gay men, and maintains contact with other European gay movements.

LEBANON: Homosexual activity is illegal, but not uncommon.

LIBYA: Homosexual activity is illegal, and the offender may be punished by being thrown from a great height. But why did you want to go to Libya anyway?

LITHUANIA: While its companion Baltic states, Estonia and Latvia, soon liberalized their sex laws after gaining independence, Lithuania dragged its feet. The Catholic Church emerged as a powerful force opposing sodomy repeal, and laws against male homosexuality were not repealed until 1993. Lesbian sex was never mentioned in the law. However, public sentiment against homosexuality still runs deep, and attitudes will take some time to catch up. The major gay organization, the Lithuanian Lesbian and Gay Association, is inactive.

LUXEMBOURG: Lesbian sex was never illegal here. Male homosexual activity has been legal since 1792, but the age of consent for gay men is set at 18, compared to 14 for lesbian and heterosexual activity. Luxembourg is socially more conservative than many countries of Western Europe, and the lesbian and gay community is not as developed. However, there is some gay nightlife in the capital, Luxembourg City.

MALAYSIA: Homosexual acts are illegal, punishable by whipping and prison sentences of up to twenty years. Even cruising is illegal, though with a more moderate sentence of two years in prison. As Islamic fundamentalists have come into power, these laws are increasingly enforced, and the social atmosphere is equally intolerant.

MALTA: Homosexual activity has never been specifically banned, but anal sex was illegal until 1973. Today gay sex is legal. The age of consent is considered to be 18 — the age of majority — although prosecution is rare from ages 12 to 17 unless there is a complaint by the younger partner, or an abuse of authority is involved. Despite these relatively lenient laws, the country is heavily influence by Catholicism; lesbians and gay men are neither popular, nor very visible.

MARTINIQUE: *See France*

MEXICO: There are no nationwide laws against homosexual activity, but individual states can pass their own laws, and some are doing their best to make life difficult for gay people — often through a selective enforcement of "public morality" laws or by condoning anti-gay violence. The 1991 conference of the International Lesbian and Gay Association had to be moved from Guadalajara to Acapulco, for example, when the mayor of Guadalajara hinted that attendees might face harassment, and stated that he would do nothing to protect them. Since 1978 the Frente Homosexual de Acción Revolucionaria (FHAR) has sought to unite gay men, lesbians, and feminists, to bring about far-reaching social change. Smaller gay organizations have also sprung up in urban areas, though often they encounter considerable hostility. Gay tourists in resort areas are seldom bothered, provided they show a minimum of discretion.

MICRONESIA: Bisexuality is widely practiced and tolerated in Micronesia, despite some anti-sex laws that are still on the books but rarely enforced. The island federation is perhaps most notable for never having accepted the younger-is-more-attractive attitude of most countries. Older and younger sexual partners are generally considered full equals.

MOLDAVIA: Gay male sex is illegal here, as it was in the Soviet Union, and that does not seem likely to change soon.

MONACO: Homosexual activity is legal for those over 16.

MOROCCO: Homosexual activity is illegal. Several writers of the 1950s and 1960s, including Jane Bowles, Paul Bowles, Tennessee Williams, and William Burroughs, visited or lived in Morocco, giving it the reputation of a homosexual mecca. The fundamentalist Islam government, however, is quite ready to enforce the law against both residents and tourists.

MOZAMBIQUE: Homosexual activity is illegal, and there is virtually no visible gay life.

NAMIBIA: Gay male sex is illegal, and there is no visible gay and lesbian community.

NETHERLANDS: The Netherlands is probably more open to sexual minorities than any other country on the globe. Laws against gay male sex were repealed under Napoleon back in 1811, when England was still hanging sodomists; lesbian sex was never outlawed. The age of consent is 16 for everybody; if the younger partner is 12 to 15 years of age, prosecutions occur only following a formal complaint. Gay people have served in the armed forces since 1974, and in 1993 the minister of defense urged more gay men and lesbians to join the services, to help break down homophobia. Amsterdam is widely considered the world's most gay-friendly city. The courts have interpreted the constitution to prohibit anti-gay discrimination, and even pedophilia is treated with a largely blasé attitude. Many cities and towns recognize same-sex marriages, and this may soon be codified into national law.

NETHERLANDS ANTILLES: Four and a half Caribbean islands make up the Netherlands Antilles: Bonaire, Curaçao, St. Eustatius (commonly called Statia), Saba, and half of St. Martin. The Antilles are considered an equal part of the kingdom of the Netherlands. Homosexual activity is legal here, with the age of consent set at 16. Gay people are generally tolerated, but it's a small community and the atmosphere is by no means as welcoming as in Holland.

NEW ZEALAND: Homosexual activity was legalized in 1986; the age of consent is 16. In 1993, the parliament passed a wide-ranging civil rights law, banning discrimination based on sexual orientation or HIV status; the law was to go into effect on Feb. 1, 1994. There has been an active gay and lesbian movement, and community, since the 1970s.

NICARAGUA: Although homosexual activity is not specifically illegal, gay people face regular persecution in Nicaragua under various pretexts, and there is little visible gay community. The lesbian and gay community held its first Pride celebration in 1991, but continued government opposition has held the movement in check.

NIGERIA: Harsh laws prohibit homosexual activity, but according to the *Spartacus* guide, "the various peoples of the country themselves pay less attention to these ominous laws than to their own cultural traditions. For example, bisexuality is a normal cultural phenomenon in the northern part of the country."

NORTHERN IRELAND: *See United Kingdom*

NORWAY: Gay male sex became legal in Norway in 1972; lesbian sex was never illegal. The age of consent is 16 for everyone. In 1981 Norway became the first country to outlaw discrimination based on sexual preference; inciting hatred of homosexuals is also illegal. In 1993, Norway legalized gay marriages, although same-sex couples cannot yet adopt children. A thriving and highly visible lesbian and gay culture is well integrated into mainstream society, including the armed forces. In short, it's practically like the Netherlands with snow.

OMAN: Both gay male and lesbian sex are illegal, and punishable by up to three years in prison. However, the law does not seem to generally be enforced against private activity.

PAKISTAN: Homosexual activity is illegal and under the country's Islamic laws can be punished with beatings and life imprisonment. Pathan culture in the Northwest Frontier province allows men to have younger men as lovers, and Karachi has a very small gay community. Otherwise, there is no visible lesbian or gay culture.

PANAMA: Homosexual activity is legal here, though the gay culture is still undeveloped.

PARAGUAY: Homosexual activity is not illegal, but reports suggest that gay people are frequently persecuted under more vaguely worded statutes. There is no active gay movement or community.

PERU: Homosexual activity is legal for adults. However, homophobia is rampant. Lesbians and gay men are sometimes persecuted under "public morality" statutes, and for those brave (or foolish) enough to come out, gay-bashing is not uncommon. This tone is set at the top: in early 1993, Peruvian president Alberto Fujimori fired 15 members of the diplomatic corps for being openly gay. Despite all this, both gay men and lesbians are coming together in a liberation movement, and a small but active gay subculture is thriving in Lima. The main support organization is the Movimiento homosexual orgollo Lima (MHOL).

PHILIPPINES: Homosexual activity is legal, and the age of consent is 18. There is a busy but discreet gay culture, but no political gay movement of note.

POLAND: Homosexual activity is legal in Poland. The age of consent is 15 — the same as for heterosexuals — and it's been that way since 1932, when prohibitions against gay male sex were dropped. (Lesbian sex was never illegal.) But this heavily Catholic country is far from being a gay mecca. Homosexuality meets with strong disapproval, gay life is virtually invisible in most cities, and even the Solidarity movement is proving as homophobic as the old regime. The general closetedness is accentuated by a severe housing shortage. Unmarried people almost always live with their parents, making carrying on a clandestine relationship a challenge. One gay man waited ten years for an apartment, but neighbors soon realized he was gay and harassed him till he moved back in with his grandmother.

Warsaw, the capital, has a nascent gay liberation movement and culture, and in 1990 the government officially recognized the Lambda Association. Progress will be slow, however, and some Polish activists report that repressive elements of their society are more free to express themselves now than they were under communism. Even Lech Walesa, in his 1990 presidential campaign, made anti-gay comments, and police in 1993 were closing down gay clubs.

PORTUGAL: This poor Catholic country lags behind the rest of Western Europe in providing equal rights to its gay citizens. Although gay male sex has been legal since 1852 (lesbian sex was never illegal), gay people are prohibited from certain jobs, as well as from the military. The age of consent is 16 for everyone, but same-sex violations can be punished more harshly than heterosexual violations. Harassment and gay-bashing are common. There is a small gay liberation movement, but it has a big job ahead of it.

PUERTO RICO: Homosexual activity is punishable by up to ten years imprisonment in Puerto Rico, which is actually a self-governing territory of the United States. However, no one can remember a case when private, consensual sex between adults was prosecuted, and there is strong legislative support for repealing the law. San Juan, the island's largest city, boasts a thriving and visible gay culture, which makes it a popular destination for gay tourists.

ROMANIA: When in Romania, do as the Romanians do: keep your mouth shut about your sexual orientation. It is the only European country where both lesbian and gay male sex is illegal, punishable by up to five years imprisonment. Gay people face constant persecution; under Ceausescu's dictatorship, torture and castration were used against known homosexuals. The recent shake-ups in Eastern Europe have raised hopes that the atmosphere in Romania will ease up. In 1992, a lesbian and gay organization named Total Relations received official recognition, and government officials promised the International Lesbian and Gay Association that they would try to abolish the sodomy law — which they said had not been enforced since Ceausescu's overthrow in 1989. But in 1993, Amnesty International reported that gay people were still frequently arrested, beaten, imprisoned, and tortured by authorities. It's likely to be many years before Romania is a comfortable place to be gay.

RUSSIA: Lesbian sex has never been illegal here; the status of gay men has changed several times.

The anti-sodomy laws of the czars were thrown out after the Bolshevik Revolution of 1917. Stalin recriminalized gay male sex in 1934. It remained illegal in Russia, punishable by up to five years in prison, for several years after the breakup of the Soviet Union; in 1989, about 500 men were imprisoned under the law. The laws were repealed in 1993, and officials said they would release men imprisoned on gay sex charges, although that's been slow to happen.

While many people identify as gay or lesbian, they still tend to be highly closeted. However, the gay movement seems to be at the beginning of a growth spurt. Russia got its first gay newspaper in 1989, and two years later, activists held the country's first conference on gay concerns. But many gay people are still closeted for understandable reasons: in 1991, over a third of the Russian population said homosexuals should be executed..

SAINT BARTHELEMY: *See France*

SAINT MARTIN: *See France*

SAUDI ARABIA: The harsh Islamic laws of this country forbid homosexual activity. For both men and women, it is punishable by whipping for the first offense; by death for a second offense. Although these sentences are rarely carried out, they ensure that no visible gay culture develops. It is common for men to have sex with one another, however, without thinking of themselves as gay. Because women are largely required to be invisible, we have no reliable information about how common lesbian contacts may be.

SCOTLAND: *See United Kingdom*

SENEGAL: Homosexual activity is legal, but there are strong social pressures against it.

SINGAPORE: Gay male sex is illegal, and can be punished by life imprisonment. There are no specific laws about lesbian sex. Singapore has a modest underground gay culture, but gays face official persecution when they become too visible.

SOUTH AFRICA: Gay male sex is illegal, punishable by life imprisonment; there are no specific laws about lesbian sex. However, many cities have open and thriving gay communities and there is a great deal of gay activism. In Johannesburg, for example, about a thousand people showed up in 1992 for the third annual gay and lesbian pride march.

SOUTH KOREA: Homosexual activity is legal, and common, but not socially accepted. Only in Seoul is there a gay community of any note.

SPAIN: Lesbian sex has never been illegal in Spain, and gay male sex was legalized in 1822. Under Franco, gay people faced heavy persecution and a repressively high age of consent of 23. In 1978, the age of consent was standardized for both homosexual and heterosexual activity: it is set at 18, but from ages 12 to 17, prosecution takes place only with a formal complaint about deception or abuse of authority. Gays have been allowed in the military since 1984. Spain now has a thriving gay culture that is increasingly, though not yet fully, accepted by the population at large. Madrid and Barcelona are the main lesbian and gay centers.

SRI LANKA: In the 1970s and early 1980s, Sri Lanka developed a reputation as a mecca of sexual openness, and many gays went there to visit, or even to live. Unfortunately, child prostitution became something of a growth industry in this atmosphere, and authorities began to enforce long-forgotten laws against gay sex, even between consenting adults.

SUDAN: Following Islamic law, homosexual activity was forbidden in 1977. The Islamic influence grew even stronger following the overthrow of President Nimeiry in 1985, and there is still no gay community or movement. As in so many Moslem countries, however, married and straight-identified men think nothing of having a discreet homosexual affair on the side.

SWEDEN: Both lesbian and gay male sex were legalized in 1944; in 1978 the age of consent was set at 15 for both heterosexuals and homosexuals. Not only are there no laws against homosexuality, but anti-gay discrimination is illegal, and the government provides financial support to gay organizations. Moreover, in 1988, Sweden became the first country to grant certain partnership rights to same-sex couples, though it fell short of providing full equality with heterosexual marriages. There is an open and thriving gay and lesbian culture, but gay people are so integrated into mainstream life — including the military — that there are fewer specifically lesbian and gay institutions than might be found in less accepting countries.

SWITZERLAND: Lesbian sex was never illegal in Switzerland. Gay male sex was decriminalized canton by canton beginning in 1937; by 1942, it was legal throughout the country, although the age of consent was higher than for straight couples. In 1992 the country revised its sex laws. The age of consent is now 16 for both heterosexuals and heterosexuals, and sex is legal between minors who are not more than three years apart in age. Marital rape is illegal, as is hard-core pornography. Gays are allowed in the There is a visible and active

gay community throughout the country, but this is a nation with a strong conservative streak, and gay people are not yet fully welcomed.

SYRIA: Homosexual activity is punishable by up to three years in prison, and there is no real gay and lesbian community.

TAIWAN: Homosexual activity is legal; the age of consent is 21. However, the social climate is not tolerant, and there is no active gay or lesbian community. According to the *Spartacus* guide, "readers have told us that ... Taiwanese soldiers who have been 'converted' to homosexuality face the death penalty," but this has not been confirmed.

THAILAND: Considering the number of countries whose Roman Catholic or Islamic traditions have resulted in harsh anti-gay laws, it is refreshing to find one where religion has had an opposite effect. Buddhism, which is practiced by 95% of the Thai population, embraces human sexuality as a natural and welcome part of life, and makes no distinction between homosexual and heterosexual acts. (The age of consent is 18 — or 15, with parental permission.) Gay sex has never been illegal in Thailand, nor does the country suffer from the ageism of Western culture. The bad news is that many Western tourists have exploited this atmosphere, acting like rich kids in a candy shop, leaving in their wake many exploited teenagers — and many cases of AIDS, for which the country is ill-prepared. Homosexuality is still accepted in Thailand, but age-of-consent laws are now strictly enforced.

TUNISIA: Homosexual activity is illegal, and entrapment is common. There is no gay movement, and only a very discreet gay underground.

TURKEY: In many respects — including laws about sexuality — Turkey is the least repressive of the Moslem nations. Homosexual activity is legal. The age of consent is 18 for vaginal and anal sex and 15 for other forms of sex, regardless of the partners' genders. But while the law doesn't discriminate, the police do. Harassment, police raids, and beatings are all too common, and in 1993, officials forced the cancellation of what would have been Turkey's first gay conference. While many men engage in gay sex, few identify as gay, and those who do face much hostility. Ibrahim Eren, a leader of the radical Green Party, started a small gay movement in Turkey in 1982, and an underground gay community can be found in Istanbul and in the resort area of Bodrum. Turkey is 98% Moslem, and while the status of women is not quite as low as in some Islamic countries, it is unheard of for women to identify themselves as lesbian.

UKRAINE: Late in 1991, the Ukraine became the first of the former Soviet states to repeal its laws against homosexual activity. The age of consent is 16. Some reports from emigrants, however, suggest that there is still a high level of intolerance and gay-bashing, which officials do not attempt to stop. The leading gay organization is named Two Colors.

UNION OF SOVIET SOCIALIST REPUBLICS: *See Russia*

UNITED ARAB EMIRATES: Homosexual activity is forbidden and can be punished by up to fourteen years in jail. Merely to be gay, even without having gay sex, is a crime. There is no gay culture, community, or political movement. As in so many Moslem countries, however, married and straight-identified men think nothing of having discreet, same-sex affairs.

UNITED KINGDOM: The United Kingdom consists of England, Scotland, Wales, and Northern Ireland. Operating on the theory that sex requires a penis, British law for many years outlawed gay male sex, but ignored lesbian sex. (This explanation is less tongue-in-cheek than it sounds. In one of the few instances that a lesbian faced legal prosecution, she had been wearing a strap-on dildo.)

England's famous Wolfenden report, in 1957, urged the legalization of gay sex. Ten years later, private consensual gay sex became legal in England and Wales. (Sodomy bans for Scotland were not lifted until 1980; for Northern Ireland, in 1982.) The government has spent the years since then looking for other ways to shackle gays, and has come up with quite a few. The age of consent is 21 for gay men but 16 for heterosexuals (lesbians continue to be invisible under the law). Gays aren't allowed in the military; gay sex is illegal with soldiers or police; it can't involve more than two people; it can only take place in one's home; and government institutions are prohibited from "promoting" homosexuality. Sexually explicit literature can be imported if it's straight; not if it's gay. Consen

S/M sex is illegal and in 1990 a judge issued jail sentences of up to four years to a group of sixteen men involved in such activities. In short, according to Peter Tatchell in his book *Europe in the Pink*, "The UK has more laws which explicitly, or in practice, discriminate against homosexuals than any other European nation, East or West." The laws are all actively, though not always consistently, enforced; and there are no laws prohibiting anti-gay discrimination. Notwithstanding all this, England has an active and open gay and lesbian culture, comparable to that in the U.S. The gay movements in Scotland, Wales, and Northern Ireland are all somewhat less advanced.

UNITED STATES OF AMERICA: Laws regarding gay sex and civil rights are passed on a state-by-state basis; homosexual activity is currently illegal in about half the states. These laws are almost never enforced against consenting private adult acts, but they can provide an excuse for both official and private harassment. Under the new Clinton administration, there is talk of a federal gay civil rights law, but passage does not seem imminent. A description of the situation in each state appears in the chapter *State Laws*.

URUGUAY: Homosexual activity has been legal since 1985. The gay movement is small, but growing.

VENEZUELA: Homosexual activity is legal, but there is still much official hostility to gay people. A small gay movement, based in the capital ˙ Caracas, is making some in- ˙ is.

WALES: *See United Kingdom*

YEMEN: Under strict Islamic law, homosexual activity is forbidden here and is punishable by death, though few reports of such punishments have reached the West. There is no gay movement or community at all.

YUGOSLAVIA: In the now-defunct country of Yugoslavia, homosexual activity was regulated by laws passed in each republic. Lesbian sex was not outlawed anywhere. Gay male sex was illegal in Bosnia-Hercegovina, Serbia, and Macedonia, though the law was rarely enforced against consenting adults. It was legal in Croatia, Montenegro, and Slovenia. When the dust and gunpowder of the current conflict settle, there's no telling what the situation will be — or even what the political boundaries will be. Slovenia was the region most tolerant of its gay population in the late 1980s, and that attitude will probably continue in whatever is left of Slovenia in the years ahead. In Serbia, anti-gay attitudes are deeply ingrained, and activists have reported that sodomy laws are enforced more often than they were in the past — often against opponents of Serbian officials.

ZAIRE: Homosexual activity is illegal, and can be punished with up to five years in prison. There is no gay community or movement.

ZAMBIA: Homosexual activity is illegal, and there is considerable official hostility toward gay people. There is no gay community or movement.

STATE LAWS

The United States is one of only a few countries in which most laws are enacted not on a nationwide level, but on a smaller level — in our case, by individual states. The following state-by-state breakdown describes major laws and executive orders that affect gay people. For each state, we've followed this longer narrative with a grade — admittedly subjective — summarizing the overall legal status of lesbian and gay citizens in that state. These grades have been used on the accompanying map to rate each state.

Most of the first states to legalize gay sex did not specifically repeal the existing laws; instead, the consenting-adult provisions were one of many provisions in an all-encompassing law reform. These reforms were usually based on the Model Penal Code of the American Law Institute, which as early as 1955 recommended decriminalizing homosexuality. It was six years before the first state, Illinois, took their recommendation, and eight more years before Connecticut became the second. Other states then followed suit more quickly.

ALABAMA: *Still has sodomy laws.* Sodomy is a misdemeanor here, and the outlook for repeal is bleak. In 1992, the state legislature readily passed a bill (signed by Gov. Guy Hunt) forbidding the use of public funds to "foster or promote a lifestyle or actions" that are illegal under the state sodomy laws. The new law was used to withhold resources from gay student groups at state universities. **F**

ALASKA: *No sodomy laws.* In August 1969, the Alaska Supreme Court ruled that the term "crime against nature" was unconstitutional. It urged a re-examination of sex laws, stating that "the courts cannot, of course, perform such a comprehensive task ... But the widening gap between our formal statutory law and the actual attitudes and behavior of vast segments of our society can only sow the seeds of increasing disrespect for our legal institutions." A decade later, as part of an overall revision of the penal code, the sodomy laws were dropped. **B-**

ARIZONA: *Still has sodomy laws.* Sodomy is a misdemeanor here. In 1976, the Arizona Supreme Court upheld the constitutionality of the state's sodomy laws, citing the Bible and stating that "the right to privacy is not unqualified and absolute and must be considered in the light of important state interests."

The year 1976 also saw a flurry of anti-gay legislation proposed in the Arizona legislature. One proposed amendment would have levied a $10,000 fine against anyone convicted of a homosexual act. Another would have made it illegal for a male to allow an erection to show through his pants. **F**

ARKANSAS: *Still has sodomy laws.* In 1975, as part of a general reform of its criminal code, Arkansas decriminalized all sexual acts involving consenting adults. When he discovered that he had inadvertently supported the repeal of sodomy laws, upset football coach and state representative Bill Stancil swept into action. He first proposed outlawing all sex that didn't involve exactly one penis and one vagina. When no one took that seriously, he more modestly introduced legislation making it a misdemeanor to have sex with someone of the same gender. The House judiciary committee quickly approved his bill by a 66-2 vote. The senate sponsor, Sen. Milt Earnhard, told fellow legislators that "This bill is aimed at weirdos and queers who live in a fairyland world and are trying to wreck family life." That was enough to convince the senate, which voted unanimously to pass the bill, and Gov. David Pryor signed it into law in 1977. Despite his words of support for gay civil rights as president, Bill Clinton made no effort to repeal Arkansas's sodomy laws during his long tenure as governor. Nor should anyone expect change soon. In 1993, a repeal measure was defeated in the state senate by a 6-1 committee vote. **F**

CALIFORNIA: *No sodomy laws. Limited civil rights law.* It wasn't easy, but on May 1, 1975, the California Senate voted to repeal the state's sodomy statutes. The initial vote was a 20-20 tie, which would have resulted in defeat. Supporters therefore telephoned Lt. Gov. Mervyn Dymally, who was in Denver, ⸺ ʰback and cast the tie-breaking ⸺ repeal. While await-

ing Dymally's arrival, opposition senators tried to break the quorum by leaving; the senate president *pro tem* locked the chamber doors to keep them inside. Eleven days later, Gov. Jerry Brown signed the bill; it went into effect January 1, 1976. In April 1980, Brown signed an executive order prohibiting anti-gay discrimination in state hiring.

A decade later, Republican Pete Wilson promised to sign a gay rights bill while he was running for governor. Once in office, under pressure from his party's right wing, he vetoed such a bill in 1991. Riots broke out, and on Sept. 26, 1992, Wilson finally signed a law prohibiting job discrimination based on sexual orientation. This was a narrower focus than the civil rights laws passed in other states, which usually banned discrimination in housing, as well. The new law went into effect January 1, 1993, and soon a complication came to light: That March, a Los Angeles appeals court ruled that the statewide law effectively nullified local anti-discrimination laws, which were often stronger. The Los Angeles law, for example, would have allowed the victims of discrimination to collect legal fees; the statewide law does not.

California's hate crimes law includes crimes based on sexual orientation. Comprehensive gay civil rights laws exist in many cities, most notably Berkeley, Davis, Hayward, Laguna Beach, Los Angeles, Oakland, Sacramento, San Diego, San Francisco, Santa Monica, and West Hollywood. **A-**

COLORADO: *No sodomy laws.* On June 2, 1971, Gov. John A. Love signed a new penal code that,

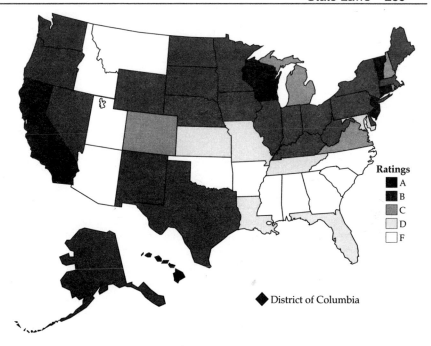

Ratings
A
B
C
D
F

◆ District of Columbia

among its many provisions, legalized homosexual acts between consenting adults. It went into effect July 1, 1972. Gay activists were concerned, however, that the new law continued to outlaw loitering "for the purpose of engaging or soliciting another person to engage in prostitution or deviate sexual intercourse."

Of course, Colorado is best known not for being the fourth state to repeal its sodomy laws, but for its later attempt to turn back the clock. In 1993, voters approved Amendment 2, a constitutional amendment that barred lesbians and gay men from receiving any civil rights protection, and that would have nullified civil rights laws in Denver, Boulder, and Aspen. As of September 1993, it seemed likely that the law would be found unconstitutional. Meanwhile, Colorado picked up the nickname "the Hate State" and became the focus of a nationwide boycott. **C-**

CONNECTICUT: *No sodomy laws. Comprehensive civil rights law.* On June 4, 1969, the Connecticut state senate approved a new penal code legalizing homosexuality; before this, it was illegal for men, but not for women. Connecticut was only the second state to abolish sodomy laws, and nine gay organizations in the state sponsored a three-day celebration when the new law went into effect on October 1, 1971. Twenty years later, in April 1991, Connecticut became the fourth state to pass a gay civil rights law, banning anti-gay discrimination in employment, housing, public accommodations, and services. Activists said a big factor in getting passage of the bill was behind-the-scenes meetings that kept the state's powerful Roman Catholic bishops from opposing it.

The state also has a hate crimes law that includes crimes based on sexual orientation, and comprehensive gay civil rights laws have been passed in Hartford, New Haven, and Stamford. **A**

DELAWARE: *No sodomy laws.* Republican governor Russell W. Peterson signed a new criminal code, dropping penalties for consenting homosexual acts, on July 6, 1972; it became law April 1, 1973. The age of consent was set at 16. Delaware's law took a new twist: Instead of dropping prohibitions against sodomy, it redefined sodomy as "deviate sexual intercourse with another person without that person's consent." The legislator responsible was also a Republican, state senator Michael N. Castle, who expressed the view that "victimless crimes — when the 'victim' is actually the person who's committed the crime, if it is a crime — are sort of outdated in this day and age." He suggested that police should spend their time on crimes where people get hurt. **B-**

DISTRICT OF COLUMBIA: *No sodomy laws.* After several false starts, the District of Columbia finally repealed its sodomy laws in 1993. The district had taken similar action once before, but in 1981 the U.S. Congress overturned that first repeal. A twelve-year battle ensued, during which time sodomy remained a felony punishable by up to ten years and/or a $1000 fine. In 1992, following protests over a police raid on a sex club, the chief of police ordered that sodomy charges would be filed only in the case of public sex, rape, and sex with a minor. The repeal was signed in May 1993 by Mayor Sharon Pratt Kelly, and became law the following September after Congress made no objection. **B**

FLORIDA: *Still has sodomy laws.* In 1971, the Florida Supreme Court struck down the state's "crimes against nature" law, under which gay sex had been prosecuted as a felony. The law was unconstitutionally vague, said the court — which in the next breath urged lawmakers to pass more specific laws against homosexual conduct. Both homosexual and heterosexual sodomy are now a misdemeanor, and the law is not expected to change soon.

Nor is the official atmosphere good in other respects. In 1976, the executive director of the Florida Public Service Commission had a private investigator search for evidence of gay employees within the commission. The investigator scoured wastebaskets, and eavesdropped on phone conversations. In 1977, the state passed laws banning same-sex marriages. Same-sex couples are banned from adopting children, although this law has been ruled unconstitutional by judges in Sarasota and Monroe counties, and could eventually be overturned on a statewide level. A 1981 law tried to withhold state funds from universities that recognized gay student groups; it was struck down by the Florida Supreme Court. The only good sign has a been a 1991 law that added anti-gay attacks to those covered by the state's hate-crimes law. Comprehensive gay civil rights laws have been passed in Key West,

Miami Beach, and Alachua County. **D-**

GEORGIA: *Still has sodomy laws.* Georgia's sodomy statutes are the best-known in the nation, having been upheld by the U.S. Supreme Court in the notorious 1986 *Hardwick* decision. They also carry one of the worst penalties: sodomy is a felony punishable by one to twenty years imprisonment. There's little reason to expect them to be abolished soon. To emphasize its homophobia, Georgia took a step in 1993 that no other state seems to have thought of. While refusing to recognize same-sex couples in any beneficial way, a 1993 law declared that such relationships *will* be recognized for the purpose of refusing alimony payments. The city of Atlanta joined in the boycott of Colorado following that state's passage of the notorious anti-gay Amendment 2; clearly they found it easier to scold another state than to clean up the mess at home. **F**

HAWAII: *No sodomy laws.* Limited civil rights law. On April 7, 1972, Hawaii governor John A. Burns signed legislation legalizing private homosexual acts between consenting adults. The law went into effect January 1, 1973.

This change came as part of a general re-evaluation by the state legislature of laws regarding sex, drugs, and gambling — often known as "victimless crimes" laws. In doing so, Hawaii went beyond what most states had done and also removed all laws against solicitation or lewd conduct.

On March 22, 1991, Gov. John Waihee signed a bill forbidding job discrimination on the basis of sexual orientation, a more narrow civil rights bill than some other states had passed.

The most intriguing news from Hawaii, however, is the 1993 ruling by the state supreme court that Hawaii's prohibition of same-sex marriages was probably unconstitutional. Unless a trial judge now finds a "compelling state interest" in such a ban, Hawaii will become the first state to legalize gay marriages. **A-**

IDAHO: *Still has sodomy laws.* Both heterosexual and homosexual "crimes against nature" are a felony here.

On March 18, 1971, Gov. Cecil D. Andrus signed a new penal code eliminating all penalties for private homosexual acts between consenting adults, and reducing solicitation to the category of a misdemeanor. It was only the third state to do so. However, religious and conservative backlash caused legislators to backpedal, and in March of the next year they passed Idaho's current "crimes against nature" law. **F**

ILLINOIS: *No sodomy laws.* Illinois was first state to repeal its sodomy laws — the repeal was passed in 1961, and became effective the following January. Illinois bans anti-gay discrimination in public employment, and in 1990, Gov. James Thompson signed a bill broadening the state's hate-crimes law to include anti-gay violence. Comprehensive gay civil rights laws have been passed in Champaign, Chicago, Urbana, and Cook County. **B+**

INDIANA: *No sodomy laws.* Consenting adult bills were introduced in both houses of the Indiana legislature in 1971. But the best of ideas don't always have the best of supporters. Democrat Richard Doyle, who introduced the measure in the House, said it was "a waste of the police officer's time" to enforce the existing laws. Further, he added, legalizing homosexuality might "give us an opportunity to study it more openly, and to see what causes it, in the hope that we can eventually eliminate it." Although that effort was unsuccessful, sodomy laws were repealed in 1976 as part of a general law reform. **B-**

IOWA: *No sodomy laws.* As part of an overall revision of its criminal code, Iowa repealed its sodomy laws on June 28, 1976; the law went into effect the first day of 1977. In addition, Iowa's hate crimes law includes crimes based on sexual orientation. The cities of Ames and Iowa City have passed comprehensive gay civil rights laws. **B**

KANSAS: *Still has sodomy laws.* Until 1970, both heterosexual and homosexual sodomy were a felony in Kansas, punishable by up to ten years of hard labor. A new criminal code, passed in 1969 and effective July 1, 1970, changed this. Sodomy was redefined as "oral or anal copulation" between persons of the same sex, and it became only a misdemeanor (with a maximum punishment of six months in jail and a $1000 fine) instead of a felony. At the same time, the new law imposed harsher penalties for sex with a minor under 16. **D**

KENTUCKY: *No sodomy laws.* Kentucky's sodomy law was struck down by the state supreme court in September 1992, in a 4-3 ruling. At the same time, the judges administered a firm slap to the U.S. Supreme Court for concluding in its 1986 *Hardwick* decision that sodomy laws were constitutional. "Equal justice under the law is more than a mere aspiration" in Kentucky, wrote justice Charles Leibson in a strongly worded decision.

It wasn't the first time that Kentucky courts had come through on gay-related issues. In 1987, the Kentucky Court of Appeals ruled that a lower court was wrong to deny child custody to a mother simply because she was a lesbian. It ordered a new custody trial in which all "relevant factors" — including the father's "undue harsh disciplining of the child" — would be considered. **B**

LOUISIANA: *Still has sodomy laws.* "Crimes against nature" by heterosexuals or homosexuals are a felony here, punishable by up to five years in prison. In 1967, the Louisiana Supreme Court ruled that oral sex between women should be considered "unnatural carnal copulation" under the laws of the state, and was punishable in the same way as sodomy between men. The court let stand a thirty-month prison sentence that had been imposed on two women. In 1975, the state supreme court ruled that the law prohibiting "unnatural carnal copulation" had acquired an "acceptable legal meaning" and was not unconstitutionally vague.

Eager to compete for the get-tough prize, a state representative proposed in 1985 that homosexual rape be punished by death. That proposal went nowhere, but in 1987, Louisiana became the first state to require HIV antibody testing as part of the application for a marriage license.

Lately the news has been slightly better. In 1992, Gov. Edwin Edwards signed an executive order that not only banned anti-gay discrimination by state agencies, but also specified that private firms doing business with the state may not engage in such discrimination. New Orleans has passed comprehensive gay civil rights laws. And a New Orleans district court ruled in 1993 that the sodomy law was unconstitutional, but that finding will apply only in the district where it was made unless it is upheld at the state level. **D**

MAINE: *No sodomy laws.* In 1975, with little dissent, Maine legislators voted to drop that state's laws against private sex acts between consenting adults, and to lower the age of consent to 14. The law went into effect March 1, 1976. A proposed gay rights bill has come close to passage in recent years, and was passed by both houses of the legislature in 1993 — only to be vetoed by Republican governor John R. McKernan. Portland has a comprehensive gay civil rights law. **B**

MARYLAND: *Still has sodomy laws.* On several occasions the state senate has passed a bill to reform its laws which make sodomy a felony. Each time, the House soundly rejected the measure. The Maryland Court of Appeals ruled in 1990 that the vaguely worded state sodomy laws applied only to homosexual activity. However, Maryland does ban anti-gay discrimination in public employment, and comprehensive gay civil rights laws have been passed in Baltimore, Gaithersburg, Rockville, Howard County, and Montgomery County. **D**

MASSACHUSETTS: *Sodomy laws not enforced. Comprehensive civil rights law.* Massachusetts often appears on lists of states that have decriminalized sodomy. It sounds logical; the country's first (Gerry Studds) and second (Barney Frank) openly gay members of Congress both came from Massachusetts. But it's not strictly true. "Crimes Against Nature," defined as bestiality and both heterosexual and homosexual anal intercourse, are still on the books as a felony, punishable by up to twenty years. Oral and anal sex by either sex are covered under an "Unnatural and Lascivious Acts" statute, also a felony, with a maximum penalty of five years in prison and a $1,000 fine. However, a 1974 ruling by the state's Supreme Judicial Court decriminalized consensual sexual conduct between adults who had a "reasonable expectation of privacy."

But there is good news, too. In 1989, Gov. Michael Dukakis signed into law the country's second statewide gay rights law. Comprehensive gay civil rights laws are also on the books in Amherst, Boston, Cambridge, Malden, and Worcester. **B**

MICHIGAN: *Still has sodomy laws.* Sodomy is still a felony here, with a theoretical possibility of up to twenty years imprisonment. In 1990, a Michigan circuit court struck down the statute on state constitutional grounds; if that ruling is upheld, it will signal the end of Michigan's sodomy laws. Michigan bans anti-gay discrimination in public employment, and comprehensive gay civil rights laws exist in Ann Arbor, Detroit, East Lansing, and Flint. **C**

MINNESOTA: *Still has sodomy laws. Comprehensive civil rights law.* Most sodomy statutes prohibit sex between a human and an animal. Minnesota, always looking to close the loopholes that others overlook, is the only state to specifically outlaw sex with birds, as well. In 1987 the state legislature came agonizingly close to repealing the law that makes homosexual sodomy a felony. A reform bill was supported by the Minnesota Bar Association, the Public Health Assocation, the League of Women Voters, and gay organizations (but not by the Audubon Society). It passed the senate judiciary committee by an 11-4 vote but was rejected in the House, 13-12.

In 1993, Minnesota governor Arne Carlson signed a gay rights bill into law, prohibiting anti-gay discrimination in housing, employment, public accommodations, credit, education, and public services. It was twenty years since such legislation had first been introduced in the state legislature. (State employees had been covered since 1991 by an executive order.) The state's hate crimes law includes crimes based on sexual orientation, and comprehensive gay civil rights laws exist in Minneapolis, St. Paul, and Marshall. **B**

MISSISSIPPI: *Still has sodomy laws.* "Unnatural intercourse," both homosexual and heterosexual, is a felony here, carrying a possible sentence of up to ten years. **F**

MISSOURI: *Still has sodomy laws.* In 1977, the state legislature approved a revised criminal code that made sodomy a misdemeanor instead of a felony; it went into effect the next year.

Missouri's sodomy law was upheld by the state supreme court in 1986, which cited the U.S. Supreme Court's *Hardwick* decision. But the Missouri court went further, and explicitly accepted the argument of state officials that the law was "rationally related to the state's concededly legitimate interest in protecting the public health," because banning gay sex could prevent the spread of diseases such as AIDS. St. Louis has passed a comprehensive gay civil rights law. **D**

MONTANA: *Still has sodomy laws.* "Deviate sexual conduct" is a felony here, punishable by up to ten years in prison and/or a $50,000 fine. Only homosexual activity is defined as "deviate." Montana is the only state in which homosexual acts are a felony while heterosexual sodomy is legal. **F**

NEBRASKA: *No sodomy laws.* On May 15, 1977, Nebraska's unicameral legislature overwhelmingly approved an overall reform of its criminal code, including a repeal of the sodomy laws. Democratic governor James Exon vetoed the law, but on June 1, the legislature overrode him. The new law took effect one year later. **B-**

NEVADA: *No sodomy laws.* In April 1977, the Nevada legislature voted with little opposition to legalize all sex between consenting adults of the opposite sex, while making same-sex acts a felony. For a time,

Nevada was one of only two states (Montana was the other) in which homosexual acts were a felony while heterosexual sodomy was legal. The statute withstood a 1987 challenge in the state supreme court, which ruled that since the law was never really enforced, the two lesbians and two gay men who had filed a suit against it "lacked standing due to insufficient threat of prosecution." On June 16, 1993, however, to the surprise of observers, the legislature repealed the state's sodomy statute. Private, consenting sex is now legal for all adults.

Nevada has also passed a hate crimes law that includes sexual orientation. **B**

NEW HAMPSHIRE: *No sodomy laws.* On June 7, 1975, New Hampshire governor Meldrim Thomson — a vocal right-winger who once unsuccessfully sought to expel a gay student group from the University of New Hampshire — signed into law a bill reforming the state's rape statute. Unknown to Thomson or most other observers, tucked into the bill was a repeal of the New Hampshire sodomy laws. The repeal went into effect Aug. 6 of that year, but no one took notice until a year later, when Washington, D.C., activist Franklin Kameny called attention to it.

A chagrined governor vowed to introduce legislation re-instating the sodomy statute. But it never happened. One quiet opponent of re-enactment was David Souter — then the state's attorney general, and later a justice on the U.S. Supreme Court — who commented that the sodomy laws were "virtu-ally unenforceable and unenforced" and were "no great loss."

On other gay-related issues, the state has sent mixed signals. New Hampshire has a hate crimes law that includes crimes based on sexual orientation. But it was also the first state to prohibit lesbians and gay men from becoming foster or adoptive parents, through legislation signed by Gov. John Sununu on May 26, 1987. Florida is the only other state to ban such adoptions. **C**

NEW JERSEY: *No sodomy laws. Comprehensive* civil rights law. New Jersey's anti-sodomy laws, which dated back to the Revolutionary War, were repealed as part of a general legislative reform on July 27, 1978.

On Jan. 19, 1992, New Jersey became the fifth state to outlaw anti-gay discrimination. Gov. James Florio signed a bill banning discrimination based on sexual orientation in housing, employment, public accommodations, credit, and public contracts. It had passed both houses of the state legislature by wide margins. **A**

NEW MEXICO: *No sodomy laws.* Sodomy laws were repealed as of July 1, 1975, with almost no dissent in the state legislature. At the same time, the definition of rape was revised to include male rape — but not the rape of one's spouse. The state also bans anti-gay discrimination in public employment. **B**

NEW YORK: *No sodomy laws.* All through the 1970s, New York law prohibited sodomy (defined as oral or anal intercourse) except between married couples. Every year, assembly members introduced legislation to repeal the laws, and every year, their efforts were defeated.

On Jan. 24, 1980, in a suit brought by the Lambda Legal Defense and Education Fund, the New York State Supreme Court did what the assembly had not. It struck down the sodomy law as violating the right of equal protection. The court held that "the distinction ... between married and unmarried individuals is impermissible under the equal protection clause."

New Yorkers still had to contend with a state law against loitering in a public place to solicit "deviate sexual intercourse." The state Court of Appeals declared that statute unconstitutional in October 1983. A statewide civil rights law passed the state Assembly in 1993, and the governor had promised to sign it, but Republicans in the state senate killed it in a closed committee hearing. Lesbians and gay men in New York are protected from discrimination in public employment, and comprehensive gay civil rights laws exist in Albany, Afred, Ithaca, New York, Syracuse, Watertown, and Tompkins County. **B**

NORTH CAROLINA: *Still has sodomy laws.* "Crimes Against Nature," both heterosexual and homosexual, are a felony here, punishable by up to ten years in prison. **F**

NORTH DAKOTA: *No sodomy laws.* The North Dakota legislature passed an extensive revision of its criminal code in 1973; it was signed by Gov. Arthur Link on March 15, 1973, but did not go into effect until July 1, 1975. One little-noted provision was a repeal of its sodomy laws, with the age of consent set at 18. "Actually the only part that was really controversial was whether to let teenagers smoke in public," said Rep. Myron Atkinson, the Republican sponsor of the code revision. **B-**

OHIO: *No sodomy laws.* Ohio governor John Gilligan signed an extensive revision of the criminal code, effective January 1, 1974. It included a repeal of the state's sodomy laws, and set the age of consent at 16. Ohio also bans anti-gay discrimination in public employment, and the cities of Cincinnati, Columbus, and Yellow Springs have comprehensive gay civil rights laws. **B**

OKLAHOMA: *Still has sodomy laws.* In 1977, an effort to repeal sodomy laws met with such a chorus of giggles that, according to local press reports, the vote was delayed. The measure was defeated, 54-36, and both heterosexual and homosexual sodomy are still a felony. **F**

OREGON: *No sodomy laws.* On July 2, 1971, Gov. Tom McCall signed a new criminal code, based on the Model Penal Law, legalizing homosexual acts between consenting adults; it went into effect Jan. 1, 1972. Oregon thus became the fourth state to eliminate its sodomy laws. At the same time, the age of consent was set at 18 (16 for partners who are within three years of the same age).

On June 29, 1981, another barrier fell when a court struck down the Oregon law that made "accosting for deviate purposes" a crime. Judge Winfred K. Liepe ruled that since "deviate" sexual acts were no longer a crime, the law violated First Amendment protections of free speech. The state has a hate crimes law that includes crimes based on sexual orientation, and the city of Portland has passed a comprehensive gay civil rights law.

All this progress was thrown into disarray, however, by the Oregon Citizens Alliance. In 1992 the OCA failed to pass strongly worded anti-gay legislation on a statewide level. The following year it introduced similar measures in the state's more conservative regions; seven cities and counties subsequently voted to ban enactment of gay civil rights laws. Activists are using both legislative and judicial tactics to fight these measures in what is likely to be a long and bitter battle. **B-**

PENNSYLVANIA: *No sodomy laws.* In 1786, following the American Revolution, Pennsylvania became the first state to revoke the death penalty as punishment for sodomy. It was the last time that Pennsylvania took the lead in this arena, however. Not until 1982 did the state repeal its sodomy laws, two years after the state supreme court struck down a law forbidding "deviant" consensual sex outside of marriage.

Pennsylvania bans anti-gay discrimination in public employment, and comprehensive gay civil rights laws are on the books in Harrisburg, Lancaster, Philadelphia, Pittsburgh, and York. **B+**

RHODE ISLAND: *Still has sodomy laws.* Sodomy laws here make both heterosexual and homosexual activity a felony; it is the only New England state with enforceable anti-gay laws. In August 1985, Republican governor Edward DiPrete issued an executive order barring discrimination on the basis of sexual orientation in state employment. The governor was so eager to avoid negative repercussions from within his party that there was no public announcement of the order; local gay activists didn't even learn about it until a week after the signing.

Rhode Island does not yet have a gay civil rights law, although it has come tantalizing close. In 1992, the governor had promised to sign such legislation, and it passed the House of Representatives, but was defeated 25-23 in the state senate, after three members who had promised their support failed to deliver. It failed again, under almost identical circumstances, in 1993. **C-**

SOUTH CAROLINA: *Still has sodomy laws.* Both heterosexual and homosexual sodomy — defined as "buggery" — are felonies here, and reform does not seem likely to come soon. **F**

SOUTH DAKOTA: *No sodomy laws.* As part of a general revision of its criminal code in 1976, South Dakota abolished its "crimes against nature" statute; the change went into effect April 1, 1977. **B-**

TENNESSEE: *Still has sodomy laws.* Homosexual sex is a misdemeanor here.

In 1979, Bradley County judge James C. Witt ruled that the state's recent revision of the sexual offenses law had, by implication, repealed the state's anti-sodomy laws. Accordingly, he dismissed charges against four men accused of soliciting gay sex at a highway rest area. But his ruling was overturned, and sodomy continued to be prosecuted as a felony for another ten years.

In 1989, the Tennessee Sentencing Commission (TSC) decided to eliminate the "archaic language" in the state's criminal code. It recommended that legislation outlawing "crimes against nature" be replaced with a specific prohibition of consensual sexual penetration with a person of the same sex. Gov. Ned McWherter signed the new legislation into law in June 1989. The punishment for such acts, however, was reduced from a felony (carrying a five-to-fifteen-year sentence) to a misdemeanor, with a maximum sentence of not more than 30 days and a $50 fine. It is routinely applied to men caught cruising in public rest areas. **D**

TEXAS: *Sodomy laws not enforced.* In 1974, maximum penalties for "homosexual conduct" were greatly reduced; instead of a potential fifteen-year jail sentence, offenders were subject to no more than a $200 fine. For a time, Texas thus had the smallest maximim penalty of any state that still outlawed gay sex. Complete relief from official homophobia had to come from the courthouse rather than the legislature, however, and it was a long battle.

That fight began in 1982, when a U.S. district judge ruled that the Texas sodomy law violated the rights of privacy. Texas attorney general Jim Mattox supported that ruling, and briefly Texas joined the list of states without sodomy laws. But Danny Hill, a county district attorney, appealed the ruling, and in 1985, the Fifth Circuit Court reinstated the law.

The law was tested again in 1990. Once again, Jim Mattox showed little enthusiasm for the century-old statue, and Judge Paul Davis found that it violated guarantees of privacy and equal protection provided in the Texas constitution. Although the law had rarely been enforced, it had often been used to justify anti-gay discrimination. The Dallas Police Department, for example, referred to the sodomy law when it refused to hire a lesbian earlier that year. That ruling was upheld on March 11, 1992, by an appeals court, which noted that the law was never enforced, and asked: "If lesbians and gay men pose such a threat to the State, why then does the State not enforce the statute on a regular basis by investigating suspected homosexuals, obtaining search warrants, making arrests, and prosecuting offenders?" The court further ruled that the police could not use the law as a pretext for anti-gay employment discrimination. In 1993 the Texas Supreme Court refused to hear an appeal on the case, which means that the Texas sodomy statute cannot be enforced anywhere in the state.

Austin, the state capital, has a comprehensive gay civil rights law. **B**

UTAH: *Still has sodomy laws.* Sodomy is a misdemeanor. While other states were debating the wisdom of gay civil rights laws, Utah was on a different course. In 1982, the Republican State Convention adopted a platform stating that homosexuals should be denied the civil, political, social, and economic rights that party guaranteed to others regardless of race, creed, sex, or religion. Sodomy laws seem likely to stay on the books for some time in Utah. Utah also bans the purchase of school textbooks that portray homosexuality in a favorable light. **F**

VERMONT: *No sodomy laws. Comprehensive civil rights law.* Vermont has repealed its sodomy laws, and has a hate crimes law that includes crimes based on sexual orientation. In 1992, it passed a wide-ranging law that banned discrimination on the basis of sexual orientation in housing, employment, public accommodations, and insurance. The Vermont Supreme Court ruled in 1993 that a lesbian could adopt her partner's children, allowing them to share parental rights. **A**

VIRGINIA: *Still has sodomy laws.* In 1975, a U.S. district court upheld the constitutionality of Virginia's sodomy laws in *Doe* v. *Commonwealth's Attorney;* that ruling was upheld the following year by the U.S. Supreme Court. Both heterosexual and homosexual sodomy are still a felony. The city of Alexandria has a comprehensive gay civil rights law. **C+**

WASHINGTON: *No sodomy laws.* Gov. Dan Evans signed into law a comprehensive reform of the criminal code in 1975; the most controversial aspect of the wide-ranging bill was that it legalized sexual acts between consenting adults. The new law took effect July 1, 1976. A year later, Rep. Ted Haley, a Republican from Tacoma, introduced the state's first proposal for gay civil

rights legislation. It has not yet passed, but public employees are protected from anti-gay discrimination. Seattle has a comprehensive gay civil rights law. **B+**

WEST VIRGINIA: *No sodomy laws.* West Virginia repealed its sodomy laws effective June 10, 1976. **B-**

WISCONSIN: *No sodomy laws. Comprehensive civil rights law.* In 1982, thanks largely to the efforts of state legislator David Clarenbach, Wisconsin became the first state in the country to adopt a gay rights bill. Signed into law that February by a Republican governor, the law added the term "sexual orientation" to existing anti-discrimination statues. Ironically, it took another year before Wisconsin abolished its sodomy laws. A consenting-adults bill was signed into law on May 5, 1983, by Gov. Anthony Earl; it set the age of consent at 18. Until then, homosexual activity had been illegal for men, but not for women.

The state has a hate crimes law that includes crimes based on sexual orientation, and Madison, the state capital, has a comprehensive gay civil rights law. **A**

WYOMING: *No sodomy laws.* In February 1977, the Wyoming legislature legalized consenting homosexual relations between adults. The measure was signed by Gov. Ed Herschler and took effect May 17 of that year. **B-**

CONGRESSIONAL REPORT CARD

These charts show how the National Gay and Lesbian Task Force has evaluated each member of the U.S. Congress for the past three sessions.

Members were rated by the percentage of the time that they voted with the NGLTF position on issues of particular importance to the gay and lesbian community; a 100% score indicates that every vote cast by that senator or representative supported the NGLTF position.

The first number following each name indicates the voting record in the 102nd Congress (1991–92). The next gives the rating for the 101st Congress (1989–90), then the 100th Congress (1987–88).

Because many members of Congress turn up in other places after they leave the House or Senate, we've included the voting records for members who recently left office. Anyone familiar with the Senate voting record of California senator Pete Wilson, for example, would not have been surprised that, once elected governor, he vetoed gay civil rights legislation that he had promised to sign.

U.S. SENATE

Name	'91-'92	'89-'90	'87-'88	Name	'91-'92	'89-'90	'87-'88
Adams (D-WA)	91	100	82	Cohen (R-ME)	64	92	54
Akaka (D-HI)	100	100		Conrad (D-ND)	20	62	46
Baucus (D-MT)	45	64	46	Craig (R-ID)	9		
Bentsen (D-TX)	36	64	45	Cranston (D-CA)	100	100	92
Biden (D-DE)	64	92	50	D'Amato (R-NY)	27	69	45
Bingaman (D-NM)	64	92	46	Danforth (R-MO)	36	77	23
Bond (R-MO)	9	38	23	Daschle (D-SD)	27	92	42
Boren (D-OK)	36	77	42	DeConcini (D-AZ)	64	67	38
Bradley (D-NJ)	73	100	70	Dixon (D-IL)	10	77	42
Breaux (D-LA)	30	42	50	Dodd (D-CT)	64	90	75
Brown (R-CO)	0			Dole (R-KS)	0	38	18
Bryan (D-NV)	18	69		Domenici (R-NM)	18	80	38
Bumpers (D-AR)	18	73	58	Durenberger			
Burdick, Q. (D-ND)	56	100	54	(R-MN)	64	77	46
Burdick, J. (D-ND)	33			Exon (D-NE)	27	54	38
Burns (R-MT)	18	25		Ford (D-KY)	9	38	25
Byrd (D-WV)	9	54	46	Fowler (D-GA)	18	75	50
Chafee (R-RI)	91	100	85	Garn (R-UT)	11	25	27
Coats (R-IN)	0	31		Glenn (D-OH)	55	92	62
Cochran (R-MS)	18	33	46	Gore (D-TN)	78	92	89

Name	'91-'92	'89-'90	'87-'88	Name	'91-'92	'89-'90	'87-'88
Gorton (R-WA)	36	69		Packwood (R-OR)	44	85	69
Graham (D-FL)	27	85	62	Pell (D-RI)	80	100	77
Gramm (R-TX)	0	23	15	Pressler (R-SD)	9	31	31
Grassley (R-IA)	0	31	31	Pryor (D-AR)	22	75	46
Harkin (D-IA)	78	92	62	Reid (D-NV)	18	77	45
Hatch (R-UT)	20	54	23	Riegle (D-MI)	64	92	62
Hatfield (R-OR)	64	80	54	Robb (D-VA)	55	92	
Heflin (D-AL)	9	31	42	Rockefeller (D-WV)	73	77	42
Helms (R-NC)	0	0	0	Roth (R-DE)	0	25	38
Hollings (D-SC)	0	69	46	Rudman (R-NH)	18	59	42
Inouye (D-HI)	82	100	83	Sanford (D-NC)	55	92	77
Jeffords (R-VT)	70	100		Sarbanes (D-MD)	73	92	62
Johnston (D-LA)	27	54	46	Sasser (D-TN)	36	83	42
Kassebaum (R-KS)	45	67	50	Seymour (R-CA)	13		
Kasten (R-WI)	9	38	38	Shelby (D-AL)	9	46	38
Kennedy (D-MA)	100	100	85	Simon (D-IL)	73	92	100
Kerrey (D-NE)	55	92		Simpson (R-WY)	18	50	31
Kerry (D-MA)	91	92	85	Smith (R-NH)	0		
Kohl (D-WI)	55	92		Specter (R-PA)	27	85	77
Lautenberg (D-NJ)	82	92	62	Stevens (R-AK)	9	58	46
Leahy (D-VT)	91	100	83	Symms (R-ID)	10	15	0
Levin (D-MI)	73	73	75	Thurmond (R-SC)	0	25	15
Lieberman (D-CT)	64	92		Wallop (R-WY)	0	0	8
Lott (R-MS)	0	8		Warner (R-VA)	27	69	25
Lugar (R-IN)	30	69	15	Wellstone (D-MN)	100		
Mack (R-FL)	0	38		Wirth (D-CO)	80	92	69
McCain (R-AZ)	0	46	38	Wofford (R-PA)	80		
McConnell (R-KY)	0	38	23	**Former members:**			
Metzenbaum (D-OH)	91	90	62	Armstrong, Wm. (R-CO)		8	8
Mikulski (D-MD)	80	100	67	Boschwitz, Rudy (R-MN)		62	54
Mitchell (D-ME)	82	92	62	Heinz, John (R-PA)		75	67
Moynihan (D-NY)	82	100	92	Humphrey, Gordon (R-NH)	0	8	
Murkowski (R-AK)	9	33	33	Matsunaga, Spark (D-HI)		100	62
Nickles (R-OK)	0	23	15	McClure, James (R-ID)		15	8
Nunn (D-GA)	36	70	46	Wilson, Pete (R-CA)		67	38

THE HOUSE OF REPRESENTATIVES

Name	'91-'92	'89-'90	'87-'88	Name	'91-'92	'89-'90	'87-'88
ALABAMA				Harris (D-7)	38	60	76
Callahan (R-1)	0	31	41				
Dickinson (R-2)	25	38	41	**ALASKA**			
Browder (D-3)	38	63		Young (R)	15	40	76
Bevill (D-4)	46	56	76				
Cramer (D-5)	38			**ARIZONA**			
Erdreich (D-6)	38	63	76	Rhodes (R-1)	17	50	53
				Pastor (D-2)	89		

Name	'91-'92	'89-'90	'87-'88
Stump (R-3)	0	0	0
Kyl (R-4)	8	13	19
Kolbe (R-5)	62	67	88

ARKANSAS

Name	'91-'92	'89-'90	'87-'88
Alexander (D-1)	64	71	93
Thornton (D-2)	58		
Hammerschmidt (R-3)	15	21	43
Anthony (D-4)	60	88	85

CALIFORNIA

Name	'91-'92	'89-'90	'87-'88
Riggs (R-1)	8		
Herger (R-2)	0	6	24
Matsui (D-3)	100	100	100
Fazio (D-4)	92	100	100
Pelosi (D-5)	100	100	100
Boxer (D-6)	100	100	100
Miller (D-7)	100	100	100
Dellums (D-8)	100	100	100
Stark (D-9)	100	100	100
Edwards (D-10)	100	100	100
Lantos (D-11)	85	100	94
Campbell (R-12)	67	87	
Mineta (D-13)	100	100	94
Doolittle (R-14)	0		
Condit (D-15)	15	92	
Panetta (D-16)	100	100	94
Dooley (D-17)	62		
Lehman (D-18)	69	100	94
Lagomarsino (R-19)	8	31	
Thomas (R-20)	15	57	63
Gallegly (R-21)	8	31	35
Moorhead (R-22)	0	19	44
Beilenson (D-23)	92	94	100
Waxman (D-24)	100	100	100
Roybal (D-25)	100	100	100
Berman (D-26)	100	100	100
Levine (D-27)	100	100	100
Dixon (D-28)	92	100	100
Waters (D-29)	100		
Martinez (D-30)	92	100	94
Dymally (D-31)	100	100	100
Anderson (D-32)	77	94	94
Dreier (R-33)	0	38	30
Torres (D-34)	100	100	94
Lewis (R-35)	36	67	62

Name	'91-'92	'89-'90	'87-'88
Brown (D-36)	92	100	100
McClandless (R-37)	0	38	25
Dornan (R-38)	0	21	20
Dannemeyer (R-39)	0	6	0
Cox (R-40)	0	31	
Lowery (R-41)	15	60	50
Rohrabacher (R-42)	8	31	
Packard (R-43)	0	20	25
Cunningham (R-44)	8		
Hunter (R-45)	0	25	0

COLORADO

Name	'91-'92	'89-'90	'87-'88
Schroeder (D-1)	100	100	93
Skaggs (D-2)	100	100	94
Campbell (D-3)	75	88	94
Allard (R-4)	15		
Hefley (R-5)	8	20	47
Schaefer (R-6)	15	19	50

CONNECTICUT

Name	'91-'92	'89-'90	'87-'88
Kennelly (D-1)	77	100	94
Gejdenson (D-2)	100	100	93
DeLauro (D-3)	92		
Shays (R-4)	69	100	94
Franks (R-5)	15		
Johnson (R-6)	58	94	76

DELAWARE

Name	'91-'92	'89-'90	'87-'88
Carper (D)	33	94	82

FLORIDA

Name	'91-'92	'89-'90	'87-'88
Hutto (D-1)	0	25	65
Peterson (D-2)	42		
Bennett (D-3)	23	56	82
James (R-4)	0	31	
McCollum (R-5)	15	25	20
Stearns (R-6)	0	19	
Gibbons (D-7)	38	75	75
Young (R-8)	15	38	53
Bilirakis (R-9)	23	21	41
Ireland (R-10)	17	29	38
Bacchus (D-11)	77		
Lewis (R-12)	8	33	35
Goss (R-13)	15	44	
Johnston (D-14)	92	88	
Shaw (R-15)	17	38	47
Smith (D-16)	85	100	94

Name	'91-'92	'89-'90	'87-'88	Name	'91-'92	'89-'90	'87-'88
Lehman (D-17)	100	100	100	**INDIANA**			
Ros-Lehtinen (R-18)	15	43		Visclosky (D-1)	69	94	100
Fascell (D-19)	85	100	94	Sharp (D-2)	62	94	76
				Roemer (D-3)	46		
GEORGIA				Long (D-4)	54	81	
Thomas (D-1)	33	63	88	Jontz (D-5)	69	100	94
Hatcher (D-2)	78	88	88	Burton (R-6)	0	6	0
Ray (D-3)	18	69	69	Myers (R-7)	23	38	40
Jones (D-4)	100	100		McCloskey (D-8)	62	100	88
Lewis (D-5)	100	100	100	Hamilton (D-9)	38	94	81
Gingrich (R-6)	0	40	31	Jacobs (D-10)	38	69	82
Darden (D-7)	46	75	96				
Rowland (D-8)	31	63	88	**IOWA**			
Jenkins (D-9)	45	44	81	Leach (R-1)	77	81	88
Barnard (D-10)	33	47	56	Nussle (R-2)	38		
				Nagle (D-3)	83	100	87
HAWAII				Smith (D-4)	85	100	86
Abercrombie (D-1)	100			Lightfoot (R-5)	8	29	60
Mink (D-2)	92	100		Grandy (R-6)	62	63	65
IDAHO				**KANSAS**			
LaRocco (D-1)	85			Roberts (R-1)	8	38	62
Stallings (D-2)	31	69	73	Slattery (D-2)	46	81	76
				Meyers (R-3)	31	50	65
ILLINOIS				Glickman (D-4)	38	81	71
Hayes (D-1)	100	100	100	Nichols (R-5)	8		
Savage (D-2)	78	93	94				
Russo (D-3)	54	81	58	**KENTUCKY**			
Sangmeister (D-4)	46	81		Hubbard (D-1)	31	53	71
Lipinski (D-5)	38	69	79	Natcher (D-2)	69	81	94
Hyde (R-6)	0	40	59	Mazzoli (D-3)	77	93	94
Collins (D-7)	92	100	100	Bunning (R-4)	0	19	31
Rostenkowski (D-8)	69	85	93	Rogers (R-5)	23	40	38
Yates (D-9)	100	100	100	Hopkins (R-6)	33	31	59
Porter (R-10)	23	63	75	Perkins (D-7)	69	81	88
Annunzio (D-11)	62	75	88				
Crane (R-12)	0	0	0	**LOUISIANA**			
Fawell (R-13)	15	19	40	Livingston (R-1)	0	25	27
Hastert (R-14)	8	27	29	Jefferson (D-2)	92		
Ewing (R-15)	0			Tauzin (D-3)	23	38	81
Cox (D-16)	100			McCrery (R-4)	18	64	
Evans (D-17)	100	100	94	Huckaby (D-5)	25	50	69
Michel (R-18)	17	47	46	Baker (R-6)	0	33	53
Bruce (D-19)	38	81	88	Hayes (D-7)	17	47	82
Durbin (D-20)	77	100	94	Holloway (R-8)	0	13	14
Costello (D-21)	31	73	88				
Poshard (D-22)	31	63					

Name	'91-'92	'89-'90	'87-'88
MAINE			
Andrews (D-1)	100		
Snowe (R-2)	23	63	76
MARYLAND			
Gilchrest (R-1)	23		
Bentley (R-2)	25	27	50
Cardin (D-3)	100	100	94
McMillen (D-4)	38	94	88
Hoyer (D-5)	92	100	100
Byron (D-6)	15	50	75
Mfume (D-7)	100	100	94
Morella (R-8)	100	100	94
MASSACHUSETTS			
Olver (D-1)	100		
Neal (D-2)	69	100	
Early (D-3)	62	93	100
Frank (D-4)	100	100	100
Atkins (D-5)	100	100	94
Mavroules (D-6)	77	100	94
Markey (D-7)	92	100	100
Kennedy (D-8)	85	100	100
Moakley (D-9)	75	100	94
Studds (D-10)	100	100	100
Donnelly (D-11)	46	81	88
MICHIGAN			
Conyers (D-1)	100	100	100
Pursell (R-2)	31	60	80
Wolpe (D-3)	92	100	100
Upton (R-4)	15	38	59
Henry (R-5)	15	67	47
Carr (D-6)	83	100	88
Kildee (D-7)	85	100	94
Traxler (D-8)	64	94	93
Vander Jagt (R-9)	15	46	56
Camp (R-10)	15		
Davis (R-11)	31	47	87
Bonior (D-12)	91	100	100
Collins (D-13)	100		
Hertel (D-14)	85	94	94
Ford (D-15)	83	100	100
Dingell (D-16)	85	87	88
Levin (D-17)	85	100	94
Broomfield (R-18)	17	40	71

Name	'91-'92	'89-'90	'87-'88
MINNESOTA			
Penny (D-1)	23	63	64
Weber (R-2)	15	38	47
Ramstad (R-3)	15		
Vento (D-4)	100	100	93
Sabo (D-5)	100	100	100
Sikorski (D-6)	92	100	94
Peterson (D-7)	38		
Oberstar (D-8)	85	100	94
MISSISSIPPI			
Whitten (D-1)	45	80	88
Espy (D-2)	69	81	94
Montgomery (D-3)	23	50	87
Parker (D-4)	15	44	
Taylor (D-5)	0	40	56
MISSOURI			
Clay (D-1)	100	100	100
Horn (D-2)	77		
Gephardt (D-3)	73	100	91
Skelton (D-4)	15	44	76
Wheat (D-5)	92	100	94
Coleman (R-6)	38	63	59
Hancock (R-7)	0	0	
Emerson (R-8)	8	25	24
Volkmer (D-9)	23	31	71
MONTANA			
Williams (D-1)	85	100	88
Marlenee (R-2)	0	6	29
NEBRASKA			
Bereuter (R-1)	31	50	65
Hoagland (D-2)	54	81	
Barrett (R-3)	23		
NEVADA			
Bilbray (D-1)	54	81	88
Vucanovich (R-2)	8	27	53
NEW HAMPSHIRE			
Zeliff (R-1)	23		
Swett (D-2)	46		
NEW JERSEY			
Andrews (D-1)	92		
Hughes (D-2)	77	94	94

Name	'91-'92	'89-'90	'87-'88
Pallone (D-3)	69	75	
Smith (R-4)	15	44	59
Roukema (R-5)	15	33	64
Dwyer (D-6)	77	100	88
Rinaldo (R-7)	15	50	65
Roe (D-8)	67	93	87
Torricelli (D-9)	77	100	94
Payne (D-10)	92	100	
Gallo (R-11)	38	81	65
Zimmer (R-12)	23		
Saxton (R-13)	15	63	65
Guarini (D-14)	50	94	94

NEW MEXICO

Name	'91-'92	'89-'90	'87-'88
Schiff (R-1)	31	81	
Skeen (R-2)	31	56	71
Richardson (D-3)	92	100	94

NEW YORK

Name	'91-'92	'89-'90	'87-'88
Hochbrueckner (D-1)	62	88	82
Downey (D-2)	83	100	94
Mrazek (D-3)	91	100	94
Lent (R-4)	8	50	65
McGrath (R-5)	8	73	69
Flake (D-6)	85	100	94
Ackerman (D-7)	100	100	100
Scheuer (D-8)	100	100	100
Manton (D-9)	77	100	86
Schumer (D-10)	100	100	94
Towns (D-11)	100	100	100
Owens (D-12)	100	100	100
Solarz (D-13)	100	100	94
Molinari (R-14)	38	90	71
Green (R-15)	100	100	100
Rangel (D-16)	92	100	93
Weiss (D-17)	100	100	100
Serrano (D-18)	92	100	
Engel (D-19)	100	100	
Lowey (D-20)	92	100	
Fish (R-21)	75	100	94
Gilman (R-22)	85	100	94
McNulty (D-23)	54	100	
Soloman (R-24)	0	25	18
Boehlert (R-25)	85	100	88
Martin (R-26)	31	56	77
Walsh (R-27)	15	73	

Name	'91-'92	'89-'90	'87-'88
McHugh (D-28)	85	100	94
Horton (R-29)	83	100	93
Slaughter (D-30)	100	100	88
Paxon (R-31)	15	38	
LaFalce (D-32)	85	80	82
Nowak (D-33)	85	88	93
Houghton (R-34)	77	83	88

NORTH CAROLINA

Name	'91-'92	'89-'90	'87-'88
Jones (D-1)	66	80	93
Valentine (D-2)	33	50	88
Lancaster (D-3)	31	73	94
Price (D-4)	50	94	94
Neal (D-5)	50	86	94
Coble (R-6)	8	19	35
Rose (D-7)	54	81	88
Hefner (D-8)	27	50	88
McMillan (R-9)	23	38	71
Ballenger (R-10)	15	25	35
Taylor (R-11)	8		

NORTH DAKOTA

Name	'91-'92	'89-'90	'87-'88
Dorgan (D)	54	81	94

OHIO

Name	'91-'92	'89-'90	'87-'88
Luken (D-1)	15	87	69
Gradison (R-2)	31	88	80
Hall (D-3)	38	67	80
Oxley (R-4)	8	47	60
Gillmor (R-5)	31	44	
McEwen (R-6)	0	25	31
Hobson (R-7)	15		
Boehner (R-8)	0		
Kaptur (D-9)	62	81	88
Miller (R-10)	0	38	29
Eckart (D-11)	85	69	53
Kasich (R-12)	15	44	65
Pease (D-13)	85	100	93
Sawyer (D-14)	85	100	94
Wylie (R-15)	15	29	47
Regula (R-16)	15	38	56
Traficant (D-17)	62	75	94
Applegate (D-18)	33	47	59
Feighan (D-19)	100	100	94
Oakar (D-20)	92	100	93
Stokes (D-21)	91	100	100

Name	'91-'92	'89-'90	'87-'88
OKLAHOMA			
Inhofe (R-1)	0	31	53
Synar (D-2)	77	100	94
Brewster (D-3)	38		
McCurdy (D-4)	46	73	82
Edwards (R-5)	20	25	59
English (D-6)	31	53	71
OREGON			
AuCoin (D-1)	100	100	93
Smith, R. (R-1)	8	25	59
Wyden (D-3)	100	100	94
DeFazio (D-4)	100	100	94
Kopetski (D-5)	100		
PENNSYLVANIA			
Foglietta (D-1)	100	100	100
Blackwell (D-2)	100		
Borski (D-3)	69	100	94
Kolter (D-4)	58	60	88
Schulze (R-5)	18	40	63
Yatron (D-6)	50	62	82
Weldon (R-7)	15	47	64
Kostmayer (D-8)	100	100	100
Shuster (R-9)	0	19	19
McDade (R-10)	54	69	88
Kanjorski (D-11)	69	81	88
Murtha (D-12)	85	81	88
Coughlin (R-13)	42	63	76
Coyne (D-14)	100	100	94
Ritter (R-15)	15	31	53
Walker (R-16)	0	19	29
Gekas (R-17)	8	19	24
Santorum (R-18)	15		
Goodling (R-19)	15	57	71
Gaydos (D-20)	62	73	88
Ridge (R-21)	15	53	80
Murphy (D-22)	46	69	94
Clinger (R-23)	54	69	76
RHODE ISLAND			
Machtley (R-1)	92	100	
Reed (D-2)	85		
SOUTH CAROLINA			
Ravenel (R-1)	23	56	64
Spence (R-2)	15	31	60

Name	'91-'92	'89-'90	'87-'88
Derrick (D-3)	77	56	71
Patterson (D-4)	31	44	71
Spratt (D-5)	38	63	81
Tallon (D-6)	8	40	76
SOUTH DAKOTA			
Johnson (D)	38	63	82
TENNESSEE			
Quillen (R-1)	0	33	64
Duncan (R-2)	0	13	
Lloyd (D-3)	15	47	65
Cooper (D-4)	62	75	88
Clement (D-5)	38	69	91
Gordon (D-6)	62	81	88
Sundquist (R-7)	8	33	36
Tanner (D-8)	15	60	
Ford (D-9)	90	100	100
TEXAS			
Chapman (D-1)	38	60	82
Wilson (D-2)	33	77	70
Johnson (R-3)	0		
Hall (D-4)	0	20	47
Bryant (D-5)	54	92	94
Barton (R-6)	0	13	0
Archer (R-7)	0	7	12
Fields (R-8)	0	19	6
Brooks (D-9)	54	75	94
Pickle (D-10)	62	88	94
Edwards (D-11)	38		
Geren (D-12)	46	69	
Sarpalius (D-13)	0	50	
Laughlin (D-14)	15	47	
de la Garza (D-15)	64	80	83
Coleman (D-16)	62	100	94
Stenholm (D-17)	15	38	63
Washington (D-18)	100	100	
Combest (R-19)	8	19	18
Gonzalez (D-20)	100	100	100
Smith (R-21)	8	29	29
DeLay (R-22)	0	19	12
Bustamante (D-23)	83	100	100
Frost (D-24)	54	94	100
Andrews (D-25)	31	69	94
Armey (R-26)	0	13	12

Name	'91-'92	'89-'90	'87-'88
Ortiz (D-27)	31	69	88
UTAH			
Hansen (R-1)	8	19	21
Owens (D-2)	83	100	88
Orton (D-3)	18		
VERMONT			
Sanders (I)	100		
VIRGINIA			
Bateman (R-1)	15	38	65
Pickett (D-2)	42	75	88
Bliley (R-3)	15	40	41
Sisisky (D-4)	38	81	82
Payne (D-5)	38	81	88
Olin (D-6)	62	81	88
Allen (R-7)	0		
Moran (D-8)	92		
Boucher (D-9)	58	88	78
Wolf (R-10)	15	31	53
WASHINGTON			
Miller (R-1)	54	100	94
Swift (D-2)	85	100	100
Unsoeld (D-3)	100	100	
Morrison (R-4)	31	88	88
Foley (D-5)			94
Dicks (D-6)	69	100	94
McDermott (D-7)	100	100	
Chandler (R-8)	25	69	94
WEST VIRGINIA			
Mollohan (D-1)	33	81	75
Staggers (D-2)	45	93	82
Wise (D-3)	62	88	88
Rahall (D-4)	42	75	82
WISCONSIN			
Aspin (D-1)	85	94	88
Klug (R-2)	46		
Gunderson (R-3)	38	94	81
Kleczka (D-4)	62	100	88
Moody (D-5)	75	100	100
Petri (R-6)	0	19	65
Obey (D-7)	83	100	81
Roth (R-8)	0	19	33
Sensenbrenner (R-9)	0	25	41

Name	'91-'92	'89-'90	'87-'88
WYOMING			
Thomas (R)	23	31	
Former members:			
Akaka, Daniel (HI: D-2)		88	93
Bartlett, Steve (TX: R-3)		33	35
Bates, Jim (CA: D-44)		100	94
Boggs, Lindy (LA: D-2)		83	88
Bosco, Douglas (CA: D-1)		100	94
Brennan, Joseph (ME: D-1)		87	88
Brown, Hank (CO: R-4)		25	41
Buechner, Jack (MO: R-2)		63	71
Clarke, James McC. (NC: D-11)		81	88
Conte, Silvio (MA: R-1)		100	88
Courter, Jim (NJ: R-12)		70	67
Craig, Larry (ID: R-1)		21	29
Crockett, George (MI: D-13)		100	94
DeWine, Michael (OH: R-7)		47	41
Douglas, Chuck (NH: R-2)			20
Dyson, Roy (MD: D-1)		56	81
Flippo, Ronnie (AL: D-5)		64	71
Frenzel, Bill (MN: R-3)		85	81
Garcia, Robert (NY: D-18)		100	94
Grant, Bill (FL: R-2)		38	93
Gray, William (PA: D-2)	100	100	93
Hawkins, Augustus (CA: D-29)		100	100
Hiler, John (IN: R-3)		33	47
Kastenmeier, Robert (WI: D-2)		100	94
Leath, Marvin (TX: D-11)		46	43
Lukens, Donald (OH: R-8)		25	7
Madigan, Edward (IL: R-15)		50	64
Martin, Lynn (IL: R-16)		53	80
Morrison, Bruce (CT: D-3)		100	100

Name	'91-'92	'89-'90	'87-'88
Nelson, Bill (FL: D-11)	44	53	
Nielson, Howard (UT: R-3)	13	12	
Parris, Stan (VA: R-8)	33	38	
Pashayan, Charles (CA: R-17)	47	82	
Robinson, Tommy (AR: R-2)	29	76	
Rowland, John (CT: R-5)	67	76	
Saiki, Pat (HI: R-1)	81	80	
Schneider, Claudine (RI: R-2)	100	93	
Schuette, Bill (MI: R-10)	33	63	
Shumway, Norman (CA: R-14)	6	6	
Slaughter, D. French (VA: R-7)	0	31	41

Name	'91-'92	'89-'90	'87-'88
Smith, Denny (OR: R-5)	15	25	
Smith, Peter (VT: R)	93		
Smith, Robert C. (NH: R-1)	13	29	
Smith, Smith (NE: R-3)	40	59	
Strangeland, Arlan (MN: R-7)	38	47	
Tauke, Thomas (IA: R-2)	50	53	
Udall, Morris (AZ: D-2)	93	94	
Walgren, Doug (PA: D-18)	80	94	
Watkins, Wes (OK: D-3)	47	88	
Whittaker, Bob (KS: R-5)	44	41	

Note: House Speaker Thomas Foley (D-WA) generally does not vote.

Keep in touch!

Letters and phone calls to elected officials do make a difference. The religious right has an efficient mechanism for churning out such responses to legislative proposals; supporters of gay civil rights have not. Here are some suggestions.

A personal letter is the most effective communication. Keep your letter brief, and focus on one issue.

Always identify yourself as a constituent, when writing to your elected officials. Give your name and address.

Avoid threats or demands. Present one or two arguments in your favor. If you can explain how legislation would affect you personally, do so. For example, if you've been subjected to anti-gay discrimination, that's an important fact to note in a letter about gay civil rights legislation.

Phone calls will be most effective if there's no time for a letter before a forthcoming vote. Identify, as clearly as possible, the bill that you're calling about.

To write your legislator:

The Honorable _____
U.S. Senate
Washington, DC 20510

Dear Senator _____:

The Honorable _____
U.S. House of Representatives
Washington, DC 20515

Dear Representative _____:

To telephone:
    U.S. Senate: 202-224-3121.
    U.S. House: 202-225-3121.

ELECTED OFFICIALS

This listing includes openly gay officeholders at all levels of government through 1985, and selected officeholders since then. We welcome information about any names that might have been missed.

NANCY WECHSLER and **GERALD DeGRIECK:** Elected to the Ann Arbor (Mich.) City Council as candidates of the radical Human Rights Party, they subsequently came out, in the fall of 1972. They were the country's first openly gay elected officials.

KATHY KOZACHENKO: Elected to the Ann Arbor City Council as an openly lesbian candidate of the Human Rights Party, April 1, 1974, by a margin of only nine votes. She was the first openly gay person to win election to public office.

ELAINE NOBLE: Elected to the Massachusetts House of Representatives, November 1974, and served for four years.

ALLAN SPEAR: A Minnesota state senator who had been elected two years earlier, Spear came out in December 1974, and repeatedly won re-election. He became president of the Minnesota senate in 1993.

GARY HESS: A member of the county board of education in Santa Barbara, California, Hess came out in late 1974.

HARVEY MILK: Elected to the San Francisco Board of Supervisors, November 1977.

JAMES D. YEADON: Served as an openly gay alderman in Madison, Wisconsin, retiring in 1979.

HARRY BRITT: Appointed to the San Francisco Board of Supervisors, January 10, 1979; he was later elected to that position. Served as president of the board, 1988–1990.

KAREN CLARK: Elected state representative in Minnesota, November 1980, and has consistently won re-election, most recently in 1992.

GERALD E. ULRICH: Elected mayor of Bunceton, Missouri, (population 437) on April 1, 1980. His homosexuality was never an issue.

JOHN LAIRD: Elected to the Santa Cruz (Cal.) City Council in 1981; as the top vote-getter, he also became vice mayor at that time. The council elected him mayor in 1983.

ROBERT GENTRY: Elected to the city council of Laguna Beach in April 1982, and unanimously chosen by other council members to be mayor the following year.

GERRY E. STUDDS: Came out publicly in July 1983, thus becoming the first openly gay U.S. congressman, and easily won re-election in 1984.

BRIAN COYLE: Elected to the Minneapolis City Council in November 1983, and later made vice president of the council. In 1991, Coyle revealed that he was HIV-positive, and he died of AIDS-related complications later that year.

DAVID SCONDRAS: Elected to Boston City Council in November 1983.

RICHARD A. HEYMAN: Elected mayor of Key West, Florida, in November 1983.

ROBERT EBERSOLE: As the town clerk (the city's highest position) of Lunenberg, Mass., Ebersole came out in 1984. He was the first openly gay Republican elected official, and later won re-election.

VALERIE TERRIGNO, JOHN HEILMAN, and STEVE SCHULTE: All three were elected to the first city council of the newly formed city of West Hollywood, California, in November 1984. Later that month Terrigno was elected by the council to become the city's first mayor. Both Heilman and Schulte later served as mayor.

CALVIN ANDERSON: Elected to Washington State legislature in 1987.

ROBERT STIPICEVICH: Elected in 1985 at age 22 to be a Fremont (Calif.) union school district trustee; he was the youngest person ever elected to the board. He came out after the election, then survived a recall attempt.

TIM MAINS: Elected to the Rochester (N.Y.) City Council in November 1985. The original count showed him defeating his opponent by 127 votes (out of 36,000 cast), but the GOP challenged some absentee ballots. In the end, a court still declared Mains the victor — but by only an 11-vote margin.

TOM NOLAN: Elected to the San Mateo (Cal.) County Board of Supervisors in 1985; became president of that body in 1987. In 1992 Nolan ran unsuccessfully for the U.S. House of Representatives.

BARNEY FRANK: U.S. congressman. Came out May 30, 1987, and easily won re-election the following year.

JUDY ABDO: Elected to the Santa Monica (Cal.) City Council in November 1988, won re-election in 1992.

RICHARD C. FAILLA: Won an uncontested election to the New York state supreme court in 1988, as an openly gay candidate, after being endorsed by the Democratic, Republican, and Liberal parties. He served until his AIDS-related death in 1993.

JOAN LOBIS: Elected to be civil court judge in New York, beginning Jan. 1, 1989, and elected to the N.Y. Court of Appeals, Nov. 3, 1992.

ROBERTA ACHTENBERG: Elected to the San Francisco Board of Supervisors, November 1990. Her lover, Mary Morgan, had become the country's first openly lesbian judge, in 1981.

CAROLE MIDGEN: Midgen, chair of the city's Democratic party, was elected to the San Francisco Board of Supervisors, November 1990. With the election of her and Roberta Achtenberg, plus Harry Britt already elected, one-third of the nine-member board consisted of open lesbians and gay men.

DALE McCORMICK: Elected to Maine's state senate, November 1990, re-elected in 1992.

DEBORAH GLICK: Elected to New York's state assembly, November 1990, re-elected in 1992.

SUSAN FARNSWORTH: Elected to the Maine legislature in 1988, re-elected in 1992.

RON SQUIRES: Elected to the Vermont legislature in 1990, re-elected in 1992.

GLEN MAXEY: Elected to the Texas legislature in 1991, re-elected in 1992.

JOSEPH GRABARZ: Elected to the Connecticut House of Representatives in 1988, came out publicly on Dec. 16, 1990.

GAIL SHIBLEY: Was appointed to fill a vacant seat in the Oregon House of Representatives, and came out publicly just hours after being sworn in on Jan. 16, 1991. Shibley said the commission that appointed her had been fully of her lesbianism. She was re-elected in 1992.

SHERRY HARRIS: Was elected to the Seattle City Council on Nov. 5, 1991, becoming the nation's first openly lesbian black elected official.

TAMMY BALDWIN: Elected to the Dane County (Madison, Wisconsin) Board of Supervisors, 1986. Elected to the Wisconsin state assembly, Nov. 3, 1992.

WILL FITZPATRICK: Elected to the Rhode Island legislature, Nov. 3, 1992.

LIZ STEFANICS: Elected to the New Mexico state senate, Nov. 3, 1992.

GEORGE EIGHMEY: Eighmey, a gay activist, was appointed to a vacant seat in the Oregon House of Representatives and took office May 6, 1993. He will have the option of running for re-election to the seat in 1994.

BILL CREWS: After serving as mayor of Melbourne, Iowa, for nine years, Crews came out during the 1993 March on Washington. One vandal spraypainted "No Faggots" on his house before his return, but most townspeople said they already suspected and didn't care.

WILLIAM J. FITZPATRICK: Was elected to the Rhode Island state senate, November, 1992. Although he was widely known to be gay while he was campaigning, Fitzpatrick did not publicly come out until after the election.

KEN REEVES: Reeves, the mayor of Cambridge, Massachusetts, was not particularly secretive about being gay, but neither had he publicly said anything about it until late 1992.

IN OTHER COUNTRIES

WENCHE LOWZOW: Elected to the Norwegian parliament in 1977 as a member of the conservative party. She publicly announced that she was a lesbian, and was renominated by her party to serve another four years.

PAUL O'GRADY: Elected to the New South Wales Upper House of Parliament in 1988.

SVEND ROBINSON: Elected to the Canadian Parliament in 1979, came out Feb. 29, 1988.

CHRIS SMITH: Elected to the British Parliament (House of Commons), 1983.

DAVID NORRIS: Elected to the Irish senate.

CHRISTIAN PULZ: Elected to Germany's state parliament, 1991.

ALBERT ECKERT: Elected to Germany's state parliament, 1989.

TRAVEL DESTINATIONS

What are the favorite destinations for gay and lesbian travelers? Here are the most popular spots named in a survey by the International Gay Travel Association, a non-profit association of gay travel professionals. For further information about the IGTA, write them at P.O. Box 4974, Key West, FL 33041.

DOMESTIC TRAVEL	INTERNATIONAL TRAVEL
1. San Francisco area	1. Amsterdam
2. Key West	2. London
3. Provincetown	3. Greece
4. New York City area	4 & 5. (tie) Australia &
5. Palm Springs	Paris
6. Hawaii	6. Brazil
7. Miami–Ft. Lauderdale	7. Vancouver, B.C.
8. W. Hollywood–Los Angeles	8. Spain
9. New Orleans	9. Thailand
10. Chicago	10. Germany

RESORT AREAS

Other popular spots, some of which are not well known beyond the local community, include:

ASBURY PARK, N.J. Just an hour south of New York City lies this small town with a beach, gay bars and clubs, and dozens of gay-related businesses.

REHOBOTH BEACH, DEL. A law passed in 1989 to prevent new bars from opening, which was widely seen as an anti-gay move, has not discouraged gay business in this resort. It has beautiful beaches, numerous nightclubs, and is just a three-hour drive from Washington.

NEW HOPE, PENN. An hour from Philadelphia, an hour and a half from New York City, New Hope has an artists' colony and a large gay population.

OGUNQUIT, MAINE. Quieter than most gay resorts, this seacoast town ninety minutes north of Boston boasts several gay-owned inns, a gay disco, the Ogunquit Playhouse, a long beach, and an active art association.

SAN PADRE ISLAND, TEXAS. This narrow island, a hundred miles off the Texas coast, offers some of the best beaches in the country, legends

Cindy Hu/S.F. Convention and Visitors Bureau

San Francisco is the #1 destination for gay and lesbian travelers. Those who make it beyond the Castro will have an opportunity to enjoy this view of the Golden Gate Bridge and Marin headlands, as seen from the Golden Gate National Recreation Area.

of lost pirate treasure, and plenty of fresh seafood. There's a gay guesthouse, Lyle's Deck, but no gay bars.

SAUGATUCK, MICH. On the eastern shore of Lake Michigan, two hours from Chicago, lies a vacation spot that few people from the coasts have heard of. Saugatuck was an artists' colony in the 1800s. It has had a gay lodge since the 1960s; it also boasts a gay beach, and a large summertime population of lesbians and gay men, as well as excellent cross-country ski trails for winter vacationers.

RUSSIAN RIVER. Sixty miles north of San Francisco, the Russian River area offers both natural scenery and gay nightlife, and a good selection of overnight accommodations.

VACATION IDEAS

ADVENTURE BOUND EXPEDITIONS. Run by David L. Johnson, this new tour agency organizes trips for gay men and women. Includes ski trips, backpacking, and river expeditions in the Colorado area, as well as more far-reaching trips of two weeks or more to the Himalayas, Machu Picchu, and other destinations worldwide. Adventure Bound Expeditions, 711 Walnut St., Boulder, CO 80302; (303) 449-0990.

ASPEN GAY SKI WEEK. Once a year, several hundred gay skiers assemble at Aspen for a week of daytime skiing and weekend partying. For dates and details, call the Aspen Gay Center, (303) 925-9249; or write or call Ron Erickson, Hillcrest Travel, 431 Robinson Ave., San Diego, CA 92103; (619) 291-0758.

ATLANTIS (at Club Med Resorts). With exclusively gay weeks at Club Med resorts in the Caribbean and Mexico, Atlantis vacations offer sun, beaches, entertainment, activities, sports, and camaraderie. For a brochure, contact your travel agent or call (800) 6-ATLANTIS.

B.W. TRAVEL. This travel agency says it's for "Boys Who Like To Travel," though women are welcome to use its services, as well. The agency puts together packages for many gay events throughout the year, most notably Gay Ski Week and Hotlanta (a summer rafting party in Georgia), as well as parties in suitably festive cities for Halloween, New Year's Eve, Memorial Day, and Labor Day. Ask to get their newsletter of upcoming events. B.W. Travel, 9 Mott Ave., Norwalk, CT 06850; (800) 288-2589 (in Connecticut, call 203-852-0200).

CAMPFEST FESTIVALS. This annual five-day women's festival includes music, comedy, outdoor activities, and workshops. Attendees are encourage to work a two-hour shift at the festival, to encourage networking and a smooth-running program. For information, write Campfest Festivals, RR 5, Box 185, Franklinville, NJ 08322.

DINAH SHORE GOLF TOURNA-MENT. Thousands of lesbians head for Palm Springs, California, each year to watch the golfers, watch each other, and party. In recent years, events for gay men have sprung up at the same time. As the organizers would hasten to tell you, the Dinah Shore Golf Tournament is not officially a lesbian event, and they won't be much help in providing information. Guest houses listed in lesbian and gay guides are a better source of details.

GUNDERSON TRAVEL, INC. Gunderson Travel offers exclusively gay Windstar Cruises in the Caribbean. For information, contact Gunderson Travel, Inc., 8543 Santa Monica Blvd., Suite 8, West Hollywood, CA 90069; (310) 657-3944.

HANNS EBENSTEN TRAVEL, INC. This gay-owned tour operator specializes in tours, cruises, and expeditions for men traveling in small groups with experienced leaders. Destinations include the Amazon, the Himalayas, Morocco, Egypt, and Russia. Although more expensive than most charter tours, Ebensten's trips have a reputation among travelers looking for more cultural and intellectual experiences. For information, contact Hanns Ebensten Travel, Inc., 513 Fleming St., Key West, FL 33040; (305) 294-8174.

HAWAII MEN'S CONFERENCE. Kalani Honua is a retreat center in the beautiful Kalapana–Black Sand Beach area of Hawaii; it offers accommodations year-round, and holds workshops in spirituality, dance, massage, and yoga. The founder, Richard Koob, is a gay man, and once a year, the center hosts the Hawaii Men's Conference, a gathering of about 100 mostly gay men. For information, contact Kalani Honua, Box 4500, Pahoa-Keheha Beach, HI 96778; (808) 965-7828. (When telephoning, remember that it's five hours earlier in Hawaii than on the East Coast, and two hours earlier than the West Coast.)

HOTLANTA RIVER EXPO. This annual weekend celebration is held the second weekend in August. It combines nightlife in Atlanta with a raft trip on the Chattahoochee River. The event has been taking place for over a decade now, and attracts thousands of people each year. Hotlanta River Expo, P.O. Box 8528, Atlanta, GA 30306; (404) 874-EXPO.

MARIAH WILDERNESS EXPEDITIONS. This travel group is a whitewater rafting and adventure travel company, committed to safe, well-organized trips that increase travelers' self-confidence and environmental awareness. For the last five years, they have offered an annual gay and lesbian rafting trip on the American River in California, and in 1993 added a Costa Rica adventure; they also offer women-only trips. Mariah Wilderness Expeditions, P.O. Box 248, Point Richmond, CA 94807; (510) 233-2303.

MEN ON VACATION. MOV offers innovative men-only tours of the South Pacific, including Australia, New Zealand, and Hawaii. Packages include airfare, hotel of your choice, and a number of perks — discounts to gyms, bars, and restaurants, and a private cruise. For a brochure and information contact Men on Vacation, 3604 Fourth Ave., Suite 1, San Diego, CA 92103; (619) 298-2285.

New Orleans's cuisine helps it win a spot in the top-ten domestic destinations. Spicy boiled crawfish with corn and potatoes are a local favorite.

MICHIGAN WOMYN'S MUSIC FESTIVAL. An annual six-day festival featuring over 40 entertainers and over 300 workshops, and set in the secluded woodlands of northwestern Michigan, this popular event offers specific-needs campgrounds and sliding-scale admission on advanced tickets. For information, send a large SASE to WWTMC, Box 22, Walhalla, MI 49458; (616) 757-4766.

OLIVIA RECORDS. A leading label in women's music has branched into the travel business, with four- and seven-day cruises, often coinciding with holidays. Olivia Records, 4400 Market St., Oakland, CA 94608; (800) 631-6277 or (510) 655-0364.

ROBIN TYLER PRODUCTIONS. Like Olivia Records, comedian Robin Tyler is branching out into cruises. Robin Tyler Productions,

15842 Chase St., North Hills, CA 91343; 818-893-4075.

RSVP CRUISES. This travel group offers Caribbean and Mediterranean cruises for gay men; their schedule has included cruises in the Caribbean, Yucatan, Mexican Riviera, and French Canada. Most are a week long, but their Halloween cruise is a three-day affair, docking in Key West. Information is available through your local travel agent.

SEASPIRIT CRUISES. This 102-passenger cruise ship offers weekly Caribbean cruises in the spring, and weekly New York to Boston cruises in the summer, with stops in Newport, Martha's Vineyard, Provincetown and Nantucket. Special-interest cruises include Single Men's Cruise, Women-Only Cruise, and even a Leather Cruise. SeaSpirit cruises are handled exclusively though RSVP Travel Productions; contact your local travel agent for details.

WINDJAMMER BAREFOOT CRUISES. This tall-ship line offers several all-gay cruises each year. For information, contact your travel agent.

WOMANTREK. Tours of Tanzania, the Galapagos Islands, and Nepal, and a bicycle tour through China are just a few of the trips that have been sponsored by Womantrek over the past several years. Plans for 1990 and 1991 include rafting in Oregon, Washington, and Idaho; a trek through the country of Sikkim, near Tibet; bicycling in China, Nova Scotia, and West Africa; and skiing, sea kayaking, and cruises. These trips are limited to women only. Participants must be in good health, but do not need to be especially athletic. Womantrek, P.O. Box 20643, Seattle, WA 98102; (206) 325-4772.

WOMEN IN THE WILDERNESS. This travel and education group offers outdoor trips from Florida to Canada, with an emphasis on learning new skills and growing closer to nature. Tours include rafting, canoeing, dog-sledding, hiking, skiing, and more. For a brochure or information on books for outdoor-minded women, contact Women in the Wilderness, 566 Ottawa Ave., St. Paul, MN 55107; (612) 227-2284.

AND DON'T FORGET... An increasing number of cities have local organizations that organize trips for gay and lesbian members. Usually these are run on a volunteer basis, and are very inexpensive. Call your nearest gay hotline, or check a local gay or lesbian paper, to find out if there's such an organization near you. For other ideas, contact a travel agent that is a member of the International Gay Travel Association.

MAJOR CITIES

We asked gay publications in 30 of the largest metropolitan areas of the country to tell us about lesbian and gay life in their area. What they told us will be helpful for anyone interested in traveling, or even relocating, to one of these cities. Among the information here is:

Information: A hotline or other phone number you can call for general information about gay and lesbian organizations and activities.

Neighborhoods: Areas of the city where gay people are especially visible, or even in the majority.

Bars: Bars and clubs with a predominantly lesbian or gay male clientele are included in these figures.

Organizations: Some of the other types of special-interest organizations that exist are noted. We especially asked about neighborhood groups and those focused around gay youth, older people, sports, leather, and political action.

Other publications: In addition to the publication supplying this information (named at the top), other publications directed at the gay community are listed.

Arts: The existence of a gay chorus, band, theater, or other arts group is noted here.

Religion: Some of the more active gay religious groups are listed. Among the most common are Dignity (Catholics), Integrity (Episcopalians), and MCC (Metropolitan Community Church). Denominational affiliations of others are given,

if not obvious from their names.

Health: If one or two major health centers are associated with the gay and lesbian community, they are listed.

AIDS: One or two major AIDS-related organizations are listed, when they exist.

Civil rights: Local and state laws protecting the civil rights of gay people are noted, if they exist.

Space limitations make it impossible to give a more comprehensive listing of businesses and organizations in each city, or to list smaller metropolitan areas. To do that would require a book in itself. Fortunately, there already is such a book: *The Gayellow Pages,* updated annually and published by the Renaissance House in New York. It's available in gay bookstores. To learn more about a particular city, call the number listed under Information, or look through one of the papers listed.

ATLANTA
as reported by Etcetera magazine
Population: 2.8 million
Information: Gay Helpline, (404) 892-0661, 6 p.m. to 11 p.m. daily
Neighborhoods: Midtown, Caudler Park/Lake Claire, Decatur, Grant Park, Virginia Highlands
Bars: about 30
Organizations: 80+ including social, political, and sports
Other publications: *Southern Voice*

Arts: Southeast Arts and Media Exchange, Gay Men's Chorus, Feminist Women's Chorus
Religion: Dignity, Integrity, MCC, and others
AIDS: NAPWA Atlanta, AID Atlanta
Civil rights: Protection within Atlanta against housing discrimination, and for Atlanta, Fulton, and DeKalb County employees

BALTIMORE

as reported by the Baltimore Gay Paper
Population: 2.3 million
Information: Gay and lesbian switchboard, (410) 837-8888, 7:30 p.m. to 10:30 p.m. daily
Neighborhoods: Mt. Vernon, Waverly, Govans, Charles Village (women), Bolton Hill (men)
Bars: about 15
Organizations: Community center; neighborhood groups; leather, older people, sports, political action; Women's Growth Center
Other publications: *The Alternative, Women's Express*
Arts: Chorus, band, theater
Religion: Dignity, Integrity, MCC
Health: Chase-Brexton Clinic
AIDS: Chase-Brexton Clinic
Civil rights: City anti-discrimination ordinance

BOSTON

as reported by Gay Community News
Population: 2.8 million
Information: Gay and lesbian helpline, (617) 267-9001, 4 p.m. to 11 p.m. weekdays, 6 p.m. to 11 p.m. weekends
Neighborhoods: South End, Jamaica Plain, Fenway
Bars: about 20

Organizations: Neighborhood groups; gay youth, leather, older people, sports, political action; Cambridge Women's Center
Other publications: *Bay Windows, Sojourner, The Mirror, The Guide*
Arts: Chorus, band, theater
Religion: Dignity, MCC, Am Tikva, and others
Health: Fenway Community Health Center
AIDS: AIDS Action Committee
Civil rights: Local laws provide protection in Boston and some surrounding communities. Massachusetts has a gay civil rights law.

CHICAGO

as reported by the Windy City Times
Population: 6.1 million
Information: Gay and lesbian hotline, (312) 929-4357, 6 p.m. to 10 p.m. daily
Neighborhoods: Lakeview (New Town), North Side
Bars: about 70
Organizations: Community center; business league; gay youth, leather, older people, sports, political action; Kinheart Women's Center
Other publications: *Gay Chicago* magazine, *Outlines*
Arts: Chorus, theater
Religion: Dignity, Integrity, MCC, Havurat Achayot, and many others
Health: Howard Brown Memorial Clinic
AIDS: AIDS Alternative Health Project, Chicago House, and others
Civil rights: Both Chicago itself and Cook County, where it is located, have gay civil rights laws.

CINCINNATI

as reported by Gaybeat
Population: 1.4 million
Information: Gay and lesbian community switchboard, (513) 221-7800, 7 p.m. to 11 p.m. weekdays
Neighborhoods: Downtown, Liberty Hill, Clifton, Northside
Bars: 11
Organizations: Gay youth, political action; women's/feminist groups; sports leagues
Other publications: *Nouveau, Gayly*
Arts: Chorus, theater
Religion: Dignity, Integrity, MCC, All Saints Chapel (Protestant), Unitarian
Health: Cincinnati Health Dept., North Kentucky Health Dept.
AIDS: AIDS Volunteers, AIDS Treatment Center
Civil rights: City anti-discrimination ordinance protects gays and lesbians in Cincinnati

CLEVELAND

as reported by the Lesbian/Gay Community Service Center
Population: 1.8 million
Information: Lesbian & Gay Hotline, (216) 781-6736, 7 p.m. to 11 p.m. weekdays, 5 p.m. to 8 p.m. Sat., 7 p.m. to 10 p.m. Sun.
Neighborhoods and suburbs: Lakewood, Cleveland Heights
Bars: about 25
Organizations: Community center; gay youth, leather, sports
Publications: *What She Wants, Gay People's Chronicle, Now Cleveland, Valentine News*
Arts: Chorus, band, square dancing
Religion: Dignity, MCC, Chevrei Tikva
AIDS: Health Issues Taskforce,

The Living Room
Civil rights: Employment protection for state employees only. State employees and job applicants are protected from job discrimination.

COLUMBUS

as reported by Stonewall Union
Population: 1.3 million
Information: Stonewall Union, (614) 299-7764, 9 a.m. to 5 p.m. weekdays, 9 a.m. to 1 p.m. Sat.
Neighborhoods: German Village, Victorian Village, Clintonville (women), Olde Towne East
Bars: about 12
Organizations: Gay youth, leather, older people, sports, political action, religious, social, business
Publications: *Gaybeat, News of the Columbus Gay & Lesbian Community, Stonewall Union Reports, Lavender Listings* (annual), *Word Is Out!* (lesbian)
Arts: Theater, Columbus Gay Writers Guild, *Momentum TV* (cable show), *Lesbian/Gay Pride Report* (cable show)
Religion: Integrity, MCC, Spirit of the Rivers Church, Affirmations (Seventh-Day Adventist), Catholic Men's Support Group, Unitarian, Spiritualist Association, Chavarah (Jewish), Lutherans Concerned, Friends for Lesbian & Gay Concerns, United Church, Evangelicals Concerned, Christ United Evangelical Church, neo-pagan group
AIDS: Columbus AIDS Task Force, AIDS Service Connection, Pater Noster
Civil rights: Anti-discrimination law covers housing, accommodations, and employment. State employees and job applicants are protected from job discrimination.

DALLAS/FT. WORTH

as reported by the Dallas Voice
Population: 3.5 million
Information: Gayline, (214) 368-6283, 7:30 p.m. to midnight; Dallas gay and Lesbian Alliance, (214) 528-4233, days; Lesbian Information Line, (214) 528-2426 (voice mail).
Neighborhoods: Oak Lawn
Bars: about 35
Organizations: Community center; Lesbian Resource Center; neighborhood groups; gay youth, leather, older people, sports, political action, women's interests; Among Friends (lesbian educational organization)
Other publications: *This Week in Texas, AIDS Update, Texas Triangle*
Arts: Men's Chorus, Women's Chorus, band, theater, gay Hispanic artists coalition
Religion: Dignity; Integrity; Cathedral of Hope MCC; Affirmation; Evangelicals Concerned; Grace Fellowship; Holy Trinity; Lutherans Concerned; Affirmation; United Church of Christ; Beth El Binah; Evangelicals Concerned; Gay, Lesbian and Affirming Disciples
Health: Nelson-Tebedo Community Clinic
AIDS: AIDS Resource Center/Oak Lawn Counseling Center; AIDS Services of Dallas; AIDS Outreach Center
Civil rights: None

DENVER

as reported by the Gay and Lesbian Community Center
Population: 1.6 million
Information: Gay and Lesbian Community Center, (303) 831-6268, 10 a.m. to 10 p.m. weekdays, 10 a.m. to 7 p.m. Sat., 1 p.m. to 4 p.m. Sun.
Neighborhoods: Capitol Hill, Broadway Terrace
Bars: about 20
Organizations: Community center; gay youth, sports, political action; Forum (monthly lesbian forum)
Publications: *Quest, OutFront, Preferred Stock, Center Lines* (community center newsletter)
Arts: Chorus, band, theater
Religion: Dignity, MCC, United Faith Ministries
AIDS: Colorado AIDS Project, Denver Dept. of Health
Civil rights: Gay civil rights protections, passed by the city of Denver, will be voided if the controversial Amendment 2 is allowed to stand.

DETROIT

as reported by Metro magazine
Population: 4.3 million
Information: Affirmations Lesbian and Gay Community Center, (313) 398-4297, 6 to 11 p.m. weekdays
Neighborhoods: Palmer Park, Ferndale, Livonia
Bars: about 40
Organizations: Gay youth, leather, older people, sports, political action, many others
Other publications: *Cruise*
Arts: Chorus, dance groups
Religion: Dignity, Integrity, MCC, Lutherans Concerned, Simcha (Jewish), Full Truth Fellowship of Christ Church
Health: Henry Ford Hospital
AIDS: Wellness Networks
Civil rights: Gay civil rights laws are in effect.

HOUSTON
as reported by the New Voice
Population: 3.2 million
Information: Gay and Lesbian Switchboard, (713) 529-3211, 3 p.m. to midnight daily
Neighborhoods: Montrose, central Houston
Bars: about 35
Organizations: Neighborhood groups; gay youth, leather, sports, political action
Other publications: *This Week in Texas*
Arts: Band, theater, chamber singers
Religion: Dignity, Integrity, MCC, Houston Mission Church, Kingdom Community Church
Health: Montrose Clinic
AIDS: Counseling Center
Civil rights: None

INDIANAPOLIS
as reported by New Works News
Population: 1.2 million
Information: Gay & Lesbian Switchboard, (317) 639-5937, 7 p.m. to 11 p.m. daily
Neighborhoods: Downtown, North Side.
Bars: about 12
Organizations: Sports, political action
Other publications: *The Mirror, Heartland, Lavender Visions* (lesbian), *IYG Reachout* (gay youth)
Arts: None
Religion: Dignity, Integrity, MCC
Health: Bell Flower STD Clinic
AIDS: AIDS Task Force
Civil rights: Anti-discrimination law in Indianapolis

KANSAS CITY
as reported by Alternate News
Population: 1.5 million
Information: Gay Talk, (816) 931-4470, 6 p.m. to 12 a.m. daily
Neighborhoods: Midtown (31st to 47th Streets), Country Club Plaza
Bars: about 15
Organizations: Leather, older people, sports, political action; Lavender Umbrella (women's group)
Arts: Chorus, band
Religion: Dignity, Integrity, MCC, L'Cha dogi (Jewish), atheist, Buddhist
Health: KC Free Health Clinic
AIDS: Good Samaritan Project
Civil rights: None

LOS ANGELES/LONG BEACH
as reported by the Gay and Lesbian Community Center
Population: 8.3 million
Information: Gay and Lesbian Community Center, (213) 993-7400, 9 a.m. to 10 p.m. Mon. to Sat.
Neighborhoods: West Hollywood, Silver Lake, N. Hollywood (lesbian), Studio City
Bars: about 95
Organizations: Community center; neighborhood groups; gay youth, leather, older people, sports, political action; several women's centers
Publications: *L.A. Dispatch, Frontiers, Edge, The Community Yellow Pages, Lesbian News, Update, Nightline*
Arts: Chorus, band, theater
Religion: Dignity, Integrity, MCC, Beth Chayim Chadashim (first U.S. gay Jewish temple), many others
Health: Edelman Health Center, Connexxus
AIDS: AIDS Project LA, AID for AIDS, AIDS Services Foundation, AmFAR, Shanti Project, Being Alive
Civil rights: Anti-discrimination

laws in Los Angeles, West Hollywood, and Laguna Beach. California has protection against job discrimination.

MIAMI/FT. LAUDERDALE
as reported by the Weekly News
Population: 2.8 million
Information: Gay Community Hotline, (305) 759-3661, 24-hour recording
Neighborhoods: Miami: Coconut Grove, Coral Gables; Ft. Lauderdale: Riverside, Victoria Park
Bars: about 30
Organizations: Gay youth, sports, political action; business association; women's group
Other publications: *David* magazine
Arts: Chorus, band, square dancing
Religion: Dignity, Integrity, MCC, Synagogue Etz-Chaim
Health: TheraFirst (Ft. Lauderdale)
AIDS: Health Crisis Network, PWA Coalition, Center One, Body Positive
Civil rights: None in Miami. Key West and Miami Beach have comprehensive gay civil rights laws.

MILWAUKEE
as reported by Wisconsin Light
Population: 1.3 million
Information: Gay People's Union Hotline, (414) 562-7010, 7 to 10 p.m. daily
Neighborhoods: East Side, Walker's Point, River West
Bars: about 25
Organizations: Gay youth, leather, older people, sports, political action; business association; Women's Coalition
Other publications: *InStep*
Arts: Chorus, theater

Religion: Dignity, Integrity, MCC, Lutherans Concerned
Health: Brady St. East Clinic
AIDS: Milwaukee AIDS Project
Civil rights: Statewide anti-discrimination law

MINNEAPOLIS/ST. PAUL
as reported by Twin Cities Gaze
Population: 2.3 million
Information: Gay and Lesbian Helpline, (612) 822-8661, noon to midnight weekdays, 4 p.m. to midnight Sat.
Neighborhoods: Loring, Kenwood, Powderhorn Park, Grand Ave. area (St. Paul)
Bars: about 8
Organizations: Gay youth, leather, older people, sports, political action; women's center
Other publications: *Equal Time, GLC Voice, Evergreen Chronicles,* GAZE-TV (cable channel)
Arts: Chorus, band, theater, Quatrefoil Library
Religion: Dignity, Integrity, MCC, Beyt G'Vurah (Jewish), Ecumenical Community Church, many others
AIDS: Minnesota AIDS Project
Civil rights: Minnesota has wide-ranging gay civil rights protection. Minneapolis also has anti-discrimination laws.

NEW ORLEANS
as reported by Impact
Population: 1.3 million
Information: Lesbian and Gay Community Center, (504) 522-1103
Neighborhoods: French Quarter, Marigny, Bywater, MidCity/Esplanade Bridge, University Section
Bars: about 40
Organizations: Leather, sports, political action; archives

Other publications: *Ambush, The Guide, The Tattler, New Voice*
Arts: Chorus, theater, *Just for the Record* (cable show)
Religion: Dignity, MCC, Grace Fellowship, Charismatic, Unitarian, atheist
AIDS: PWA Coalition, AIDSLaw, The Lambda Center, New Orleans AIDS Task Force
Civil rights: Limited city anti-discrimination ordinance

NEW YORK CITY
as reported by the Gay Switchboard
Population: 8.5 million
Information: Lesbian Switchboard, (212) 741-2610, 6 p.m. to 10 p.m. weekdays; Gay Switchboard, (212) 777-1800, 10:30 a.m. to midnight daily
Neighborhoods: East Village, Upper West Side, West Village
Bars: about 40 in Manhattan; hundreds in greater metropolitan area
Organizations: Community center; neighborhood groups; gay youth, leather, older people, sports, political action
Other publications: *Sappho's Isle, Conditions, Equal Times, Gay Scene, Parlee Plus, Womanews, Women's Network*
Arts: Chorus, band, theater
Religion: Dignity, Integrity, MCC, Temple Beth Simchat Torah, Lutherans Concerned, Methodists, many others
Health: Gay Men's Health Crisis, Community Health Project
AIDS: Gay Men's Health Crisis, PWA Coalition
Civil rights: As early as 1972, then-mayor John Lindsay issued a "policy directive" stating that "private sexual orientation" could not be considered in city employment procedures. Today, gay people in New York City are covered by an anti-discrimination ordinance.

NORFOLK/VIRGINIA BEACH
as reported by Our Own Community Press
Population: 1.4 million
Information: Gay Information Lines, (804) 622-GAYS and 623-BARS, 24 hours
Neighborhoods: Ghent (Norfolk), Colonial Place
Bars: about 10
Organizations: Gay youth, sports, political action
Other publications: *Out and About in Virginia, Out in Virginia*
Religion: Dignity, MCC, Unitarian Church
AIDS: Tidewater AIDS Crisis Task Force
Civil rights: None

PHILADELPHIA
as reported by the Philadelphia Gay and Lesbian Switchboard
Population: 4.8 million
Information: Gay Switchboard, (215) 546-7100, 6 p.m. to 11 p.m. daily
Neighborhoods: Center City
Bars: about 25
Organizations: Community center; gay youth, leather, older people, sports, political action; Sisterspace
Other publications: *Au Courant, Labyrinth*
Arts: Chorus, theater, poetry group
Religion: Dignity, Integrity, MCC, atheist group
AIDS: Action AIDS, AIDS Task Force, BEBASI
Civil rights: Pennsylvania bans

anti-gay discrimination in public employment, and the Human Rights Ordinance in Philadelphia covers gay rights.

PHOENIX
as reported by Western Express
Population: 1.9 million
Information: Lesbian/Gay Community Switchboard, (602) 234-2752, 10 a.m. to 10 p.m. daily
Neighborhoods: North-central Phoenix
Bars: about 25
Organizations: Gay youth, leather, older people, sports, political action; professional women's group; business association; FLAC (support group for women)
Other publications: *Phoenix Resource, The Transformer, The Echo*
Arts: Band, theater
Religion: Dignity, Integrity, MCC, Lutherans Concerned, Affirmation (Mormons)
Health: Phoenix Clinic
AIDS: Community AIDS Council, Arizona AIDS Project, Shanti Project
Civil rights: None.

PITTSBURGH
as reported by Out magazine
Population: 2.3 million
Information: Gay and Lesbian Community Center, (412) 422-0114, 6:30 p.m. to 9:30 p.m. weekdays, 3 p.m. to 6 p.m. Sat.
Neighborhoods: Shadyside, Mexican War streets area
Bars: about 12
Organizations: Community center; gay youth, leather, older people, sports, political action, professionals, cross-dressers, country/western
Other publications: None

Arts: Chorus, film festival, gay cable network, theatre, radio
Religion: Dignity, MCC, Beth Tikva (Jewish), Integrity, Lutherans Concerned, Presbyterians for Lesbian and Gay Concerns, Affirmation, Unitarian
AIDS: Pitt Men's Study, Pittsburgh AIDS Task Force, Pitt Treatment Evaluation Unit, Shepherd Wellness Community
Civil rights: Pennsylvania bans anti-gay discrimination in public employment, and Pittsburgh has a comprehensive gay civil rights law.

SACRAMENTO
as reported by Mom, Guess What!
Population: 1.3 million
Information: Lambda Community Center, (916) 442-0185, 10 a.m. to 9 p.m. weekdays, 12 p.m. to 4 p.m. Sat.
Neighborhoods: Midtown (Lavender Heights), South Natomas
Bars: about 10
Organizations: Community center; gay youth, leather, sports, political action; business group; women's center; professional groups
Other publications: *Latest Issue*
Arts: Chorus, theater, square dancing
Religion: Dignity, Integrity, MCC, Ahvat Zion, Lutherans Concerned
AIDS: Sacramento AIDS Foundation
Civil rights: City anti-discrimination ordinance. California has protection against job discrimination.

ST. LOUIS
as reported by the Gay News–Telegraph
Population: 2.4 million

Information: Gay and Lesbian Hotline and Action Line, (314) 367-0084, 6 to 10 p.m. daily
Neighborhoods: Central West End, Lafayette Square, Soulard, South Grand Area, Benton Park
Bars: about 20
Organizations: Gay youth, older women, leather, sports, political action
Other publications: *This Week in St. Louis*
Arts: Chorus
Religion: Dignity, MCC, Affirmation (Methodist), others
AIDS: Effort for AIDS
Civil rights: St. Louis has some of the strongest gay civil rights laws in the nation.

SAN DIEGO
as reported by Update
Population: 2.2 million
Information: Lesbian and Gay Men's Community Center Information and Counsel Line, (619) 692-4297, 6 p.m. to 10 p.m. Mon. to Sat.
Neighborhoods: Hillcrest, North Park
Bars: about 30
Organizations: Community center; gay youth, leather, older people, sports, political action; women's center
Other publications: *San Diego Gay Times, San Diego Lesbian Press, Bravo, The Voice*
Arts: Chorus, band, theater
Religion: Dignity, MCC, Yachad (Jewish), others
Health: Ciaccio Clinic
AIDS: AIDS Project, Ciaccio Clinic
Civil rights: Anti-discrimination protection in San Diego. California has protection against job discrimination.

SAN FRANCISCO/OAKLAND
as reported by the San Francisco Sentinel
Population: 3.4 million
Information: Gay and Lesbian Switchboard, (510) 841-6224, 10 a.m. to 10 p.m. weekdays, noon to 4 p.m. Sat., 6 to 9 p.m. Sun.
Neighborhoods: Castro, Polk, Noe Valley, Valencia, Mission District
Bars: about 200
Organizations: Gay youth, leather, older people, sports, political action; women's building
Other publications: *Bay Area Reporter, Bay Times, The Gay Book* (quarterly directory)
Arts: Chorus, band, theater, chamber singers, twirling corps
Religion: Dignity, Integrity, MCC, Congregation Sha'ar Zahav
AIDS: San Francisco AIDS Foundation
Civil rights: In 1972, San Francisco banned discrimination in city hiring, as well as by any firms doing business with the city or county. There is a citywide anti-discrimination ordinance, and California has protection against job discrimination.

SEATTLE
as reported by the Seattle Gay News
Population: 1.7 million
Information: There is no hotline. The *Gay News* (206-324-4297) will make referrals and answer brief questions, as will the Lesbian Resource Center, (206) 322-3953.
Neighborhoods: Capitol Hill, Queen Anne, Wallingford
Bars: about 30
Organizations: Gay youth,

leather, older people, sports, political action; lesbian resource center; business club; antique car club
Other publications: *Stranger, Twist, LRC Community News* (lesbian)
Arts: Chorus, band, theater, film
Religion: Dignity, Integrity, MCC, Congregation Tikvah Chadashah, Affirmation, Pentecostals
Health: Seattle Gay Clinic, Arradia Women's Clinic
AIDS: Northwest AIDS Foundation, Bailey-Boushay House, Seattle Treatment and Education Project
Civil rights: City anti-discrimination ordinance covers employment, housing, and public accommodations

TAMPA/ST. PETERSBURG
as reported by the Weekly News
Population: 1.9 million
Information: Tampa: Gay Hotline, (813) 229-8839, 7 p.m. to 11 p.m. daily; St. Petersburg: The Line, (813) 586-4297, 7 to 11 p.m. most days.
Neighborhoods: Hyde Park (Tampa), Seminole Heights
Bars: about 15
Organizations: Leather, older women, sports, political action; business guild; The Salon

(women's group); women's center
Other publications: *Womyn's Words, Gasp of Tampa Bay, Gazette, Reach Out*
Arts: Chorus
Religion: Dignity, MCC
AIDS: Tampa AIDS Network
Civil rights: None

WASHINGTON, D.C.
as reported by the Washington Blade
Population: 3.5 million
Information: Gay and Lesbian Hotline, (202) 833-3234, 7 p.m. to 11 p.m. daily
Neighborhoods: Dupont Circle, Georgetown, Capitol Hill, Adams Mogan
Bars: about 30
Organizations: Community center; neighborhood groups; gay youth, leather, older people, sports, political action; women's center
Arts: Chorus, band
Religion: Dignity, Integrity, MCC, Bet Mishpachah, many others
Health: Whitman Walker Clinic
AIDS: Whitman Walker Clinic
Civil rights: The District of Columbia Human Rights Ordinance covers gay men and lesbians.

NATIONAL PUBLICATIONS

This listing includes national publications that focus on gay or lesbian concerns, as well as selected other titles that will be of interest to many readers. The address and telephone are for the main editorial office; for subscriptions and advertising, you may be referred elsewhere.

In general, this listing does not include newsletters of national organizations or regional publications. Except as otherwise noted, the information here was recently supplied or confirmed by each publication.

Ad information: This is printed to provide a general sense of the rates for each publication. Anyone planning to advertise should request a complete rate card, showing other sizes, discounts, availability of color, and complete terms.

Circulation: All prices are, of course, subject to change, but most publishers will fill subscriptions and sample-copy orders at the prices shown here through 1994. Subscription rates are usually higher for first-class delivery and for non-U.S. addresses. Circulation figures are what was reported to us by the publisher; where a publisher provided verification of these figures, that is indicated.

THE ADVOCATE, 6922 Hollywood Blvd., 10th floor, Los Angeles, CA 90028; (213) 871-1225; fax (213) 467-0173
Founded 1967. Biweekly magazine for gay men and lesbians, with national and international news, features, health coverage, letters to the editor, arts and entertainment reviews, interviews, and opinion columns. Editor in chief: Jeff Yarbrough
Ads: $2950 for black-and-white full page (7"x10⅛"); business classifieds only, at $6 per line
Circulation: About 60% through subscriptions; 40% through retailers. $3.95 cover price; $39.97 for one-year (26 issues) subscription. Sample copy, $5.20 by mail. 85,000 copies per issue; about 200,000 readership.

AIDS TREATMENT NEWS, P.O. Box 411256, San Francisco, CA 94141; (800) 873-2812
Founded 1986. Biweekly newsletter for health professionals and PWAs with news and reports on experimental and standard treatments. Editor: John S. James
Ads: None
Circulation: 100% through subscription. One-year subscription for institutions, $230; for individuals, $100; for nonprofit groups, $115; for HIV-positive and low-income, $45. 5,000 copies per issue.

ANYTHING THAT MOVES, 2404 California St., #24, San Francisco, CA 94115; (415) 564-2226
Founded 1991. Quarterly magazine published by the Bay Area Bisexual Network, ATM is a multicultural, sex-positive magazine for men and

women, covering anything of interest to bisexuals: features, interviews, health, the arts, groups and resources, fiction, poetry and more. Acting Editor: Gerard Palmeri
Ads: $275 for full page (9.5"x6.75")
Circulation: About 87% through retail sales; 13% through subscriptions. $6 cover price; $25 for one-year subscription. Sample copy, $6 by mail. 4000 copies per issue; 65% of readership is in California.

ASIANS & FRIENDS—NEW YORK, P.O. Box 6628, New York, NY 10163; (212) 674-5064
Founded 1987. Monthly magazine for Asian and Pacific Islander gay men with news, features, letters to the editor, reviews, fiction, poetry, drawings, photos, classifieds, and editorials. Editor: Bradley Frome
Ads: $110 for full page (8"x10"); $3 per line for classifieds at 33 characters per line
Circulation: About 99% through membership in organization; 1% through subscriptions. $25 for one-year subscription in U.S., $30 outside of U.S. Sample copy, $2.75 by mail. 350 copies per issue (verified).

BAD ATTITUDE, P.O. Box 390110, Cambridge, MA 02139; (508) 372-6247
Founded 1984. Bimonthly erotic magazine for lesbians — with an emphasis on S/M and B/D — with news, features, letters to the editor, reviews, fiction, poetry, drawings, and photos. Editor: Jasmine Sterling
Ads: $200 for full page (7⅛"x9¾"); personals, $10.
Circulation: About 50% through subscriptions; 50% through retailers. $6 cover price; $30 for one-year

subscription. Sample copy, $6 by mail. 5,000 copies per issue.

BISEXUALITY, P.O. Box 20917, Long Beach, CA 90801; (310) 597-2799
Founded 1988. Bimonthly newsletter for bisexual men and women with news, features, letters to the editor, reviews, poetry, drawings, and photos. Editor: Gary North
Ads: $200 for full page (8½"x11"); $.85 per word for classifieds
Circulation: 100% through subscriptions; also distributed at special events. $33 for one-year subscription. Sample copy, $5 by mail. 200–5,000 copies per issue.

BLK, P.O. Box 83912, Los Angeles, CA 90083; (213) 410-0808
Founded 1988. Monthly magazine for black gay men and lesbians with news, features, letters to the editor, cartoons, and photos. Editor: Don Thomas
Ads: $380 for full page (7½"x10"); $.40 per word for classifieds
Circulation: About 30% through subscriptions; 70% through retailers. $1.95 cover price. $18 for one-year subscription. Sample copy, $2 by mail. 11,000 copies per issue (verified).

BOOKED FOR BRUNCH?, c/o A Different Light, 489 Castro St., San Francisco, CA 94114; (415) 431-0891
Founded 1979. Newsletter for gay men and lesbians with book reviews, published 2–4 times per year. Editor: Richard Labonté
Ads: None
Circulation: About 20% through retailers; 80% through mail. Free. Sample copy, $1 by mail. 14,000 copies per issue.

BRIDGES, P.O. Box 18437, Seattle, WA 98118; (206) 721-5008

Founded 1989. Biannual journal for Jewish feminists with features, letters to the editor, reviews, fiction, poetry, drawings, and photos. Managing Editor: Clare Kinberg

Ads: $125 for full page (6"x9")

Circulation: About 75% through subscriptions; 25% through retailers. $7.50 cover price; $15 for one-year subscription. Sample copy, $7.50 by mail. 3,000 copies per issue.

CHIRON RISING, P.O. Box 2589, Victorville, CA 92393

Founded 1986. Bimonthly magazine for mature gay and bisexual men with erotica, news, features, letters to the editor, reviews, fiction, poetry, drawings, and photos. Publisher: Patrick H. Colley; editor: Charles Chiarelli

Ads: $600 for full page (7"x10"); $.30 per word for classifieds

Circulation: About 30% through subscriptions; 60% through retailers; 10% through mail-order. $5.95 cover price; $38 for one-year subscription. Sample copy, $3 by mail. 10,000 copies per issue.

CHRISTOPHER STREET, P.O. Box 1475, Church St. Station, New York, NY 10008; (212) 627-2120

Founded 1976. Monthly magazine for gay men and lesbians with features, letters to the editor, reviews, fiction, poetry, drawings, and photos. Editor: Tom Steele

Ads: $1,200 for full page (8¼"x11⅛"); $10–$15 per line for classifieds

Circulation: About 75% through subscriptions; 25% through retailers. $3 cover price; $27 for one-year subscription. Sample copy, $3 by mail. 4,000 copies per issue.

COMMON LIVES/LESBIAN LIVES, P.O. Box 1553, Iowa City, IA 52244

Founded 1981. Quarterly magazine for lesbians with reviews, fiction, poetry, drawings, and photos. Editor: Collective

Ads: $100 for full page (4"x7"); $.20 per word for classifieds

Circulation: About 70% through subscriptions; 30% through retailers. $5 cover price; $15 for one-year subscription. Sample copy, $5 by mail. 1475 copies per issue.

CONNEXIONS DIGEST, P.O. Box 158, Station D, Toronto, ON M6P 3J8 Canada; (416) 537-3949

A quarterly, nonprofit magazine featuring news and analysis of social and environmental issues, reviews, information, resources, and services for nonprofit groups. Materials featured in the digest are based on a grassroots social-change perspective, and relate in some way to Canada.

Ads: $175 for full page (17.5cm x 54.5cm); $.25 per word for classifieds

Circulation: Mostly through subscriptions. $2.50 cover price; $25 for one-year subscription. Sample copy, $2.50 by mail. 1200 copies per issue.

DENEUVE MAGAZINE, 2336 Market St., #15, San Francisco, CA 94114;(415) 863-6538

Founded 1991. Bimonthly magazine for, by, and about lesbians, with news, features, poetry, reviews, and fashion photos. Editor: Frances Stevens

Ads: $720 for full page (7.5"x10"); National Resource Guide, $10 per issue; free classifieds up to 30 words

Circulation: Mostly through subscription. $22 for one-year subscription.

DUNGEONMASTER, P.O. Box 410390, San Francisco, CA 94141; (415) 252-1195
Founded 1980. Bimonthly magazine for gay men into S/M with how-to articles. Editor: Anthony Deblase
Ads: Call for rate card.
Circulation: About 22% through subscriptions; 73% through retailers; 5% through mail-order. $4.95 cover price; $24 for one-year subscription. Sample copy, $6.50 by mail. 5,500 copies per issue.

DYKES, DISABILITIES & STUFF, P.O. Box 6194, Boston, MA 02114. Quarterly journal for disabled lesbians and feminists with news, features, letters to the editor, reviews, fiction, poetry, and drawings. Editor: Catherine Odette
Ads: $200 for full page (8"x10½"); contact for classified rates.
Circulation: About 95% through subscriptions; 5% through retailers. $3 cover price; $8–$20 for one-year subscription. Sample copy, free with self-addressed, stamped envelope by mail. 630 copies per issue.

FAG RAG, P.O. Box 331, Kenmore Station, Boston, MA 02215; (617) 661-7534
Founded 1970. Annual magazine for gay men with features, letters to the editor, fiction, poetry, drawings, and photos.
Ads: None
Circulation: About 25% through subscriptions; 75% through retailers. $4 cover price. Sample copy, $4 by mail. 5,000 copies per issue.

FEMINIST BOOKSTORE NEWS, P.O. Box 882554, San Francisco, CA 94188; (415) 626-1556. Fax (415) 626-8970
Founded 1976. Bimonthly magazine for feminist and lesbian feminist booksellers and publishers with news, features, letters to the editor, reviews, and drawings. Editor: Carol Seajay
Ads: $695 for full page (6⁵⁄₁₆"x7³⁄₈"); $2 per 25 characters for classifieds
Circulation: 100% through subscriptions. $65 for one-year subscription. Sample copy, $6 by mail. 800 copies per issue.

FRONTIERS: A JOURNAL OF WOMEN STUDIES, Mesa Vista Hall 2142, University of New Mexico, Albuquerque, NM 87131-1586; (505) 277-1198. Fax (505) 277-0267.
Founded 1975. Feminist, academic journal published three times a year. Editor: Jane Slaughter
Ads: Academic presses and exchange journal ads only
Circulation: 95% through subscriptions; 5% through retail. $8 cover price; $20 for one-year subscription. Sample copy, $8 by mail. 1,000 copies per issue.

GAY COMMUNITY NEWS, 62 Berkeley St., Boston, MA 02116; (617) 426-4469
Founded 1973. Weekly newspaper for gay men and lesbians with news, features, letters to the editor, reviews, and photos. Features editor: Chris Wittke
Ads: Contact for rates.
Circulation: About 50% through subscriptions; 35% through retailers; 15% through other means. $1.25 cover price; $39 for one-year subscription. Sample copy, $1 by mail.

GENRE MAGAZINE, 8033 Sunset Blvd., #261, Los Angeles, CA 90046; (800) 576-9933
A glossy, national bimonthly magazine with features on fashion, travel, arts and entertainment, fiction, and celebrity interviews. Editor: Richard Settles
Ads: $4158 for full-page, black-and-white ad (7"x9.5"); classifieds are $220 per inch or $5 per word
Circulation: 50% through subscription; 50% through newsstands. $3.95 cover price; $15 for one year subscription. Sample copy, $5 by mail. 100,00 per issue.

GOLDEN THREADS, P.O. Box 60475, Northampton, MA 01060-0475.
Founded 1985. Worldwide contact quarterly for lesbians over 50, but younger women are not excluded. Each issue include resources, reviews, editorial, and poetry. Editor: Christine Burton.
Ads: $10 for business-card-sized ads
Circulation: 100% through subscriptions. Sample copy discreetly mailed for $5. 300 copies per issue.

HAG RAG, P.O. Box 93243, Milwaukee, WI 53203; (414) 372-3330
Founded 1986. Bimonthly magazine for radical lesbian feminists with news, features, letters to the editor, reviews, fiction, drawings, and photos. Editors: Mary Frank and Lance Link
Ads: $100 for full page (7¼"x10"); $.50 per line for classifieds
Circulation: About 25% through subscriptions; 75% through retailers. $2 cover price; $10 for one-year subscription. Sample copy, $2 by mail. 1,000 copies per issue.

HERESIES: A FEMINIST PUBLICATION ON ART AND POLITICS, P.O. Box 1306, Canal Street Station, New York, NY 10013; (212) 227-2108
Founded 1977. Biannual political and cultural journal for feminists, lesbian feminists, and artists with fiction, poetry, drawings, photos, essays, page art, and experimental writing. Editor: Heresies Collective
Ads: $250 for half page (7½"x5" or 3-5/8"x10")
Circulation: About 33% through subscriptions; 33% through retailers; 33% through sale of back issues. $8 cover price; $27 for four-issue subscription. Sample copy, $8 by mail. 3,500 copies per issue.

HIKANE: THE CAPABLE WOMON, P.O. Box 841, Great Barrington, MA 01230
Founded 1989. Quarterly magazine for disabled lesbian feminists and their wimmin friends with news, features, letters to the editor, reviews, fiction, poetry, and drawings. Also available on cassette and in braille. Editor: Jodi
Ads: Contact for rates.
Circulation: About 90% through subscriptions; 2% through retailers; 8% through community events. $4 cover price; $14 (sliding scale) for one-year subscription. Sample copy, $4 by mail. 275 copies per issue.

HOT WIRE: THE JOURNAL OF WOMEN'S MUSIC & CULTURE, 5210 N. Wayne, Chicago, IL 60640; (312) 769-9009
Founded 1984. Magazine, published three times a year, for lesbians and feminists with news, features, letters to the editor, drawings, and photos

pertaining to women's music, theater, writing, film, and video. Editor: Toni Armstrong, Jr.

Ads: $250 for full page (7½"x9⅜"); $20 one-time classified rate

Circulation: About 30% through subscriptions; 65% through retailers; 5% through other means. $6 cover price; $17 for one-year subscription; $19 in Canada. Sample copy, $7 by mail. 15,000 copies per issue.

IN TOUCH FOR MEN, 13122 Saticoy St., North Hollywood, CA 91605; (818) 764-2288.
Founded 1973. Monthly erotic magazine for gay men with news, features, letters to the editor, reviews, fiction, poetry, drawings, and photos. Assistant Publisher: Glen Bassett

Ads: $1,300 for color full page (7"x10")

Circulation: About 40% through subscriptions; 60% through retailers. $5.95 cover price; $49.50 for one-year subscription. Sample copy, $5.95 by mail. 26,00 copies per issue; estimated 70,000 readership.

JAMES WHITE REVIEW, P.O. Box 3356, Butler Quarter Sta., Minneapolis, MN 55403; (612) 291-2913
Founded 1983. Quarterly literary journal for gay men with reviews, fiction, poetry, drawings, and photos. Editors: Phil Willkie and Greg Baysans

Ads: $400 for full page (11"x16")

Circulation: About 50% through subscriptions; 50% through retailers. $3 cover price; $12 for one-year subscription. Sample copy, $3 by mail. 2,500 copies per issue.

JOURNAL OF HOMOSEXUALITY, The Haworth Press, Inc., 10 Alice St., Binghamton, NY 13904; (607) 722-8169
Founded 1974. Quarterly academic journal for gay and lesbian professionals and scholars with news and reviews. Editor: John P. DeCecco, PhD.

Ads: $300 for full page (4⅜"x7⅛") for profit organizations; $150 for nonprofit organizations.

Circulation: About 97% through subscriptions; 3% through retailers. One-year subscription for individuals, $40; for institutions, $95; for libraries, $160. Sample copy, $4 by mail. 1,200 copies per issue.

JOURNAL OF HOMOSEXUALITY, C.R.E.S., San Francisco State University, San Francisco, CA 94132; (415) 338-1137
Founded 1974. Quarterly academic journal for gay men and lesbians with features, reviews, and articles. Editor: John P. DeCecco

Ads: $100 for full page (6"x 7")

Circulation: About 90% through subscriptions; 10% through retailers. $35 for one-year subscription. Sample copy, free from publisher by mail.

JOURNAL OF GAY AND LESBIAN PSYCHOTHERAPY, Editorial office: 1439 Pineville Rd., New Hope, PA 18938; circulation office: Haworth Press, 10 Alice St., Binghamton, NY 13904
Founded 1988. Academic journal for psychotherapists and other mental health professionals involved in treating gay and lesbian patients and clients. Each volume consists of four issues, published irregularly. Editor: David Scasta, M.D.

Ads: Contact Haworth Press for details.

Circulation: 100% through subscriptions. $15 for one-year subscription. Sample copy, free by mail. 410 copies per issue.

LAMBDA BOOK REPORT, 1625 Connecticut Ave. NW, Washington, DC 20009; (202) 462-7924
Founded 1987. Bimonthly magazine for gay men and lesbians with news, features, letters to the editor, reviews, and fiction relating to gay and lesbian literature and publishing. Editor: Jim Marks
Ads: $800 for full page (7¼"x9⅞"); $1.50 per word for classifieds
Circulation: About 45% through subscriptions; 45% through retailers; 10% through sale of back issues. $3.95 cover price; $19.95 for one-year subscription. Sample copy, $3.95 by mail. 11,000 copies per issue.

LAW AND SEXUALITY: A Review of Lesbian and Gay Legal Issues, Tulane Law School, 6801 Freret St., New Orleans, LA 70118; (504) 865-5835
Founded 1990. A yearly journal devoted exclusively to legal issues concerning the lesbian and gay community, and featuring articles, essays, research pieces, casenotes, and legal comments. The journal's main audience is the legal community, but it's accessible to interested lay readers.
Ads: None
Circulation: Almost 100% through subscriptions. $12 for one-year subscription; $8 for students. About 1,200 copies per issue.

LESBIAN/GAY LAW NOTES, c/o Lesbian and Gay Law Association of Greater New York (LeGaL),799 Broadway, Room 340, New York, NY 10003; (212) 353-9118
Founded 1984. Published eleven times a year. Newsletter for gay men and lesbians with current news on court cases, court decisions, and new developments in the law as they pertain to lesbians, gay men, and AIDS. Contains a bibliography of law periodicals of interest to the gay community and PWAs. Editor: Arthur S. Leonard
Ads: None
Circulation: About 60% through membership in various law groups; 10% through libraries; 30% through subscriptions. $20 for one-year subscription. Sample copy, free with stamped, self-addressed, business-size envelope. About 1,000 copies per issue.

LESBIAN CONNECTION, Elsie Publishing Inst., P.O. Box 811, E. Lansing, MI 48826; (517) 371-5257.
Founded 1974. Nationwide forum of news and ideas for, by, and about lesbians.
Ads: Write for rates.
Circulation: 90% through subscriptions; 10% distributed free of charge. $18 suggested donation for one-year subscription (more if you can, less if you can't). Sample copy, free by mail. 20,000 copies per issue.

LILITH, 250 W. 57th Street, #2432, New York, NY 10107; (212) 757-0818
Founded 1976. Quarterly magazine for Jewish feminists with news, features, letters to the editor, reviews, fiction, poetry, drawings, and photos. Editor: Susan Weidman Schneider
Ads: $700 for full page; $.75 per word for classifieds

Circulation: About 75% through subscriptions; 20% through retailers; 5% through special sales. $3.50 cover price; $14 for one-year subscription. Sample copy, $4.50 by mail. 10,000 copies per issue.

MAIZE: A Lesbian Country Magazine, P.O. Box 130, Serafina, NM 87569
Founded 1983. Quarterly magazine for lesbians with features, reviews, and drawings relating to country living and politics. Editor: Lee Lanning.
Ads: Contact for details.
Circulation: About 70% through subscriptions; 30% through retailers. $3.50 cover price; $10 for one-year subscription. Sample copy, $3.50 by mail.

NEW YORK NATIVE, P.O. Box 1475, Church Street Station, New York, NY 10008; (212) 627-2120
Founded 1981. Weekly newspaper for gay men and lesbians with local and national news, features, letters to the editor, reviews, fiction, and photos. Editor: Mark Stromberg.
Ads: $950 for full page (11"x17"); $21 minimum for classifieds
Circulation: About 35% through subscriptions; 65% through retailers. $2 cover price; $39 for one-year subscription. Sample copy, $2 by mail. 11,000 copies per issue.

NEWSLETTER OF THE ASSOCIATION OF GAY AND LESBIAN PSYCHIATRISTS, 1439 Pineville Rd., New Hope, PA 19838
Founded 1978. A quarterly academic newsletter for psychiatrists who are gay or lesbian and/or are involved in treatment of gay and lesbian patients. Editor: David Scasta, M.D.
Ads: $200 for full page (8.5"x11").
Circulation: 100% through subscriptions. $15 for one-year subscription. 600 copies per issue.

OFF OUR BACKS, 2423 18th St., NW, 2nd floor, Washington, DC 20009; (202) 234-8072
Founded 1970. Monthly newspaper for feminists and lesbian feminists with news, features, letters to the editor, reviews, drawings, and photos. Editor: off our backs collective.
Ads: $400 for full page (13"x17½"); $.40 for classifieds
Circulation: About 66% through subscriptions; 33% through retailers. $2 cover price; One-year subscription for individuals, $19; for institutions, $30. Sample copy, $3 by mail. 7,000 copies per issue (verified).

ON OUR BACKS, 526 Castro St., San Francisco, CA 94114; (800) 845-4617
Founded 1984. Bimonthly erotic magazine for lesbians offers news, features, letters to the editors, reviews, fiction, poetry, and photos. Editor: Heather Findlay
Ads: $1400 for full page (8½"x11")
Circulation: About 30% through subscriptions; 70% through retailers. $5.95 cover price; $34.95 for one-year subscription. Sample copy, $7 by mail. 12,000 copies per issue; 35,000 readership.

OPTIONS, P.O. Box 470, Port Chester, NY 10573; (914) 939-2111
Founded 1982. Magazine focusing on the gay and lesbian side of bisexuality. Features news and reviews, health updates, advice, and sexually stimulating reading. Published 10 times per year. Editor: Don Stone
Ads: $450 for full page, black-and-white ad (5-3/8"x8-1/4")
Circulation: 97% retail sales; 3% subscriptions. $35 for one-year subscription. Sample copy, $5 by mail. 30,000 copies per issue.

OTHER COUNTRIES, P.O. Box 3142, Church Street Station, New York, NY 10008; (212) 864-4905.
Founded 1986. Annual journal for black gay men with features, reviews, fiction, poetry, drawings, and photos.
Ads: None
Circulation: About 30% through subscriptions; 30% through retailers; 40% through other means. $10.95 cover price. Sample copy, $12 by mail. 3,000 copies per issue.

OUR WORLD, 1104 N. Nova Rd., #251, Daytona Beach, FL 32117; (904) 441-5367
Founded 1989. Monthly, glossy travel magazine for gay men and lesbians, with worldwide listings of tours, trips, cruises, inns, resorts, features, departments and photos. Editor: Wayne Whiston
Ads: $585 for full page (7"x9.75")
Circulation: About 50% by subscription; 50% by retail sales. $4.95 cover price; $44 for 12 issues. Sample copy, $4.95 by mail. 20,000 copies per issue.

OUT, 110 Greene St., Suite 800, New York, NY 10012; (212) 334-9119
Founded 1992. Glossy bimonthly magazine for gay men and lesbians featuring news, culture, politics, travel, fashion and health. Editors: Michael Goff and Sarah Pettit
Ads: Call for a rate card; display ads and classifieds offered.
Circulation: About 50% through subscriptions; 50% through retailers. Cover price $4.95; 24.95 for one-year subscription. 100,000+ per issue.

PAZ Y LIBERACION, P.O. Box 66450, Houston, TX 77266.

Founded 1978. Quarterly newsletter about gay and lesbian news and events in Latin America, Asia, Africa, and Arab lands. Spanish and Asian editions published semi-annually; Arab/African edition published annually. Editor: John Hubert
Ads: Free worldwide classifieds included.
Circulation: $10 for four issues.

RFD, P.O. Box 68, Liberty, TN 37095; (615) 536-5176
Founded 1974. Quarterly magazine for gay men with news, features, letters to the editor, reviews, fiction, poetry, drawings, and photos. Editor: Short Mountain Collective
Ads: Call for information.
Circulation: About 55% through subscriptions; 45% through retailers. $5.50 cover price; $18 for one-year subscription sent second class, $25 sent first class. Sample copy, $5 by mail. 3,300 copies per issue.

SINISTER WISDOM, P.O. Box 3252, Berkeley, CA 94703
Founded 1976. Tri-annual political journal for radical lesbian feminists with letters to the editor, reviews, fiction, poetry, drawings, and photos. Editor: Elana Dykewomon
Ads: $200 for full page (4½"x7"); $.40 for classifieds
Circulation: About 39% through subscriptions; 60% through retailers; 1% through other means. $5 cover price; $17 for one-year subscription (four issues). Sample copy, $6 by mail. 3,000 copies per issue.

SOJOURNER: THE WOMEN'S FORUM, 42 Seaverns Ave., Jamaica Plain, MA 02130; (617) 524-0415
Founded 1975. Monthly newspaper of politics and culture for feminists with news, features, letters to the editor, reviews, fiction, poetry, drawings, and photos. Editor: Karen Kahn
Ads: Contact for rates.
Circulation: About 60% through subscriptions; 30% through retailers; 10% free/promotional. $2.50 cover price; $19 for one-year subscription. Sample copy, $2 by mail. 12,000 copies per issue.

TRADESWOMEN, P.O. Box 40664, San Francisco, CA 94140; (415) 821-7334
Founded 1981. Quarterly magazine for women in nontraditional blue-collar work with news, features, letters to the editor, reviews, fiction, poetry, drawings, and photos. Editor: Janet Scoll Johnson
Ads: $1,000 for full page (7½"x 10"); $.50 per word for classifieds
Circulation: About 95% through subscriptions; 5% through retailers. $3.50 cover price; $35 for one-year subscription for individuals (includes membership in Tradeswomen, Inc. and monthly newsletter); $50 for one-year subscription for institutions. Sample copy, $4 by mail. 1,500 copies per issue.

TRIBE, Columbia Publishing Co., 234 E. 25th St., Baltimore, MD 21218; (410) 366-7070
Founded 1989. Quarterly literary journal for gay men with essays, fiction and poetry. Editor: Bernard Rabb
Ads: None
Circulation: About 20% through subscriptions; 80% through retailers. $8 cover price; $28 for one-year subscription. Sample copy, $8 by mail. 3,000 copies per issue.

TRIVIA, P.O. Box 606, Amherst, MA 01059; (413) 367-2254
Founded 1982. Magazine for lesbian feminists with news and reviews published 2-3 times a year. Editor: Lise Weil.
Ads: $130 for full page (4½"x6"); $.25 per word for classifieds
Circulation: About 50% through subscriptions; 50% through retailers. $5 cover price; $14 for one-year subscription. Sample copy, $6 by mail. 1,500 copies per issue.

WASHINGTON BLADE, 724 9th St. NW, 8th floor, Washington, DC 20001; (202) 347-2038
Founded 1969. Weekly newspaper for gay men and lesbians with local and national news, features, letters to the editor, reviews, and photos. Editor: Lisa M. Keen
Ads: $695 for full page (9¾"x13¼"); $.40 per word for classifieds
Circulation: About 9% through subscriptions; 1% through retailers; 90% free. Free in Washington, D.C., area, $.75 elsewhere; $25 for one-year subscription. Sample copy, $1 by mail. 27,600 copies per issue (verified).

WOMEN'S REVIEW OF BOOKS, Wellesley College, Wellesley, MA 02181; (617) 283-2087
Founded 1983. Monthly literary newspaper for lesbians and feminists with letters to the editor, reviews, and poetry. Editor: Linda Gardiner
Ads: $1445 for full page (10"x15"); $..80 per word for classifieds
Circulation: About 80% through subscriptions; 20% through retailers. $2 cover price; $18 for one-year subscription. 14,500 copies per issue.

YELLOW SILK, Box 6374, Albany, CA 94706; (415) 644-4188
Founded 1981. Quarterly erotic magazine for all sexual persuasions with a focus on fine arts with reviews, fiction, poetry, artwork, and photos. Editor: Lily Pond
Ads: Contact for rates.
Circulation: About 50% through subscriptions; 50% through retailers. $7.50 cover price; $30 for one-year subscription. Sample copy, $7.50 by mail. 15,000 copies per issue.

ORGANIZATIONS AND HOTLINES

The organizations listed here operate on a national level. Some provide services directly to individuals; others to local groups.

When requesting information from any of these organizations, we suggest you enclose a stamped, self-addressed, business-size envelope.

Listings are arranged alphabetically within the following categories:

AIDS- and Health-Related   Legal and Political
Business and Professional   Religious
Educational   Special-Interest

AIDS-RELATED

AIDS ACTION COUNCIL, 1875 Connecticut Ave., NW, Suite 700, Washington, DC 20009; (202) 986-1300
Founded: 1985
Purpose: To work with the federal government to create a sound national AIDS policy, and lobby for funding of AIDS care, research, prevention, and treatment.

AIDS COALITION TO UNLEASH POWER, 135 West 29th St., 10th Floor, New York, NY 10001; (212) 564-2437; fax (212) 594-5441
Founded: 1987
Purpose: A diverse, nonpartisan group united in anger and committed to direct action to end the AIDS crisis. Largely autonomous local chapters have been formed in many cities.

AMERICAN FOUNDATION FOR AIDS RESEARCH (AmFAR), 1515 Broadway, Suite 3601, New York, NY 10036; (212) 719-0033; or 5900 Wilshire Blvd., 2nd Floor, East Satellite, Los Angeles, CA 90036; (213) 857-5900
Founded: 1985
Purpose: To provide funding for research into the cure, prevention, and treatment of AIDS, and to produce educational materials for the general public, medical and scientific professionals, and people with AIDS.

AMERICAN RUN FOR THE END OF AIDS, 2350 Broadway, New York, NY 10024; (212) 580-7668
Founded: 1985
Purpose: To provide public education about AIDS and fund raising for AIDS service groups.

NATIONAL ASSOCIATION OF PEOPLE WITH AIDS, 1413 K St,. NW, #10, Washington, DC 20005; (202) 898-0414; fax (202) 898-0435
Founded: 1987
Purpose: To provide information and referrals to member organizations and to advocate for rights for people with AIDS.

NATIONAL COALITION OF FEMINIST AND LESBIAN CANCER PROJECTS, P.O. Box 90437, Washington, DC 20090; (202) 332-5536
Purpose: To provide support to community-based women's health organizations, and information about starting such a group.

NATIONAL LEADERSHIP COALITION ON AIDS, 1730 M St., NW, #905, Washington, DC 20036; (202) 429-0930; fax (202) 872-1977
Founded: 1987
Purpose: To increase public and private sector cooperation on AIDS issues. Works especially to improve the response of employers and employees to AIDS and to encourage balanced and informed consideration of public policies affected by the disease.

PROJECT INFORM, 1965 Market St., Suite 220, San Francisco, CA 94103. Hotline: (800) 822-7422; in California: (800) 334-7422; in San Francisco: (415) 558-9051
Founded: 1985
Purpose: To serve as a clearinghouse for information about alternative treatments for AIDS. Through its hotline, Project Inform provides advice about which treatments for AIDS currently seem most promising. It is also active politically in trying to speed up drug testing, and providing more options for people facing the life-threatening disease.

BUSINESS/PROFESSIONAL

AMERICAN ASSOCIATION OF PHYSICIANS FOR HUMAN RIGHTS, 273 Church St., San Francisco, CA 94114; (415) 255-4547

Founded: 1980
Purpose: To provide an organization in which lesbian and gay physicians and medical students can find a source of professional and personal support and affiliation.

GAY AND LESBIAN PRESS ASSOCIATION, P.O. Box 8185, Universal City, CA 91608; (818) 902-1476
Founded: 1981
Purpose: To insure and promote ethical journalistic standards among its members; to increase understanding and communiation with the gay and lesbian community and with the community at large; to promote a healthy business environment; to foster the growth and development of the gay press; and to protect and defend the rights and integrity of the gay press. Sponsors annual Media Awards.

GAY AND LESBIAN ROUNDTABLE of the SOCIAL RESPONSIBILITIES TASK FORCE of the AMERICAN LIBRARY ASSOCIATION, 50 East Huron, Chicago, IL 60611
Founded: 1970
Purpose: To put more and better gay materials into libraries and to oppose discrimination against gay librarians and library users. Quarterly newsletter is available; write to ALA for information.

HIGH TECH GAYS, P.O. Box 6777, San Jose, CA 95150; (408) 993-3830
Founded: 1982
Purpose: To increase awareness of the presence of gays in the high-tech industry, and to provide support to members. Publishes a newsletter focusing on San Jose area.

LESBIAN, GAY, AND BISEXUAL PEOPLE IN MEDICINE, 1890 Preston White Dr., Reston, VA 22091; (703) 620-6600
Founded: 1976
Purpose: To give support to lesbian and gay medical students.

NATIONAL ASSOCIATION OF LESBIAN AND GAY ALCOHOLISM PROFESSIONALS, (213) 381-8524
Founded: 1979
Purpose: To create and sustain a support network for alcoholism professionals, and to advocate a non-homophobic treatment of chemically dependent lesbians and gay men.

NATIONAL ORGANIZATION OF GAY AND LESBIAN SCIENTISTS AND TECHNICAL PROFESSIONALS, P.O. Box 91803, Pasadena, CA 91109
Purpose: NOGLSTP seeks to promote communication among people employed in scientific and high-tech fields, and to work within these professions to oppose anti-gay discrimination and stereotyping. Among the issues it has tackled are anti-gay security clearance policies, mandatory HIV antibody testing, and computer threats to privacy. Several pamphlets on these and other topics are available from either office listed above.

EDUCATIONAL

CAMPAIGN TO END HOMOPHOBIA, P.O. Box 819, Cambridge, MA 02139; (617) 868-8380.
Founded: 1986
Purpose: To build and support a network of people working together to end homophobia and heterosexism through education. This work is done through conferences, educational resources and materials, publications, networking, and consultation on educational strategies.

FEDERATION OF PARENTS & FRIENDS OF LESBIANS AND GAYS, INC., 1012 14th St., NW, #700, Washington, DC 20005; (202) 638-0243
Founded: 1981
Purpose: To help parents and friends of gay men and women understand homosexuality through education and support. To provide education for individuals and the community at large on the nature of homosexuality; to fight for the civil rights of gay people.

NATIONAL FEDERATION OF PARENTS AND FRIENDS OF GAYS, 8020 Eastern Ave., NW, Washington, DC 20012; (202) 726-3223
Founded: 1980
Purpose: To provide educational materials to anyone searching for an improved understanding of issues surrounding human sexuality. NF/PFOG groups have mailed educational material to thousands of churches and high school counselors and administrators, urging them to address the concerns of the gay people they serve.

NATIONAL GAY YOUTH NETWORK, P.O. Box 846, San Francisco, CA 94101-0846
Founded: 1979
Purpose: To serve as a networking resource for the exchange of infor-

mation among its member groups. The Network conducts research, creates educational programs, offers technical assistance, and makes information available to and about member groups.

NATIONAL LESBIAN/GAY HEALTH FOUNDATION, P.O. Box 65472, Washington, DC 20035; (202) 797-3708
Founded: 1978
Purpose: To provide comprehensive information and service delivery models to the lesbian and gay community and to the American health care system.

LEGAL AND POLITICAL

ACLU LESBIAN AND GAY RIGHTS PROJECT, 132 W. 43rd St., New York, NY, 10036; (212) 944-9800, ext. 545
Founded: 1986
Purpose: To defend the civil rights of lesbians and gay men. Since its inception, the Project has furthered the ACLU's long-standing commitment to lesbian and gay equality by organizing the nation's most extensive program of advocacy for civil rights for lesbians and gay men. The project undertakes precedent-setting litigation, policy advocacy, and public education.

FAIRNESS FUND. The Fairness Fund was absorbed by the Human Rights Campaign Fund in March 1988.

GAY AND LESBIAN ADVOCATES AND DEFENDERS, P.O. Box 218, Boston, MA 02112; (617) 426-1350
Founded: 1978

Purpose: To provide litigation, advocacy, and education in support of gay and lesbian civil rights, and the rights of persons with HIV/AIDS.

GAY AND LESBIAN ALLIANCE AGAINST DEFAMATION, 150 West 26th St., New York, NY 10001; (212) 807-1700
Founded: 1985
Purpose: To discourage stereotypes and misinformation about lesbians and gay men, through organizing grass-roots responses to public bigotry and by working with the media to improve coverage of issues that concern gay people.

GAY AND LESBIAN VICTORY FUND, 1012 14th St. NW, Suite 707, Washington, DC 20005; (202) VICTORY; fax (202) 289-FUND.
Founded: 1991
Purpose: The Victory Fund is a political network that empowers our community by supporting openly gay and lesbian candidates for public office. The Fund recommends candidates to its members, who are then free to choose which candidates they would like to financially support.

GAY RIGHTS NATIONAL LOBBY. GRNL encountered financial difficulties in the mid-1980s, and was absorbed into the Human Rights Campaign Fund in December 1985.

HUMAN RIGHTS CAMPAIGN FUND, 1012 14th St., NW, 6th floor, Washington, DC 20005; (202) 628-4160
Founded: 1980
Purpose: To educate and elect congressional candidates who support

The National Gay and Lesbian Task Force, shown here at a Pride Day march in Washington, came back from several financial and morale problems in the early 1980s to take a central role in the gay movement.

lesbian and gay civil rights and full funding for AIDS research and treatment. In 1989 it became the fourth largest independent political action committee (PAC) in the country; unlike many PACs, however, HRCF spends much of its income on lobbying, media work, and persuading individual voters to make themselves heard. Only 18% of the group's funds actually are contributed to candidates.

LAMBDA LEGAL DEFENSE AND EDUCATION FUND, 666 Broadway, New York, NY 10012; (212) 995-8585
History: LLDEF was founded in 1973 in New York. It opened a Los Angeles office in 1990, and one in Chicago in 1993.
Purpose: To pursue test-case litigation that will protect the rights of lesbians and gay men, and to educate government, the legal profes-

sion, and the public about anti-gay discrimination. In recent years, Lambda has also focused heavily on AIDS issues.

LESBIAN MOTHERS NATIONAL DEFENSE FUND, P.O. Box 21567, Seattle, WA 98111; (206) 325-2643
Founded: 1974
Purpose: To secure fair and equitable judgments in child custody and visitation disputes based on the best interests of the children and to completely eliminate the consideration of sexual preference in court decisions regarding custody and visitation. The network offers information, attorney referrals, and emotional support for lesbians in matters including custody and visitation cases, donor insemination, adoption, and parenting issues.

NATIONAL CENTER FOR LESBIAN RIGHTS, 1663 Mission St., 5th floor, San Francisco, CA 94103; (415) 621-0674

Founded: 1977, as the Lesbian Rights Project; in 1989, the project went national and changed its name.

Purpose: To achieve full civil and human rights for all lesbians through a national program of litigation, judicial education, public policy advocacy, resource publications, and community forums.

NATIONAL GAY AND LESBIAN TASK FORCE, 1734 14th St., NW, Washington, DC 20009; (202) 332-6483

History: Dr. Howard J. Brown, a prominent health official who had only recently come out, announced the founding of the National Gay Task Force on Oct. 15, 1973. Dr. Bruce Voeller was named the first executive director of the group. The NGTF (the word *Lesbian* was added to the name later) quickly became the country's leading gay-rights advocacy group.

Purpose: NGLTF is a national organization that lobbies, organizes, educates, and advocates for gay and lesbian civil rights and for responsible AIDS policy. As of 1990, the NGLTF has two full-time lobbyists in Washington, one of whom works on health issues. It has special projects focusing on anti-gay violence and sodomy law repeal; and in coalition with other groups is part of the Military Freedom Project.

NATIONAL ORGANIZATION FOR WOMEN, 1000 16th St. NW, Suite 700, Washington, DC 20036; (202) 331-0066; TTY (202) 331-9002

Founded: 1966 by Betty Friedan

Purpose: Now the largest women's rights organization in the country, NOW's purpose is to take action to bring women into full participation in the mainstream of American society, in truly equal partnership with men. This mission involves a wide variety of issues, such as lesbian and gay rights, ERA, violence against women, and racism.

ONE, Inc.

History: Founded in 1952, taking its name from the quote "A mystic bond of brotherhood makes all men one." Dorr Legg, one of the seven cofounders, is still a guiding force behind ONE.

Purpose: Originally founded to provide support to the homophile community, while educating the outside world, One has served many functions in the four decades since then.

PARTNERS TASK FORCE, P.O. Box 9685, Seattle, WA 98109; (206) 784-1519

Founded: 1986.

Purpose: To create publications and videos that provide information, support and advocacy for the diverse community of same-sex couples and those who serve them. Partners Task Force asserts that gay and lesbian couples are families who need and deserve the same rights and privileges accorded heterosexual married couples.

RELIGIOUS

AFFIRMATION: United Methodists for Lesbian, Gay and Bisexual Concerns, P.O. Box 1021, Evanston, IL 60204; (708) 475-0499

Founded: 1976
Purpose: To eliminate homophobia, racism, classism, and sexism from the United Methodist Church and from society in general, and to be a support group for lesbians, gay men, bisexual persons, and their friends.

AFFIRMATION: Gay and Lesbian Mormons, P.O. Box 46022, Los Angeles, CA 90046; (213) 255-7251
Founded: 1977
Purpose: To provide a social and support group for gay and lesbian Latter-Day Saints.

AMERICAN BAPTISTS CONCERNED, 870 Erie St., Oakland, CA 94610
Founded: 1972
Purpose: To provide education and support for gay and lesbian members of the American Baptist Church, as well as to their friends and families.

AMERICAN GAY AND LESBIAN ATHEISTS, P.O. Box 66711, Houston, TX 77266; (713) 862-3283
Founded: 1983
Purpose: To support and maintain the separation of Church and State; to stand as a guardian of the First Amendment promise of free thought for all people; and to attain equality for gay men and lesbians.

BRETHREN/MENNONITE COUNCIL FOR LESBIAN AND GAY CONCERNS (BMC), P.O. Box 65724, Washington, DC 20035; (202) 462-2595
Founded: 1976
Purpose: To provide support for Brethren and Mennonite gay men

and lesbians, their families, and friends, and to provide accurate information about homosexuality to the churches.

CONFERENCE FOR CATHOLIC LESBIANS, P.O. Box 436, Planetarium Station, New York, NY 10024; (813) 822-5030
Founded: 1982
Purpose: Originally an offshoot of (what they felt was) the predominantly male-oriented Dignity/USA, the Conference was created to foster community among Catholic lesbians, and to help them find a spirituality that speaks of who they are and their lived experiences. There are a number of these groups across the country (and one in Canada). They sponsor biannual conferences.

DIGNITY/USA, 1500 Massachusetts Ave., NW, #11, Washington, DC 20005; (202) 861-0017
Founded: 1970
Purpose: To unite all gay and lesbian Catholics to develop leadership, and to be an instrument through which they might be heard by the Church as well as by society at large. Dignity has over one hundred chapters nationwide where members gather for worship and for social purposes.

FRIENDS FOR LESBIAN AND GAY CONCERNS, P.O. Box 222, Sumneytown, PA 18084; (215) 234-8424
Founded: 1972
Purpose: An organization for gay and lesbian Quakers and their friends, including those who would like to know more about Quakers. A newsletter is available at $8 for four issues.

GAY, LESBIAN AND AFFIRMING DISCIPLES ALLIANCE, P.O. Box 19223, Indianapolis, IN 46219-0223
Founded: 1979
Purpose: To provide support, outreach, education, and advocacy for lesbian, gay, bisexual, and affirming laity and clergy of the Christian Church (Disciples of Christ). The Alliance maintains a visible presence at all levels of the denomination. It also sponsors an annual retreat for members and supporters.

INTEGRITY, P.O. Box 19561, Washington, DC 20036; (718) 720-3054
Founded: 1974
Purpose: Integrity is the gay and lesbian justice ministry of the Episcopal Church. It has sixty-five chapters in the U.S., with nonaffiliated chapters in some other countries.

METROPOLITAN COMMUNITY CHURCH. *See* Universal Fellowship of Metropolitan Community Churches

NEW WAYS MINISTRY, 4012 29th St., Mt. Rainier, MD 20712; (301) 277-5674
Founded: 1977
Purpose: To provide a ministry of advocacy and justice for lesbian and gay Catholics and the larger Christian community.

PRESBYTERIANS FOR LESBIAN AND GAY CONCERNS, c/o James Anderson, Box 38, New Brunswick, NJ 08903; (908) 249-1016
Founded: 1974
Purpose: An organization for Presbyterians and others who care for lesbian and gay people, and who desire the full participation of lesbian and gay people in the Presbyterian Church.

SECULAR GAYS AND LESBIANS/HUMANIST FELLOWSHIP, P.O. Box 620219, San Diego, CA 92162; (619) 236-0984
Purpose: To provide support for gay people who feel shut out from most religions. Discussion groups are comprised of atheists, deists, agnostics, and humanists. For a group near you, send an SASE to the above address.

SEVENTH-DAY ADVENTIST KINSHIP INTERNATIONAL, INC., P.O. Box 3840, Los Angeles, CA 90078; (213) 876-2076
Purpose: A worldwide organization of gay Christians. Provides intellectual, spiritual, and social fellowship for new or existing members.

UNITARIAN/UNIVERSALISTS FOR LESBIAN AND GAY CONCERNS, 25 Beacon St., Boston, MA 02108; (617) 742-2100, ext. 250
Founded: 1971
Purpose: To integrate and educate, and to make gay and lesbian influence felt in the Unitarian Universalist Church and in society at large.

UNITED CHURCH COALITION FOR LESBIAN AND GAY CONCERNS, 18 N. College St., Athens, OH 45701; (614) 593-7301
Founded: 1972
Purpose: To provide a special ministry to and to promote justice for lesbian, gay, and bisexual members of the United Church.

UNIVERSAL FELLOWSHIP OF METROPOLITAN COMMUNITY CHURCHES, 5300 Santa Monica Blvd., #304, Los Angeles, CA 90029; (213) 464-5100; fax (213) 464-2123
Founded: 1968
Purpose: An ecumenical religious denomination which welcomes all worshippers, with a special outreach to the gay and lesbian community.

WORLD CONGRESS OF GAY AND LESBIAN JEWISH ORGANIZATIONS, P.O. Box 3345, New York, NY 10008-3345
Founded: 1980
Purpose: To prepare materials for dissemination in the wider Jewish gay and lesbian community to combat homophobia and anti-Semitism. To function as the center of a communications network of member organizations. To provide advice and assistance to new and existing groups.

SPECIAL-INTEREST

AFRICAN AMERICAN LESBIAN AND GAY ALLIANCE, P.O. Box 50374, Atlanta, GA 30302; (404) 755-7731
Founded: 1986
Purpose: To organize the African-American gay community and to bridge the gap between the African-American community and the African-American gay community as well as the gap between African-Americans and other groups within the gay community.

BLACK GAY AND LESBIAN LEADERSHIP FORUM, 1219 South La Brea Ave., Los Angeles, CA 90019;

(213) 964-7820
Founded: 1989
Purpose: Responsible for a national biannual conference for black gay men and lesbians. On a local level, the forum works on AIDS education issues. It holds workshops, gives referrals, and produces a safer-sex poster series.

EDUCATION IN A DISABLED GAY ENVIRONMENT, P.O. Box 305, Village Station, New York, NY 10014
Founded: 1986
Purpose: To provided support for lesbians and gay men with impaired sight or hearing; amputees; people with cerebral palsy; and others.

GAY AND LESBIAN ARABIC SOCIETY, P.O. Box 4971, Washington, DC 20008
Founded: 1988
Purpose: To provide a support network for gays and lesbians of Arabic origin or descent, and their supporters, and to dispel negative stereotypes of Arabs.

GAY AND LESBIAN ASSOCIATION OF CHORUSES (GALA), 4016 SW 57th Ave., Portland, OR 97221
Founded:
Purpose: Plans annual conferences for directors and managers. Produces a choral festival every three years.

GAY AND LESBIAN HISTORY ON STAMPS CLUB (GLHSC), P.O. Box 230940, Hartford, CT 06123; (203) 653-3791
Founded: 1982
Purpose: To foster interest in philatelic material depicting men and

women who are thought to have been gay, lesbian, or bisexual, or depicting other topics of significance to gay people. Publishes the *Lambda Philatelic Journal.*

GAY AND LESBIAN PARENTS COALITION INTERNATIONAL, P.O. Box 50360, Washington, DC 20091; (202) 583-8029
Founded: 1979
Purpose: To unify leadership and represent gay and lesbian families by advocating civil rights, and by commissioning and disseminating research and resources. Newsletter and children's newsletter available upon request.

GAY FATHERS COALITION, P.O. Box 19891, Washington, DC 20036; (202) 583-8029
Founded: about 1981
Purpose: The coalition consists of many local groups, which provide support and social contact for gay fathers. In many cities, the local groups have grown so large that they are themselves broken into smaller units.

GAY VETERANS ASSOCIATION, 346 Broadway, #814, New York, NY 10013; (212) 787-0329
Founded: 1984
Purpose: To advocate for the civil rights of gay men and lesbians presently in military service and for former members of military service.

THE GAYLACTIC NETWORK, P.O. Box 127, Brookline, MA 02146-0001
Founded: 1986, as the Gaylaxians, based in Boston. In 1992, eight different Gaylaxian chapters united as the Gaylactic Network.

Purpose: To promote recognition of the need for gay, lesbian, and bisexual characters and themes in the science fiction, fantasy, and horror genres.

INTERNATIONAL ADVISORY COUNCIL FOR HOMOSEXUAL MEN AND WOMEN IN ALCOHOLICS ANONYMOUS, P.O. Box 90, Washington, DC 20044
Founded: 1981
Purpose: To provide support to gay people in AA, and to assist the professional community with questions about gay people and alcoholism. The Council also publishes a world directory of lesbian and gay AA groups.

NATIONAL COALITION OF BLACK LESBIANS AND GAYS, P.O. Box 19248, Washington, DC 20036
Founded: 1978
Purpose: To help black gay men and lesbians in local organizing efforts, networking, and empowering one another. The NCGLG is also now defining AIDS education as a top priority.

NATIONAL LATINO/A LESBIAN AND GAY ORGANIZATION (LLEGO), P.O. Box 44483, Washington, DC 20026
Founded: 1987
Purpose: To develop a leadership, advance a progressive political agenda, and formulate a national HIV/AIDS policy that reflects the needs and concerns of gay and lesbian Latinos/as. LLEGO also sponsors a newsletter and conferences.

NETWORK OF GAY AND LESBIAN

Vince Langmann

Stonewall Climbers provides an opportunity for lesbian and gay rock climbers to meet and climb together.

ALUMNI/AE ASSOCIATIONS, P.O. Box 15141, Washington, DC 20003
Founded: 1985
Purpose: To serve as a clearinghouse for college lesbian and gay alumni organizations and to eliminate homophobia within universities.

NORTH AMERICAN MAN/BOY LOVE ASSOCIATION (NAMBLA), P.O. Box 174, Midtown Station, New York, NY 10018; (212) 353-9656
Founded: 1978

Purpose: To organize support for men and boys who have or desire consensual and emotional relationships and to educate society on their positive nature.

SENIOR ACTION IN A GAY ENVIRONMENT (SAGE), 208 W. 13th St., New York, NY 10011; (212) 741-2247
Founded: 1977
Purpose: An intergenerational social service organization providing information, education, and resources on lesbian and gay aging

nationwide. SAGE provides direct services for older gay men, lesbians, and PWAs in the New York metropolitan area.

STONEWALL CLIMBERS, P.O. Box 445, Boston, MA 02124
Founded: 1988
Purpose: To promote the sport of rock climbing among lesbians, gay men, bisexuals, and their friends; and to enable members to climb together on trips throughout the U.S. and world. The Climbers are currently organizing a sport climbing event at the Gay Games in 1994.

TRIKONE, P.O. Box 21354, San Jose, CA 95151; (408) 270-8776
Founded: 1986
Purpose: Trikone, a support and social group for gay and lesbian South Asians, also publishes a newsletter four times per year.

HOTLINES

NATIONAL AIDS HOTLINE: (800) 342-AIDS. Sponsored by the American Social Health Association. Operates twenty-four hours a day. Provides information about AIDS, and referrals to other groups, especially local AIDS organizations and hotlines.

PENPALS FOR LESBIAN AND GAY TEENAGERS

Alyson Publications, a gay-owned publisher of literature for lesbians and gay men, runs a letter-exchange service to help gay teenagers get in touch with others who would like to correspond. If you'd like to participate in this, here's what to do:

1. Get an address where you can receive this mail. If you can use your home address, fine. Otherwise, some possibilities are: (a) ask at the post office how much it costs to rent a box there, or whether you can have mail addressed to you at General Delivery in the town where you live, and pick it up at the post office; (b) find a friend, perhaps an older gay person, who will let you use their address.

2. Write a letter introducing yourself, and be sure your address is on the letter. Put it in an envelope with a first-class postage stamp but without an address; do not seal the envelope. Then put *that* letter and envelope along with a cover letter into a larger envelope and mail it to us:

Alyson Publications
(letter exchange)
40 Plympton Street
Boston, MA 02118

We'll seal this letter and forward it to someone else who has expressed interest in exchanging correspondence.

In the cover letter, which will be for our confidential files, you should (a) give your name, address, age, and sex; (b) state that you are under 21; (c) give us permission to have mail sent to you; and (d) sign your name at the bottom.

3. When we get your letter, we'll forward it on to someone else who has expressed interest in corresponding. We'll also keep your name on file to get someone else's letter eventually. Once you've established correspondence with someone you should mail letters directly to them; you'll only go through us to get that initial contact.

4. Be patient. It may take a while to get a first response. If no one replies, it could be that someone has received your letter but is having problems at home or for some other reason isn't able to write back; in that case, try again.

5. There's no charge for this service, but we do ask that it be used only by gays and lesbians under 21 years of age.

SELECTED BIBLIOGRAPHY

Austen, Roger. *Playing the Game.* New York: Bobbs-Merrill, 1977.

Bérubé, Allan. *Coming Out under Fire.* New York: Free Press, 1989.

Boswell, John. *Christianity, Social Tolerance, and Homosexuality.* Chicago: University of Chicago Press, 1980.

Curtin, Kaier. *"We Can Always Call Them Bulgarians."* Boston: Alyson Publications, 1987.

D'Emilio, John. *Sexual Politics, Sexual Communities: The Making of a Homosexual Minority in the United States.* Chicago: University of Chicago Press, 1983.

Duberman, Martin Bauml, Martha Vicinus, and George Chauncy, Jr. *Hidden From History: Reclaiming the Gay and Lesbian Past.* New York: New American Library, 1989.

Dynes, Wayne. *Homolexis: A Historical and Cultural Lexicon of Homosexuality.* New York: Gai Saber, 1985.

Dynes, Wayne R. *Encyclopedia of Homosexuality.* New York & London: Garland, 1990.

Faderman, Lillian, Brigitte Eriksson. *Lesbian-Feminism in Turn-of-the-Century Germany.* Weatherby Lake, MO: Naiad Press, 1980.

Faderman, Lillian. *Surpassing the Love of Men.* New York: Morrow, 1981.

Fadiman, Clifton. *The Little, Brown Book of Anecdotes.* Boston: Little, Brown, 1985

Foster, Jeannette H. *Sex Variant Women in Literature.* Tallahassee, FL: Naiad Press, 1985.

Gaia's Guide (various editions). London & New York: Gaia's Guide.

Garde, Noel I. *Jonathan to Gide: The Homosexual in History.* New York: Vantage Press, 1964.

Gmünder, Bruno, and John D. Stamford. *Spartacus International Gay Guide* (various editions). Berlin: Bruno Gmünder Verlag. For men; extensive listings, plus some background on each country.

Grahn, Judy. *Another Mother Tongue: Gay Words, Gay Worlds.* Boston: Beacon Press, 1984.

Green, Frances. *Gayellow Pages: The National Edition.* New York: Renaissance House, 1992.

Hepburn, Cuca, Bonnie Gutierrez. *Alive and Well: A Lesbian Health Guide.* Freedom, CA: Crossing Press, 1988.

Homosexual Posters. *Gay Men's Diary.* London: Gay Men's Press, 1984.

Katz, Jonathan. *Gay American History.* New York: Thomas Y. Crowell, 1976.

Katz, Jonathan. *Gay/Lesbian Alma-*

nac. New York: Harper & Row, 1983.

Kellner, Bruce. *The Harlem Renaissance: A Historical Dictionary for the ERA.* New York: Methuen, 1987.

Kennedy, Hubert. *Ulrichs: The Life and Works of Karl Heinrich Ulrichs.* Boston: Alyson Publications, 1988.

Kepner, Jim. *Becoming a People.* Hollywood: National Gay Archives, 1983.

Kinsey, Alfred C., Wardell B. Pomeroy, Clyde E. Martin, and Paul H. Gebhard. *Sexual Behavior in the Human Female.* Philadelphia: W.B. Saunders, 1953.

Kinsey, Alfred C., Wardell B. Pomeroy, and Clyde E. Martin. *Sexual Behavior in the Human Male.* Philadelphia: W.B. Saunders, 1948.

Lauritsen, John, and David Thorstad. *The Early Homosexual Rights Movement (1864–1935).* New York: Times Change Press, 1974.

Likosky, Stephan. *Coming Out: An Anthology of International Gay and Lesbian Writings.* New York: Pantheon Books, 1992.

Mendola, Mary. *The Mendola Report: A New Look at Gay Couples.* New York: Crown Publishers, 1980.

Odysseus Enterprises. *Odysseus '93.* Port Washington, NY: Odysseus Enterprises, 1993.

Rodgers, Bruce. *The Queen's Vernacular* (later reprinted as *Gay Talk*). San Francisco: Straight Arrow Books, 1972.

Rutledge, Leigh. *The Gay Decades.* New York: Plume, 1992.

Tannahill, Reay. *Sex in History.* New York: Stein & Day, 1980.

Tatchell, Peter. *Europe in the Pink.* London: GMP Publishers, 1992.

Tripp, C.A. *The Homosexual Matrix.* New York: Signet/New American Library, 1976.

Van Hertum, Aras. Ongoing columns in the *Washington Blade,* 1992-1993.

Weiss, Andrea, and Greta Schiller. *Before Stonewall: The Making of a Gay and Lesbian Community.* Tallahassee, FL: Naiad Press, 1988.

Wockner, Rex. Ongoing syndicated columns, 1990–1993.

INDEX